Foreign Employees
in Nineteenth-Century Japan

Foreign Employees
in Nineteenth-Century Japan.

EDITED BY

Edward R. Beauchamp
and Akira Iriye

Westview Press
BOULDER, SAN FRANCISCO, & LONDON

Westview Special Studies on East Asia

This Westview softcover edition is printed on acid-free paper and bound in library-quality, coated covers that carry the highest rating of the National Association of State Textbook Administrators, in consultation with the Association of American Publishers and the Book Manufacturers' Institute.

Published in 1990 in the United States of America by Westview Press, Inc., 5500 Central Avenue, Boulder, Colorado 80301, and in the United Kingdom by Westview Press, Inc., 13 Brunswick Centre, London WC1N 1AF, England

Library of Congress Cataloging-in-Publication Data
Foreign employees in nineteenth-century Japan / edited by Edward R.
  Beauchamp and Akira Iriye.
    p. cm.—(Westview special studies on East Asia)
  Bibliography: p.
  Includes index.
  ISBN 0-8133-7555-X
  1. Alien labor—Japan—History—19th century. 2. Technology
transfer—Japan—History—19th century. I. Beauchamp, Edward R.,
1933–   . II. Iriye, Akira. III. Title: Foreign employees in 19th-century Japan.
IV. Series.
HD8728.5.A2F67 1990
331.6'2'0952—dc19   88-4974
                                                             CIP

Printed and bound in the United States of America

 The paper used in this publication meets the requirements of the American National Standard for Permanence of Paper for Printed Library Materials Z39.48-1984.

10   9   8   7   6   5   4   3   2   1

Contents

Part Three
Case Studies: Japanese Views

Part Four
Archival Resources

Foreword: *"Za" Yatoi—*
An Appreciation

The importance of foreign advisers hired by central and local governments in late Tokugawa and early Meiji Japan is widely recognized by students of Japan's modern development. Definition of the *yatoi* phenomenon and the systematic analysis of *yatoi* activity has been greatly enhanced in the past twenty years by the collaborative effort of a cluster of dedicated scholars in and outside of Japan.

In the United States the opening up of the William Elliot Griffis archive at Rutgers University, through the efforts of Ardath Burks, signaled the existence of a treasure house of historical materials capable of illuminating the interplay between Western and Japanese individuals in what is often called the "Westernization" of Japan. William Elliot Griffis (1843-1928) was only one of many examples, but the nature of his appointments in Japan and the richness of the documentary materials he left behind are such that he has stimulated many scholars to take up the study of Griffis and other advisers.

Fortunately, at the same time on the Japanese side, scholars in the Kyoto-Osaka region had for some years been engaged in a continuing seminar on *yatoi* studies. The prime organizers were Motoyama Yukihiko and Umetani Noboru. The latter's book on the subject, published in English in 1971, helped to define the field from the Japanese perspective. To this should be added the work of Hazel Jones, who wrote on the *yatoi* for her doctoral dissertation at the University of Michigan, subsequently published in 1980 as *Live Machines* (University of British Columbia).

A third dimension to this effort was the Fukui connection. Fukui, the location of Griffis' first employment, provided the backdrop for his early life in Japan, adding the local dimension to his experience. Kanai Madoka of the University of Tokyo, an authority on both Tokugawa and Meiji government foreign relations, provided a comprehensive overview of Fukui under the local *daimyo*.

All of these elements were woven together in 1967 in a conference organized by Ardath Burks at Rutgers University. The results of this conference were published in 1985 as *The Modernizers: Overseas Students, Foreign Employees and Meiji Japan* (Westview Press). This is a unique contribution to the field, not only for the information it contains, but also for the pattern of collaboration between scholars from Japan and abroad.

The 1967 conference built up a momentum in the field of *yatoi* studies that led to a second conference held at Fukui University in 1985. Many of the previous participants contributed papers, but the second gathering brought together a much larger diversity of interest. Many more papers were presented in Japanese and a greater effort was made to study the overall impact of *yatoi* activity as a general phenomenon.

The results of this second conference have been published in Japanese, and now non-Japanese language readers have the opportunity of reading the Fukui papers in English. Those who have read the 1967 symposium volume will find this new collection of papers all the more enlightening.

John Whitney Hall
Yale University

Introduction

Edward R. Beauchamp and Iriye Akira

The study of the *oyatoi gaikokujin* (foreign employees) in Meiji Japan has a long and honorable history going back to the very beginnings of the phenomenon. Over the years, many scholars have contributed to our understanding of this important chapter in Japanese-American cultural relations, but we would be remiss if we did not single out one individual who has made a particularly singular contribution to the field of *yatoi* studies.

Professor Emeritus Ardath W. Burks, of Rutgers University, is clearly the major figure among contemporary Western *yatoi* specialists. Professor Burks has not only written widely in this area, but has encouraged younger scholars to work in the field. In addition, he has accomplished valuable archival work in a number of depositories, but particularly with the William Elliot Griffis Collection at Rutgers and, finally, he has been instrumental in organizing two major *yatoi* conferences during the last two decades.

Professor Burks was responsible for what was, to the best of our knowledge, the first *yatoi* conference held in the United States, at Rutgers University in 1967. The great success enjoyed by that conference led to a resurgence of interest in the role played by foreign employees in early modern Japan. As the scholarly contributions of a new generation of scholars began to appear in the 1970s, Professor Burks played a major role in persuading the Japanese that the time was ripe for a second conference. As a result of his superb contacts in Japan, and the eloquence of his proposal, Fukui University readily agreed to host a second conference in the autumn of 1985.

Immediately prior to the Fukui conference, the University of Hawaii's Japan Endowment Fund generously supported a small, two day pre-conference in Honolulu. This event featured several papers that were also presented at Fukui, and was marked by the participation of the Consul General of Japan, Endo Tetsuya, as well as a lively discussion of the issues raised by the papers.

The extremely well-attended Fukui conference received extensive national coverage in both the print and electronic media in Japan. The conference was characterized by the meticulous planning and superb hospitality that one has learned to associate with conferences held in Japan. The intellectual excitement generated by the conference resulted in two decisions. First, there was general agreement that there should be periodic *yatoi* conferences held, alternately in Japan and the United States. A second decision mandated the publication of selected conference papers in both Japanese and English.

A few months before Japanese and Western *yatoi* specialists gathered in

Fukui, the revised papers presented at the earlier Rutgers conference were published under the title, *The Modernizers: Overseas Students, Foreign Employees, and Meiji Japan* (Westview Press, 1985). This volume, edited by Professor Burks, is clearly a labor of love. Painstakingly edited, with detailed transitional chapters, *The Modernizers* is a model to be emulated and has had a profound influence on the organization of this volume.

Professor Burks' several transitional chapters provide such an excellent contextual background for the papers in *The Modernizers* that the editors of this volume have decided that, rather than rewriting essentially the same material, it is best to simply refer readers to the earlier volume. In several important ways, this volume is therefore an extension of *The Modernizers*.

The editors extend their thanks to all the participants in the Fukui conference, and especially to the Japanese organizing committee, chaired by President Shimada Tadashi, President of Fukui University. The hard work of Shimada-sensei and his committee made the conference an outstanding success. The editors would also like to thank the University of Hawaii's Japan Endowment Fund for its support of the pre-conference held in Honolulu and especially for its financial support for the preparation of this manuscript. In this regard, the editors are especially grateful to Professor Patricia Steinhoff, chair of the University of Hawaii's Council for Japanese Studies, and Professor Sharon Minichiello, chair of the University of Hawaii's Japan Endowment Committee, for their encouragement and support. Last, but not least, the editors are indebted to Ms. Cheryl Feagins for her dedication, competence and hard work in helping us see this book through to completion. Cheri not only typed the manuscript and provided excellent advice, but applied her extensive computer literacy to the solution of problems which often seemed insoluble. Her unfailing cooperation and good sense saved us from several potential disasters and we are grateful to her.

In writing Japanese names, the standard form is used, with family name first, followed by the given name. Although purists may fault this decision, the editors have not used macrons to mark long vowels. Japan specialists will undoubtedly recognize where they should be used, and non-specialists will not be interested in this detail.

Finally, the individual authors accept responsibility for the contents of the volume, and editors accept responsibility for format and style.

PART ONE

THE *YATOI* PHENOMENON

1

The *Yatoi* Phenomenon: An Early Experiment in Technical Assistance

Ardath W. Burks

In Japan's history there have been two—historians might say, three—periods when the island-nation could be likened to developing countries in our day. In these periods Japan sought what today we call "foreign aid": Japanese leaned heavily on the advice of alien advisers (in other words, they sought "technical assistance"). Japan sent students abroad and then retrained them at home to become the "counterparts" of foreign counselors.

The first example, of interest mainly to specialists, began at the time of the Great Reform (*Taika*, seventh and eighth centuries) and lasted roughly until the twelfth century. During this period, Japanese learned from the Chinese principles of the Confucian ethic, mastered the rudiments of administration ("institution-building," we would call it in modern jargon), and studied the religious tenets of Buddhism. In old Nara and in the new capital of Kyoto, Japanese learned how to lay out a metropolitan-capital. They were taught by Chinese and Koreans how to construct temples, how to fashion statuary glorifying Buddha, and how to communicate in written (ideographic) language. Japanese went off to the continent, there to be impressed by the T'ang example.

The second example, which has been relatively neglected, was during the late Tokugawa period (1853-1868)* and early Meiji era (1868-1900). In this historical time frame Japanese sought the advice of foreign employees (*oyatoi gaikokujin*, or *yatoi* for short) and dispatched students (*ryugakusei*) abroad.

The third example was during the Occupation of Japan (1945-1952) which, not surprisingly, has been more thoroughly reviewed. Almost as soon as the

Presented at the Hawaii pre-conference, held at the Center for Korean Studies, University of Hawaii (September 30, 1985).
*Japanese refer to this period as the "twilight of the shogunates" (*bakumatsu*).

Allied, overwhelmingly American, Occupation got under way, a significant political effect of developments that led to the surrender became apparent. Because they were Americans, the occupationaires launched with reformist zeal a program of what Robert Ward has called "planned political change."[1]

It is possible, of course, to overemphasize the role of the occupationnaires, more than forty years ago. Some still debate whether General MacArthur walked on water to reach the island-nation. Revisionist historians, on the other hand, have increasingly emphasized the link between Occupation policy and the cold war.[2]

Suffice it to say that the "miracle" of the 1960s and Japan's well-publicized contemporary success is certainly not unconnected with the Occupation. Curiously called the "reorientation" of Japan by MacArthur's headquarters and often dubbed the "democratization" of the Japanese (terms no political scientist understands), the remarkable experiment called the Occupation is perhaps best defined as *directed change* or *planned development*.

For purposes of this discussion, it should also be said that the Occupation involved "foreign aid," the use of "alien advisers," and the dispatch of "Japanese students," in short, "technical assistance." In broader terms, the planned transformation was at best well-meaning, relatively gentle, and marked by cooperation between Japanese and occupationnaires. At worst, it was patronizing on the part of those occupying Japan. The two parties emerged from the experience with a reservoir of good will.

In fact, Meiji Japan's employment of foreign advisers in the process of modernization was also remarkable. Indeed, the foreign advisers—the *yatoi gaikokujin* or *yatoi*—were ancestors of the occupationnaires, just as the Meiji modernizers—the Japanese founding fathers of the nineteenth century—were the grandparents of Japanese leaders today. The Meiji experiment was "indeed a striking, possibly the earliest, historical example of the use of technical assistance in development."[3]

Little attention has, however, been paid to the Meiji experience in this light. By way of exception, in 1954 Merle Curti and Kendall Birr wrote an essay on "Missions to Japan" in their interesting book *Prelude to Point Four*, a study of American technical missions overseas between 1838 and 1938.[4]

In drawing a parallel between the Occupation and the Meiji transformation, the result of the latter was *not* the "Westernization" of Japan, just as Japanese experience from the seventh to the twelfth centuries did *not* constitute the "Sinification" of Japan. Similarly the Occupation, forty years ago, did *not* result in the "Americanization" of Japan. These comments lead to the first very general conclusion to be drawn from experiments with aid and development. The *successful* modernizing or developing nation attains or retains *independence*. If the results were otherwise, then we would be talking about development in a dependent unit, in a colony—for example, India under the British *Raj,* depicted in "The Jewel in the Crown"—or in a "semi-colonial" environment—Mao Tse-tung's description of nineteenth century China comes to mind. Now some critics (both Japanese and foreigners) have held that Japan *is* still an American "colony" as a result of the Occupation, or at least lies within the "sphere of influence" of the United States.

On some occasions, such as the symposium on *yatoi* held in Fukui in 1985, it is understandable, even appropriate, to celebrate the role of foreign employees and their contributions during the Meiji modernization. Some Japanese have continued to emphasize the *primary* contribution by foreigners, whom a few observers during the nineteenth century called "the makers of modern Japan." Not to denigrate that role, but such a view tends to overlook the *preparation* toward modernity during the "Great Peace" of the Tokugawa era, the contributions by *Japanese* forerunners, leaders, and subleaders and the extent to which *Japan* controlled the transformation. Moreover, rarely have the hidden lessons of the Meiji experience been applied to contemporary technical assistance doctrine.

To digress into the present, more often "the Japanese model" (the Tokugawa-Meiji transition) is indiscriminately applied to other developing nations in the contemporary world. For example, parallels are often drawn between Japan of the 19th century and Korea in the 1960s, or in our day, Hong Kong, Taiwan, and city-state of Singapore.[5] The comparison between Japan today and a developed country like the United States will be postponed to the conclusion of this essay.

To return to the *yatoi* and so-called "technical assistance" in 19th century Japan, one must refer to the work of Professor Hazel Jones, who has written the definitive study of the *yatoi* and who contributed an up-date at the conference on foreign employees held in Fukui. She called the *yatoi* "live machines." Of the Meiji experiment she wrote:

> While Japan's leadership drew heavily on the resources of other nations, as many developing nations do today, at the same time they marshalled indigenous resources, selected from among the successful nineteenth-century Western models of modern development, adhered firmly to a policy of Japanese control and management, assumed total responsibility for the cost of modernizing, and carried out their decision to replace foreigners with trained Japanese as rapidly as possible.[6]

This statement certainly implies that perhaps attention should be turned from the *yatoi* over to study of *Japanese* and their place in the process of modernization in the nineteenth century.

The *yatoi* are, however, still worthy of attention. Professor Jones estimated that they lent Japan some 9,500 man-years of aid, counsel, and cooperation. Many of the alien advisers had a hand in training what Dr. Robert Schwantes of the Asia Foundation had called their "counterparts" among Japanese modernizers.[7] In any case, the experiences of the foreigners make a fascinating story.

Historically, their roles well illustrate the perils and promise in technical assistance, the lessons to be learned from one of the first examples of development, modernization, and foreign aid. As is well known, those who do not learn from history are doomed to the process of reinventing the wheel or worse, repeating the failures of the past.

It is a brave or an ignorant person who would try to summarize the doctrine of technical assistance at a gathering (the pre-conference on *yatoi*) held in the very shadow of the East-West Center. The center has, of course, been a prime practitioner in the field of foreign aid, either by training guests in Honolulu or by extending assistance to nations spread across the Pacific basin. Nonetheless, the attempt will be made, if only to ascertain what the Meiji experiment with foreign employees has to offer in the way of lessons. In reviewing the literature on technical assistance, one is struck by the fact that this historical sample is scarcely mentioned, scarcely remembered.

Americans, especially, have been prone to a desire to tinker with the world. Converted to the doctrine of improvability and with a firm faith in a protestant ethic of hard work, they have long displayed an "idea of mission"[8]—which is not simply a religious drive—and they have responded to the "call." Again, the "call" was heard not only by missionaries, but also by laymen who set out to investigate, to cooperate, and to ameliorate. Today this American idealism has been somewhat tempered in the fire of experience. Many broad aid programs have been disappointments both to those who thought Americans ought to try to rebuild the world and to those who later thought we ought to leave it alone.

To turn to the more narrowly defined field, technical assistance involves the supply of expert and professional personnel to, in our day, developing nations. "Its object is to provide those countries with the expertise needed to promote development."[9] It includes training, at home in the developing country or in the nation offering aid. Technical assistance may also embrace research, carried out by experts from the developed country or cooperatively with fledgling specialists in the developing nation. In summary, technical assistance usually involves teaching skills and problem-solving in areas of specialization: agriculture, irrigation, fisheries, forestry, education, law, public administration, the conduct of foreign relations and organization for security, and many, many other fields. By the way, sometimes governments offer aid to depressed areas and populations within their own jurisdiction. The "Bootstrap" operation in Puerto Rico in New Deal days and federal assistance to the American Appalachian area come to mind.

To the extent that technical assistance prior to World War II has been identified at all, emphasis was placed on private (both religious and secular) effort and aid. The *yatoi* in nineteenth century Japan (like their counterparts elsewhere) were often first, missionary-educators and later, secular assistants. In the realm of public health, the Rockefeller Foundation and its activities in China have been most frequently and favorably cited.

Although colonialism was once a major channel for the diffusion of knowledge and application of technical assistance, since the nineteenth century it has been increasingly unpopular. Thus recent programs have as their objectives not only development but also popular sovereignty, self-determination, and equality. Today one speaks not of "underdeveloped," but of "developing" nations. Similarly, plans more often refer not to "aid" but to "cooperation."

For example, the United States has its International Cooperation Administration; France, its Ministry of Cooperation; and Britain, its Department of Technical Cooperation. In the case of Great Britain, technical assistance has gone to the other extreme: in a majority of cases, British assistants do not "advise" or train "counterparts" but simply "do the job." It is the opinion of David Lilienthal, however, that if training does not go along with assistance, the project is not worth doing.[10]

Since World War II the diffusion of knowledge and the extensions of skills have been normal operations. The effort began in December 1946 with the Economic and Social Council of the United Nations General Assembly and its Expanded Program of Technical Assistance. President Truman's famous Point Four plan appeared in 1949. In January 1950 the Colombo Plan of Economic Development of Southeast Asia was born. Meanwhile, Japan very shrewdly mounted a long-range program of assistance and training, in lieu of reparations, directed at the former colonies of Southeast Asia. Although one seldom thinks of them as such, personnel from Southeast Asia, who are studying in Japan, have been the modern *ryugakusei*, this time non-Japanese students in Japanese universities. Japan itself, now a developed nation—even an advanced "Western" industrial-democracy—has a program of Official Development Assistance (ODA) and even a corps of modern-day Japanese "*yatoi*" working abroad.[11]

The largest technical assistance programs, administered by the United Nations and its various agencies, have concentrated on four major areas: (1) agricultural production. (2) basic resource surveys and administrative services, (3) health services, and (4) education. Of these, improvement of agriculture has been the leading area of United Nations emphasis. As early as 1956, however, studies have shown that "a large amount of valid knowledge on local agricultural possibilities may be accumulated through the empirical methods of non-literate societies."[12]

Now to turn back to the Meiji experiment, Japan was scarcely "non-literate" at the time; and traditional Japanese agricultural methods did supply "a large amount of valid knowledge." In fact, yield per acre in Japan has risen only slightly in the modern era although total production has been raised with sharply decreased labor force in the agrarian sector. In the Meiji era, emphasis on agricultural development occurred mainly in Hokkaido, with the aid of American technical assistance and "extension services." Indeed, the results of William S. Clark's remarkable work in Hokkaido are visible in the northern island even today, and Clark is, among the *yatoi*, still most fondly remembered by the Japanese. Agricultural reform under the Occupation, which also involved some technical assistance, is another story: again, the result was not so much an increase in yield per acre as it was a monumental social and political reform.

To conclude these brief comments on technical assistance doctrine, what can be learned from extensive post-war experience? First, there is a large and growing literature which documents the fact that technical innovation (including assistance) is accompanied by cultural and social change. Leading figures in Asian planning organizations have concluded that technical assistance has a dual purpose: to develop self-sufficiency in the manpower required for development and to build institutions that accelerate self-sustained growth.[13]

As to personnel involved in technical assistance, certain factors have been identified as useful to recruiters in the field: first and above all, technical skill; second, a belief in the particular mission; third, cultural empathy, what in sociological jargon is known as "cultural relativity"; fourth, some sophistication in politics and in organizational ability.[14] In one of the most succinct statements about requirements, Francis X. Sutton has concluded, "How effective aid by an expert will be depends on his capacity to make generalized use of his competence."[15]

Without such elaborate doctrine, derived from several decades of post-war experience, how, then, would the *yatoi* in nineteenth century Japan, have measured up to the standards applied today? It has been this author's opinion that contributions to Meiji Japan made by the foreign employees were marginal, perhaps incremental is a better word. From the beginning the Japanese controlled the experiment and since, by the early twentieth century most of the *yatoi* were phased out of their assignments, the foreign employees can scarcely be said to have been "the makers of modern Japan," as the Englishman Basil Hall Chamberlain called them.

The *yatoi*, however, worked on the very cutting edge of technical innovation, which was accompanied by profound cultural and social change in Japan. They helped the Meiji modernizers open the Pandora's box of modernization. Nonetheless, like present-day agents of change, they had little control over (to shift the figure of speech) the genie of change who popped out of the box. Modernization led to showy red brick structures on, and gas lights over, the Ginza; it also led to Zero aircraft over Pearl Harbor and B-29s over the homeland. It is a moot point among scholars, whether the rapidity of modernization led inevitably to "absolutism," militarism, imperialism, war, and the disaster of defeat in World War II. A more sanguine view would see the foundations laid down in the Meiji Restoration for the spectacular successes of contemporary Japan.

As hands-on observers of the very beginning of the process of alteration, the *yatoi* in their memoirs, histories, and travel accounts have willed to us original sources for the study of the transition from traditional Tokugawa to traditional-modern Meiji culture. They were the first of the "Old Japan Hands," the first amateur historians of modern Japan.[16] This may have been the major theme of the Fukui conference, held in October 1985. In their writings *yatoi* often revealed an ambivalence, a nostalgia for the "Old Japan" alongside a faith that it was being displaced by the "New Japan." Unknowing, they wrote in effect the first guide books for technical assistance. They were pre-Peace Corps peace corpsmen, operating in Japan over a century ago.

In almost everything the foreign employees did, they set examples and thus, were teachers. They not only aided in training the manpower required for development; they also helped establish the institutions needed for sustained growth.

The *yatoi* were successful in one way: by and large they saw to it that training (the requisite defined by Lilienthal) accompanied technical assistance. In an essay prepared for an earlier conference by Dr. Robert Schwantes, Vice President of the Asia Foundation, it was pointed out that the foreign employees helped produce their Japanese "counterparts." Dr. Schwantes studied the transition in the medical faculty of the institution which was predecessor to Tokyo Imperial University. In the 1870s *To-dai* (Tokyo University) was entirely staffed by medical experts from abroad, mainly from Germany. By the 1880s the major chairs were filled by Japanese, who had trained in Europe or who had interned under foreign doctors in Japan.[17] Benjamin Smith Lyman, who worked for the Colonization Commission (the *Kaitakushi*) on the frontiers of Hokkaido, insisted upon training his own Japanese surveyors.[18] As is well known, Edward S. Morse first went to Japan to study brachiopods, in a tiny coastal laboratory in Enoshima. Through his good offices, Thomas Mendenhall and Ernest Fenollosa came to Japan. Of equal significance, it has been said that progress in all the sciences in Meiji Japan sprang from Morse's 90 most promising Japanese students. The *yatoi* provided, in modern terminology, self-sufficiency in Japanese manpower required for development.

In Meiji Japan, as in contemporary developing societies, attention of foreign advisers was directed to agricultural development. Efforts were devoted, as has been mentioned, first to the frontier of Hokkaido. There the Americans in particular used classic nineteenth century practice, what is now called "extension education," which was nurtured by the post-Civil War Morrill Act in the United States. The work of William S. Clark, Horace Capron, Benjamin Smith Lyman, Edwin Dun, and many others has been thoroughly documented.[19]

In the field of medicine and health services the *yatoi* simply built on the foundation already laid down by Japanese during the Tokugawa era. Underground medical research, linked to Dutch Studies *(Rangaku)* had already proceeded apace. For example, vaccination was being practiced in Kaga-*han* as early as 1850.[20] Hashimoto Sanai, a domain surgeon in Fukui and later, a pre-Restoration martyr-hero, was already exploring Western medicine long before Perry arrived.

Among the *yatoi*, Americans tended early on to specialize on matters of education. Two men, both from Rutgers College, may be cited as examples. William Elliot Griffis recruited by Guido Verbeck, set up a curriculum in the natural sciences, both in Fukui and in Tokyo at the Kaisei Gakko (predecessor of Tokyo Imperial University). During his first stay in Japan, Griffis began his avocation, compiling data on the first unofficial history of activities of the *yatoi*. David Murray cooperated with Mori Arinori in designing an early scheme called the Education Ordinance (*Gaku-rei*, 1879). As documented by the late Professor Shiro Amioka of the University of Hawaii, the ordinance was a revolutionary plan, which began to steer Japan in the direction of universal education.[21] In modern terms of development, the *yatoi* thus participated in founding the infrastructure of self-sustained growth.

In conclusion, what can be said in summary about the *yatoi* themselves? It must be admitted that at first, these foreign employees were engaged in imperialism, even if the description is softened by calling them cultural imperialists. From the first, *yatoi* came to Japan sponsored by their respective nations and were, wittingly or unwittingly, partners to the pressure being applied to a vulnerable Japan. Before the new Japanese government asserted its autonomy, hired foreigners were linked with unequal treaties, extraterritoriality, and exclusive trade arrangements. In the beginning the aliens, who occupied special residential areas (*kyoryuchi*) and enjoyed the protection of special police (*bettegumi*), were beyond Japanese law. Indeed, in attitude many were arrogant. Richard Henry Brunton, whom Griffis called "the typical *yatoi*" and who built the first lighthouses along Japanese shores, once described the atmosphere in which the aliens lived:

> Their high pay, their different mode of living, their want of disciplinary power, and the knowledge of the Japanese that foreigners were more or less indispensable to them, rendered their European assistants most impractical and difficult to deal with. [22]

Basil Hall Chamberlain was even more acerbic in his comment:

> There is nothing picturesque in the foreign employee. With his club, and his tennis-ground, and his brick house, and his wife's piano, and the European entourage which he strives to create around him in order sometimes to forget his exile, he strikes a false note. . . . He was a sojourner in Lotus-land.[23]

In fact, nineteenth century *yatoi* may have been the predecessors of the "Ugly American" in both senses of the phrase.

One cannot, however, fault most of them for their motivation. The majority of the "Japan helpers"—these early foreigners who were engaged in technical assistance—often displayed qualities which modern recruiters would look for among potential peace corpsmen. Most held, above all, a firm faith in progress and supreme confidence that they could help it along.

The Americans had a particularly strong "sense of mission." Sometimes, the drive stemmed from a religious "call," for example: in the hopes of Guido Verbeck, who turned from converting Christians to educating future leaders in Nagasaki; in the often pious attitudes of William E. Griffis, who taught in Fukui and in Tokyo; in the writings of Edward Warren Clark, who worked in Shizuoka; in the activities of William S. Clark, who conducted Bible study with his charges in Hokkaido; in the quiet work of James C. Hepburn, who taught future leaders, prepared one of the first dictionaries, and established a dispensary in Yokohama; and in the labor of Samuel R. Brown, who established an interpreters' school in Yokohama.

More often the *yatoi* had faith in their technical skills, which were formidable, and in their secular "mission" to convert Japan into a modern nation, for example: in the scientific attitudes of Griffis, who taught chemistry and natural science; in the pragmatic experiments of Clark in Hokkaido; in the linguistic ability of Hepburn; in the pioneering efforts of the agnostic, Morse, in the biological sciences and in the introduction of the Japanese to Darwinism; and in the pioneering work of the equally skeptical Lyman to survey the natural resources of Hokkaido.

Some of the Japan helpers developed, partly out of their liberal education before coming to, partly out of their experience in, Japan, a remarkable sense of cultural relativism. Even Griffis, the confirmed Christian, came to see that Japanese had evolved a remarkable culture, without benefit of the Old Testament. Hepburn, Fenollosa, Morse, and Lyman tried to learn the language.

As Dr. Griffis came to realize, the foreign guests who learned how to adapt to conditions in Japan were most useful to the Japanese. They became dedicated "servants" of the Japanese, to cite Griffis' description. This attitude, according to Hazel Jones, made up the "Griffis thesis" on the *yatoi*.[24]

On the negative side, those who tried to dominate the Japanese were soon dismissed.

Finally, "generalized use of competence"—to cite the modern criteria for experts in technical assistance—marked the work, above all, of Guido Verbeck in the early period, and of Henry Denison, "the shadow of the Foreign Office," in the later stages of modernization. Both learned the ultimate lesson of working in Japan, to remain modest, to speak in low key, to stay in the background behind the screen, and to cooperate with the group.

So far as the eventual goal was concerned, rapid modernization (some sought the "Westernization" of Japan), both the *yatoi* and the Japanese were markedly successful. Without elaborate plans, with a pay-as-you-go fiscal policy, without complicated screening, recruitment, and personnel regulations, the technical assistance "took." Would that Ford Foundation, the Japan Foundation, or the East-West Center, in our day, could identify and support so successful a venture.

This logically leads to the final point, whether Japan can serve as a "model" for other, even the developed, nations. Not at all facetiously, some Americans have looked forward eagerly to Japanese technical assistance to help in the construction of a high-speed rail line on the California coast. New York businessmen have pored over management texts that have been modelled on Japanese practices in organization. The nineteenth century experiment does show, however, that wholesale importation of culture traits is neither desirable nor possible.

Technological change does mean cultural alteration and in this transition we are all involved. At the present time, Japan and the U.S. are both entering upon a new frontier, the change into post-industrial, high-tech, information societies. The adjustments are on occasion painful. It helps to share experiences. In this broadest possible sense we can learn what the most perceptive of the *yatoi* came to realize: that we are all human beings under the the four corners of heaven.

Notes

[1]Robert E. Ward, "Reflections on the Allied Occupation and Planned Political Change in Japan," in Robert E. Ward, editor, *Political Development in Modern Japan* (Princeton, 1968).

[2]The following is a sample of recent publications on various aspects of the Occupation: for a "conservative-revisionist" view, explanatory notes by Eto Jun, editor, *Senryo shiroku*, [*Occupation Documents*] 4 vols. (Tokyo, 1981-1982) and the cluster-review by Ray A. Moore in *The Journal of Japanese Studies*, 10,1 (Winter 1984). Also John W. Dower, *Empire and Aftermath: Yoshida Shigeru and the Japanese Experience, 1878-1954* (Cambridge, 1979); and, with an emphasis on particular reforms, Theodore Cohen, *Nihon senryo kakumei: GHQ kara no shogen* [*Revolutionary Aspects of the Occupation of Japan: The GHQ Point of View*] (Tokyo, 1983).

[3]Ardath W. Burks, ed. *The Modernizers: Overseas Students, Foreign Employees, and Meiji Japan* (Boulder, 1985), p. 187.

[4]Merle Curti & Kendall Burr, *Prelude to Point Four: American Technical Missions Overseas 1838-1928* (Madison, 1954), chapter 3.

[5]Often called the "four little tigers," (South) Korea, Taiwan, Hong Kong and Singapore followed in the footsteps of Japan. See Richard Holbrooke, "East Asia: the Next Challenge," *Foreign Affairs*, vol. 65, no. 2 (Spring 1986).

[6]Hazel J. Jones, *Live Machines: Hired Foreigners and Meiji Japan* (Vancouver, 1980), Introduction, p.xiii.

[7]Robert S. Schwantes, "Foreign Employees in the Development of Japan," in Burks, *The Modernizers*, pp. 207-217.

[8]Edward McNall Burns, *The American Idea of Mission* (New Brunswick, 1957).

[9]Technical Assistance," Micropedia, vol. 11, *Encyclopedia Britannica* (Chicago, 15th edition, 1985).

[10]Francis X. Sutton, "Technical Assistance," *International Encyclopedia of the Social Sciences* (New York, 1968), volume 15, pp. 565-576.

[11]Established in 1965 and inspired by activities of the U.S. Peace Corps, the Japan Overseas Cooperation Volunteers (JOCV) first went to work in Southeast Asia. Their successors have been active throughout Africa, the Pacific, Central and South America, and Asia. For recent developments, see the report of Murakawa Ichiro, "Japanese Volunteers in Africa," in *Liberal Star* (an organ of the Liberal-Democratic Party), 16 (June 10, 1987), p. 14.

[12]Study by Pierre de Schlippe (1956), in Sutton, pp. 568-569.

[13]Report adopted in Bangkok (1965), in Sutton, pp. 570-571.

[14]Harlan Cleveland, Gerald J. Mangone and John Clark Adams, *The Overseas Americans* (New York, 1960); see also John D. Montgomery, *Foreign Aid in International Politics* (Englewood, N. J., 1967), p. 74, n. 10.

[15]Sutton, pp. 573-575.

[16]Professor Umetani Noboru, the dean of Japanese scholars devoted to the study of *yatoi,* listed six significant introductory works written by early foreign

employees. The authors, who helped introduce Japan to the West, included William E. Griffis, David Murray, Edward Warren Clark, Henry Dyer, Etienne de Villaret, and Karl Rathgen.

[17]Schwantes, "Foreign Employees," in Burks, pp. 207-217.

[18]The Benjamin Smith Lyman Collection in the Forbes Library, Northampton, Massachusetts, is made up of field notebooks, letters and papers. Most have been microfilmed, with copies in the Griffis Collection, special Collections & Archives, Alexander Library, Rutgers University.

[19]See John M. Maki, "The Japan Helpers," in Clark Beck, Jr. & Ardath W. Burks, eds. *Aspects of Meiji Modernization: The Japan Helpers and the Helped* (New Brunswick, 1983); also in the same volume, Fujita Fumiko, "Understanding of a Different Culture: The Case of Benjamin Smith Lyman."

[20]Yoshiko N. & Robert G. Flershem, "Kaga, A Domain That Changed Slowly," in Burks, ed. *The Modernizers*, cited, chapter 5.

[21]Shiro Amioka, "Changes in Educational Ideals and Objectives (From selected Documents Tokugawa Era to the Meiji Period)," pp. 323-357; and Kaneko Takashi, "Contributions of David Murray to the Modernization of School Administration in Japan," in Burks, *The Modernizers*, pp. 301-321.

[22]R. Henry Brunton, "Pioneer Engineering in Japan: A Record of Work in Helping to Re-lay the Foundations of the Japanese Empire (1868-1879)," unpubl. ms., Griffis Collection, Alexander Library, Rutgers University. This work, edited and annotated by Edward R. Beauchamp, will be published by Paul Norbury Publications in England.

[23]Basil Hall Chamberlain, *Things Japanese* (London, 1890), pp. 184-185.

[24]Jones, *Live Machines*, pp. 90-93.

2

Live Machines Revisited

Hazel J. Jones

Introduction

Contemporary research on *yatoi* was initiated by Japanese. Of the many who could be mentioned, the late Saigusa Hiroto and his colleagues should be remembered for their fine work in the history of Japanese modern technology and Ogata Hiroyasu in education. The person who provided the impetus to wide-scale exploration of the theme is Umetani Noboru, whose *Source Materials on Foreign Employees*[1] is of great value. The Kashima kenkyu shobokai *Oyatoi gaikokujin* series is a major contribution (17 vols. 1968-76). But another name comes to mind, Shigehisa Tokutaro. In 1939 Professor Shigehisa published the first contemporary compilation of names of foreigners in Meiji Japan, a list which includes many who were employed by the Japanese government. His list may be said to be the beginning of contemporary *yatoi* studies.[2] In addition to the Kashima series, there are at least two monographs which deserve publication in English to be made available to persons who are not specialists *per se* in Japanese studies; that by Tanaka Tokihiko on the politics of railway construction and that by Ishizuki Minoru on Japanese overseas students.[3]

Research Milieu

Any discussion and study of the Meiji event and hired foreigners is not without immense contemporary significance. Modernization, Europeanization, Westernization have become value-laden terms in the academic world. But Meiji efforts were initially an experience in internationalizing. This need is again being focused upon in contemporary Japan's development.

In *Japan's Modern Century*, a book of considerable scholarship which did long service as a college textbook, Hugh Borton writing in 1955 presented to a broad readership this thesis: "The record also shows clearly that a drive to dominate China was one of the basic determinants of Japanese foreign policy throughout the past century."[4] Categorical statements of this nature are being made again by persons wielding considerable influence.

Gradually many fine books have brought a balance into the study of modern Japan. Perhaps it is as American *yatoi* adviser on international law, E. Peshine Smith (1871-76)[5] wrote in private correspondence in 1850: "The Press is the only University worth mentioning in these latter days."[6] But progress has been made.

The field is indebted to the research of Professor Sakata Yoshio published in the late 1950s and early 1960s on the nature and grouping of Meiji Japanese leadership; what he calls "the modern bureaucratic faction" and "the new knowledge bureaucrats."[7] Both were progressive. In the Meiji era there was certainly polarization in leadership, as illustrated by these major factions. The configuration of leadership was more an ellipse than a full circle. But there was no rupture. Bernard Silberman's studies of attitudes and values of Meiji leaders confirms an integral progressiveness in their thinking. This important statement by Silberman is part of enduring scholarship: "By 1880 it is clearly evident that internal development rather than external expansion was the primary goal."[8]

In the past decade and more particularly at present, the words international and internationalization are given frequent expression in the mass media as leaders urge international consciousness. The future is not something distant nor even just around the corner. In the throes of rapid change, the future is upon us as technological advances touch every aspect of human life and society. In part this is the much-touted phenomenon of "future shock." The present era should heighten our appreciation of the Meiji event, both its virtues and its faults. A great deal is heard today about frayed nerves and failures in tension management. We live with the nuclear threat under the nuclear umbrella. What was the situation in Meiji Japan?

Background: Confluence of Powers

A hundred and twenty years ago, Japan and especially the decision-making segment, plunged into future shock. In the words of one of the *bakufu* advisers, the mist that gathered over China threatened to settle as hoar frost over Japan.[9] The necessity of fighting against colonization and of establishing full sovereignty accounts for the rapid tempo of the era. Opinion seems in consensus that the modern transformation of Japan would have taken place eventually. But faced with foreign pressure, the decision to use foreign expertise drastically reduced the time factor.

While this is not the place to go into details of the numerous legal constraints under which Japanese officialdom labored in this era of the unequal treaty system, it is necessary to be aware of them. Western power was dominant; treaty revision was contingent on foreign unanimity; import tariffs were limited to a flat five percent. The psychological ramifications of these three points are still staggering. How does a nation stand up against superior firepower, how is foreign unanimity obtained, how is massive internal expansion financed without external revenue or home industries protected without import controls?

Review of the Yatoi *Phenomenon*

The Term

Officially, private foreigners in Japan were not called *yatoi*. While *kanyatoi* (government employee) and *shiyatoi* (private employee) are used in Foreign Ministry records, the use of *yatoi* by itself, that is, *oyatoi* or *oyatoi gaikokujin* invariably refers to government employees. As an English loanword in the foreign community, usage was that given by *yatoi* Captain Frank Brinkley (1867-80) in his *Japanese-English Dictionary*, originally published in 1896: "a government employe (not a regular official); lowest grade of officials."[10] This specific usage is confirmed in English language newspapers throughout the Meiji era. The irony of being a hired man was a subject of much discussion and chagrin among *yatoi*. In the Showa era the term *yatoi* had been broadened by some writers to include foreigners engaged in non-government employment.

Numbers

During the *bakumatsu* era (1853-68), some 200 foreigners were employed by bakufu and han, principally for language and technology training.[11]

By the Meiji government, some 300 foreigners were employed for education, government, and technology.[12]

This figure represents close to half of all foreigners resident in Japan during the period. Some of these hired foreigners were inherited from the previous regime. These *yatoi*, as they came to be called, were drawn from some twenty-six national groups. All in some sense were teachers and informants. The majority were practical teachers of science and technology, but all fields of knowledge were addressed by the *yatoi*. Most were in fact well-educated and energetic. There were large numbers of skilled, semi-skilled, and unskilled laborers for mechanical maintenance, machine work, time keeping, track laying, lighthouse tending, farming, timber cutting, etc. These were accustomed to the work pattern and systems of their respective countries; *yatoi* often preferred their own nationals as laborers. Another major group of significance was the cadre of foreign lawyers, all highly experienced.

In the early years it was necessary to get rid of ne'er-do-wells. Mistakes were made in hiring, but Japanese officials, at least the upper echelon, learned quickly. Actually until 1875, the Japanese had to pay dearly to release a foreigner under contract. However, by 1875 not only had a careful and reasonable system been worked out for contracts, but Japanese officials had acquired finesse and courage in dealing with foreign diplomats and consular court intervention.[13] Their tasks were rendered easier by changes taking place in international policy and by evolutions in international legal theory. The expertise of *yatoi* lawyers assisted greatly in the assertion of Japanese sovereignty.

Length of Employment

In a base sample of over 2000 *yatoi*, length of employment stretched from a few months to many years. The overall average stands at five years. The average for upper level *yatoi* was more than nine years. About a hundred served twenty years; more than a dozen served a quarter of a century, a few even longer. Peak employment was registered in the mid-1870s. A significant fact is that those in technology were actively engaged at work sites, only fifteen percent were office or administrative staff.[14] In actual duties in the sample of over 2000 *yatoi*, there were 350 cases of simultaneous or multiple inter-ministry employment. Intra-ministry employment by more than one bureau runs twice that count. These two points speak to the effective and heavy use of foreign employees.

Salaries

These foreign employees were paid well. The upper seven percent received between $500 and $2,000 a month (the real span is to $1,200); nineteen percent received $300-$400 a month; and seventy-four percent received $200 or less. These percentages are close to a breakdown that can be made from published figures in the *Imperial Japan Statistical Yearbook* (*Nihon teikoku tokei nenkan*), though names are not in context.

But what do these pay scales mean? Certainly the expenditure on the part of the government was onerous, and political capital was made of it. *Yatoi* salaries were often a third of expenditures, and at one point they were sixty-six percent of the Public Works Ministry (*Kobusho*) expenditures.[15] Was this a contributing factor in the demise of that ministry? These salaries are quite apart from housing and hiring and work related travel expenses, and other emoluments.

A few examples may be given from continuing research. Horace Capron (1871-75) received $3,000 per annum as U. S. Commissioner of Agriculture, and $10,000 per annum as Superintendent for Hokkaido. Erastus Peshine Smith earned $2,000 a year in the United States and was paid $10,000 a year by Japan's Foreign Ministry. The genius chemist Thomas Antisell (1871-74) left U. S. government service at $2,000 per annum for $8,000 in Japanese service. Many *yatoi* were hired for long terms in shipping. In that era the usual rate for shipmasters was $80 a month. In Japanese employ foreign shipmasters received $350 a month. In checking several categories of skilled and semi-skilled labor as well as professional positions, the increase was triple to quadruple. Thus, it is needless to point out that *yatoi* received more than their

Japanese counterparts, but most received even more than their Japanese superiors. All *yatoi* were paid in hard coin, some in gold even after Japan opted for the silver standard. Upper rank Japanese officials were paid between 400 and 800 yen a month; actually the government often resorted to salary moriatoria under financial stress, and in any case part of all salaries was paid in rice.

Assessment

Besides construction projects and systems designs, the presence and expertise of *yatoi* served as a catalyst.[16] In the Japanese reaction innate and latent energies were released. By contract, official treatment, and duties, *yatoi* were molded into quasi-civil servants by Japanese modernizers, and they were worked hard. In many ways *yatoi* bore with their employers the stress and the burden of the day's heat in building Modern Japan. The most tangible even quantifiable contribution was the number of Japanese they taught in government offices, in field work, and in schools. *Yatoi* and Japanese who had studied with *yatoi* and Japanese who studied abroad trained in Tokyo University alone a cadre of leadership models in the 12,235 graduates between 1876 and 1912: 33% in law; 23% in engineering; 16% in medicine; 13% in letters; 9% in agriculture; 6% in natural science. There were many more from private and public institutions.

Some Study Considerations

In looking again at the large scale employment of foreigners in the Meiji era, there are a number of areas for further consideration.

Okuma Shigenobu's interests were perhaps broader than any of the Meiji statesmen. Shibusawa wrote that Okuma thought nothing was impossible.[17] Okuma did early service as Finance Minister, and in the Okuma papers, a sizeable manuscript collection in Waseda University, his sustained interest in world economy is reflected. Okuma set American banker and financial adviser, George B. Williams (1871-75) to monitor bankruptcies and economic conditions world-wide.

Little connection has been made as yet between such actions as this and world conditions of the time. The West experienced a severe depression in the early 1870s with another nadir in the 1880s, and recovery was not made until the mid-1890s. The hiring of foreigners needs looking into from the aspect of economic history and sociology. To what degree, for example, was world-wide depression a factor in the availability of so many competent technologists for Japan? Incompetents are always available. Many *yatoi* had field experience abroad and many were engaged in home projects before coming to Japan. Deflation in the employment market and in home economies appears a special factor in motivation for employment in Japan.

Meiji foreign employees (*yatoi*) and their Japanese contemporaries were not only participants in the building of Modern Japan, but they were keen observers as well. Part of the elan which still evokes special interest in Meiji Japan is due to the enthusiasm of the participants. Articulate eye witnesses really pioneered the study of Modern Japan. Their writings, memos, personal correspondence, published personal accounts, and analyses of the Meiji event, are live sources which have scarcely been tapped.

Compiling and subjecting information to method is time-consuming. Why cannot the Meiji method be used? Enlist the energies and talents of everyone, especially undergraduate students world-wide should be encouraged. Segments could then be drawn together from each country into an integrated pattern. Collections such as Toyo Bunko in Tokyo, the Manuscript Division of the Library of Congress, the Okuma Monjo at Waseda, the Edward House Collection in the University of Virginia, national biographic encyclopedias, and "local" collections everywhere are the kinds of things tapped most easily by local residents. Such endeavor would be a practical experience in internationalization.

Private correspondence of the time reveals attitudes and practices affecting relations of foreigners and Japanese officials, particularly the important sense of trust. The widespread practice of investment and currency speculation among *yatoi* and foreign diplomats in Japan was certainly known to Japanese officials. It puts in a new light the strong injunction in *yatoi* contracts against business involvement, and needs to be studied. Likewise family squabbles among foreigners need looking at for their effect on working relations. Some were aired in the press, but more can be found in private correspondence and in complaints sent through the diplomatic pouch. Information can be found in national archives because of the close relation of foreigners to their national legations.

In Deborah Church's doctoral dissertation, it seems that part of Henry W. Denison's malaise with life as a consular official may be found in relations with the household of Thomas Van Buren. Not only was Denison passed over for promotion to Consul-General, the post going to Van Buren, but Mrs. Denison already in delicate health became a victim of Mrs. Van Buren's mentally deranged accusation.[18] In the end, Denison's move to Japanese government service was of great benefit. He became the most distinguished adviser on international law, serving from 1880 to 1914. It is interesting that this quiet but extremely competent man was content to be hired at what for the times was a moderate increase of salary. Over the years he literally worked himself up the ranks by achievement. Digging into personal relations within the foreign community will reveal more of what the *yatoi* were really like in temperament and character.

Also in Church's dissertation there is inference that while legal *yatoi* Eli Sheppard (1877-79) refused to divulge "secrets," U.S. Minister John Bingham was kept informed.[19] In any case Sheppard was not retained long. To what extent did camaraderie of former consular and other government officials affect their positions as *yatoi*? Japanese heavy emphasis on the maintenance of secrets clause in contracts for advisers to government may be seen in a new light.

An in-depth study of *yatoi* educational backgrounds and later careers would give a clearer picture of expertise and accomplishment. A case in point is the German shift in agriculture. The shift to German employees from 1878 has been tied to mounting hostility toward British intransigence on treaty revision. But there were tremendous German advances in agricultural chemistry and veterinary science. The actual state of science in Western countries of the time needs evaluating. Study suggests that German *yatoi* were better educated in agriculture (licentiates and doctorates) than American and British *yatoi*. German *yatoi* evidenced considerable energy, and many had made major contributions to the field before coming to Japan. What influence was the fact that agricultural planning was already being highly structured in Bismarck's Germany?

In agriculture, a few Americans were retained in Hokkaido, but all British, except language teachers, were released. Some British *yatoi* do appear particularly inflexible. Farm bailiff James Begbie in the Komaba College experimental farm had to be told that he was not in charge. In government correspondence, he is described by his Japanese superior, Sekizawa Akekio, as having assumed a stance that the reprimand placed him in a position of "irresponsibility." Begbie absented himself from meetings and refused to make written reports. He repeated in memos that he would answer inquiries verbally. He was dismissed "because he insisted on his own biased opinion."[20] This case and others show the importance of mutual respect in working relations. But the charged political atmosphere seems to have affected British *yatoi* more than Japanese officials. For example in the early 1870s a large group of British *yatoi* was dismissed from the Navy. The timing was political, but also the Japanese were shifting to fewer foreign employees but ones with more expertise. British engineers and British shipping specialists were retained through the turn of the century. Thus, in agriculture the German shift appears more due to desire for progress.

Another example of the importance of background study of *yatoi* is that of the volatile but highly useful adviser on international law, E. Peshine Smith. He was strong on national rights and innovative and faithful to the Japanese on this point. Recent studies show the importance of his *Manual of Political Economy*, published in 1853.[21] It had formative influence on Republican Party policy through William H. Seward. The book went through nine printings, was adopted as a textbook at Cornell and Princeton, and was translated into French and German. Smith's protectionism thesis was not only at the center of New York protectionists dominating American politics of that era, but he gave the best of his advice to the Japanese.

Early legal advisers, many of whom had been consuls for their own countries, viewed Japanese jurisdiction with objectivity in areas that did not conflict with their homeland's national interests. In this regard mention may be made of Hollander Anthony Bauduin and American Eli Sheppard. Other legal specialists may be said to have been fully objective in regard to treaty revision and other legal questions, but they took their viewpoint from the school of law they professed. This tended to carry a national bias. For this and other reasons the Japanese very early became international in their approach. Whatever the inquiry at hand, legal or work projects, they put each question to several *yatoi*. It was from a broad information base that action was taken. More work is called for on the Japanese approach to *yatoi* and the use of their services. Japanese management had special characteristics in the Meiji era as it has today, especially in psychological finesse, incentives and rewards.

Yatoi in legal studies and *yatoi* in education deserve major focus in future studies. Given the international conditions of legal complexity and constraint in early Meiji, it may not seem surprising that the Japanese would give priority to legal study. Yet the Chinese did not nor did the Ottoman Empire similarly faced with external pressure. Amidst the numerous interpretations of the Meiji event, perhaps what stands out most is this penchant for study. And it was carried out in a foreign language milieu. In *bakumatsu* and early Meiji Japan, the French language was used. Thereafter the English language was the vehicle of modernizing. Not only were rocks unearthed but pebbles were scrutinized. The Japanese proclivity for eclecticism just as evident today as then is surely a component of internationalization.

Georges Bousquet, the first *yatoi* lawyer, commented that the Japanese studied and trained so exasperatingly intensively to prevent further humiliation. He also wished that they would slow down, as did many of the *yatoi*. Contemporary sociologist Tsurumi Kazuko asserts that study is natural to the fiber of the Japanese. The Japanese did study, and they did not succumb to the mixed court system and many other legal pitfalls.

Interpretations of Japanese accomplishments in the field of law still stress foreign model dominance. Japanese themselves still speak of Germanification of Japanese law at the turn of the century. Noda Yoshiyuki has called this a myth, although a widespread and deeply imbedded one. The influence of foreign law in Japan certainly goes back as far as Nishi Amane and Tsuda Mamichi studying Dutch law in Leiden. Yet already in 1860 the *Bansho shirabesho* had dropped Dutch in favor of English, French, German, and Russian. In 1872 the law school in the Justice Ministry began French law. After eight years of training thirty-seven students were graduated. In 1873 the Kaisei School introduced the first English law course, and it was taught in English. American *yatoi* advisers were prominent in international law throughout the Meiji era, and British *yatoi* advisers were widely used in industrial and tax laws. However, for internal law revision the French model was dominant to 1881. Mitsukuri Rinsho and Kurimoto Juon translated the Code Napoleon. In 1882, the French model penal and criminal codes were promulgated. Adaptation of the Civil Code also proceeded in this period with the help of French *yatoi* Georges Bousquet (1872-76), Albert C. DuBousquet (1868-82), and especially Emile G. Boissonade de Fontarabie (1873-95). There were other *yatoi* as well.[22]

It was after the Civil Code dispute that German law came to the fore in 1899. According to Noda Yoshiyuki, this was in good part because of the myth that the New Civil Code was drawn entirely from German law. In actuality Japanese customary practices, German theory, English and French ideas were embodies in the code. Further, Japanese practices were developed based on French and Anglo-American law principles for both the penal and civil codes.

Given the myth that Japanese law was German law, a look at course offerings in Tokyo University School of Law and in private institutions reveals an amazing breadth of French and Anglo-American law coverage. Interest in these fields remained high. Until 1916 no Japanese chaired a department of foreign law in Tokyo University. In that year Sugiyama Naojiro took charge of French law. It is from 1916 that serious work has gone forward in comparative jurisprudence.[23] In Tokyo University alone between 1874 and 1919, there were four *yatoi* professors of German law and sixteen *yatoi* professors in French and Anglo-American law (eight in each field).[24] In a total of eighty-three years of teaching by these *yatoi*, Germans gave eighteen man years, British and Americans thirty-two years, and the French thirty-three man years.

The whole of Meiji education needs further consideration. What actually did foreign teachers teach? What effects did their teaching have on their students? For example, Hozumi Yatsuka is often credited with a shift to German constitutional law. However, he was a student of Yale University law professor, Henry T. Terry (1876-1912). During two substantial periods in Japan, Terry imbued Japanese students with John Austin's theories of law as sovereign command, separate from moral judgment. Social Darwinism, popularized in Japan by American *yatoi* Edward S. Morse, was also significant in Hozumi's development. Hozumi's political thinking came full circle with some aspects of German legal positivism and more so with national studies. Richard Minear has helped demythologize the asserted dichotomy of British-American democratic liberalism vs. German authoritarian conservatism.[25] This type of study points up the need to ascertain the curriculum pursued by *yatoi* teachers.

In the Meiji era for an institution to be accredited by the Ministry of Education as a *semmon gakko* (special college), and accreditation involved funding, it was necessary to have a *yatoi* on staff. In the Taisho era this prestige pattern was discontinued. But again today there is promotion of internationalization in education. Study may be pursued to Showa *yatoi*. The milieu briefly is that, the United Nations University is in Japan, and there are many foreign students in Japanese universities with alterations being made in the system to accommodate them, and the Japan Foundation has assumed an active role in research and educational exchange. In the Japanization of government universities in the Taisho and early Showa eras, *yatoi* professors and lecturers were term appointments. However, in August 1982 the Diet passed a 'Special Legislative Measure for the Appointment of Foreign Nationals as Faculty Members at National and Public Universities.' These institutions are now legally able to appoint foreign nationals as professors with voting rights in faculty meetings, etc. The legislation is an effort toward internationalization. It is hoped that university faculties will carry forward. Kyoto University and National Museum of Ethnology have begun the process with three appointments from April 1983. Two are from the United Kingdom and one from China.[26]

The above are only a few topics, but very rewarding would be a study of the psychological milieu, Meiji Japan's 'future shock'. The following commentary is from a lecture *Gendai Nippon no kaika* (The Enlightenment of Contemporary Japan) given in 1911 by Natsume Soseki.

Japan's enlightenment should have been the natural product of a process generated by the internal dynamics of our society, like a natural wave generates another wave which in turn gathers the water and pushes it into another rolling wave. Regrettably, however, the process of enlightenment of Japan was not generated by such internal dynamics. As I mentioned earlier, due to the pressure to save her energy on the one hand, and to expend it on the other, Japan could achieve only a mark of 20 under normal conditions. However, given the external pressure for rapid development, we had to make a leap to reach a mark of 30. Like a man fleeing helter-skelter with a *tengu* (a long-nosed goblin) hard on his heels, we ran and jumped for our lives, hardly conscious of how we did it. . . . We had to achieve in ten years something which took European countries a century, and to do so in such a way as would make it appear genuinely self-motivated, not hollow. This entailed serious consequences. Even to a novice who had been barely initiated in the rudiments of arithmetic it was plain to see that in order to gain in ten years the experience which took others one hundred years, we had to expend our energy at ten times the rate of Europeans. This can best be illustrated by the example of the pursuit of learning. . . . Leaving aside those who acquired a superficial knowledge of new Western theories and loudly denounced them as lies, let us suppose that we reached by dint of the hard training we received during the forty or fifty years after the Restoration, a level of specialization which had taken Westerners one hundred years to attain. Let us suppose we did so by advancing from theories of A to those of B and then to those of C as a natural result of step-by-step studies, by comprehension and reasoning, and through spontaneous and graduated internal development, not newfangled pretentiousness. Even if you discount the difficulties inherent in the pioneering studies of a field of knowledge, if we could claim that we, who as a people are blessed with less vigor and brain power than Westerners, had accomplished in half the period that which took Westerners one hundred years, we could be proud of this as a stupendous achievement. At the same time, however, this exertion would necessarily reduce the people involved to a state of complete exhaustion in which they would be slumped, as it were, on the wayside gasping for breath. Any college professor who goes about his teaching hammer and tongs for a decade could easily wear himself out. It may be too much to say that those who are still full of life after ten years of teaching are a sham, but it seems to me that any hard-working professor is bound to become exhausted after teaching for so long. . . . [27]

Soseki's thesis is provocative. His last comment above may be applied to the Japanese nation. This capsuling of time produced tremendous tension. *Yatoi* themselves were caught up in it. Many felt as did British *yatoi* Edmund G. Holtham (1873-81) that "everywhere was tension, fatigue, and a cry for relief."[28] Japanese exhaustion, the total experience of social fatigue, has had psychological effects throughout this century. Several of Soseki's points lend themselves to analysis. To look at only one, what marks should Meiji Japan receive? Soseki seems to suggest a barely acceptable mark for the first ten years and at least academic par by the end of Meiji. With all that is known of advances in the Tokugawa era, modernization theorists would likely give the early Meiji learning base and potential half marks and, despite imbalances which are found in any development, high pass by the end of Meiji. Other schools of thought may offer other assessments. But what marks the *yatoi* will be given is in the hands of future researchers.

Notes

[1]UNESCO Higashi Ajia Bunka kenkyu senta [UNESCO East Asia Culture Research Center], *Shiryo oyatoi gaikokujin* [Source Materials on Foreign Employees] (Tokyo, 1975). See Review, H. J. Jones, *Monumenta Nipponica* 30, 4 (1975), pp. 465-68.

[2]Shigehisa Tokutaro, "Meiji jidai ni okeru seiyojin no bunka jigyo" [Cultural Activities of Westerners in the Meiji Period], *Doshisha kosho ronso* [Doshisha Commerce Essays] 20 (1939), pp. 134-48.

[3]Tanaka Tokihiko, *Meiji ishin no seikyoku to tetsudo kensetsu* [Railway Construction and the Political Situation of the Meiji Restoration] (Tokyo, 1963). Ishizuki Minoru, *Kindai Nihon no kaigai ryugakusei* [Modern Japan's Overseas Students] (Kyoto, 1972).

[4]Hugh Borton, *Japan's Modern Century* (New York, 1955), p. vi.

[5]Dates cited after *yatoi* names refer to years of employment.

[6]Deborah C. Church, "The Role of American Diplomatic Advisers to the Japanese Foreign Ministry, 1872-1887" (Ph.D. dissertation, University of Hawaii, 1978), p. 79.

[7]Sakata Yoshio, *Meiji zenhanki no nashonarisumu* [Early Meiji Nationalism] (Tokyo, 1958), pp. 12-14.

[8]Bernard S. Silberman, "Bureaucratic Development and the Structure of Decision-Making in the Meiji Period: The Case of the Genro," *Journal of Asian Studies* 27, 1 (1967), pp. 84-85.

[9]R. H. Van Gulik, "Kakkaron, a Japanese Echo of the Opium War," *Monumenta Serica* 4 (1939-40), pp. 481-511.

[10]Brinkley's *Japanese-English Dictionary* 2 vols. (Ann Arbor, 1963), 2, p. 1621.

[11]H. J. Jones, "Bakumatsu Foreign Employees," *Monumenta Nipponica* 29, 3 (1974), pp. 305-27.

[12]Cf. H. J. Jones, *Live Machines: Hired Foreigners and Meiji Japan* (Vancouver, 1980).

[13]H. J. Jones, "The Formulation of Meiji Government Policy Toward the Employment of Foreigners," *Monumenta Nipponica* 23, 1-2 (1968), pp. 9-30.

[14]Toyohara Jiro, "Kobusho to oyatoi gaikokujin ni tsuite: Meiji sangyo kindaika no issetsu" [Public Works Ministry and Foreign Employees: A Chapter in Meiji Industrial Modernization], *Shodai ronshu* [Commercial College Papers] 60, 1 (1964), pp. 35-56.

[15]Nishikawa Midori, "Meiji shoki ni okeru Kobusho setchi no igi" [Significance of the Establishment of the Public Works Ministry in Early Meiji], *Shiron* 10 (1962), pp. 719-36.

[16]See Ardath W. Burks, editor, *The Modernizers: Overseas Students, Foreign Employees, and Meiji Japan* (Boulder, 1985); H. J. Jones, "Meiji seifu to oyatoi gaikokujin" [The Meiji Government and Foreign Employees], *Meiji bunka kenkyu* [Studies in Meiji Culture] 3 (Tokyo, 1969), pp. 139-55.

[17]Shibusawa Eiichi, *Jijoden* [Autobiography] (Tokyo, 1937), p. 797.

[18]Church, p. 164.

[19]*Ibid.*, p. 157.

[20]Gaimusho kiroku [Foreign Ministry Records], Gaikokujin yatoiire toriatsukai sankosho, Folio 3, Sekizawa Akekio-James Begbie Correspondence (Tokyo, Japan Foreign Ministry Records Bureau).

[21]Church, p. 79; Michael H. Hudson, "E. Peshine Smith: A Study in Protectionist Growth Theory and American Sectionalism," (Ph.D. dissertation, New York University, 1968), pp. 23-24.

[22]Numata Jiro, "Rangaku kara Eigaku e" [From Dutch Studies to English Studies], *Nihon rekishi* [Japanese History], 14: pp. 3-15: 4 (1949), pp. 30-35; pp. 47-51; Mukai Ken and Nobuyoshi Toshitani, "The Progress and Problems of Compiling the Civil Code in the Early Meiji Era," *Law in Japan* 1 (1967), pp. 25-59.

[23]Noda Yoshiyuki, "Comparative Jurisprudence in Japan: Its Past and Present, Part I," *Law in Japan* 8 (1975), p. 5. *Hogaku Kyokai zasshi* [*Education Law Magazine*] (1972), pp. 1244-1290.

[24]*Ibid.*, Part II, *Law in Japan* 9 (1976), 33.

[25]Richard A. Minear, *Japanese Tradition and Western Law: Emperor, State and Law in the Thought of Yatsuka Hozumi* (Cambridge, 1970).

[26]Kitamura Kazuyuki, "The Internationalization of Higher Education in Japan," *Law in Japan* 16 (1983), pp. 135-40.

[27]Noda, Part I, *Law in Japan* 8 (1975), p. 32.

[28]Edmund G. Holtham, *Eight Years in Japan, 1873-1881* (London, 1883), pp. 216, 271, 312-13.

PART TWO

CASE STUDIES:
NORTH AMERICAN VIEWS

3

William Elliot Griffis:
The Tokyo Years, 1872-1874

Edward R. Beauchamp

I

Upon his death on February 5, 1928, the respected liberal American journal, *The Nation*, eulogized William Elliot Griffis (1843-1928) as "an authority on things Japanese," and "the first, if not the only, American to live in Japan during the feudal days, [when] he helped to lay the foundation of the existing Japanese school system."[1] Griffis' work, *The Mikado's Empire,* was in a sense a religious calling. Although never serving as a missionary in Japan, Griffis suggested, shortly before his death in 1928 that

> Providence so ordered that I should see, when almost a baby, the launching, in 1850, of Commodore Perry's [sometime] flagship, the frigate *Susquehanna*; that I should have as a classmate the son of our American Minister [to Japan] Pruyn. . . ; that I should during my four years at Rutgers College . . . teach the first Japanese students in America; that I should spend another four years in educational work in the interior of *Dai Nippon*; that my sister Margaret Clark Griffis, should be the principal of the first government school for girls; and that I should remain on constant terms of intimacy with Nippon's sons and daughters ever since meeting them at my home, at the Asiatic Society [of Japan] and in a hundred ways.[2]

These words contain in large measure the essence of William Elliot Griffis; he was a man secure in his belief that he was God's chosen instrument to assist in bringing the blessings of Western civilization (material and spiritual) to Japan, and in explaining Japan and the Japanese to his fellow countrymen.

Griffis' career can be divided into three separate, yet overlapping phases. First, as a popular historian and analyst of Japan to the English-speaking world. Second, as an early and talented practitioner of what has come to be called international education; and finally, as one of the earliest of the *oyatoi gaikokujin*, or "foreign employees" of a Japan emerging from two-and-one-half centuries of virtual isolation. This chapter concentrates on a single phase of this last dimension--Griffis' two years as a teacher in Tokyo from February 1872 to July 1874--and attempts to describe, in his own words, his experiences as a teacher in one of the predecessors of what was to become Tokyo Imperial University.

William Elliot Griffis arrived in Japan on December 29, 1870 after having been chosen by the Board of Foreign Missions of the Dutch Reformed Church in New York "to establish a scientific school on the American principle and teach the natural sciences" in Fukui, the provincial capital of Matsudaira Shungaku.[3] After only a year in Fukui, Griffis was able to successfully arrange a transfer to Tokyo to assist in the establishment of a new technical school. Shortly after arriving in the capital in February 1872, Griffis learned that the new school would not open at the scheduled time. This development gave him time to pursue his study of Japanese, to become deeply involved in the establishment of the new Union Church in Yokohama, and to become acquainted with the members of the American Scientific Commission in Japan, including the commission's head, General Horace Capron, former United States Commissioner of Agriculture in the administration of President Grant. Further delays in opening the new school prompted Griffis to remark, "I find it the best philosophy to wait patiently and improve my leisure time for myself, although I am sorry that the Japs have to pay me for doing nothing."[4] He did, however, some teaching, although not at the technical school. The Meiji government had established in February 1870 the so-called *Daigaku Nanko* (School for Western Studies) at which Mr. Edward House, an American who became editor of the *Tokyo Times*, taught. When Griffis arrived, he found House confined to his home with an attack of gout, and thus taught House's classes for several days until he recovered.

It was about this time that Griffis received further bad news about his expected teaching duties. The technical school would not be opening, and he was to take up different duties. "It never opened," he wrote, "because the scholars were too few for the Prof. of Law and Astronomy, while for me, although they were plenty (20 or so) the students were really of a grade of education & ability inferior to those in the College. I was then offered a position with the Department of Public Works, to instruct the young Japanese engineers in an outline of Chemistry, or the post of Prof. of Chem. at the Yedo College [*Daigaku Nanko*]. I chose the latter."[5]

His agreement to switch from the proposed technical school to *Daigaku Nanko* was the cause of an eventual dispute with the *Mombusho*, [Ministry of Education] and indirectly at least, a major cause for his leaving Japan in the summer of 1874. However, he was pleased at the time of the switch because "I occupy a position second only to Mr. [Guido] Verbeck the President."[6] His responsibilities consisted of teaching "Chemistry, Physiology, and Comparative Philology. . . . I teach in the three higher classes [and] all my pupils are bright, eager and industrious. They range from 16 to 21, and they will, in the future, be the leading men in Japan. [This work] is my highest joy."[7]

II

In early 1872 when Griffis began to teach, *Daigaku Nanko* was really "a replica of an American grammar school."[8] The school's English division included about 500 students,[9] and these students were "of every age, and from every quarter of the empire."[10] Griffis left a colorful description of conditions in the school upon his first arrival in January 1871, and it is doubtful the picture had changed significantly by the time of his return a year later.

> The middle-aged and old men, who wished to learn merely to read and translate, and not to speak, a foreign language, were mostly in the "meaning school." The younger, though some were over thirty, learned the alphabet, spelling, conversations, writings, and, in the higher classes, geography, arithmetic, and simple history. The buildings were rows of sheds with glass windows, deal desks and seats, and unpainted wood partitions.[11]

If the students were unlike those in Western institutions, the teachers were even more colorful. As one student of the period has written, "It is an unalloyed truth to say that the majority of the 'Professors' in the schools of . . . [Tokyo] were graduates of the dry-goods counter, the forecastle, the camp, and the shambles, or belonged to a vast array of unclassified humanity that floats like waifs in every seaport."[12] Warming to his task, he accused these teachers of "Coming directly from the bar-room, the brothel, the gambling saloon, or the resort of boon companions, they brought the graces, the language and the manners of those places into the school room."[13]

The quality of teachers in *Daigaku Nanko* had improved substantially by the late winter of 1872. Perhaps the Japanese had grown more selective in hiring foreigners to teach, and certainly, the supply of qualified men outstripped the relatively limited demand. For example, when Griffis first considered having his sister Margaret join him in Japan, he had no doubt that he could find her a position without difficulty. Within a short time after her arrival in 1873, however, both brother and sister agreed that finding a teaching position would be a long and difficult process. By the opening of the school term in Fall, Griffis was besieged with requests from people in America who were seeking positions, but as Margaret confided to her sisters in Philadelphia, "there is nothing for them here. The government has enough foreigners on hand."[14] The days when almost any foreigner could land a position, despite his qualifications, were at an end. Japan was anxious to hire as few foreigners as possible and to phase out, as soon as possible, as many of those employed as possible. As many developing nations are learning today, expatriate teachers may possess badly needed skills, but there comes a time when their value reaches a point of diminishing returns. Professor Hazel Jones aptly describes the Japanese policy:

> Recognizing the use of foreign employees as a stop-gap measure, Japanese officials began to stress education of Japanese to replace foreigners as quickly as possible. Of all the means open to the Japanese to modernize, the employment of foreign specialists may be seen as one wing, but the other was the education of Japanese at home and abroad. [The Meiji oligarchs] made clear that the primary purpose of foreign employees was to educate Japanese to replace them.[15]

In terms of cost alone, Nagai Michio points out that in 1873 the Japanese government was devoting 14% of the total education budget for the salaries of foreign teachers. Some of these men "were paid up to ¥600 per month when the school was founded four years later."[16]

The teachers already hired at *Daigaku Nanko* came from a wide variety of backgrounds and countries. The faculty appears to have been divided into English, French, and German departments and was composed of at least eleven foreign teachers.[17] In a letter written home prior to his sister's arrival in Tokyo, Griffis described how "I enjoy fully the presence and contact of kindred souls" during meals in "the mess." This was "an assemblage of the four German, one English, one Dane, and three American teachers."[18] This organization, which appears to have been an eating club, provided food and good fellowship for $25 per week.

III

Griffis' letters and diary reveal little about his teaching in Tokyo, and his sister's letters are silent on this phase of their life in Japan. We do know, however, that soon after his arrival from Fukui in early 1872, Griffis asked that two copies of Professor George Baker's chemistry textbook be sent to him as soon as possible and it appears that this was the book he relied upon for his chemistry teaching.

It seems reasonable to assume that Griffis saw no reason for changing the method of teaching chemistry that he had employed in Fukui. He described this method as being based largely on "the blackboard system of instruction" in which "all the teaching has been by experiments and lectures."[19] Thus, most of his formal teaching consisted of his either lecturing or demonstrating an experiment, and using the blackboard for listing formulae or illustrating various points. The only difference was that in Tokyo his students had a better working knowledge of English, enabling him to dispense with a translator. Presumably this allowed him to cover more material more efficiently than in Fukui, where he was forced to rely on a translator or his limited knowledge of Japanese.

Virtually nothing is known, however, about his methods of teaching his other classes in geography, literature, etc. Since his educational theory placed the teacher at the center of the learning process and the students as the receivers of knowledge, it seems reasonable to assume that he lectured a great deal. We do know that he introduced some sort of "Game of Authors" to his literature class, but this was less than two months before his return to America, which casts some doubt about how "innovative" his teaching had been in this period.

It is worth noting, however, that Griffis was highly critical of the Japanese teachers of the Tokugawa period whose major qualification was their knowledge of the Chinese classics. His view of the approach of these teachers has a contemporary ring. Griffis wrote that their "chief duty was to stuff and cram the minds of...pupils. To expand or develop the mental powers of a boy, to enlarge his mental visions, to teach him to think for himself, would have been doing precisely what it was the teacher's business to prevent."[20] What Griffis opposed, however, was neither the centrality of the teacher to the learning process nor even his propensity "to stuff and cram the minds of his pupils." Instead, he argued that "the native teacher of the future must depend less on traditional authority, and more on the resources of a *richly furnished* mind."[21] He suggested that while the "old teacher was a drillmaster; the new one must be that and more. The old one stifled questioning; the new one must encourage it."[22] Griffis' concern, then, was one of primarily modifying the traditional lecture method in ways which would make it more effective. He was a reformer, not a radical.

Griffis was not the type of teacher who put in his several hours of classroom time each day and spent the rest of his time in pursuing his own interests. From the time he moved into his new house in the European quarter of Tokyo, he had several young Japanese students living under his roof. Their numbers fluctuated from time to time, but they were always present in significant numbers. During Christmas 1872, for example, Griffis informed his family that in order to celebrate Christmas properly, "I shall have my five Japanese boys in my house hang up their stockings on Xmas eve, and on Xmas day we shall have a children's party."[23]

One of the most interesting aspects of Griffis' teaching in Tokyo was his characteristic trait of taking on many more responsibilities than he could legally be expected to assume. Although he was contracted to teach chemistry and physics at *Daigaku Nanko*, he also voluntarily taught geography, physiology, literature, and, later, law. Probably as a result of the tight financial situation in which he found himself, Griffis successfully secured a ¥30 per month salary increase based on this extra teaching.

An interesting aspect of the educational reforms of the early Meiji period was the Emperor's personal interest in their progress. The Emperor often received foreign teachers in a formal ceremony and even visited the schools in Tokyo, not only as a political gesture but also because of his concern in their well-being. One of his visits to *Daigaku Nanko*, which Griffis describes in his diary, took place on May 7, 1872.

. . . the Mikado visited the school today arriving at nine A.M. and
remaining till 12:30. He witnessed a number of experiments in physics
and chemistry, and listened to the students read, answer questions in
English, French and German. Several of his cabinet ministers were
present, and about twenty of his courtiers in court costume. His Majesty
was dressed in a wide long robe of heavy white silk with bloomer-like
trousers of red silk. His hair was cut round to his head, on which rested a
cap of shining black material with a plain ornament of fluted gold with
an upright projection several inches high. According to prescribed
etiquette his countenance was passive, lacking expression, except
occasionally when his interest was excited sufficiently to show a firm
and manly, but not handsome face. As I stood for nearly an hour within
six feet of him, I studied his face carefully. So far as I could judge there
was neither profound wisdom nor deep-set purpose in countenance. It
was that of an intelligent, earnest Japanese. The exercise having been
finished, those present remained respectfully seated. The Mikado and the
courtiers proceeded to the reception room His Majesty advancing first,
along the passage. As I turned I came within three feet of a collision
with the august personage. I sheered off backward to a side recess, hiding
my diminished head until [the Emperor] had passed by. The Emperor
returned his thanks to his foreign servants by a letter and banquet.[24]

IV

Of all of Griffis' experiences in his 1,297 days in Japan, the one that both
seared him the most, and which offers the student of the period the greatest
insights, was the events leading up to his departure from Japan in July 1874. A
major conflict erupted between Griffis and the *Mombusho* over the
interpretation of Griffis' contract in Tokyo, and especially his situation
resulting from the failure of the technical school to open in the late winter of
1872. The event that appears to have triggered the whole affair grew out of the
American teachers' celebration of their July 4 Independence Day holiday
in 1873. These teachers, living in the European compound, were determined
to celebrate their national holiday with the traditional fireworks in spite of
the Japanese officials' injunction just a day earlier against such a display.
The Japanese authorities were justifiably concerned over the fire hazard that
the American celebration would pose to the flimsy wooden structures which
made up the bulk of the capital's structures. The Americans, on the other hand,
felt that the concept of "extraterritoriality" prevented the Japanese from
interfering. In any event, the fireworks display took place on the night of July
4th with Griffis watching it from a friend's residence. On the following day,
Griffis' diary records that a Mr. Wilson, presumably one of the teachers
suspected of complicity in the affair, was "questioned" by the police and school
authorities.

One must keep in mind that the Japanese were extremely jealous of their sovereignty and were looking for ways in which to have the unequal treaties with the Western powers abrogated. The American defiance of Japanese regulations undoubtedly was irksome to the government officials. It appears that the Japanese, stung by this turn of events, looked for an occasion to reassert their authority over the foreigners. The result was the so-called "Sunday Question."

Soon after, the school officials announced that they were shifting the teachers' Sunday holiday to conform to the Japanese holidays. As Griffis summed up the situation in a letter home:

> The educational authorities have determined to enforce the observation of Japanese holidays, and to require all foreign teachers to disregard Sunday. The Japanese holidays are the 1st, 6th, 11th, 16th, 21st, 26th of each month. Such a rule would give us more holidays, but we should have to teach on Sundays. It was given out that in all new contracts, the anti-Sunday clause would be inserted. A few weeks ago, a request from the *Mombusho* was sent asking us to teach on Sunday. We replied, "no, not for $10,000 per month."[25]

Griffis, secure in his knowledge that righteousness was on his side, immediately began to rally his compatriots in opposition to this decision. He wrote, "I went to see the English-speaking teachers, both British and American. All agreed to protest against the changing rest days from Sunday to [the Japanese system]."[26] The Japanese authorities, according to Griffis' account of the incident, did not take kindly to his activities.

> This action [on my part], though done with all courtesy...immediately aroused the wrath of the [Minister of Education, Tanaka Fujimaro] then in control who stands in memory as the typical Japanese politician and spoilsman, about as closely resembling the American "boss" as any creature ever met with.[27]

Much to his surprise, Griffis received notice on July 15, that his contract was not to be renewed. The communication not only shocked him, but must have also angered him. He was a hardworking, conscientious professor, well liked by his students, with the best interests of Japan at heart. He had led his family to believe that he might stay in Japan for a long time and, in addition, he saw himself doing God's work in opposing the shift of rest days from Sunday to the Japanese system. Griffis' initial response to this unwelcome news was to fight back, and he immediately brought his case to the attention of Mr. Charles De Long, the American Minister to Japan, and other influential foreigners. He wrote a private letter to the editor of the *Japan Mail* (Mr. William Howell), complaining about the situation and received this reply:

I have said a few words this week upon the Sunday question, which I
hope may do some good. But I know the Japanese are in a very
uncomplying mood . . . [and] have a class of men in office who delight
to answer a foreign ministers [sic] remonstrance on such a subject with a
snub. For a long time they were servile when their seat was yet insecure.
Now they are insolent—like all ill-bred grooms as half of them are—or
little better.[28]

In addition, he began to contact influential political figures in the Japanese
government to protest what he considered unfair treatment at the hands of "a
petty underling."[29] Years later, in 1900, he wrote that solving the problem was
a simple matter. "I dropped a note to Mr. Iwakura [Tomomi], the junior prime
minister, simply stating the case. The matter was very quickly settled to my
satisfaction. Another position of equal honor and emolument for three years
was offered me, which I declined with thanks."[30] As in much of what Griffis
wrote, there is truth in this interpretation, but he selectively omitted much
which would have cast his actions in a different, even unfavorable, light. In the
first place, Griffis' diary and correspondence indicate that, in addition to seeking
the intercession of Iwakura, he also contacted Mori Arinori, Matsudaira
Shungaku, Judge Horace Bingham, the new American Minister to Japan, and
others.

In late July 1873, he informed his family:

This will most probably finish my career in Japan, and I am not sorry
that I have so good a reason for leaving the Japanese civil service. I am a
little sorry, as I should like to have remained six months longer at least.
After near three years service in a foreign land, I have in the bank now,
just enough to take me home. For the future however, I have no sort of
fear, and though I never expect, nor care to be a rich man, not making
wealth an object, I expect to win a name and place in my native land.
The tide in the affairs of Japan may turn, but at present, it is most
decidedly anti-Christian and reactionary.[31]

An examination of the available correspondence between Griffis and
Minister of Education Tanaka indicates that their differences clearly revolved as
much around the interpretation of Griffis' contract as on the burning question of
whether foreign teachers should teach on the Western sabbath. It seems that
Griffis felt very strongly that he was brought to Tokyo to fill a specific
position in the proposed polytechnical institution which, for various reasons,
failed to open at the scheduled time. On the other hand, Griffis had been
"willing to volunteer . . . to teach the 1st class students at old *Nanko* (now
Kaisei Gakko), until that special school was opened." With the school now
opened in the *Kaisei Gakko*, Tanaka pointed out, "you have . . . been
appointed, as promised, as the professor of the same, that is to say, Law and
Physics,"[32] so the contract was fulfilled. Moreover, the government had even

added ¥30 per month to his salary "so that our contract to engage you as professor at the special school was wholly and satisfactorily fulfilled."[33]

Upon receiving this letter, Griffis felt compelled to reply "because silence on my part would be misunderstood."[34] The major thrust of Griffis' disagreement with Tanaka revolved around three aspects of the contract. First, Griffis reiterated his stand that he was hired for a specific position, i.e., in the technical school, and when that school failed to open, he "could have waited, had I so chose, doing nothing, until the Educational authorities were ready to carry out their contract with me."[35] He claimed to have "volunteered" for *Nanko* in order to be useful, and "on the condition that I should have my proper postion as Professor of Chemistry and Physics, for the term contracted for, i.e., two years."[36] Griffis seemed especially agitated over the Education Minister's interpretation of the reason for paying him ¥30 per month extra. Griffis contended, with apparent justification, that the extra ¥30 was due to *extra* chores that he had voluntarily taken on, above and beyond his normal contractual duties. "I never asked for any increase of salary, " Griffis told Tanaka, "nor do I want any, except as honest payment for honest extra work, done outside my contract." He petulantly concluded by informing his antagonist that if he persisted in his interpretation of this matter, "I do not wish, nor will I receive, the extra 30 yen per month, recently added."[37]

The available evidence indicates that Griffis' students fully supported him in his battle with the *Mombusho*, and this cheered him. Between August 20-22, they wrote four letters of support to Griffis, and perhaps to Tanaka also, although there is no evidence of the latter. The self-interest of the students is in the forefront of their letters, but there is also real, if muted, affection for their *sensei*. One class requested his "mercy to continue in teaching us as you have done during a year and a half, that is to teach us on the other branches besides Chemistry. Indeed . . . it would be beyond your proper duty to the school. But we shall be very happy if you grant this request."[38] His students in the First Legal Class appealed to his pedagogical pride, telling him that no matter how "greatly learned teachers we may have in the future, it is quite certain that we shall not get the teacher like you who has great skill in teaching according to the character and ability of each scholar."[39] Perhaps the most poignant appeal came from his "affectionate scholars of the 2nd Legal Class":

> In this school, many teachers are of different classes of men, some are soldiers, some are sailors and others are mere drinkers or very bad men, though there are a few educated teachers who are very kind, such as you and two other gentlemen. There is a great difference between the lower classes of men whose only objects are to make money and the educated teachers whose purpose are to help the Japanese in advancing in civilization. But if the officer think all to be the same object, he is quite mistaken. Of course, we honor you as our dear teacher and distinguish you from lower classes of men.[40]

This support from his students must have buoyed Griffis' spirits considerably in his battle with the *Mombusho*. Be that as it may, the fact remained that Griffis' contract had not been renewed and he had an extremely small financial cushion to fall back on in the event of a real emergency. He undoubtedly had this in mind when he wrote to Iwakura Tomomi again on September 11.[41] There is no record of the contents of this letter, but a reply to it was written by the busy official's son on September 19, 1873. Young Iwakura acknowledged Griffis' letter and apologized that his father was unable to see him at that time owing to his "exceedingly busy" schedule which, his son complained, left him "no time to talk even to us."[42] Lest this be interpreted as a lack of interest on the Foreign Minister's part, it should be pointed out that the summer and autumn of 1873 saw the eruption of Japan's "Korean Crisis."[43] These events kept him constantly involved with weighty matters of state, and a foreign teacher's contractual problems had to take second place. Griffis had been the Rutgers teacher of Iwakura's son and thus Iwakura undoubtedly did what he could under the circumstances.

By October 10, it appears that there was some movement in the negotiations between Griffis and Tanaka. In a letter of that date, Tanaka reaffirmed his basic position that Griffis had "no reason . . . of any dissatisfaction on your part," but added the significant phrase, "if you have anything to be proposed, please give it in detail to the Director of the Kaisei gakko, and whether your service after the expiration of your term is left to the convenience of the school. . . ." In this letter Tanaka appears to be backtracking somewhat from his previous hard line. We cannot be sure, but it was possible that between Griffis' last letter of September 11 and Tanaka's letter of October 10, Iwakura had contacted Tanaka in an attempt to work out some sort of face-saving compromise.

A proper explanation of the details of the negotiations after this point is not possible because of the constraints of time, but Griffis reaffirmed his original position and contended that "I do not wish to force myself on the Japanese officers," and if the *Mombusho* "cannot carry out your contract with me, I shall return to my own country and tell everyone that a contract with the *Mombusho* is worth nothing."[44] Despite this strong language, he offered the compromise suggestion that his contract run only until October 1, 1874, rather that July 10, 1875. After further complex negotiations and the apparent intervention of Hatakeyama Yoshinari, a friend of Griffis since student days at Rutgers and newly appointed director of the Kaisei Gakko, the impasse was resolved by extending Griffis' contract to July 1874.

This episode ended with the National Superintendent of Education David Murray's letter to Griffis on January 24, 1874.

Allow me to express the pleasure I feel in seeing the matters at issue are settled in an honorable and satisfactory manner, and on which must be regarded as highly complimentary to you, and I must add creditable to the Japanese officials.[45]

A question bound to occur in the assessment of any teacher's career is that of influence. What difference did he or she make? Questions of this sort are fraught with danger; the intellectual quicksand surrounding questions of influence should be approached with great caution, and any answers to the question must be viewed with more than a healthy skepticism. In Griffis' case, however, it is probably fair to suggest that his unique position as a bearer of Western science and modernity, in a society consciously seeking to emulate these attributes, ensured that his impact on his students would be more than an average one.

In later years, Griffis was to claim, "I know personally every one of the fifty-five men who made up the new [Meiji] government."[46]This, indeed, may have been true since we know that through his connections with Dr. Verbeck and by virtue of his position in Tokyo, Griffis moved in the same social circle as the Japanese leaders. We also know that Griffis was a member of the so-called *Meirokusha* ("Meiji Six Society"), a "literary society for the encouragement of western studies,"[47] which was composed of "the leading students of the West and the most progressive thinkers of the day."[48] Among the original founders of this society were Mori Arinori, Fukuzawa Yukichi, Nishi Amane, Nishimura Shigeki, Naura Masano, Kato Hiroyuki, Tsuda Masamichi, and Mitsukuri Rinsho, or, in Donald Shively's phrase, "the private scholars and officials best informed about the West."[49] Many of these scholars were also prominent members of the government at various times during the period. Griffis' participation in this context is important not only because it brought him into direct contact with some of the best minds of Meiji Japan and informed his voluminous writing about Japan, but also because it gave his ideas an entree into influential Japanese minds. The measure of his influence eludes our calipers, but since the *Meirokusha* was "for several years perhaps the most important channel for the introduction of information and ideas from the West," we can be assured his ideas moved in Japan's highest circles.[50]

We also know that Griffis was proud of his contacts with influential Japanese government figures and powerful Americans who interacted with the Japanese government. On a least three occasions Griffis dined with Iwakura Tomomi (whose son he had taught at Rutgers), whom Edmond Papinot describes as "Until his death, . . . the most conspicuous politician in Japan."[51]

Whatever influence Griffis had on individual Japanese was probably most forcefully exerted on his students in Tokyo. Perhaps the most prominent of them was Komura Jutaro, whom Griffis described as "my star pupil in the University of Tokyo from 1872 to 1874," to whom he taught law and "often discussed American ideas and policy."[52] Upon completing his studies at Tokyo, Komura was sent to Harvard Law School on a government scholarship. On his return to Japan, he began his career as a judge before taking a minor position in the Ministry of Foreign Affairs. In 1893, however, he was posted to Peking to represent Japanese interests in the international conference there. As a reward for his services, Komura was named Minister of Foreign Affairs in the first Katsura cabinet in 1901. He played a major role in the 1902 Anglo-Japanese Alliance. The high point of his career came in 1905 when he was named Japanese plenipotentiary to the Portsmouth Peace Conference, which concluded the Russo-Japanese War. In 1908 he became Foreign Minister for a second time and played an important role in the annexation of Korea.[53]

Another of Griffis' students in Tokyo was Viscount Kuroda, and there is evidence of Griffis' influence on his future. In a letter to Griffis, dated 12 April 1915, he wrote:

> I often say that without your help I could never have been successful in accomplishing my course of study at the University and...I could never get my present position with the Imperial Household.[54]

Takahashi Korekiyo was another recipient of Griffis' hospitality. In an unpublished manuscript Griffis credited Takahashi with reading to him a "good deal of native Japanese literature."[55] Takahashi later became president of the Bank of Japan, twice his nation's Prime Minister, and Finance Minister who stabilized the yen in the early 1930s. He was assassinated by fanatics in the 26 February (1936) Incident because of his opposition to the army's actions in China.

Not all of Griffis' students were influential or prominent. A number of them were merely successful in the various endeavors to which they chose to devote themselves. A certain Nishimura, a student in Fukui, edited a journal, *Gakusei (Student)*, devoted to young people. In a letter to Griffis, dated 5 March 1915, the young editor asked his former teacher for a short contribution to his journal. and his assistance in tracking down a copy of a book Nishimura had written, *A History of Japanese Vessels in the United States*, that had been published in America.[56] Another of his students who falls into this category was also from Fukui, Karl Kasahara, who lived in Griffis' house, and later became manager of the Kobe Pier Co., Ltd.[57]

We would be remiss if we did not mention two of Griffis' many students from Rutgers who have become at least a footnote to history. The first, Kusakabe Taro, was a brilliant student at Rutgers who, unfortunately, died of tuberculosis just prior to his graduation in 1870. It was Griffis' sad duty to present Kusakabe's Phi Beta Kappa key to his grief-stricken parents when he arrived in Japan a few months later.

Another of his Rutgers "boys" was Hatakeyama Yoshinari. Although he did not graduate, he returned to Japan and acted as an interpreter with the Iwakura Embassy before serving as an administrator at the University of Tokyo soon after its founding and later in the Ministries of Education, Home, and Foreign Affairs. He also died at an early age because of tuberculosis.

If a teacher is, indeed, known by the students he has taught, William Elliot Griffis was a success in that calling.

Notes

[1]"Obituary," in *The Nation*, No. 126 (February 22, 1928), p. 199.

[2]William Elliot Griffis, "Japan at the Time of Townsend Harris," in W. E. Griffis and Hugh Byas, *Japan: A Comparison* (New York, 1923), p. 12.

[3]Foster Rhea Dulles, *Yankees and Samurai: America's Role in the Emergence of Japan* (New York, 1965), p. 156.

[4]William Elliot Griffis, "Diary," February 24, 1872, in Griffis Collection, Rutgers University Library (hereafter GC).

[5]Letter, WEG to Margaret Clark Griffis (hereafter MCG), April 21, 1872, GC.

[6]*Ibid.*

[7]*Ibid.*

[8]Robert Schwantes, *Japanese and Americans: A Century of Cultural Relations* (New York, 1955), p. 157.

[9]Aoki Hideo, "The Effect of American Ideas Upon Japanese Higher Education" (Unpublished Ph.D. dissertation, Stanford University, 1957), p. 174.

[10]William Elliot Griffis, *The Mikado's Empire* (New York, 1913), Volume II, p. 372.

[11]*Ibid.*

[12]Harold S. Williams, *Foreigners in Mikadoland* (Tokyo, 1963), p. 84.

[13]*Ibid.* Also see William Elliot Griffis, *Verbeck of Japan: A Citizen of No Country* (New York, 1900), p. 240.

[14]Letter, MCG to Sisters, September 21, 1872, GC.

[15]Hazel J. Jones, "The Meiji Government and Foreign Employees, 1868-1912," (Unpublished Ph.D. dissertation, University of Michigan, 1967), p. 77. See also Hazel J. Jones, *Live Machines: Hired Foreigners in Meiji Japan* (Vancouver, 1980).

[16]Nagai Michio, *Higher Education in Japan: Its Takeoff and Crash* (Tokyo, 1971), p. 23, quoting Ogata Hiroyasu, *Seiyo Kyoiku Inyu no Hoho [A Plan for the Introduction of Western Education]*, (Tokyo, 1961), p. 142.

[17]An undated document in Griffis' hand in the Griffis Collection lists the following Nanko faculty: English Department--W. E. Griffis (Chemistry), P. V. Veeder (Physics), D. B. McCartell (Natural History), Horace Wilson (Mathematics), and Rev. J. A. Summers (Literature); French Department--X. Maillot (Physics and Chemistry), G. Fontaine (Literature), and P. Fougue (Mathematics); German Department--[?] Ritter (Physics), E. Knipping (Mathematics), and C. Schenck (unknown subject).

This document obviously reflects the composition of the school's faculty at a particular point in time; other evidence (Aoki, p. 174) indicates that men such as Guido Verbeck (Algebra and Moral Philosophy), Edward House (English), and others also graced its faculty, and at least some of the men on Griffis' list taught subjects other than those listed next to their names. For example, Griffis taught law in addition to chemistry.

[18]Letter, WEG to MCG, March 18, 1872, GC.

[19]Letters, WEG to MCG, September 9 and December 3, 1871, GC.

[20]William Elliot Griffis, "Education in Japan," in *The College Courant*, May 16, 1874, n.p., GC.

[21]*Ibid.*

[22]*Ibid.*

[23]Letter, WEG to Sisters, December 23, 1872, GC.

[24]William Elliot Griffis, "Extra Notes," May 7, 1872, GC.

[25]Letter, WEG to Sister, July 29, 1873, GC.

[26]Griffis, *Verbeck of Japan,* pp. 269-270.

[27]*Ibid.*, p. 270.

[28]Letter [signature and date unclear but probably William Y. Howell] to WEG, July 19, 1873, GC.

[29]Griffis, *Verbeck of Japan,* p. 271.

[30]*Ibid.*

[31]Letter, WEG to Sisters, July 29, 1873, GC.

[32]Letter, Tanaka Fujimaro to WEG, August 16, 1873, GC.

[33]*Ibid.*

[34]*Ibid.*

[35]*Ibid.*

[36]*Ibid.*

[37]*Ibid.*

[38]Letter, "Sincere Pupils" (fourteen pupils of Griffis' First Scientific Class), to WEG, August 20, 1873, GC.

[39]Letter, students of Griffis' First Legal Class to WEG, August 20, 1873, GC.

[40]Letter, students of Griffis' Second Legal Class to WEG, August 22, 1873, GC.

[41]Letter, WEG to Iwakura Tomomi, September 11, 1873, GC.

[42]Letter, T. S. Iwakura [son of Iwakura Tomomi] to WEG, September 19, 1873, GC.

[43]For details, see Hilary Conroy, *The Japanese Seizure of Korea,* 1868-1910 (Philadelphia, 1960), and Marlene J. Mayo, "The Korean Crisis of 1873 and Early Meiji Foreign Policy," in *Journal of Asian Studies,* XXXI, No. 4 (1972), pp. 793-819.

[44]Letter, WEG to Tanaka Fujimaro and a certain Ban [*Mombusho* official?], October 13, 1873, GC.

[45]Letter, David Murray to WEG, January 24, 1874, GC.

[46]"Dr. W. E. Griffis Brings Message from the East," (unidentified newspaper clipping, probably 1911-1912), GC.

[47]George Sansom, *The Western World and Japan: A Study in the Interaction of European and Asiatic Cultures* (New York, 1950), p. 197. See also, William Reynolds Braisted, *Meiroku Zasshi: Journal of the Japanese Enlightenment* (Tokyo, 1976).

[48]Donald Shively, "Nishimura Shigeki: A Confucian View of Modernization," in *Changing Japanese Attitudes Toward Modernization*, edited by Marius Jansen (Princeton, 1965), p. 197.

[49]*Ibid.*, p. 209.

[50]*Ibid.*

[51]Edmond Papinot, *Historical and Geographical Dictionary of Japan* (Tokyo, 1972), p. 220.

[52]Letter, WEG to *New York Herald Tribune*, August 9, 1924, GC.

[53]Okamoto Shumpei, *The Japanese Oligarchy and the Russo-Japanese War* (New York, 1971), pp. 26-27.

[54]Letter, Viscount Kuroda to WEG, April 12, 1915, GC.

[55]William Elliot Griffis, "The Rise of the New Japan," (unpublished manuscript, n.d., GC), p. 14.

[56]Letter, Nishimura [?] to WEG, March 5, 1915, GC.

[57]Letter, Karl Kasahara to WEG, May 1, 1916, GC.

4

Science and Civilization in Early Meiji Japan: The "Autobiographical Notes" of Thomas C. Mendenhall

Richard Rubinger

Introduction

Any attempt to assess the role of the *oyatoi* in the introduction of modern science in early Meiji Japan immediately suggests a number of broad and fundamental questions: Why has Japan been so successful in developing Western technology? To what degree did Tokugawa traditions help prepare the way? Did they, on the other hand, retard or set limits to the process? Did individuals matter or were institutional and ideological factors paramount? Once committed, did the Japanese government put its funds into basic research or applied science? Why was the matter settled as it was? These and other basic problems form the core of a rich literature on the history of science in modern Japan dominated by the work of Nakayama Shigeru, Watanabe Masao, Sugimoto Isao, Koizumi Kenkichiro, James Bartholomew and others.

Although informed by the issues in the scholarly literature, this chapter does not presume to make contributions to the on-going debates among specialists. Furthermore, since the scientific achievements of the subject of this essay, Thomas C. Mendenhall, have been amply documented and described by Professors Nakayama, Watanabe, and Koizumi, among others, emphasis will be placed on setting a broad context for evaluating Mendenhall's contributions to Japanese science on the one hand, and to our understanding of Meiji society and the world of the *oyatoi* professors on the other.

This chapter establishes two broad contexts from which to view Mendenhall's work in Japan: the body of experience, training, and skills which he brought to Tokyo; and the institutional development of science at the University where his professional activities took place. The paper then focuses

The author is grateful to Professor Gerald Curtis and to the Toyota Fund at the East Asian Institute, Columbia University, for travel funds to attend the 2nd International Symposium in Fukui, Japan, October, 1985, on *yatoi* at which this chapter was presented.

on Mendenhall's account of his experiences as recorded in his extensive "Autobiographical Notes." These are important primary materials which, although known by specialists, have never been mined for anything but biographical information and narrowly scientific content.

The Autobiographical Notes

The following account of the life and work of Thomas Corwin Mendenhall (1841-1924) is based on extensive materials currently housed in the Niels Bohr Library of the American Institute of Physics in New York City.[1] They contain approximately 4,000 items—manuscripts, correspondence, published articles, photographs and memorabilia—occupying twelve feet of shelf space. The materials were deposited there in June 1964 by Mendenhall's grandson and namesake, Thomas Corwin Mendenhall II, an historian and former president of Smith College. Particular use was made of the multi-volume "Auto-biographical Notes" which Mendenhall wrote by hand, apparently from detailed diaries kept in numerous small volumes (the diaries are extant but barely readable), during his convalescence in Europe from 1901 to 1911.[2]

The section on Japan is only a small part of the whole which begins with the lineage of the Mendenhall family, traces in detail the author's illustrious career as educator, administrator, and scientist, and ends with Mendenhall's resignation from the United States Coast and Geodetic Survey in 1889 to accept the presidency of Worcester Polytechnic Institute. The opening lines reveal something of the character of the man and the nature of the Notes themselves;

> These notes are not and will not be written for the "public eye," but solely with the idea that they may some times be of interest to some of my descendants—direct or collateral—in case my direct line should be interrupted. They will, therefore, be very informal in character and often very personal in their references to myself, my own experiences and to others with whom I may have come in contact. They will be of that confidential nature which would characterize a free and unembarrassed talk over old times in the privacy of the family circle.[3]

Indeed, it is the anecdotal nature of the Notes and the candor with which experiences and relationships in Japan are discussed that make them valuable to the social historian. The "Notes" were written not long after Basil Hall Chamberlain had remarked of his fellow foreigners in *Things Japanese* (1890) that "not to have written a book about Japan is fast becoming a title to distinction." Thus, Mendenhall's reticence was uncharacteristic for his group.

The "Notes" end with Mendenhall's resignation from government service in protest over the appointment of men to high positions as political favors rather than for scientific competence. Mendenhall had been a tireless promoter of high standards in science and engineering education and integrity in the pursuit of scientific knowledge during a long career that spanned university professorships at Ohio State University and Tokyo University, leadership in the National Academy of Science and the American Association for the Advancement of Science, and university presidencies at Rose Polytechnical Institute in Indiana and Worcester Polytechnic Institute in Massachussetts. He is the only American teacher in Japan in the early Meiji period who is listed among the some 1800 names of those considered by the American Institute of Physics to have made significant contributions to physics.[4]

He was not, however, known as an originator of ideas or for his contributions to scientific theory. In the late 19th-century debates among the scientific community in America over the merits of theoretical and abstract science as opposed to experimental and applied science, Mendenhall, with Alexander Graham Bell and some others, took strong public stands against the American tendency at the time to despise the useful and practical in science and to worship European successes in theoretical work.[5] In this Mendenhall may have been in the minority in his own country but his professional attitudes and interests—formed early in life, as we shall see—were well-suited to Japanese needs during the late 1870s when Western scientific knowledge was sought to solve the numerous practical problems of early industrialization.

In 1901 Mendenhall resigned as president of Worcester Polytechnic Institute due to illness and travelled to Europe to recuperate. He remained there for over ten years during which time he completed his massive Autobiographical Notes. The long section describing the trip to Japan and three years of life and work there was written at different times during 1905 and 1906 in places like Capalago, Switzerland and Florence, Italy. The Japan section has been fully transcribed from handwritten manuscript as reference material for this chapter; it amounts to about seventy-five double-spaced typewritten pages.[6]

Mendenhall returned to Ohio in 1912 and worked actively in retirement as a member of the board of Trustees of Ohio State University until his death in 1924.

Early Life and Career[7]

Mendenhall was born on a farm near Hanoverton, Ohio on 4 October, 1841. He was named after the popular governor of the state at the time, Thomas Corwin. His formative first twenty years were spent in the hills of eastern Ohio during the politically tense period preceding the Civil War. His family were Quakers and abolitionists and proudly traced their ancestry back to members of the Pennsylvania colony who arrived in America in 1686.

Because his father was a farmer and carriage-maker it is likely that Mendenhall's early interest in tinkering with gadgets came from the practical nature of his early home education. He worked the lathe in his father's shop, ran the engine at his brother's steam saw mill, assisted his mother with farm chores, and watched the mining of coal from nearby hills.

Unlike some of the *oyatoi* professors Mendenhall's formal education was not of the elite variety; he was, in fact, largely self-educated. He attended the usual primary schooling but pursued mathematics on his own after that. Reversing the usual order, he first became an assistant principal (at the age of 17!) and then the next year attended a teachers' institute for formal training. In 1861 at the age of 20, Mendenhall entered Southwest Normal School in Lebanon, Ohio and graduated in a year with the degree of Instructor Normalis—the only formal course degree he ever received.

Following graduation Mendenhall taught mathematics and science in various high schools in Ohio while studying physics and advanced mathematics on his own. On July 12, 1870, when he was 29, he married Miss Susan Allen Marple, a student at the high school where he was teaching. On August 1, 1872 they had their first child, a boy named Charles, who accompanied his parents to Japan as a small child and later became a well-known physicist in his own right.

In 1873 Ohio Agricultural and Mechanical College, one of the first Morrill Land Grant institutions,[8] opened its doors and needed someone to fill the chair of physics and chemistry. Under a broad definition of a university professor set out by President D. C. Gilman of Johns Hopkins University at the time—namely, "a student who can also teach"—Mendenhall qualified. Though he had never attended a university Mendenhall was hired as the first professor of physics and mechanics at what would become Ohio State University.

In many ways the conditions and nature of work as the first professor of physics at Ohio Agricultural and Mechanical College were ideal preparation for the responsibilities of inaugurating modern science pedagogy and research at Japan's first university five years later. In the 1870s the two schools were not far apart. Science and physics were in their infancies in both Tokyo and the American midwest; the pedagogy of science had not yet been born in either. Both schools needed someone who could incorporate experimental research into classroom teaching, provide guidance in the construction of scientific apparatus and a physics laboratory, and develop public support for science through lectures in the community and the organization of professional societies. The ideas and methods that Mendenhall had devised as a self-taught high school teacher in Ohio five years earlier, he now expanded, systematized and introduced as a professor in Japan.

The Call to Japan

In early spring 1878 Dr. Edward Sylvester Morse returned briefly to America from Japan for a speaking tour. He stopped in Columbus, Ohio to lecture on Japanese homes and Japanese art and to see his friend, Thomas C. Mendenhall. His intentions were more that casual; Morse, who occupied the chair of zoology at the newly consolidated Tokyo University, carried with him a commission from the Japanese government to find suitable professors for the chairs of philosophy and physics. Ernest F. Fenollosa was offered the position in philosophy and Mendenhall was asked to take the physics chair. The Autobiographical Notes state, "I talked it over with my wife and agreed."

The decision could not have been made so easily. Mendenhall tells us that he had to resign his position at Ohio State. Furthermore, the family had to sell all of their household effects except for essential equipment difficult to find in Japan, which was packed to take along. The latter included Mendenhall's scientific library, volumes of the *Encyclopedia Britannica*, the old 'Edinburgh' Dictionaries, books on physics and mathematics, silver table ware, pillows, bedding, a fine microscope and other scientific equipment.

Although considerable inconvenience was involved, Mendenhall also provides hints of what some of the enticements might have been for what he called, "the then almost unheard of journey to the Orient." There was certainly the element of curiosity. Mendenhall suggests that the exhibition of porcelain and other arts which the Japanese had made a the Philadelphia Exhibition of 1876 "has been a revelation to most people and everyone was interested to learn something of the customs and character of this curious people."[8]

There were more tangible considerations as well. For one thing, although nothing could be put on paper, Mendenhall was given to believe that his position at Ohio State would be waiting whenever he returned. For another, the Japanese were offering considerable compensation. The agreement made with the Ministry of Education was for two years, renewable if both parties agreed, with a salary of $3500 Mexican dollars per year plus $450 Mexican for roundtrip travel, a residence and vacations. Mendenhall remarks, "I considered the proposition very liberal and even if the compensation offered had been less I should have welcomed the opportunity for making the acquaintance of the Japanese people under such favorable conditions."[10]

First Encounters

On August 1, 1878, the sixth birthday of son Charles, the three Mendenhalls set off on the overland leg of their journey to Japan. The six day trip by sleeper train from Chicago to San Francisco was uneventful except for the first encounter with "our clients," the Japanese, at the weigh-in counter of the baggage check-in at Omaha, Nebraska. Two Japanese men were having difficulty communicating in English and Mendenhall went to their assistance and successfully straightened matters out. They turned out to be two future statesmen who had just graduated from America's most prestigious eastern universities: Dan Takuma was returning to Japan from MIT and Kaneko Kentaro had just graduated from Harvard.[11] Mendenhall describes Dan as "a modest man" and mistakenly consigns him to an early death a few years later. In fact Dan, though he was assassinated in 1932, was still alive six years after Mendenhall passed away, and had an extraordinary career as executive director of the Mitsui enterprises. Kaneko is described as "a much less modest man," and as if to illustrate this Mendenhall recounts an episode in San Francisco when Kaneko came down with an unknown disease which required visits to a doctor and caused considerable concern to everyone. Though Kaneko continued to insist it had come from his drinking too much "eggnog" while visiting the Seal Rock not far from San Francisco, Mendenhall's conclusion after consulting the doctor, written with gracious good-humor, was that "it had been nothing more or less than a plain drunk."[12]

First Impressions

One of the things one misses travelling in the jet age is the thrill of sighting land after a long voyage and the sense of anticipation that inspires. 19th-century travel literature, unlike that of the present day, is filled with flights of rhetoric, lofty reflections and metaphorical symbols of fulfillment that often reveal more about the traveller than about his new land. One is reminded of the sense of excitement and anticipation that filled the young Siebold's account of his arrival in Nagasaki in the 1820s despite the fact that his ship was headed for the tiny confines of Dejima and the shoreline he was passing was lined with cannon and armed guards.[13] One thinks, too, of John Russell Young's record of the arrival of General Grant's party into Nagasaki Bay at the same time the Mendenhalls were in Tokyo. At the end of a long and arduous journey around the world the writer can hardly contain himself:

> Through green and smooth tranquil waters we steamed into the bay of Nagasaki, and had our first glimpse of Japan. Nagasaki is said to be among the most beautiful harbors in the world. But the beauty that welcomed us had the endearing quality that it reminded us of home. . . .It was this school-boy sense of pleasure that came with my first view of Japan. All the romance, all the legends, the dreams I had dreamed and the pictures I had seen; all the anticipations I had formed of Japan were immersed in this joyful welcome to the green that I had not seen since leaving England. . . .All that I saw of the coast was the beauty of the green, which came like a memory of childhood, as a memory of America, and in which I rejoiced as in a mere physical sensation, like bathing, or swinging on the gate, or dozing under the apple-tree in the drowsy days of June.[14]

First impressions may reveal the hopeful anticipations of a young man seeking adventure; or, they may stir reveries of home and childhood for the weary traveller. They may also, however, simply borrow the vocabulary of an accepted idiom. In such cases they reveal little about the traveller and much about the accepted genre of travel writing in a particular period. This is what Mendenhall has provided us. Descriptions of his first impressions of Japan are filled with stereotypes and observations that abounded in his day:

> . . . finally on the 20th day out we were all on deck and anxiously waiting for the cry of "Land" which was expected to be seen soon. And at last it came, from the mast head, and a little later we could ourselves make out, but dimly on the horizon, the "snow-tipped" summit of the most beautiful mountain in the world, the great "Fujiyama" of Japan,

known on nearly every fan, or plate or other work of art coming from that country. It gave us our first, as three years later it gave us our last glimpse of Japan.[15]

As he enters the town of Yokohama, Mendenhall observes the "queer architecture" of the villages and towns, the "naked men" in the fishing craft, the crowds of curiously costumed people, strange noises and the special delight of most foreign visitors at this time—the "jinrikisha," which Mendenhall describes as a "small two-wheeled over-grown baby carriage."

This is all quite familiar and Mendenhall's descriptions, one suspects, reflected what he had learned to see, what he had been taught to see by the Japanology of his day. Almost immediately, however, Mendenhall embarked upon his professional work and for this there was no literature available he could rely on; his observations are shaper, truer, more original and more valuable to us.

When Mendenhall arrived at Tokyo University two days after he stepped off the boat at Yokohama he brought with him not only his books and scientific instruments but a background of education, skills, attitudes about science and about Japan that strongly influenced his professional behavior and the structure of his thought. The institutional setting in which he was to work, although recently reorganized and upgraded to university level, also had a history of development that would sharply define the contours of Mendenhall's scientific work in Japan.

Following the proclamation of the Imperial Restoration by the emperor on January 3, 1868, the new government's immediate concerns were to consolidate its authority and extend its control over the entire country. It was not until the abolition of the han and establishment of prefectures (*hihan chiken*) on August 29, 1871 that these goals were realized and a true national administration became possible. On September 2, a Ministry of Education (*Mombusho*) was established with the responsibility of planning a national system of education. There was little question that the Mombusho's first priority was to establish a system of higher education that would replenish the leadership group with the best talent in the country and import and disseminate advanced science and technology from abroad.

By 1878 when Mendenhall arrived at Tokyo University (created the year before from an amalgam of lesser institutions) considerable progress had been made in consolidating national resources in science under the auspices of a single centrally controlled institution. The curriculum, no longer organized around languages (as it had been since pre-Meiji days), now had programs in specialized disciplinary areas. But there were constraints as well. The university had only recently been upgraded from the level of a preparatory school Thus, students and staff with specialized training and skills were few in 1878; laboratory facilities were primitive; and the science of physics continued to be seen as a tool for the solution to practical problems rather than as an academic and theoretical science in its own right. There was also the constraint of instruction in a foreign language. For Mendenhall and other *oyatoi* instructors lecturing in their own language was an enormous convenience; for their students it was a considerable obstacle. Mendenhall not only survived the situation he found himself in, he flourished and made important contributions to the further development of Japanese physics and science education.

Teaching and Research at the University

The state of the physics program at the University became clear to Mendenhall on his first day of work, two days after arriving in Tokyo. He found there was not much for him to do since he was required to put in only seven hours per week instead of the seven times that amount he was used to at Ohio State. It is quite possible that part of the motivation to initiate a high level research oriented physics program was to keep himself busy: "before many weeks I had rearranged the schedule of work in the Department of Physics so that my time was pretty well occupied—for I was young, strong, and loved work."[16]

Mendenhall's teaching responsibilities came to include a large lecture course of 100-150 students that met two or three times a week. It was a general introductory course and was required for all students in the engineering and science course. The students then met in smaller sections with Mendenhall's "assistant," Yamagawa Kenjiro[17] for "textbook work." All the lectures were in English and Mendenhall states that the students were well trained in the language, having prepared under foreign instructors at the "Yobimon."[18] This large lecture course was probably not very different from the general courses that had been taught at the predecessors of Tokyo University by other *oyatoi* like William E. Griffis.

In addition to the general course Mendenhall soon initiated a laboratory course which became required for all engineering and physics students. It met for four hours per week and became an essential part of the physics course. Although laboratory work of some kind had existed before, Mendenhall upgraded and modernized it (to the extent that he claims to have "created" it). Making experimental work in the laboratory an integral and required part of the training of all science students was clearly an innovation and stands as one of Mendenhall's significant contributions to the pedagogy of science at the University.

Within a few years a small group of "special students" were ready to embark upon advanced studies. They spent most of their time with Mendenhall and relationships developed that continued after his return to America. He singles out two students in particular who became University professors, were instrumental in educating the next generation of Japanese physicists, and who made important and original contributions to physics through publications in leading scholarly journals in later years. Fujisawa Rikitaro (1861-1933) became a prominent mathematician and taught many younger scholars at the

University. Tanakadate Aikitsu (1856-1952), often called the "father of Japanese seismology and geophysics," was Mendenhall's best known student. He was prominent among the first generation of Japanese physicians and also led a movement to romanize the Japanese language based on a system of his own invention.

Of the students in general Mendenhall also had high praise:

> I cannot speak too highly of the excellence of these young men in the performance of all duties coming upon them as students. They were a select class, there being many more demands for admission to the university than there were places in it—and all recognized that success in their work was the key to success in their after careers, for Japan was then looking for men with a knowledge of Western science and art, preferring to take her own sons whenever possible. Thus, in many respects, the conditions under which we were doing our work, were almost ideal. Always fond of teaching and always enjoying my college work, I cannot but look upon my three years with these well-mannered, good tempered, ambitious and intellectually strong young men as being in most respects the pleasantest and best of all my professional years.[19]

These comments, while clearly reflecting Mendenhall's perspective as professor, also tell us something of the early Meiji university: it was highly selective and admissions was already competitive; it had become meritocratic and an important determiner of future success in life; the *oyatoi* would inevitably be replaced by young Japanese trained by people like himself. All of these things Mendenhall saw as positive contributions to an almost ideal professional environment.

Mendenhall went out of his way several times in the Notes to praise the administration of the University and the officials of the Ministry of Education for fairness and reasonableness in all matters of mutual concern, including his contract, a sore point for some other *oyatoi*. He does not, however, have high praise for everyone he worked with. One who is damned with faint praise was his "assistant," Yamagawa. Of all Mendenhall's associates at the University Yamagawa undoubtedly achieved the greatest success. At the time Mendenhall was writing the Autobiographical Notes Yamagawa was serving as president of Tokyo Imperial University and later became the only man ever to serve concurrently as president of two imperial universities—Tokyo and Kyoto in 1914-15. Mendenhall consistently refers to him in his memoirs as his "assistant" despite the fact that Yamagawa had been appointed assistant professor of physics in the Kaisei Gakko in 1876 and then professor of physics at the University in 1879, the first Japanese to achieve that rank.

Mendenhall['s initial comments on Yamagawa is that he is "one of the tallest Japanese of my acquaintance." He goes on to remark that Yamagawa was of "fair ability," who:

belonged to a family of excellent rank (samurai of good standing) and
while he had much less real talent than several of the younger men who
were my special students while there, his good looks and dignified
presence, added to his really good sense and rather practical mind marked
him out for a successful career.[20]

It is difficult to know whether Mendenhall's insights here on social
class stem from his American biases as to what "really matter," or whether
he has caught some of the nuances of change in the transition from
Tokugawa to Meiji in Japanese education. We know, in any case, that
during Mendenhall's tenure at the University students with samurai backgrounds were the overwhelming majority. One scholar estimates that 77% of
the student body at Tokyo University were of samurai origin in 1879.[21] As in
the late Tokugawa period when they began pouring into the private Dutch
academies, in early Meiji as well it was the samurai who felt the civic
responsibility to strengthen the country by acquiring specialized knowledge in
Western science. Mendenhall, in focusing his comments on Yamagawa's family
background, was very likely also describing the social origins of most his
students.

Although Mendenhall initiated a number of new courses, spent time
constructing a new laboratory, and guiding his advanced students, the fact that
there was not yet a regular collegiate program in physics meant that he had
time of his own for private study and experimental research. During his three
years in Japan Mendenhall continued to read. The books included a number of
mathematics textbooks, works on differential and integral calculus, analytical
mechanics, a book on optics, several treatises on electricity, and other areas of
physics.

In the laboratory, which was assembled with considerable difficulty owing
to the remoteness from places where construction or purchase of instruments
was possible, Mendenhall carried on his experimental work. With a
spectrometer which he was sent from America he did optical experiments of
some interest. These involved a long series of wave length measurements of the
principal dark lines of the solar spectrum. This occupied him and several of his
special students for about one year and the results were published in monograph
form by the University.

Mendenhall's life-long interest in the measurement of gravity by means
of various pendulum developed at this time. In August 1880 he completed
the research he is best known for in Japan: an estimate of the mass of the
earth based on calculations by pendulum of the force of gravity at sea level
in Tokyo and at the summit of Mt. Fuji. The scientific results were
published in the *American Journal of Science* and many of the
detailed calculations were published as a monograph by university
authorities. The device experimented with in Japan was perfected from 1890
to 1891 and used as the standard measure by the United States Coastal
Survey.

The Promotion of Science

In addition to teaching and research Mendenhall worked tirelessly as a promoter of science outside the narrow confines of the University. He helped to found a seismological society in Japan and played a role in the establishment of a meteorological observatory. Two aspects of his efforts to extend interest in Western science are described at some length in the Autobiographical Notes: his participation in a public lecture series and his private contacts with influential individuals.

Mendenhall had been contacted before he left Columbus about speaking on Western science in a public lecture series and was asked to participate in his first on the day after he arrived in Japan. The lectures were on Sunday afternoons (the only time when the Japanese could attend). Since the foreign missionaries objected the regular foreign lecturers became Mendenhall, Morse, and Fenollosa—a formidable trio. The foreigners lectured in English and their words were interpreted into Japanese because very few members of the audience knew English. Mendenhall's interpreter was Kikuchi Dairoku[22] who had studied mathematics and physics at Cambridge and was able to very skilfully explain words and concepts for which the Japanese as yet had no vocabulary; in a process that Mendenhall describes in some detail.

Gatherings of interested Japanese listeners around foreign experts in science were not new in Japan and had their origins going back to the 17th century, in the meetings Dutch physicians on Dejima had with Japanese medical men. They reached their high point during the time of Siebold when, accompanying the Dutch Factor to Edo, he would stop off in cities along the way and consult with interested Japanese physicians, stimulating wider interest in Western medical techniques. These get-togethers both earlier in Tokugawa times and in early Meiji with men like Mendenhall considerably expanded public knowledge and further stimulated public interest in the latest advances in Western science.

Besides lecturing to large and enthusiastic audiences Mendenhall's activities on behalf of the promotion of science extended to private contacts with influential individuals. In one interesting story in the Autobiographical Notes along this line, Mendenhall claims to have introduced the telephone to Japan.

Mendenhall was contacted one day by Kaneko Kentaro (the man who had too much "egg-nog" in San Francisco) and invited to the villa of a "Prince" of the Tokugawa family. Mendenhall suspects that it is a pair of telephones he had with him that had brought the invitation:

> I had brought with me from America a pair of telephones just then coming into use in a small way, a year or two after the invention had been brought to the attention of the public. I had the first and then the only telephones in Japan, although within a year the original pair had multiplied into many made by native workmen, although there was no attempt to put them into practical use. I suspected that my telephones were invited to see the Prince and my suspicions were confirmed when

Kaneko, a day or two before our appointed visit casually and almost carelessly remarked that perhaps I might take my telephones along as the Prince might like to see them.[23]

At the villa the telephones were set up in two rooms and connected with copper wire. As soon as this was done the Prince had the satisfaction of talking over the line with Kaneko in another room. The Prince, Mendenhall notes, was especially pleased in finding that the instruments would "talk Japanese." What is more significant than the Prince's evident delight at this new discovery are the long discussions which Mendenhall had with him in which he found him greatly interested and quite well informed of developments in science. When the talk on the telephone was completed Mendenhall spent several hours explaining the principles involved in the construction and operation of the device.

How widespread such unofficial and private contacts were or how much information flowed during them is difficulty to measure, but they were very likely a significant, if largely unreported, part of the educational influence of the *oyatoi* during their brief tenure in Japan.

Japanese Tradition and Modern Science

Mendenhall brought with him to Japan the mind of a professionally-trained Western scientist and there are numerous occasions throughout the Notes when his observations of Japanese culture reflect his training. Not only does he describe physical objects in elaborate and precise detail but he notices the curious way that science and Japanese culture seemed at times to be mutually supportive. When he visited a traditional Japanese house, for example, and observed the apparatus holding the kettle over a charcoal brazier in the center of the room, he noted:

> The kettle was adjusted as to height by means of an ingenious "clutch" which I examined with interest and which, to my great surprise, I found identical with the "clutch" for holding the upper electric light carbon which Mr. Brush had invented and patented in America and which was an important feature of his electric lamp. In Japan it was very old but I am sure Mr. Brush had never heard of it.[24]

Again, invited to a duck hunt, Mendenhall commented on the use of a telegraph system to announce the arrival of the ducks at the desired location where the hunters waited:

> It was interesting to see that the operation of hunting ducks by one of the most ancient of methods (falconry)—now all but obsolete everywhere—had been facilitated by the use of the application of modern science. There had been erected a series of telegraph poles around the

lake and on these wires had been strung "keys" at each pole and all connected with a battery and bell in our tea hut.[25]

Finally, on the celebrated expedition to the summit of Mt. Fuji to make scientific measurements Mendenhall twice gives credit for the success of the venture to those who appear to be the least "modern" segment of the Japanese population: Shinto priests. The first incident occurred when the climbing party became fatigued about half way up the mountain. They were able to continue only because they fell in with a band of pilgrims in white flowing gowns. Completely exhausted, they learned the religious prayers and the rhythmic and synchronized method of walking and resting and only by so doing were able to continue to the top.

Later, at the summit a heavy wind made it impossible to set up the scientific instruments and the mission was about to be abandoned when a mountain priest agreed to let his shrine be used for the measuring devices. Mendenhall shows surprise that the traditional dualism between science and the "more civilized religions" of the West appeared not to operate in Japan—that science and religion could accommodate each other:

> I have always taken much pleasure in this liberal-minded Japanese who allowed me to transform a holy shrine of one of the oldest religions in the world into a laboratory of modern science and to substitute for his sacred images the most recent devices for the accurate measure of time. I fancy that few priests of more civilized religions would have been equally accommodating.[26]

Domestic and Social Life

Mention has been made of Mendenhall's comments on some of his Japanese students and colleagues; he also described his impressions of some of the foreign teachers who lived in close proximity to him in the Kaga *yashiki*. His view may help to flesh out the portraits of some of these *oyatoi* gained from other sources.

The Morses, of course, were the foreign residents the Mendenhalls knew best. It was at Morse's invitation that Mendenhall had gone to Japan; it was the Morses who met them at the dock in Yokohama; and it was the Morses with whom they stayed (as paying guests, Mendenhall is careful to point out) for three months until alterations were completed on their own place. It is possibly because he knew them so well that comments on the Morses in the Autobiographical Notes are few.

The Mendenhalls eventually moved into House #2 in the Kaga *yashiki*; it was second in order from the entrance to the compound. Mendenhall describes it as a "semi-tropical" house of ample size with a frontage of 100 feet to the main street and 200 feet in the back. When they first arrived Dr. E. W. Syle, who taught English and history, was on one side of them. Mendenhall thought highly of the English language ability of Dr. Syle's students but saw him as a "relic of the first decade of foreignization of the University when missionaries, being available, were taken in to teach various subjects." One senses here some of the cleavages that must have existed among the foreigners in the compound due to differences in backgrounds, social styles, and intellectual orientations.

The neighbors on the other side in House #1 were the Fenollosas. Mendenhall's views on this most distinguished of the *oyatoi* professors is worth quoting at length:

Ernest F. Fenollosa was a young man very recently graduated from Harvard University where he won distinction. He was appointed to the chair of philosophy in the University at Tokyo and married a very good-looking woman from Salem, Mass. just before going there. He was an unusually talented young man with great artistic instincts and himself a painter in oils of considerable merit. He was fond of music and led or directed rather (as he did not sing much himself) our "quartet"consisting of Morse and Mrs. Fenollosa, my wife and myself.

Although somewhat dreamy in disposition he was most agreeable in personality and I became very fond of him. We often took long walks together and I always valued and enjoyed my association with him. He remained in Japan for several years after I left, devoting himself to the study of Japanese and Chinese art, which he came to esteem above that of any European nation. Returning to the US he lived in Boston for a time but was unfortunate in his domestic relations; was divorced from his wife and married another who had first made his acquaintance by sending a letter of appreciation for his Phi Beta Kappa forum read at a Harvard commencement. Later he returned to Japan as an agent for art dealers and an altogether promising career seems to have come to an unfortunate ending through failure in domestic relations, not entirely to be charged to him, however, as I believe.[27]

Mendenhall mentions that his other neighbors were Professor Atkinson, Professor of Chemistry, in House #4; the Morses in House #5; and in House #6 Professor Chaplin, a West Point graduate who became a professor of civil engineering in Maine before coming to Japan. Professor Chaplin accompanied Mendenhall on the Mt. Fuji expedition and Mendenhall had high praise for his character and competence. Chaplin left Japan after five years and taught civil engineering at Union College, then at Harvard; later he became president of Washington University in St. Louis. The rest of the group that formed the circle of the Mendenhalls' friends and associates among the resident foreigners consisted of two or three English teachers in the engineering department and two or three German professors in the medical college and a professor of economics who moved next door after Dr. Syle left. Typically, Mendenhall sums up his feelings about life in the Kaga *yashiki* by putting the best face on a less than ideal social environment:

> Social life under such conditions was rather monotonous, but not unpleasant. There was little variety in our meetings of a social character, but the people were generally cultivated and agreeable.[28]

Conclusion

Tributes to the *oyatoi* come in many forms. A special collection of *oyatoi* documents has been meticulously maintained and catalogued at Rutgers University in the name of William E. Griffis—an honor to the man and a boon to scholars. William S. Clark has a statue on the campus of Hokkaido University and even a coffee shop named after him in Kyoto (Kuraaku Hausu)—a sure sign of public acceptance. Mendenhall never published anything of note on Japan nor did he ever utter so catchy a slogan as "Boys be ambitious," so his name is not generally remembered. There is, however, a laboratory and a fellowship in physics in his name at Tokyo University, so he is not entirely without honor. But should public recognition be the measure of the man or of his achievements?

Professor Watanabe, in a useful article, provides some comparative perspective.[29] Putting aside the lack of early formal education and the distinction of his later career, Mendenhall was typical of American *oyatoi* by Professor Watanabe's criteria of measurement. Mendenhall's term of employment of three years was close to the average for all American teachers; the means by which he was employed was like most others—personal invitation; his age at the time of arrival in Japan was 37, just above the average age of 33. Like most of the *oyatoi* professors (with several notable exceptions) Mendenhall did not complain bitterly about the conditions of his employment; he did his work competently and with enthusiasm, and got along well with colleagues and employers.

This essay presents Mendenhall's achievements in Japan within a still broader framework, defined by the convergence of a unique personal history with institutional requirements themselves determined by a particular context of historical development. With this as background, Mendenhall's Autobiographical Notes—his private record of experiences in Japan—is analyzed. What do we learn from this?

The Autobiographical Notes are written with clarity and candor. They provide a rare glimpse from the perspective of an important participant into the world of science and scientists at Tokyo University at a formative stage of its development. Mendenhall was a scientist, however, who not only carefully described physical phenomena and practical matters, but was not averse to jotting down gossipy vignettes of his colleagues at the University, many of whom later emerged as statesmen of Meiji Japan.

But Mendenhall's Notes are primarily of value for the rich details of Japanese social life provided through the cold and empirical eye of the 19th century scientist. Mendenhall was the kind of man who, when an earthquake hit took out his notebook and kept detailed records of the occurrence: the time, duration, the physical sensation. He described how the water in glasses shivered, how the lanterns swung, how the timbers of the houses creaked, how the dogs in the neighborhood became disoriented. And he described how the Japanese instinctively ran to open sliding doors and windows as if each was an amateur seismologist. Such insights suggest that the judgement of the writer on the *oyatoi* who remarked that "aesthetic sensitivity is a better approach to the Japanese than ruthless logic," may be misleading.[30] Mendenhall's Autobiographical Notes show that the ruthless logic, the cool and calculating mind of the late-nineteenth century mind could also add significant new data to the social history of modern Japan.

Ultimately, however, the value of the private record of a man of science is in reminding us that the scientist is more complex than our one-dimensional stereotypes of him. Although Mendenhall patiently recorded with scientific precision everything he could about the jolt of earthquakes and made important contributions to seismology both in Japan and later in America, he was at the same time deathly afraid of them. Here are his very last words upon departing from Japan at the end of his three year stay:

> Except for the earthquakes we were very reluctant to leave Japan where we had spent three very happy and useful years. . . . Although I had been one of the charter members of the Seismological Society of Japan—to which we owe the great advances in the scientific study of earthquakes during the past 25 years—I was really glad to get away from them, and I remember saying as we sailed away from the beautiful shore of the bay of Yeddo [sic], that the earthquakes were the only thing that reconciled me to leaving so beautiful a land, such a mild and wholesome climate and so charming and hospitable a people.[31]

In the final analysis the Autobiographical Notes are a record of a sensitive, hard-working, practical man of the 19th century whose descriptions of life in Japan reveal a number of profound ambivalences suggesting that the assessment of the *oyatoi* and their place in modern Japanese history may be more difficult than many of us have believed.

Notes

[1]The author would like to thank the staff of the Niels Bohr Library at the American Institute of Physics for their assistance in gaining ready access to the Mendenhall Papers.

[2]Hereafter page references to the Autobiographical Notes will indicate

volume and page as they appear in the original manuscript. The Autobiographical Notes will also be abbreviated as AN.

[3]AN, Volume I, p. 2.

[4]Watanabe, Masao, *Oyatoi Beikokujin kagaku kyoshi* [*Science Across the Pacific*], (Tokyo, 1976), p. 518.

[5]Daniel J. Kevles, *The Physicists: The History of a Scientific Community in Modern America*, (New York, 1978), p. 50.

[6]Richard Rubinger (editor), *An American Scientist in Early Meiji Japan: The Autobiographical Notes of Thomas C. Mendenhall* (Honolulu, 1989).

[7]This material on Mendenhall's early life relies on a summary from the Autobiographical Notes appearing in Henry Crew, "Biographical Memoir of Thomas Corwin Mendenhall, 1841-1924," *National Academy of Science Biographical Memoirs* Vol. XVI, (1935), pp. 331-351.

[8]Morrill Land Grant colleges were established in 1862 by the Morrill Act which provided federal assistance for the establishment of public colleges of agricultural and mechanic arts. They were especially important in extending opportunities for higher education to youth in rural areas.

[9]AN, Volume IV, p. 102.

[10]AN, Volume IV, p. 106.

[11]Dan Takuma (1858-1932). Born in what is now Fukoka prefecture, he accompanied the Iwakura Mission to the United States where he remained, graduating from the Massachusetts Institute of Technology (MIT) in 1878 with a degree in mining engineering. Upon return to Japan he taught briefly at Tokyo University then joined the Ministry of Public Works as an engineer in the government-owned Miike coal mines in Fukuoka; he joined the Mitsui Company when it took over the mine in 1888. He eventually became executive director of all Mitsui operations. Considered too pro-West by the ultra-nationalists in the 1930s, Dan was assassinated by Hishinuma Goro in 1932.

Kaneko Kentaro (1853-1942). Born to a samurai family in Fukuoka, he went to Harvard in 1871 and graduated in 1878 having concentrated in political science and law. After returning to Japan, he lectured for a time at Tokyo University and in 1880 was appointed secretary to the *Genroin* (Senate). In 1884 he was invited to work on drafts of the Meiji Constitution and became secretary to Ito Hirobumi who became Japan's first prime minister in 1886. He went back to Tokyo University as a lecturer, served in several ministries and was sent to Washington during the Russo-Japanese War as spokesman for Japanese interests. In this connection he met and became friendly with Theodore Roosevelt. He became a baron in 1900.

[12]AN, Volume IV, pp. 112-113.

[13] von Siebold, Dr. Philipp Franz. *Manners and Customs of the Japanese in the Nineteenth Century* (Rutland, and Tokyo, 1973), pp. 16-17.

[14]John Russell Young, *Around the World With General Grant*, (New York, 1879), Volume II, p. 473.

[15]AN, Volume IV, p. 117.

[16]AN, Volume IV, p. 144.

[17]Yamakawa Kenjiro (1854-1931). Born in Aizu han he attended the han school, Nisshinkan, from the ages of 8 to 14. Following the Restoration Yamakawa went to Tokyo and studied English, algebra and geometry at several schools. He went to America as a junior high school student and stayed on to enter Yale University in May 1872. He returned to Japan in 1875 as assistant professor at Tokyo *Kaisei Gakko*; then became full professor at Tokyo University in 1879. In 1911 he was president of Kyushu University; 1913-20 President of Tokyo University, and 1914-15 also president of Kyoto University.

[18]Yobimon or more properly, Tokyo Daigaku Yobimon, was the preparatory institution for Tokyo University. Originally part of the Kaisei Gakko, it became Tokyo Eigo Gakko when the English department separated from Tokyo Gaikokugo Gakko in 1874. With the establishment of Tokyo University in 1877 it became Tokyo Daigaku Yobimon, a mandatory preparatory institution for the University. It became independent of Tokyo University in 1885.

[19]AN, Volume IV, pp. 148-149.

[20]AN, Volume IV, pp. 144-145.

[21]Kikuchi Joji, "The Emergence and Development of a National Educational System in Modern Japan," unpublished paper presented at International Sociological Association conference, (Paris, August 1980).

[22]Kikuchi Dairoku (1855-1917), born in Edo, attended the Bansho Shirabesho. From 1866 to 1868 he studied in England, then again in 1870 he studied at Cambridge specializing in physics and mathematics. Returning in 1877 he became a professor at Tokyo University and established the new mathematics program. From 1898 to 1901 he was President of Tokyo University; and from 1901 to 1903 Minister of Education. His English-language book, *Japanese Education*, remains a standard work on the pre-war educational system.

[23]AN, Volume V, p. 7. Bell received a patent for the telephone in 1876 and immediately began commercial production. Kevles, *The Physicists*, p. 47.

[24]AN, Volume V, p. 11-12. Mr. Brush is Charles Francis Brush (1849-1929) an American pioneer in the investigation of electric lighting. He invented the Brush electric arc light in 1878 and patented over fifty other instruments, including the storage battery.

[25]AN, Volume V, p. 14.

[26]AN, Volume V, p. 53.

[27]AN, Volume IV, pp. 140-142.

[28]AN, Volume IV, p. 143.

[29]Watanabe Masao, "American Science Teachers in the Early Meiji Period," *Japanese Studies in the History of Science*, 15 (1976), pp. 127-144.

[30]Robert S. Schwantes, *Japanese and Americans: A Century of Cultural Relations*, New York, 1955, p. 160.

[31]AN, Volume V, pp. 97-99.

5

William Smith Clark, *Yatoi*, 1826-1886

John M. Maki

As a foreign employee of the Japanese government, William Smith Clark did not play a central role in the developing drama of Japan's modernization in the mid-1870s. He was one of a small band of Americans who served on what was then the remote frontier in Hokkaido. He did not advise on or participate in the creation of the modern army and navy, the bureaucratic government, the financial system, the industrial structure or any of the other elements of the structure and infrastructure of the modern society that Japan was becoming. Moreover his term of service was only eight and a half months in contrast with the years and even decades of some of his fellow *yatoi*.

Nevertheless his achievements as an educator, an adviser, an innovator in agriculture, and as a molder of the minds and characters of the small group of students who came under his influence created for him a lasting position in Japanese popular culture. All Japanese are familiar with his "Boys, be ambitious!," supposedly his final words of farewell to his students. Brief accounts of his life and work in Japan still appear in Japanese textbooks. Reverent Japanese appear in Amherst, Massachusetts, where he attended college and taught, to pay homage at his grave. In 1981, ninety-five years after his death, a long television documentary on his life was shown on a national network. His name is far better known throughout Japan than in his native town and state.

The foundation of his success in Japan lay in the fact that the first fifty years of his life had unintentionally ideally prepared him for his brief mission. He left for Japan as the President of Massachusetts Agricultural College (MAC), one of the early land-grant colleges in the United States. He had come to his presidency after years as a leading professor at Amherst College, a position to which he had been appointed after earning a doctorate in Germany. He had also become widely known for his work in both the local and state agricultural societies. At both MAC and Amherst College he was famous as an outstanding teacher. He had also fought in the Civil War as an outstanding officer and hero. As a person he was possessed of enormous physical energy, a keen mind rich in the production of practical ideas, and a driving determination.

But Clark's achievements as a *yatoi* resulted from a unique circumstance. Armed with a most effective blend of personal characteristics and professional training, he entered a society in the process of rapid change at the precise moment when he could make a maximum contribution. Furthermore this society was in a position to respond effectively. Like his fellow *yatoi* he was a facilitator of change in a society in transition from a self-contained world of its own to a nation-state in the international arena.

William Smith Clark was born in Ashfield, Massachusetts, a tiny village in the western part of the state on July 31, 1826. Both his father, Atherton Clark, and his mother Harriet, were the offspring of country doctors. Clark grew up in Ashfield and two nearby villages, Cummington and Easthampton. As a boy, he early revealed a capacity of intense physical activity, a characteristic throughout his life until the broken health of his final years. A friend once quoted Clark as saying that as a boy "he always made it a rule to run faster, jump farther and higher, fight harder and swim more strongly than any of his companions." Of more significance he became in boyhood and adolescence an avid collector of bird skins, dried flowers and mineral specimens, a foreshadowing of his career in science.

After his graduation from Williston Academy in Easthampton as a member of the school's first class, Clark entered Amherst College. There he came under the influence of two leading scientists, Professor Charles Upham Shepherd, a mineralogist, and President Edward Hitchcock, a geologist. Under Professor Shepherd's guidance Clark greatly expanded his interest in mineral specimens, eventually earning enough money from their sale to finance his education. He was graduated from Amherst College in 1848 as a member of Phi Beta Kappa and with a reputation as an orator which he was to enjoy for the rest of his career. He then taught for two years at Williston Seminary.

In 1850 apparently with the advice and perhaps financial assistance of Samuel Williston, a wealthy businessman, founder of the seminary bearing his name, and the benefactor of Amherst College and Clark's future father-in-law, he decided to go to Germany to earn a doctorate in chemistry. En route to Germany he stopped in England where he was much impressed by Kew Gardens which strengthened his interest in botany. After two years of study at Georgia Augusta University in Göttingen, he was granted his doctorate with a dissertation on the chemical composition of meteorites. His letters home from both England and Germany clearly reveal his talent for close and accurate observation of foreign societies, a talent that later served him well in Japan.

Clark returned in 1852 to an appointment at Amherst College as professor of analytical and agricultural chemistry and an instructor in German. He immediately made his presence known on the faculty by establishing a well-thought-out Science Department. College records show that only a few students enrolled in what may possibly have been one of the first such departments in the United States.[1] The significance of Clark's first curricular venture is that it showed at the beginning of his academic career his interest in and talent for curricular planning, a skill manifested later at both MAC and Sapporo Agricultural College (SAC).

Clark soon became involved in the affairs of the college beyond the classroom. He proved to be highly successful as a fund-raiser for both library and building purposes. In his fund-raising his relationship with Samuel Williston (whose adopted daughter, Harriet Keopuolani Richards, Clark married in 1853) proved to be of considerable value.

He was also becoming increasingly active beyond the walls of the college. In 1859 he was appointed a member of the powerful and influential State Board of Agriculture, an association that was to continue for many years. A year later he became president of the local Hampshire Agricultural Society, a position to which he was elected on three subsequent occasions. Although he was no farmer himself, he was deeply interested in the application of scientific knowledge, particularly chemistry, to agriculture. It was this involvement in agriculture that equipped him effectively for his work at both MAC and SAC.

Like millions of his fellow Americans, he interrupted his career to fight in the Civil War. In August, 1861, he accepted the position of major of the Twenty-first Regiment of Massachusetts Volunteers. He saw his first action in February and March, 1862, at the battles of Roanoke Island and Newbern. His bravery and leadership under fire were mentioned in both the *New York Times* and the *New York Daily Tribune* and he was officially commended in both actions.[2] As a result he was promoted to lieutenant-colonel.

By the spring of 1863 he had risen to the rank of colonel and had been recommended for promotion to brigadier general. However, because of manpower losses his 21st Regiment was threatened by reorganization out of existence. Confronted with that situation Clark resigned from the army and returned to Amherst. His resignation and return were perfectly, though unwittingly, timed to involve him in an operation that profoundly influenced his career and eventually led him to Japan.

On April 29, 1863, just a week after his resignation, the General Court of the Commonwealth of Massachusetts (the state legislature) enacted a law incorporating the trustees of Massachusetts Agricultural College, the enabling legislation that was to lead to the creation of the college itself. The General Court had acted in accordance with the provisions of the Morrill Act of 1862 which had created the system of the land-grant colleges.

Early in 1864 the new Board of Trustees set off a competition among several towns, of which Amherst was one, to become the site of the proposed agricultural college. Clark immediately became a leader in his town's campaign. After leading his town to victory, he then headed a fund campaign to raise the needed money which was also to provide the means to build the school. Here, too, the town was successful.

Clark's success in the two campaigns led to the end of his career at Amherst College and to his appointment as the first professor at the still unopened new college. Six months later in August, 1867, the trustees elected him president and the school opened early in October after just under two years of preparatory work under two other presidents.

The college was tiny with a faculty of three (including Clark) and less than fifty students in the first class. From the beginning Clark threw himself into the development of the school with all his abundant energy and drive. At MAC, even more than at Amherst College, he was recognized as an outstanding teacher. He also worked tirelessly on the construction of additional buildings, and the recruitment of more students. From the outset he strove to have the General Court increase his school's budget, essential to his goal of making MAC into a liberal arts college, not simply a training school for farmers' sons.

Clark's first contact with Japan and the Japanese came in 1867. As his career at Amherst was ending, Joseph Hardy Niishima, whom Clark later described as his "first Japanese student," appeared at the college.[3] Niishima fled from Japan prior to the fall of the Tokugawa regime and found his way eventually to New England principally through the assistance of a New Englander from whom came his decidedly non-Japanese names. Niishima later founded Doshisha College in Kyoto which Clark visited en route home in 1877. Clark's brief initial contact with Niishima did nothing more than to bring his attention to the existence of the distant and then almost unknown land.

A few years later a chain of events developed that inevitably drew Clark to Japan. In 1870 Kuroda Kiyotaka, who had crushed the last of the pro-Tokugawa resistance in Hokkaido, went to the United States on a mission with the objective of learning the secrets of western power and of how to set Japan on the road to modernization which would surely place the country on a footing of equality with the west. While in the U.S. Kuroda met and travelled extensively with Horace Capron, U.S. Commissioner of Agriculture. As a result of that relationship Capron left his American position and became principal foreign adviser to the Japanese government office, the *Kaitakushi* (Development Office), responsible for the development of Hokkaido.[4] Kuroda had been appointed the head of the *Kaitakushi* and concurrently governor of Hokkaido on his return to Japan.

Capron, while still Commissioner of Agriculture, wrote to Clark in the spring of 1871 that he had recommended to Mori Arinori, the *Chargé d'affaires* at the Japanese ministry in Washington, D.C., that the Massachusetts Agricultural College would be the best educational institution for "a Japanese youth of high rank." He requested Clark to relax "the stringency of your regulations for admission" in regard to the youth, Naito Seitaro.[5] Naito was soon admitted becoming not only MAC's first Japanese student but later Clark's interpreter in Hokkaido.

Within two years five additional young Japanese had followed Naito to MAC, but the critical event that pointed Clark toward Japan occurred in the summer of 1872. At that time Mori visited his friend and protege, Naito, at MAC. In the course of a tour of the campus under Clark' guidance the two men observed the students in military drill. According to a newspaper account of the visit, Mori, struck by the scene, turned to Clark and said, "This is the kind of an institution Japan must have, that is what we need, an institution that shall teach young men to feed themselves and to defend themselves."[6]

It was not strange that Mori should be thus impressed for it was the American land-grant college with its combined emphasis on agricultural and industrial arts and instruction in military tactics that fit exactly into Japan's needs, particularly in respect to Hokkaido. This island required agricultural development, and was of strategic importance, situated as it was Imperial Russia to the north. Four years were to elapse before Clark went to Japan, but his meeting with Mori was undoubtedly of decisive importance.

When Clark signed his contract with the Japanese government on March 3, 1876 to be president of a proposed agricultural college in Sapporo, Mori had already been gone from Washington for almost three years and so the Japanese signatory was his successor, Yoshida Kiyonari. The provisions of the contract not only reveal the dimensions of Clark's responsibilities but also, by implication at least, some of the difficulties that had arisen in the Meiji government's relations with its foreign employees in the early years.[7]

The contract provisions bearing directly on Clark's work were: the contract period was from May 20, 1876 to May 20, 1877; his position was to be assistant director, president and professor of agriculture, chemistry, mathematics and the English language at the proposed agricultural college; he bound himself to "observe, and to the best of his ability, carry out all the instructions and directions, which may be issued from time to time by the *Kaitakushi* officers;" his workday was to be at least six hours, excepting Sundays and special Japanese "resting days;" his compensation was 7,200 Japanese gold yen (the virtual equivalent of $7,200 at the current rate of exchange) plus a house, although Clark was to bear the cost of furnishings and household expenses.

Additional provisions which bound Clark but seem to reflect broader problems with foreign employees included: a commitment that he would not engage, directly or indirectly, in any trade or commerce; cancellation of contract on three months' notice by either party; if cancellation was at the *Kaitakushi*'s initiative Clark was to be paid two months' separation pay; if at his initiative he would be paid only for services rendered; travel expenses both ways for Clark, but if the contract were cancelled while he was in Sapporo expenses would cover only travel to Tokyo or Yokohama; and the government's right to dismiss Clark in the event of neglect of duties, disobedience of instructions or commission of unsatisfactory acts with compensation only to the date of dismissal and no payment of return passage.

The contract contained one insertion of note, written in by Clark and initialled by Yoshida. The text read that Clark was to be "head teacher (namely, 'assistant director, and professor')," but Clark inserted "president" after "assistant director." He always used the title "president," while at SAC and later; the Japanese always used "head teacher" or, occasionally, "assistant director." Fortunately, the difference never led to a dispute, undoubtedly because the working relationship between Clark and the *Kaitakushi* officials was always smooth.

When Clark signed his contract in Washington he was accompanied by two of his MAC students, William Wheeler of the class of 1874 and David P. Penhallow, class of 1875. Both signed two-year contracts, Wheeler as professor of civil engineering, mechanics, mathematics and the English language at an annual salary of 3,000 gold yen and Penhallow as professor of chemistry, botany, agriculture, mathematics and the English language at 2,500 gold yen. Soon after his arrival in Sapporo, Clark was authorized to add a third member to his staff. He chose William P. Brooks, class of 1876, who signed a two-year contract at 2,500 gold yen as professor of agriculture and superintendent of the college farm which Clark had just established.

Clark, Wheeler and Penhallow left Amherst on May 21, 1876 and arrived in San Francisco via Philadelphia and Washington on May 29. After a busy few days there they sailed for Yokohama on June 1. They landed on June 28, went up to Tokyo on the 29th and had their first interview with General Kuroda on the 30th. After a month of sightseeing, socializing, conferences, interviews with prospective students, purchasing of supplies and inspection tours, the triumvirate set sail for Hokkaido on July 25. With them were the students selected in Tokyo, a small group of young women workers being sent to Hokkaido and, most significantly, General Kuroda, Clark's superior and soon-to-be friend.

During the trip by steamship Clark and Kuroda became involved in what fortunately turned out to be a minor and inconclusive confrontation. Because problems of student conduct, drinking and carousing especially had arisen in the temporary school that had been established in Tokyo as the predecessor of the Sapporo school, Kuroda had become concerned with the issue of moral training for the students. On the ship Kuroda asked Clark if he would assume responsibility for such training in the new school. Clark agreed to do so, but insisted that the basis of the training would have to be the Bible which was to him the source not only of moral training but of morality itself. Kuroda objected because although the long-standing proscription of Christianity had been lifted a few years earlier, it was still unthinkable that the Bible be used in a government school which is what the soon-to-be-opened agricultural college would be.[8] Clark had with him some 30 English Bibles which had been given him, for the students in Sapporo, by the Reverend Dr. Luther Gulick, a pioneer American missionary.[9]

The discussion was inconclusive because neither man would budge from his position, but later events demonstrated that a decision either way was unnecessary. Clark used the Bibles to good effect in the moral instruction of the students. Thus, Kuroda achieved his goal with respect to the students without openly approving the use of the Bible. Clark, of course, could not but feel that he had won an important concession, if not victory.

On July 31, 1876, Clark's fiftieth birthday, the group arrived in the village of Sapporo after spending the night at Otaru on the coast. Thus started eight and a half months of almost frantic, but highly productive, work by Clark, his young MAC associates and the Japanese officials in the *Kaitakushi*. In that brief period he fulfilled his contractual obligation by opening, operating and teaching in the agricultural college, a task which alone would have justified his generous salary. In addition, through a logical extension of his work with the college, he created for himself a role of technical advisor to the Kaitakushi which enabled him to make a major contribution to the agricultural development of Hokkaido. Finally, as a teacher and moral and spiritual guide he played a vital role in the training of his small group of students who were destined to become leaders both in Hokkaido and throughout Japan.

A week after their arrival Clark accompanied Kuroda on a minor expedition up the Ishikari River to inspect coal mines. The trip apparently cemented the relationship between the two men. On his return to Sapporo, Clark wrote to his wife as follows:

I had a most delightful excursion with the Governor and had a splendid opportunity of becoming intimately acquainted with his private and public life and his views on many subjects of education, politics, and religion. He is a very remarkable man and in many respects of admirable character. Though born a poor boy and trained only as a private soldier he has become one of the ablest statesmen and generals of the empire. He is now thirty-six . . . [and a] Major General in the regular army, one of the seven members of the imperial council selected by the Mikado, and chief of one of the ten departments of government.[10]

Clark and Kuroda seem to have been completely compatible in spite of the considerable gap in their ages. That they were temperamentally akin was demonstrated by their military service. Clark's record in the Civil War showed clearly that he was not an unwilling warrior in spite of his eventual disillusionment with war. Kuroda was a military man by both birth and career. He was a man of powerful physique with strong, handsome features adorned with a thick mustache and a slight beard. Contemporary photographs of the two men indicate that they were not too dissimilar in appearance.

Their ability to get along well was a major contributing factor to Clark's outstanding accomplishments. At a minimum he never had to waste time trying to get along with his superior. On the other hand, Kuroda was more than willing to give Clark a free hand if for no other reason than he was doing what had to be done not only for the new school but also for the development of Hokkaido itself for which Kuroda, as governor, was officially responsible.

On August 14, 1876, just two weeks after his arrival in Sapporo, Clark presided over the opening ceremony of the agricultural college which under Kuroda's general supervision had undergone three years of evolutionary development in Tokyo and one in Sapporo. Present were Governor Kuroda, Zusho Hirotane, director of the school and Clark's immediate superior, the small faculty, the twenty-four students, and a group of military officers and invited guests.[11]

Clark's remarks which he described in a letter to his wife as being extemporaneous were later set down in writing and published.[12] In a section addressed to the students Clark made some remarks which not only made a lasting impression on them, but also foretold both the mission and the accomplishment of the school.

> Let everyone of you, young gentlemen, strive to prepare himself [*sic*] for the highest positions of labor and trust and consequent honor in your native land which greatly needs your most faithful and efficient service. Preserve your health and control your appetites and passions, cultivate habits of obedience and diligence, and acquire all possible knowledge and skill in the various sciences which you may have an opportunity to study. Thus, you will prepare yourselves for important positions, which are always in waiting for honest, intelligent and energetic men, of whom the supply is uniformly less than the demand in this as in every other country.

The second sentence made a lasting impression on the students some of whom quoted it many years later. Of greater significance is that they did prepare themselves for the responsible positions they later filled.

The school had a total of 50 students, 24 in the college proper and 26 in the preparatory class. Clark taught two hours of English and two of botany six days a week. Wheeler taught two hours of algebra and Penhallow two hours of chemistry daily in the college. The two also taught two hours of English and arithmetic to the preparatory students who also studied Chinese and Japanese under Japanese instructors.[13]

Two weeks after the school opened Clark presented to Director Zusho a comprehensive four-year curriculum for the college. It was ambitious, covering mathematics, half-a-dozen sciences, the English and Japanese languages, civil engineering, mechanics, agriculture and horticulture, and assorted lesser subjects. Obviously, such a curriculum would demand a larger faculty as well as physical plant. However, what was involved was not a complex of academic department in the various disciplines, but a somewhat larger faculty which could teach a variety of subjects at the level then required.

The work of developing the school remained one of Clark's continuing preoccupations. Throughout his stay he ordered books and a wide variety of supplies for the school. He won the approval of the authorities for the construction of a chemical laboratory which he regarded as both an educational necessity and a means by which the college could contribute to the agricultural and economic development of Hokkaido. His program for the college made it clear that he perceived it not as a narrow educational institution but a vital instrument for the development of the area.

On September 8, 1876, five weeks after his arrival in Sapporo, Clark addressed an important memorandum to Governor Kuroda in which he urged that a well-equipped farm be established and "placed under the exclusive control of a foreign Professor of Agriculture, who shall be under the direction and authority of the President of the College."[14] This marked the beginning of his second major activity, serving as technical adviser to the *Kaitakushi*.

Clark stated that the farm should be established to further the proper training of the students in practical agriculture, "especially in the correct mode of farm management, with due regard to the economy of labor, the production of profitable crops and the maintenance of fertility in the soil." The farm should be operated in such a way that income from the sale of livestock and produce could be used to defray the farm expenses. In other words, it should be run as a money-making operation. In addition, he recommended that human labor "should be replaced by agricultural machines and the working of horses and cattle;" this provision obviously calling for considerable technological innovation. Finally, almost as an afterthought he recommended the carrying out of experiments with new crops, fertilizers and machines and with manufactures such as silk, sugar, beer and wine. What Clark had in mind was clearly an operation with a potential far beyond what it could provide in the training of students.

Clark soon won from Governor Kuroda not only approval of the experimental farm, but also the responsibility for managing it. In addition, the foreign professor to control the farm turned out to be his student, William P. Brooks. He wrote to his wife:

Governor Kuroda consults me constantly and always follows my advice. Yesterday he turned over to me the great model and experimental farm near the capital where more than a hundred men are employed.[15]

Several weeks later he again wrote to his wife describing both the satisfactory progress of his work and the degree of responsibility he had been granted:

My health is excellent, my work abundant and not above my capacity, my employers liberal and appreciative, and my achievements satisfactory to myself and so far as I know to the government. I believe I am the first foreigner who had been entrusted with the entire control of valuable property, with full power to buy and sell, employ and discharge help, build and make improvements, and draw money from the treasury with my official seal, without the slightest supervision from a Japanese officer.[16]

Within a few weeks 200 men were at work on the farm. Clark decided to enclose it entirely with a fence some three miles in length and surrounding an area of about 250 acres. In addition, a ditch about a mile long, a little less than five feet wide at the top and varying from a foot to three feet deep was dug to serve the double purpose of drainage and irrigation. Existing roads and ditches were obliterated to facilitate the use of farm machinery and a new road was laid out. Altogether the farm was an imposing operation.[17]

The most impressive building on the farm was the model barn, built on plans and specifications prepared by William Wheeler which were based on the college barn at MAC. Clark intended the barn to be the model for others to be constructed throughout Japan, but it remained unique. It stands as a metaphor for the process of modernization already initiated in Japan: the plan was western, but the construction was done by Japanese hands. It still stands on the campus of Hokkaido University as a national cultural property and demonstrates the rapidity with which the Japanese builders were able to adapt their traditional techniques to the construction of an edifice of a type hitherto completely unknown to them.

To Clark the barn was not simply an architectural exercise; it was a central element of the broader problem of animal husbandry as an integral segment of the development of Hokkaido agriculture. Clark was not responsible for the introduction of farm animals in the American style. Horace Capron a few years earlier had urged the importation of farm animals and was responsible for the appointment of a young cattle farmer from Ohio, Edward Dun, to develop the farm animal program.[18] Dun and Clark knew each other, but there is no record of how or if they worked together.

Clark acknowledged Dun's work, but made a number of recommendations of his own. He advised against the importation of shorthorn cattle and thoroughbred horses on the reasonable ground that Japanese farmers were not yet prepared to develop and maintain their breeds. Instead he recommended the rapid introduction of large numbers of "clean and hardy cattle from California" to be used as both work animals and for dairy products. In addition, he advocated the importation of Ayrshires as "undoubtedly the best breed for the production of milk, butter and cheese." After his return to Amherst he purchased and shipped about half-a-dozen Ayrshires to the Sapporo Farm.

He also recommended the importation of Nambu stallions from northern Japan for breeding purposes, but only after a vigorous program for the castration of native Hokkaido horses had been carried out. In addition, he recommended the importation of both stallions and mares from California in order to breed horses for heavy work. He also argued for the importation of sheep from California instead of China which the Japanese government had favored. In regard to swine he believed that the initial step should be to persuade the farmers that "it will pay to keep them."

Clark also recognized from the beginning that if the animal husbandry program was to succeed emphasis would have to be placed on the creation of adequate supplies of fodder which, of course, should come from the experimental farm. Soon after the farm had been authorized he ordered from America some twelve hundred pounds of seed of a variety of fodders. The seeds were used in experimental plantings to determine the varieties most suitable for Hokkaido and the best methods of cultivation.

While Clark certainly did not found animal husbandry in Hokkaido, both his recommendations and his work contributed significantly to its development. It was as a result of the work of Capron, Dun and Clark that Hokkaido became and has remained a principal dairy-farming region in Japan.

Clark found the farm to be ideal for general farming terming the land to be "most admirable tillage land in perfect condition." Under Clark's direction the farm, in addition to fodder, produced wheat, barley, oats, rice, beans, Indian corn, Chinese indigo, potatoes, flax and hemp.

At MAC Clark had become interested in developing sugar beets as a crop in the Amherst area. He transferred his interest to Hokkaido and became convinced that sugar beets would become an excellent source of farm income. In his first annual report on SAC Clark argued vigorously for the establishment of a sugar beet industry. He believed that Hokkaido was ideal sugar beet country listing a number of reasons: ideal soil and climatic conditions, cheap labor, suitable cultivating techniques, adequate fuel and water for processing the beets into sugar, and the existence of the College whose resources could be used to develop the industry. Although the *Kaitakushi* attempted to develop the industry after Clark's departure, it was found that beets with the necessary sugar content could not be grown. Sporadic attempts were made to establish the industry but they came to naught.[19] Eventually a modest sugar beet industry came into being, but it never reached the scale that Clark envisaged.

Early in his mission Clark submitted two memoranda to Governor Kuroda which, although they did not result in concrete programs unlike most of his memoranda, nevertheless serve as good illustrations of the scope of his activities. Apparently during the expedition up the Ishikari River, Kuroda brought up the interesting idea of the establishment of an American colony in Hokkaido. Clark's response was a series of questions he presented to the governor in writing.[20]

Would the government grant public land for a settlement of at least thirty young men and their families? Would the government accept the colonists on the condition that they renounce their American citizenship and become Japanese subjects? Would the government exempt the colonists from taxation and military service for a term of years and allow the colonists the right of self-government without Japanese interference? Would the settlers be permitted to engage in trade, manufacturing, fishing, mining and other pursuits with the rights and privileges of Japanese citizens?

In spite of his questions Clark believed that such a colony would contribute significantly to the development of Hokkaido and made some concrete suggestions as to how the venture could be initiated. However, there was no further mention of the project, possibly because of Clark's penetrating questions and their implications. It is highly unlikely, however, that the Japanese government would have ever approved of such an idea, especially if the colonists were to be granted the rights and privileges suggested by Clark.

In a memorandum recommending a series of broad changes in food, clothing and housing in Hokkaido, Clark declared that housing was inappropriate for the climate and listed a number of changes to guard against the cold. Similarly for clothing he urged the use of wool and leather boots and shoes; in food he recommended a diet which would include meat. His recommendations were based not on the idea that Japanese living conditions as he observed them were inferior in some abstract faction, but that improvements would mean better health conditions and an increased capacity for labor, especially in winter. His recommendations were not adopted, but they are interesting examples of Clark's ability to make accurate and penetrating observations.

In the closing weeks of his stay Clark submitted a long memorandum on forestry and forest management in Hokkaido.[21] Its only flaw was his prediction that Hokkaido forest resources would be sufficient for its needs for the next century.

At the end of his stay he agreed with the *Kaitakushi* to write a report on the salmon canning industry in the United States with the *Kaitakushi* paying the expenses of an inspection trip to Astoria at the mouth of the Columbia River, some seven hundred miles north of San Francisco. After his arrival in San Francisco Clark undertook the long and uncomfortable journey by horse-drawn wagon and wrote a detailed report covering everything from the best species of salmon for commercial purposes through the technical problems of the canning process to the final recommendation that England be targeted as the market for Hokkaido's future salmon industry.[22]

One of Clark's final acts before leaving Sapporo was the completion of the first annual report of Sapporo Agricultural College. This lengthy document is an invaluable record of both Clark's accomplishments and the inaugural year of the little college.[23]

Finally, there was his relationship to the work of his three young assistants, Penhallow, Wheeler and Brooks.[24] They must be given full credit for their own very considerable achievements. But it was Clark who selected them and recommended their appointments. Above all he created the conditions under which it was possible for them to accomplish what they did. For example, his smooth working relationship with Governor Kuroda and the *Kaitakushi* undoubtedly eased their work. The powerful example of Clark's driving energy and creative planning surely inspired them.

As president of SAC and adviser to the *Kaitakushi*, Clark made significant contributions to the development of Hokkaido, but it was his molding influence on his students that assured him a lasting place in the modern history of Hokkaido. Beyond question what he did for his students was one of Clark's major, though unplanned and unanticipated achievements.

An objective observer at the time undoubtedly would have concluded that the chances for a truly productive relationship between Clark and his students would not have been promising if for no other reason than the language problem. As for Clark, he had made the deliberate decision not to attempt to learn any Japanese because of the time it would require. He had acquired a few words during the voyage across the Pacific, but they were of no practical use.

It was the students who bridged the language gap. All had studied English and most had had the advantage of studying it in Tokyo where the best instruction was available. In addition, Clark and his MAC assistants placed great stress on English language proficiency in the interviews in both Tokyo and Sapporo. The fact that they were intellectually able, as proved conclusively by their subsequent careers, was undoubtedly of considerable assistance in their mastery of English. They were fortunate also in that Clark's language teaching extended beyond the classroom. He corrected their English compositions and notebooks in detail and in the evenings would go over them with the individual students.

The evening sessions with Clark in his comfortable quarters which the *Kaitakushi* provided made a lasting impression on the students.[25] He would speak informally with them while darning socks or engaging in similarly homely tasks and eating mandarin oranges for which he apparently developed a passion. He would also regale them with tales of his war experiences.

His teaching extended beyond the classroom in other ways as well. He introduced at SAC a practice that he had already developed at MAC: the requirement that students had to work on the farm for small wages. This had a peculiar relevance at SAC. Most of the students had come from samurai families and it had been part of the warrior ethos that neither manual labor nor cash wages was acceptable. Here was a breaking of tradition that was enabling the young students to feel even more at ease with the new currents of modernization.

Field trips under Clark's leadership to collect botanical and mineral specimens were novelties not only to the students but to the interested villagers who observed the processions of teachers and students. The trips were part of both the introduction of the students to science and the further cementing of the student-teacher relationship.

As foretold in his shipboard discussion with Governor Kuroda and in his inaugural speech, Clark devoted a considerable amount of time to moral training both in and out of the classroom. As he had told Kuroda he would do, he used the Bible. At the beginning of each school day he would devote about fifteen minutes to reading from the Bible and would have the students memorize passages from it. During the evening sessions in his quarters he would also discuss the Bible.

On Sundays Clark led services for the students. According to one of them, the services were varied, including reading from the Bible by both Clark and the students, fervent prayer by Clark, the reading of sermons and essays from newspapers and books, but no singing although Clark occasionally read hymns. One student attested to the power of his eloquence on such occasions by writing:

> He was naturally an eloquent speaker. His speech was always full of fire. When he spoke, it was so powerful that we felt as if the whole building were shaken by his energy. Even dogs outside were frightened and barked and barked while he was preaching. At other times he gave us gentle talks . . . as a father talks to his children.[26]

The same student on another occasion wrote that Clark's religion appealed to his students because it was a "practical religion, unlike that taught by ordinary missionaries" and was "religion without the odor of religion."

Clark's efforts as an informal missionary were crowned by the signing by all his students of what he termed the "Covenant of *Believers* in *Jesus*."[27] The signing, he wrote to his wife, is "the nearest I can come to organizing them into a church." The signers affirmed their belief in Jesus Christ, God, and the Bible and committed themselves to adhere to eight "commandments" which included the majority of the original ten in paraphrase and several of Clark's devising. They also constituted themselves into an association to be known as the "Believers in Jesus" for mutual assistance and encouragement.

Although all his "boys" had committed themselves to the Christian faith, Clark did not see them formally become Christians. That did not take place until almost six months after his departure from Sapporo when members of both the freshman and sophomore classes were baptized by an American missionary. Subsequently, about half of the group abandoned their faith, but the rest succeeded in establishing the Sapporo Independent Christian Church in 1882. The church members wanted to be independent of both foreign missionaries and foreign churches. From Amherst, Clark supported them both by letters and a cash contribution. In 1914 ten of the original signers of the covenant raised funds for the construction of "The William S. Clark Memorial Church" which eventually opened in 1922. Although the church was eventually relocated, it has continued under its original title.

Clark himself provided no reasons for his decision to engage in what turned out to be such a successful effort at proselytization. However, a number of circumstances seem to have led him to it. He was, of course, a devout church-goer in Amherst, but apparently no more so than his fellow townspeople. He was a part of an America that was much concerned about bringing the word of God to the heathen peoples of the world among whom were the Japanese. The gift of the Bibles to be presented to his students undoubtedly was a signal to Clark that it would not be out of place to attempt to convert them. Then there was also the circumstance that a few days after his arrival, an American missionary converted a young Japanese (who was to become an SAC student) in Clark's quarters when no other location was permitted. Finally, the close relations between Clark and his students undoubtedly led him to think of strengthening the bonds between them by making them fellow Christians.

Clark's own students carried on the work by successfully converting members of the second class who arrived about the time that the baptism of the former occurred. A total of 31 eventually signed the covenant, 17 from the first class and 14 from the second. Among them was Uchimura Kanzo who, in time, became Meiji Japan's leading Christian thinker.

Governor Kuroda and the *Kaitakushi* and behind them the Japanese government had to have been more than gratified with what Clark had achieved during his brief stay in Sapporo. The *Kaitakushi* apparently sounded Clark out on the possibility of extending his contract. However, he was bound to return to MAC for his leave of absence was for only a year. At any rate, the negotiations never reached a serious stage, although the *Kaitakushi* offered Clark a three-year extension on his contract.

In mid-April, 1877, Clark left Sapporo, but only after appropriate official farewells which included the exchange of mutually congratulatory letters between Clark and Director Zusho. Governor Kuroda had left Sapporo to command the government troops in the Satsuma rebellion which had broken out in distant Kyushu and which he successfully subdued.

On April 16, Clark said good-bye to Sapporo, SAC and especially his students. Clark, the faculty, all the students and several Japanese officials left his quarters on horseback in the morning bound for the village of Shimamatsu, now a Sapporo suburb, about twelve miles away. After luncheon and a ramble over the hills, reminiscent of the field trips at the college, Clark mounted his horse and bade farewell to his students, ending with a ringing, "Boys, be ambitious!"[28]

The three-word injunction has become permanently associated with Clark. However, it is only one of several similar phrases which his "boys," writing years later, attributed to him as he bade them farewell. Among them are: "Boys, be ambitious like this old man!," "Boys, be ambitious for Christ!," "Boys, be ambitious for good!" and in the longest version "Be ambitious not for money or selfish aggrandizement, not for that evanescent thing which men call fame. Be ambitious for the attainment of all that a man ought to be!" It is not too difficult to see why the shortest version has prevailed.

After his farewell Clark went on to visit another *Kaitakushi* model farm.[29] He went on to Hakodate where he boarded an English ship for Nagasaki where he visited wounded men from the battlefields of the Satsuma rebellion. He then went on to the Kobe-Osaka-Kyoto area where he visited the Reverend Joseph Hardy Niishima, his first Japanese student, at his newly established college. Arriving in Tokyo in May 17, he spent a busy week centering on a series of farewell dinners at one of which he and Kuroda had their final meeting. On May 24, Clark sailed from Yokohama for San Francisco which he reached on June 9.

He was never to return to Japan but his contacts with Hokkaido were by no means ended. He continued for almost three years to work on behalf of the *Kaitakushi.* He wrote a series of reports: the one on salmon canning already mentioned; another on fish oil and the curing of fish; and two on a raw silk sample which had been sent to him and on wood pulp. He also corresponded from time to time with Kuroda and several of his students.[30]

After his return to Amherst he delivered a number of lectures which revealed his fondness and admiration for Japan and its people and the soundness of his observations. Unfortunately, only newspaper accounts of his lectures remain. He did write a monograph on the agriculture of Japan which stands as the only formal record of his observations on Japan.[32] In his correspondence, the accounts of his lectures and his monograph, Clark stands as a firm Japanophile. It is clear that his work, his relationships with his students, Kuroda and the *Kaitakushi* and his general experience of the country made his year in Japan the richest and most rewarding of his life. He gave much and received much.

The brief months in Sapporo were climactic. What went before had been a necessary prelude; what followed was anticlimax. On his return to MAC he found the college in difficulty, no surprise for the situation had been far from rosy long before his departure for Japan. The difficult budgetary problems had become exacerbated by an increasing reluctance on the part of legislators to appropriate the sums that were necessary for a stable operation, to say nothing of the achievement of the ambitious goals in building, enrollment and curricular breadth still envisaged by Clark.

Under the circumstances relations between Clark and his board of trustees steadily deteriorated. He finally resigned early in 1879, just before a special alumni committee issued a report on the college which, without mentioning Clark by name, was critical of the state of the college, particularly of the management of its finances. In effect, the report simply brought to public attention the difficulties that Clark had partly created and partly had been created for him and that he seemed not about to solve.

If the situation of the college was a negative motive for resignation, Clark also had a positive one, his acceptance of the presidency of a floating college to be organized in New York City.[32] The brain-child of a wealthy young Ohio businessman, the floating college was to be a modern steamship, complete with a carefully selected faculty under Clark's leadership and a student body of young males whose fathers could pay the very substantial sum of $2,500 for a two-year cruise around the world with shipboard lectures and visits to and field trips from dozens of ports. It was clearly the kind of academic venture that would have strong appeal for Clark with his record of educational innovation going back to his scientific department of his first year at Amherst College. Besides, his beloved Japan was on the itinerary.

Unfortunately, the venture soon foundered in spite of extensive and favorable publicity. It became apparent that to recruit 250 students (already reduced from the original goal of 300) at $2,500 a head was an impossible task. Then the promoter suddenly died and in spite of Clark's best efforts the project was soon cancelled, leaving him without his presidency. Thus ended his long career as an academic.

While he was attempting to get the floating college under way, Clark met John R. Bothwell, the publisher of a newspaper devoted to mining affairs, and in the spring of 1881, the two men opened the firm of Clark & Bothwell at the corner of Nassau and Wall Streets, specializing in the ownership, management and operation of mines.[33] Shortly the firm was involved with mines stretching from Nova Scotia to Northwestern Mexico with the principal ones in Utah, Nevada, and California. Clark immediately plunged into their operation and in the course of a little over a year made five transcontinental trips to oversee the mines.

In the first year Clark earned a considerable fortune, but because of the precarious nature of the mining business at the time and specific difficulties encountered by some of the mines, the company and its investors soon found themselves in serious difficulty. The company collapsed and Clark's partner disappeared. It soon came to light that Bothwell had a long record of dubious financial operations. Warrants for the arrest of both men were issued in New York, but were never executed. Bothwell had disappeared and Clark was able because of his immediate efforts to salvage the operation to establish his innocence in the affair.[34] Not only did Clark lose the apparent fortune he had gained during the brief operation of the company but hundreds, if not thousands, of investors lost sums ranging from a few dollars to several thousands.

Soon after his return to Amherst—scarcely a happy one since dozens of his fellow townspeople had invested in his company—he suffered a severe illness, but speedily recovered. But he enjoyed only a brief respite. For the almost four years that remained of his life, ill health kept him in virtual seclusion, the local newspaper noting his rare appearances outside his home. On March 9, 1886 he died in Amherst from the heart disease which had kept him in confinement in his home for so long.[35]

Sources

The basic sources on Clark are to be found in the archives of the libraries of Amherst College, Hokkaido University and the University of Massachusetts (Amherst). The Amherst College collection includes material on his activities as both a student and professor there and some on his Civil War experience. Hokkaido University has what appears to be a virtually complete file of his official correspondence with the Kaitakushi and the correspondence between Clark and his students after his departure. The University of Massachusetts has the most complete file of his letters and a considerable amount of secondary material on his life as well as microfilm of local newspapers which contain accounts of Clark's activities.

Clark's letters provide good coverage of his student years at Amherst College, his Civil War service, his study in Germany, and his stay in Sapporo. His letters from Sapporo to his wife exist only in typed copies made many years later, but the style and content are entirely consistent with the few letters he wrote to his children. Unfortunately no letters remain that deal with his presidency, the faculty years at Amherst College, his University of Massachusetts floating college and the mining venture.

The single book-length biography in Japanese was written before many of Clark's letters became available and without access to the useful newspaper material relating to Clark.

The present author has written a typewritten manuscript entitled *William Smith Clark: A Yankee in Hokkaido* which is in the University of Massachusetts Archives. Professor Takaku Shin'ichi of Hokkaido University shortened and translated the manuscript which was published by the Hokkaido University Press in 1978 under the title *Kuraaku: Sono Eiko to Zasetsu* [*Clark: His Glory and Collapse*].

The Hokkaido Broadcasting Company in 1981 as a part of its thirtieth anniversary celebration prepared and presented on a national network an excellent 90-minute documentary on Clark's life. It was carefully researched and shot on location, including Germany and the United States. It is particularly valuable for material relating to his study in Göttingen and to one of the mining sites in Utah, material previously unknown. There is an English version narrated by Professor Takaku who was the commentator in the original.

Notes

[1]*Catalogue of the Officers & Students of Amherst College for the Academic Year of 1852-3* (Amherst, 1853), pp. 24-28.

[2]*New York Times*, February 13, 1862 and *New York Daily Tribune*, March 19, 1862.

[3]Anon., "W. S. Clark Hakase no Saisho no Nihonjin no Seito" [Dr. William S. Clark's First Japanese Student,"] *Neesima Kenkyu* 21 (April, 1960), pp. 13-15.

[4]For Capron's account of his service in Japan see *Memoirs of Horace Capron*, 2. (Ann Arbor: University Microfilms, unpublished manuscript).

[5]*Amherst Record*, May 17, 1871.

[6]*Springfield Republican*, July 18, 1872.

[7]The contract in both English and Japanese is in the University of Massachusetts Archives. For a translation of the Japanese government's instructions on hiring foreigners, see Appendix 1, pp. 155-6, in Hazel J. Jones, *Live Machines: Hired Foreigners and Meiji Japan* (Vancouver: University of British Columbia Press, 1980).

[8]On the Clark/Kuroda discussion see p. 10 in Miyabe Kingo, "William Smith Clark," unpublished manuscript in the University of Massachusetts archives, translated by Dr. George Rowland and revised by William Smith Clark II under Dr. Miyabe's direction.

[9]On the gift of the Bibles see WSC's letter of August 5, 1876, to Captain William B. Churchill, a brother-in-law.

[10]WSC letter to his wife, August 14, 1876.

[11]Clark's own account of the opening ceremony is in his letter to his wife, August 14, 1976. The English text of WSC's speech is in Sapporo Nogakko Gakugeikai, *Sapporo Nogakko* [Sapporo Agricultural College], (Tokyo, 1892).

[12]See unique copy of pamphlet on Sapporo Agricultural College inaugural ceremony in Hokkaido University archives.

[13]*Sapporo Agricultural College, First Annual Report, 1877* (Tokyo, 1878).

[14]WSC memorandum to Kuroda, September 8, 1876 (Hokkaido University archives).

[15]WSC to his wife, September 10, 1876.

[16]WSC to his wife, October 22, 1876.

[17]See *SAC, First Annual Report*, (Hokkaido, n.d.), pp. 10-15 for a description of the farm and pp. 19-21 for a description of the barn.

[18]See Edwin Dun, *Reminiscences of Nearly Half a Century in Japan.* Unpublished manuscript (Ann Arbor: University Microfilms, n.d.).

[19]WSC's thoughts on sugar beets are in *SAC, First Annual Report*, pp. 27-32.

[20]WSC memorandum to Kuroda, September 12, 1876.

[21]WSC memorandum to M. Yamada, March 8, 1877.

[22]WSC to Hori Motoi, June 29, 1877.

23See citation in note 13.

24See Chapter 13, "American Professors at the Sapporo Agricultural College: Their Role as Technical Specialists in the Development of Hokkaido" by Akizuki Toshiyuki.

25On his students' reactions to Clark see Oshima Shoken (Masatake), "Reminiscences of Dr. W. S. Clark," *The Japan Christian Intelligencer*: 1, 2 (April 5, 1926) and his "Kakuretaru Korosha: Kuraaku-sensei: Sapporo Nogakko no Sosetsusha" [The Hidden Man of Distinction: Clark-sensei, the Founder of Sapporo Agricultural College"], a six-part article in *Jiji Shimpo*, in August, 1922.

26On Clark's sermons see Oshima, cited above.

27The original of the Covenant is in the archives of the Sapporo Independent Christian Church.

28On the "Boys, be ambitious!" variations see Oshima in Note 24; Anon., "'Boys, be ambitious' ni tsuite" in *The Hokkaido University Library Bulletin*, 29, (June, 1972): pp. 4-5; and Tanaka Shinichiro, "Kuraaku no Kyokun" [Clark's Injunction], *Gakushikai Kaiho* 715 (1972) II, pp. 12-13.

29Akizuki Toshiyuki, "Kuraaku-hakase no Kiro" [Dr. Clark's Return Journey], *Hoppo Bungei* 61, 7 (July, 1973), pp. 3-5.

30The reports and correspondence are in the Hokkaido University archives. For the correspondence between WSC and two of his students see Saito Masahito, Onishi Naoki and Seki Hideshi, *Kuraaku no Tegami: Sapporo Nogakko Seito to no Ofuku Shokan* [Clark's Letters: The Correspondence of W. S. Clark and his Japanese Students] (Sapporo, 1986). Contains facsimiles of the original letters, English transcriptions and commentary.

31*Agriculture in Japan* (Boston, 1879).

32On the floating college see *New York Times*, December 2, 1878, March 27, 28, 1879, and April 3, 4, 10, 18, May 19, July 12, 1879; *New York Daily Tribune*, June 3, 1879; *Amherst Record*, April 23, May 7, 28, June 11, 18, July 30, 1879; and Anon., "A Floating College to Circumnavigate the Globe," a discussion of the prospectus in an unidentified magazine in the University of Massachusetts archives.

33Material on the firm of Clark & Bothwell is to be found in the *New York Times*, the *New York Daily Tribune*, the *Amherst Record*, the *Springfield Republican*, the *Hampshire Gazette* and the *Boston Daily Globe*, between the spring of 1881 and the spring of 1882.

34WSC's account of the affair appears in a lengthy deposition in the *Amherst Record*, June 18, 1882.

35The principal obituaries were in the *Amherst Record* (by Professor W. S. Tyler of Amherst College), March 10, 1886; *Proceedings of the American Academy of Arts and Sciences, 1886*; *Springfield Daily Republican*, March 10, 1886; *Boston Daily Globe*, March 9, 1886; *The Christian Union* (by Uchimura Kanzo), April 22, 1886; and *Amherst*

Record, June 23, 1886 (eulogy by Professor H. D. Goodell delivered at MAC alumni dinner).

6

Encounters with an Alien Culture: Americans Employed by the *Kaitakushi*

Fujita Fumiko

Introduction

In a world closely bound together by highly developed technology and communication, encounters with alien cultures have become extremely common, and it has become almost a cliche to emphasize the importance of mutual understanding between different cultures. While people faced with alien cultures are compelled to grope for ways to deal with them, historians are tempted to look backward and examine past cases of intercultural transactions in an attempt to learn from them. This chapter is concerned with one such case: Americans employed by the Japanese government in the 1870s for the development of Hokkaido, the northernmost of Japan's four main islands.

In 1869 the newly established Meiji government, deeply concerned about the possible threat of a Russian advance over Japan's northern frontier, while at the same time hopeful about the potential resources of the area, created a department called the *Kaitakushi*, which was specifically designed to administer, defend, and develop Hokkaido. In the spring of 1871, Kuroda Kiyotaka, Deputy Commissioner of the *Kaitakushi*, went to Washington to ask the U.S. government for help in securing able advisers. The sixty-six year old General Horace Capron, U.S. Commissioner of Agriculture, agreed to head an American mission to Hokkaido. Subsequently, until its abolition in 1882, the *Kaitakushi* employed forty-eight Americans, in addition to seventeen Europeans and thirteen Chinese. The corps of American experts played a far more important role than the other foreigners, not only because of their number, but also because of their pivotal positions in the *Kaitakushi*.

Fortunately for historians, the prominent members of the group left copious records in the form of reports, private as well as official letters, diaries, unpublished memoirs, and articles. Three of these men will be discussed here: Horace Capron, Commissioner and Adviser to the *Kaitakushi*; Benjamin Smith

Lyman, mining engineer; and Edwin Dun, agricultural expert. This chapter is primarily concerned with what these Americans thought, through their experience in Japan, about an alien culture, about their own country, and about their mission to transplant Western techniques and practices in an alien soil. To understand their experience and thoughts during their stay in Japan, their lives before coming to Japan will be also taken into consideration. It is hoped that, by dealing with the Americans employed by the *Kaitakushi* as a case study, this chapter will shed some light upon the larger issues of cultural confrontation.

The American Image of Japan

Before discussing the encounter of American experts with Japan, it may be worthwhile to consider the American image of Japan, specifically revealed in connection with Capron's mission. When Capron decided to accept the mission, he was keenly aware of America's interest in the island empire which the arrival of Perry's "black ships" had forced out of a long seclusion, and he was convinced that the "friendly spirit existing in this country . . . would be gratified at seeing its citizens engaged in building up the prosperity of the Great Empire of Japan."[1]

Capron's friends in Washington agreed with him. Finding Japanese solicitation of American assistance "extremely flattering" to the United States, Secretary of the Navy George M. Robeson expressed his belief that Capron's mission would "result in cementing the friendship, and in widening and making valuable to both the intercourse between the two governments." General William T. Sherman, Commanding General of the U.S. Army, joined Robeson in expressing his hope that the mission "will tend to bring that people into more intimate and friendly relations with those of Our country." Joseph Henry, secretary of the Smithsonian Institution, one of the few who had known of Capron's mission before it became public, and worked hard to search for Capron's assistants, extolled the mission as "a means of extending the blessings of high civilization and more Christianity to a very interesting portion of the human family."[2] Finally, President Grant also conveyed his high expectations to Capron:

> I look upon the department [of agriculture] as a very important one, and full of benefit to the country if wisely administered. But with all its importance it is not equal in value to your country to your new mission. From it I expect to see early evidence of increased commerce and friendly relations with a hitherto exclusive people, alike beneficial to both.[3]

The American press was even more enthusiastic about the so-called "American Commission."[4] Newspaper stories exaggerated Capron's position and described it as "not only one of dignity, but also of incalculable influence."

His salary was somehow doubled and reported as twenty thousand dollars a year. Also, the impression was given that his task concerned all Japan, not merely Hokkaido. While a few newspapers such as the *New York Times* accurately wrote that Capron's party was employed for the development of the agricultural and mineral resources of Hokkaido, many did not report the limits of Capron's mission. Some newspapers instead said that he would "make a thorough mineralogical and agricultural survey of that country," and others wrote: "His mission is nothing short of the reconstruction of Japanese productive industry."

The press moreover praised the Japanese as "the most intelligent and practical of Oriental nations, the Yankees of Asia," and wrote of Japan: "Instead of allowing itself to be crushed by the march of progress it proposes to keep step with it." Americans in turn flattered themselves by thinking that the Japanese "naturally look[ed] to the most progressive people in the world for ideas of progress." The *Prairie Farmer* wrote: "It must be a matter of pride to all Americans that the most enlightened of the Eastern Nations looked to this country, and not to the Nations of Europe, to find a representative of the most advanced civilization." It seems that Americans were generous in praising the Japanese exactly because the latter did not fail to "recognize the superiority of our progressive civilization."

The press took it for granted that the mission would result in many and enduring benefits to the people of Japan: "The Japanese will learn the arts that have made us a mighty nation in a single century." At the same time the press was unanimous in expecting that the mission would bring abundant material returns to Americans at home. They predicted: "One of the first results of this movement will be a great enlargement of our trade with Japan, and a great increase in our manufacturing operations." The *New York Times*, which knew the limits of the scope of Capron's mission, also reported that "in results to us this Commission is regarded as the most promising; far more so, indeed, than the Burlingame Chinese mission, since it will affect directly our foreign commerce, and perhaps afford the opportunity of regaining in the Pacific what we have lost in other seas." According to the *New York Times,* the leading manufacturers were eager to provide the commission with models of machinery, samples of their manufactures, catalogues, and illustrated price lists. *Pittsburgh Gazette,* referring to a possible Japanese demand for the products manufactured in the United States, simply wrote: "Imagination cannot picture the magnificent results which this mission of General Capron may accomplish."

The American image of Japan was abstract in the sense that the description similar to "the most intelligent and practical of Oriental nations" or "the Yankees of Asia" seems to have been applied to almost any people who acknowledged the American superiority and asked for their help. The American experts employed by the *Kaitakushi* would soon find out how close such an American image of Japan was to the realities.

The Case of Horace Capron

A Long Prelude

Horace Capron, born on August 31, 1804, in Attleboro, Massachusetts, was the fifth generation in descent from a French Huguenot who emigrated to Rhode Island in 1656.[5] His father, who had served in the Revolution in his youth, was a physician. When Horace was two, his family moved to Oneida County, New York, where his father erected a cotton mill and a woolen mill. Encouraged by handsome profits during the War of 1812 and motivated by patriotic zeal as well, he organized another cotton mill, but his factories could not survive the free admission of foreign manufactured goods after the war was over. In 1825 he moved to Orange County where he worked with others to establish the manufacturing village of Walden. The great disappointment for Horace was that he could not afford to go to college; he instead started to learn the manufacturing business as an apprentice at his father's and other large mills. In 1829 he was entrusted with the supervision of several textile factories in Maryland, and his successful management soon brought him into favorable notice in the area.

After marrying a daughter of a wealthy family in Montpelier, Maryland, Capron organized in 1836 a cotton mill on his wife's estate and over the years helped establish the flourishing village of Laurel. The factories he built gave employment to over seven hundred people and supported a population of over two thousand. At the same time he set out to renovate a large piece of land near the settlement, worn out by successive cultivation of tobacco and corn. When Capron developed a prosperous dairy farm, he became widely known as a progressive scientific agriculturalist and was elected as Vice President of both the Maryland State Agricultural Society and the U.S. Agricultural Society.

Capron, however, suffered severely from the tariff of 1846, and in 1850 he had to give up his estate as well as his share of the manufacturing corporation. After serving as special agent to the Indians in northern Texas for two years, he settled in Illinois in 1854, where he devoted himself to the breeding of cattle and the raising of horses. As "the country's most famous breeder of Devon cattle,"[6] Capron was appointed to the executive committees of state and national agricultural societies. But his peaceful life was suddenly interrupted by the Civil War. Although nearly sixty years old, Capron, commissioned to raise the 14th Illinois Cavalry, took part in thirty-four engagements. Wounded severely in the fall of 1864, he was discharged with the rank of brigadier-general. All his three sons went to war; the eldest was killed, while two others came home wounded. Since his neglected farm had fallen into poor condition, Capron had to find other means to support his family.

His friends, including governors and senators of Maryland and Illinois intervened to get him the position of Commissioner of Agriculture, vacant since the death of the first Commissioner. With his national reputation in the field of farming and breeding and his Middle Western and conservative border state support, Capron was an acceptable candidate and was confirmed by the Senate in November 1867.[7] The Department of Agriculture, established in 1862, still, faced the traditional fears of centralized control and a widely-shared suspicion that the Department would be another refuge for partisan job-hunters. Capron sought to display his commitment to economy by dismissing a considerable number of employees and by erecting a new building for the Department within the original appropriation. At the same time, he not only expanded practical services for farmers but also established the division of botany under a scientific botanist, thus demonstrating his appreciation of professional work. Capron thus maintained the confidence of the farming interests, Congress, and the administration so fully that there was no thought of replacing him until Capron himself decided to resign to head the mission to Japan.[8]

Capron's background suggests that he took the *Kaitakushi* job in the conviction that his varied and extensive knowledge would be of the greatest value for the development of the Japanese frontier. Also, stories of the Revolutionary War in which his father fought, the memory of the War of 1812 when his father proudly built American factories, the Civil War in which Capron himself fought for his country, and his subsequent service for the federal government—all made Capron an American proud of his country and concerned with its prestige. The task offered by the Japanese government certainly appealed to patriotic Capron, for he believed, like his Washington colleagues, that its execution by Americans would contribute to the expansion of American influence and the strengthening of friendly relations between the United States and Japan. It cannot be denied, however, that Capron had pecuniary needs in mind too; his youngest son, severely burnt in a hotel fire the previous winter, became totally blind and had to depend financially upon his father.[9] Capron's salary ($3,000) as Commissioner of Agriculture was far from sufficient, and the generous remuneration Capron received from the Japanese government ($10,000) was most helpful for his family.

A "Semi-barbarous" Country

Before Capron left the United States, his image of Japan was simply one of "a far-off and semi-barbarous country," of which "so little is really known."[10] When he arrived in Japan, accompanied by his three assistants, in August 1871, he was indeed overwhelmed by the novelty and peculiarity of the people and society, feeling as if Japanese customs and temples took him some centuries back in history. Two months after arrival, he wrote his son: "Everything is so strange, and so entirely different from anything I ever saw before that I must acknowledge some bewilderment."[11]

First of all, Capron observed, many activities, even the most common ones, displayed "exactly the reverse of all European or American ideas." For example, a Japanese mounted his horse from the right side instead of the left; he drew a saw up, instead of pushing it down; he drew a plane towards him, instead of pushing it away from him; and he passed people on his right (in this case, like an Englishman) instead of on his left, "like an enlightened American."[12] Japanese music, entirely different from Western music, struck Capron as "an infliction." After attending a dinner at which Japanese music was performed, Capron wrote in his journal: "Never did I before experience greater agony ... than through this lengthy performance. I did not, although I tried to do my best, detect the slightest approach to a tune." Therefore he was "almost led to laughter to see at the closing of each piece the applause and greater distinction it met with from the Japanese portion of the assembly."[13]

Capron was far more favorably impressed by Japanese crafts, landscape, and some of its architecture. He saw many temples and shrines "decorated in the highest Japanese art." He described them "truly magnificent," "truly works of art," "superb," and "beyond description." Especially when he observed figures of gods carved in wood, he marveled at the fact that so much expression could be given to a block of wood. "No sculpture in marble, or painting upon canvas," Capron thought, "could convey a better idea of the peculiar virtue or passion they were intended to represent, such composure, such majesty, so much heavenly expression in one and agony in another."[14]

In Capron's mind, however, these temples and shrines, with all their beauties, belonged to the past. When it came to progressive civilization, Capron confirmed his original image of Japan as a "semi-barbarous" country when he actually saw that Japan was "deficient in nearly all the comforts and conveniences of civilized life." In clothes, the ordinary Japanese appeared to him "all nearly naked, both male and female." In basic foodstuffs, they were limited to rice and fish, supplemented by a few roots such as *daikon,* "the great worthless fibrous turnip radish," and a few varieties of fruit.[15] Furthermore, Capron discovered that the Japanese, employing human muscle as their only motive power, were entirely deficient in the use of "the ways and means by which foreign nations have reached such a high state of civilization." He was amazed to find the propelling of drays upon the streets, the hulling of rice, the manufacturing of silk and cotton, and even the transportation of people all done either by hand or by foot. Capron wondered: "How it is that a people naturally so intelligent, ingenious, appreciative, and so capable of imitating everything they see, should remain so long in a state of semi-barbarism, is perfectly incomprehensible."[16]

Yet, in spite of their deprivation in the benefits of civilization, Capron noticed "cheerfulness and good nature" among the Japanese. The experience "to pass through the throngs which filled the streets and witness so much happiness"—"cheering beyond expression"—led Capron to think: "Truly these are a happy people having few wants and these easily supplied, and many, very many sources of innocent amusement." He even wondered "how much their happiness will be augmented by their intercourse with "outside barbarians." Also, when he was favorably impressed by the Ainu living in Hokkaido, he again asked himself "how far the introduction of the wants, habits and ideas of civilized society, with all its concomitant of evils and vices, may add to their real happiness in this world." The Japanese attitudes in adversity seemed to Capron even more "commendable." Observing, at the scene of a fire, that there was "not a word of murmur at their lot, not a tear or complaint but a calm resignation . . . and an almost cheerful submission to their fate," Capron was moved to remark, "Truly a most wonderful people."[17]

There were such rather rare moments when Capron seemed to find some value in the non-Western way of life, but most of the time he was deeply committed to his mission to introduce Western civilization in Japan. In fact, the westward movement of civilization seemed to Capron to be a matter of inevitability. He wrote an American editor: "The great tidal wave of civilization which . . . was sweeping across the American continent, seems only to have paused upon the western coast to gather strength for its passage over the broad Pacific in its westward progress around the world. It has reached the Asiatic continent."[18] Capron was aware that a change was about to take place in Japan: "There is a wonderful determination to break the shakles [sic] which have bound them for ages" and to "emmerge [sic] from a state of barbarism to a state of highest civilization." It gave Capron a thrilling sensation to consider himself a messenger of "the light of the most advanced civilization."[19]

Capron was moreover convinced of the potential of the Japanese drive for progress: "An immense field will be opened to the commerce of the world." For he had a vision of about thirty million Japanese who were "without nearly all of the requirements of a highly civilized people" but "destined at some future day to attain" them. "They [the Japanese] want everything," Capron reported to his former colleague in Washington, "from a cambric needle to a steam engine, every kind and description of farming implement and machine, from the hoe (inclusive) up, also all kinds of stock, and every description of wearing apparel, from a shirt collar, to the most elaborate toggery you can put on."[20] Capron naturally expected that his mission to help the Japanese would also help the Americans who dreamed of expanding markets for their ever-increasing production.

Inefficient and Conceited Japanese

Under the employ of the *Kaitakushi* for nearly four years, Capron provided the department with plans and advice, while supervising his foreign assistants. As an agricultural expert, he devoted himself to the introduction of a variety of food, plants, improved breeds of horses and cattle, and farm implements and machinery, and as the chief adviser to the *Kaitakushi*, he stressed the importance of "systematic," "scientific," "practical," and "economical" operations as essential to the successful development of Hokkaido. As part of practical and economical agriculture, for example, Capron urged that settlers switch from the traditional Japanese staple, rice, to wheat, for not only was wheat more suitable to a northern climate than rice, but also rice, "the most expensive" in the cost of production, was "the least nutritive of the food grains." Such changes in food habits, he believed, would help Hokkaido become self-sufficient in food production and at the same time would make the settlers sturdier.[21]

Capron, however, realized that there was an enormous gap between his ideal and the *Kaitakushi* operations, especially during his once-a-year visit to Hokkaido. He particularly abhorred the waste and inefficiency characteristic of the *Kaitakushi* operations, which he attributed in part to supernumerary officials. When he inspected salmon fisheries, for instance, he found "one official for every hundred fish taken, and at some of the landings to every ten." At the *Kaitakushi* farm in Nanae, he found spacious buildings erected for the accommodation of eighteen officials whose duty was to oversee eighteen laborers. When the whole army of officials received him and escorted him over the place, Capron "could not disguise [his] astonishment and perfect disgust of the whole matter," thinking that "one good American farmerman and his two sons on a farm of 40 acres, with a yoke of oxen, a pair of horses and a cow, would have produced better results."[22]

According to Capron's observations, no sooner was anything started and fairly got under way before an important official made his appearance and took charge, and trouble would start at once. For example, although Capron rejoiced to see a great Illinois breaking-plow drawn by six bulls "cut a straight handsome furrow in the virgin soil of Japan," he was dismayed when an official, a "pest" in his word, appeared and appointed assistants "to an unlimited number" while money was "lavished, recklessly spent in searching and bringing forward bulls from all parts of the country" just for one breaking-plow. The establishment of a simple blacksmith's forge on the American plan was another such example. While it required one smith and two coolies as strikers, Capron was surprised to see an office opened at once and two or three officials take their seats upon the floor with a Japanese writing table before them, thus assuming the appearance of a great business; in fact these officials succeeded in making any business, even the supply of one horseshoe nail, cumbersome. Capron had to wonder whether the introduction of a machine or an implement intended to save labor and money could perform its function or rather just help officials to spend money in an extravagant way.[23]

Another cause for the waste and inefficiency of the *Kaitakushi* operation was also obvious to Capron; Japanese failure to consult him and obtain his sanction beforehand. Capron was frustrated at what he conceived as "the want of candor on the part of the officials of this Department, and entire exclusion from [him] of all information touching the designs or plans of operations, or the means appropriated in whole or in part to carry out those plans." He found the communication between him and the *Kaitakushi* extremely "one-sided." He was constantly interviewed on a vast scope of American topics, from farm management to government organization, but, when he thought his turn had come to ask questions about the task in hand, the interview was closed. He was therefore "compelled to grope [his] way in the dark, expected always to be prepared to advise and cooperate."[24] He considered such a situation not only a violation of his contract,[25] but also a great loss to the *Kaitakushi*. "How much greater benefit I could have been to you and to this people," Capron appealed to Kuroda, "could the terms of my contract have been adhered to and I received your full countenance and support."[26]

Capron saw "overweening vanity" in the Japanese who did not humbly admit their incompetence and ask for his guidance. In his view, the canal of the Toyohira River and the pier at the harbor of Mori were good examples. While Capron was in Tokyo, Japanese constructed the canal at the junction of the large Ishikari River and the Toyohira River, which cut its way through the town of Sapporo with a rapid current. In the summer of 1873, when Capron visited Sapporo, the Japanese showed him a large bulkhead which they had constructed, expecting it both to stand as a bulwark against all freshets in the river and to regulate the supply of water which was to flow through it into the canal. Capron, "surprised and amazed and mortified" to see their "great work," told them that the bottom of the gates of the bulkhead and of the canal was so far above the level of the stream that no water could enter in, and that the dam at the point would not stand a moderate rise of the river because of the low banks. A large force immediately set to filling up bags with sand in order to raise the water to a sufficient level. But, when the officials raised the gates with a cheer, water rushed down the steep grade of the canal with such force that, in less than two hours, it ripped and tore away the banks, carrying away the sheathing of plank.[27] Then the winter floods of 1873-74 entirely cleaned out the bulkhead.

In the summer of 1874, when Capron inspected the Toyohira River again, he found the new bulkhead "a great improvement" in its location and construction. Nevertheless, he was still repelled by Japanese vanity, for they "attempted to deceive [him] into the belief that it was the same old work." When he discovered the whole structure of the original bulkhead some distance below the banks of the river, he found it "quite amusing to see the duplicity of these Japanese officials." He "called their attention to it afterwards, and they slunk away without any remarks."[28] Also, finding fault with another part of the canal, Capron pointed out the defect to the Resident Governor. While the Japanese again immediately set to repairing it, he was sure that they would have to fall back onto the old channel or maintain a battery of sandbags certain to be washed away every time there was more water than would run through the gates. Giving all the details of the Japanese work, Capron asked his assistant, Benjamin Lyman, "Did you ever in your life come across such a stupid affair?"[29]

As for the pier at Mori, Capron admitted that the plan (given the Japanese by his American assistant) was good but pointed out that the structure would rot in a few years because the material used was perishable, and that, worst of all, it was constructed where it could never be of any use. On learning of the importance of having a sufficient depth of water to float a vessel along the side of the pier, the Japanese continued adding to the pier until it reached far out into the sea. Capron observed, "It now stands as a monument of their egregious folly and self conceit."[30]

Capron thought that both these projects originated not from any Japanese intention to interfere with his plans, but from the "great defect in the Japanese character," that is, "overbearing confidence in their own judgment, and overweening vanity, which pushes them forward to cover up an error in their judgment when their attention is brought to it and to squirm out of it in some way at whatever cost." Capron, specifically referring to the canal and the pier, wrote: "In two cases of this character they have gone from bad to worse, expending vast sums to cover errors which have only ended in disaster." About the contrast between his competence and Japanese incompetence, he bluntly told Kuroda: "There is not an item of expense that has ever been made by my advice that has not proved an entire success . . . on the other hand all that has been done outside of me and without my approval has proved a failure."[31]

What particularly exasperated Capron was to find himself made "the 'scape goat' for all the delinquencies of the *Kaitakushi*" and "subjected to the daily criticism of the press and by individuals both in this country and America."[32] Criticism in the American press was especially disheartening for Capron, who viewed himself as working in Japan with "pride and responsibility in sustaining our [U.S.] national reputation and interest."[33] In order to clear his reputation which he "value[d] more than gold," Capron meticulously and repetitiously condemned the projects which he had not approved in his reports and his letters to Kuroda and to other *Kaitakushi* officials. "In all these cases," Capron consoled himself, "the records of the *Kaitakushi* will show my condemnation of them."[34]

A Firm Belief in the Success of His Mission

That Capron's four-year Japanese experience, after all, did not affect his belief in the superiority and universality of Western civilization was demonstrated in the speech he made in Washington in 1876. He first told the audience that the Japanese were "quiet, good natured, easily controlled, and measurably happy and contented, notwithstanding the absence of almost everything the average American or European considers essential to personal comfort." In other words, Capron explained, the Japanese were contented exactly because of their "blissful ignorance of the luxuries of the outer world." Therefore, "intercourse with foreigners and an intimate acquaintance with their luxurious and expensive habits may . . . effect discontent and consequent unhappiness among [the Japanese]." But taking notice that the seeds of Western civilization had been already sown and Japanese leaders were eager to "become better acquainted with our more advanced humanity," he asserted that "Whatever the result, the change was necessary for the elevation of the race to a higher condition of civilized life and to position and power among Christian peoples, and therefore attempts to render it permanent are in the highest degree justifiable." Calling the Japanese "the most industrious known," "incomparably frugal," possessing "ambition . . . in an eminent degree," and skilled in "all works of art requiring delicate manipulation," Capron predicted that "[Japan's] skilled labor will, if rightly utilized, advance the empire to wealth and power."[35]

Capron was fully convinced that his work had "resulted in much good" to Japan. First of all, by way of introducing Western plants, fruit, vegetables, crops, improved breeds of livestock as well as labor-saving machines and implements in agriculture and industry, his mission inaugurated "a complete revolution . . . in the system of labor and the character of the food supply." Moreover, his party had "the right to claim also the inauguration of the first regular system of geological, mineralogical and land surveys ever attempted in Japan, and the first successful lithographing of maps." The work of the *Kaitakushi* "exclusively under American direction" thus enlarged the boundaries of Japan to the extent of the domain of Hokkaido which "up to the period of 1871, when this Island was first taken in hand by the American Commission, was an encumbrance to the nation." He further pointed to the training of Japanese youths in useful trades and professions under the guidance of American experts. In his view, the good effects of the American work were not confined to Hokkaido; in modifying and improving the habits and conditions of the people, they were "of incalculable value to the Japanese as a nation."[36]

To Capron's satisfaction, the Japanese did not forget his contributions to their country. In January 1884 the Japanese government, in the name of the Emperor, conferred upon Capron the Decoration of the Second Order of the Rising Sun. He especially valued the Diploma which recited the results of his labors in Japan and the benefits derived by the country. "In fact," Capron wrote his son,"I don't see how any one can find fault with my work there after this endorsement by the Emperor after so many years experience in following up the plans laid out by me for the development and settlement of that long neglected but splendid Island."[37] One year later, on February 22, 1885, Capron died at the age of eighty.

The Case of Benjamin Smith Lyman

An Established Geologist

Born on December 11, 1835, in Northampton, Massachusetts, Benjamin Smith Lyman was an eighth-generation American.[38] His British ancestor arrived in Boston in 1631, and the subsequent Lymans were mostly "worthy men, respected in the rural community."[39] Both Benjamin's grandfather, a graduate of Yale, and his father, a graduate of Harvard, served the courts of Northampton for over forty years.

Benjamin attended Phillips Exeter Academy and Harvard. During his college days, he thought of entering into the mercantile business. Upon graduation in

1855 at the age of nineteen, however, he did not take up work but made many excursions in order to cure him of "a troublesome tendency of blood to the head."[40] Half a year later, considering his health satisfactory, he taught temporarily at Deerfield Academy in Massachusetts. For the following few years he was engaged in various assignments and he accompanied J. Peter Lesley, his uncle by marriage and an eminent geologist, on topographical geological surveys in Pennsylvania; he travelled extensively to collect statistics on iron-works for Lesley; and he also joined the Iowa State Geological Survey as assistant geologist. Lyman found the profession of a geologist appealing to his studious nature. "If this business would give me better opportunities of studying then trade would," he wrote his uncle, "I think I should prefer it."[41] In the fall of 1859, he thus left for Europe to obtain a first-rate geological education. He studied at Ecole Imperiale des Mines in Paris for two years, and then at the Royal Academy of Mines in Freiburg for one year.

During his stay in Paris, the Civil War broke out at home. Lyman, an abolitionist, was disappointed in the U.S. government, which showed "no disposition . . . to improve the opportunity of abolishing slavery." He was also opposed to "the attempt to conciliate any part of any state by avoiding emancipation." After his return home in September 1862, Lyman remained critical of the government; he was, for example, "quite disgusted" to learn that Lincoln, addressing to the deputation of blacks, called attention to the inherent inequality between whites and blacks, and felt "disinclined to much sacrifice for a government with such views."[42] He therefore took up civil employment such as doing survey of coal lands in Cape Breton for a Canadian client, and after the war, he kept on doing surveys, including a survey of the petroleum fields in the Punjab, India, for the British government.

While Lyman headed home from India, another opportunity to go to Asia was waiting for him. When Joseph Henry, searching for Capron's assistants, asked Lesley to recommend a young geologist and topographer "well-skilled in the practical operation of his profession, as well as fully informed in its theoretical principles, of strict integrity, good judgment, industrious habits, gentlemanly deportment, Lesley immediately recommended Lyman, writing Henry that "I know but one person who will meet your numerous requirements." Lyman, however, turned down the offer because he thought an annual salary of $3,000 to $4,000 "decidedly insufficient."[43]

One year later, Lyman was again offered the same position due to the dismissal of one of Capron's original assistants. This time he accepted it, although he still considered the increased salary, $7,000 a year, "rather lower than it should be." While he felt "pretty well content to stay in America," his "great interest in exploring so new a country" as Japan and his hope that he might "accomplish something of use to science" enticed him to the mission to Japan.[44]Lyman was at the time a thirty-six-year-old bachelor and vegetarian.

Lyman was the very kind of person whom Henry hoped to get for the Japanese government; an expert with a highly creditable academic background and rich practical experience. Lesley assured Henry that Lyman was not only capable but exceptionally industrious:

> His maps show genius. His *exactness* is his chief charm for me. His integrity is unshakable, and penetrates all his science. I consider him the best field worker we have in America, but he is *slow*. On the other hand he does not know what fatigue means. He works from sunrise to sunset. His enthusiasm is of that sturdy & unwavering kind that never is thrown over by any excitement.[45]

Besides, Lesley added that Lyman's "complete sympathy with the poor, & cordial benevolence to the suffering" would exert an exemplary influence upon the Japanese.[46]

Nightmarish Experience

Arriving in Tokyo in January 1873, Lyman was "very well pleased not only with [his] cordial reception . . . but with the general prospect." He was favorably impressed by Kuroda, "a very intelligent looking man." Moreover, he found his Japanese assistants—most were the students of the *Kaitakushi* Temporary School and a few *Kaitakushi* officials—"so bright, so anxious to learn, so quick at understanding outlandish things, so good humored, so polite." During the survey of mineral resources in Hokkaido, they continued to satisfy their teacher, bearing many hardships cheerfully."[47] While diligently and energetically performing his duties, Lyman, with his studious nature and interest in an alien culture, spent a great deal of time studying the Japanese language. In retrospect Lyman's first year in Japan was like a lull before a storm.

While Lyman accepted the Japanese mission primarily with his own interests in mind, he soon came to view Japan as "the Sleeping Beauty, that the young Prince (America) came to awaken to fresh life and renewed loveliness."[48] This meant that Lyman could not overlook what struck him as deficiencies of what ought to be a princess. In April 1874, he started by urging Kuroda to abolish the "oppressive" regulation of the *Kaitakushi* Temporary School, which required its students to serve the *Kaitakushi* for a certain number of years after graduation in return for their free education and an allowance for living expenses. To Lyman, it appeared that the *Kaitakushi* students "had virtually been sold into what might prove in some cases an irksome slavery however attractive the condition might be." Since "there is no better sign of enlightenment in a government than a jealous regard for the personal liberty of the individual," Lyman told Kuroda, "the known existence of it in Japan would lead quicker than anything else to the abolition of the exterritorial rights of foreigners."[49]

Lyman soon drafted another letter to an unnamed *Sangi* [Councilor of State], which revealed his extremely critical stance toward the *Kaitakushi*. First of all, seeing Kuroda as responsible for the wasteful expenditure of money appropriated to the *Kaitakushi*, Lyman expressed his belief that Kuroda "has either connived at robbery of the government or that he has through intellectual incapacity been unable to prevent it." In short, Lyman declared, "he is either a knave or a fool; and on either account is wholly unfit to act as the head of a department." Lyman then attacked again the oppressive regulation of the *Kaitakushi* Temporary School. This time Lyman indicated that his objection to the regulation had much to do with his own interests too, for he brought up a proposal of marriage he had made to a girl student of the *Kaitakushi* School; Lyman had apparently found out that a school regulation obliged the girl student to marry a graduate of the school and work together with him for the development of Hokkaido. Lyman charged that Kuroda, and both the principal and the superintendent of the school interfered with his proposal. The superintendent had also annoyed Dutch women teachers at the girls' school. Lyman then concluded his lengthy letter both with a demand that Kuroda, the principal, and the superintendent be all dismissed from the *Kaitakushi* and with a threat that the whole matter "would disgrace the empire if published to the world."[50]

Lyman did not, however, send the letter. He instead demanded Kuroda to dismiss the Superintendent on a charge of "gross rudeness" to a Dutch teacher, interference with Lyman's proposal of marriage, and "so bad a character" in general as to make him unfit for his position. The relationship between Lyman, who repeated his accusation, and Kuroda, who supported the Superintendent, deteriorated to such a degree that Lyman thought of resigning.[51]

The subsequent conflicts between Lyman and the *Kaitakushi* were mostly concerned with the issue of Lyman's authority over his assistants. In the summer of 1874, during a survey in Hokkaido, Lyman ordered a *Kaitakushi* official, who served as his interpreter, to go to the party of his American assistant. But the interpreter protested on the ground that, as an officer of the *Kaitakushi*, he had to adhere to the order of the department which had assigned him to Lyman, and the interpreter got the support of the *Kaitakushi* authorities. Since Lyman, regarding the interpreter as an assistant, believed that "there is no court in the civilized world that would not justify me in saying that . . . in my work I was to have undisputed control of my assistants," he demanded to the *Kaitakushi* that they should either give him "undisputed control" of his assistants or accept his resignation. When Kuroda called attention to Lyman's contract which specified his obligation to obey all orders issued to him by the authorities of the *Kaitakushi*, and pointed out that Lyman ought to have consulted the Department about the change beforehand, Lyman was even more determined to be released from his engagement, "so ruinous to my reputation"; he also demanded compensation until the end of the full term of three years as well as heavy damages. Capron, who was determined to keep

Lyman, managed to get Kuroda to recognize Lyman's "full and exclusive right to direct the work of all the assistants assigned to him," and the conflict, which had lasted for three months, seemed to have been solved.[52]

However, this was not the end of frictions between Lyman and the *Kaitakushi*. Lyman in fact continued to fight with the *Kaitakushi* authorities over one issue after another. In December 1874, Lyman learned that one *Kaitakushi* official who had accompanied him during the survey was assigned to the *Kaitakushi* office instead of continuing to work with him. Harboring "not only a complete distrust of the *Kaitakushi* but a thorough disgust with its management," Lyman felt he had no choice but to demand a complete release from the department which was "so blind to its own promises."[53] The decision of the *Kaitakushi* to move a large part of its office to Sapporo became another source of friction. Since the decision meant that Lyman's party would remain in Hokkaido all year around, Lyman sent a strong note of protest to the *Kaitakushi*, arguing: "I could have demonstrated to the satisfaction of the dullest comprehension that the winter work of the survey could be done at Yedo [Tokyo] far more economically, satisfactorily and conveniently than at Sapporo."[54]

Capron, deeply concerned over the growing friction between Lyman and the *Kaitakushi* authorities, advised Lyman to go on with his work rather than demand a release, reminding him of the great task he was engaged in and the strong possibility that the British would come in and take credit for what Lyman had done if he left in the middle of his work. Lyman answered, "I don't care so much for the English or for myself, and have no fear that any one will steal the credit of what has been done." But he did care to "leave [his] assistants sufficiently grounded in our method to be able to make geological surveys by themselves and fix the method permanently in Japan and indeed all eastern Asia." Lyman expressed his profound feeling of disappointment and sorrow to Capron: "That has been my dream, but this cursed *Kaitakushi* changes all to a nightmare."[55]

While Lyman fought with the *Kaitakushi* mostly over his authority to control his assistants, he continued to be sharply critical of the whole operation of the department. Lyman, who believed in individual initiative and free competition as primary forces in developing Hokkaido, considered the major role of the *Kaitakushi* should be to expand opportunity for all by promoting internal improvements. But, in his view, the *Kaitakushi* not only fell far short of performing such a role but obviously hindered the progress of Hokkaido. After his three-year service for the *Kaitakushi*, he was convinced that Hokkaido would be "better off" without the department. Lyman argued that a half decade under the jurisdiction of the *Kaitakushi*, Hokkaido was left "without schools, without roads, with living made dear by practical monopolies that the *Kaitakushi* has created by loans to merchants . . . and with the best land kept out of the hands of immigrants." "Give Yesso [Yezo, on Hokkaido] the same government advantages as the rest of the empire has already," urged Lyman, so that the settlers in Hokkaido could have for themselves "at least something better than this petty disposition of an almost independent little viceroyalty."[56]

Lyman was subsequently employed by the Interior Department and Public Works Department for two and a half years. While he found his relationship with officials much better than in the *Kaitakushi*, he still had occasional frictions over such issues as the salaries of his assistants, the digging of trial wells by the government, and the rising influence of a young German geologist, Edmund Naumann. Lyman thus came to the conclusion that the Japanese were, after all, "so ignorant of modern methods of business, and so different from Anglo Saxons in temperament." To a friend who had expressed an interest in seeking employment in Japan, Lyman, a long-time bachelor, gave a warning, by describing his experience vividly: "Serving them is like being subjected to a lot of girls—ignorant, arbitrary, fickle, vain, willful, faithless." Also, observing these Japanese officials, he could not but wonder, "How little brain it takes to run a government of thirty odd millions."[57]

The "Unreflective" and "Warlike" People

After his return home in May 1881, Lyman, who had studied the Japanese language and closely observed Japanese life during an eight-year stay in Japan, had chances to speak and write about the country. Among his writings, the fifty-page article on "The Character of the Japanese" in the *Journal of Speculative Philosophy* (1885) most clearly presents his view of Japan.

In terms of intelligence, Lyman explains, the most outstanding characteristic of the Japanese is that, while they are "remarkably quick" in "external perception," thus excelling as imitators, they are in fact "unreflective and not deep in reasoning and originality." Lyman believed that "they have for ages adopted the civilization of others without any important additions of their own," that their discoveries and inventions were "none but those of a kind that needs little deep thinking," and that "we may confidently expect that a profound discovery will rarely at any future time be made by the present race of Japanese."[58]

Japanese art, Lyman argues, also shows "the same love of outward observation, and the same lack of the profounds" as is characteristic of Japanese intelligence. In literature, "original traces of profound wit or wisdom are looked for almost in vain." The Japanese certainly excel in decorative art, in the painting of flowers and birds, and especially in landscape gardening, but the "high art" is hard to be found. Japanese temples contain many wooden "grotesque rather than majestic" images of gods and bronze images of Buddha which, "however interesting as specimens of foundry-work and ingenuity, have no great merit as sculptures." Japanese pictures show "an endless variety of admirably skillful trifles . . . but never a combination into anything grand or thoroughly and consistently beautiful." Japanese lacquer-ware, bronzes, pottery, and cloisonne also exhibit "the same tendency to lightness, variety, pleasing colors, and graceful decoration; but the more difficult merit of fine form is often lacking." Worse still, Japanese art lacks not only "the profound that is essential to high art," but also originality, mostly consisting of imitations of the Chinese art.[59]

Finally, discussing Japanese behavior, Lyman explains that their ruling principle is "regard for others rather than self-respect." He admits that this "genuine readiness to comply with the will of others" made the Japanese more amiable and agreeable than those Anglo-Saxons driven by "conscientiousness and self-respect." This regard for others also enables Japanese to "get along together without disagreeable friction." Lyman highly praises the Japanese in this regard: "If the word civilization as distinguished from enlightenment means natural or trained adaptation and skill for human association, then the Japanese are among the most highly civilized races in the world. However, Lyman warns, the very respect for others, coupled with their hierarchical values, carries with it a dangerous tendency to make Japanese "ready to be subjects of despotic power." In fact, "their Government has ever been 'an absolute despotism tempered by assassination.'" Furthermore, remarkable Japanese politeness has its limit because they are "polite out of regard for others' opinion and not out of self-respect." Therefore, they can be "extremely rude and overbearing" or "even treacherous" toward those for whom they do not have any particular respect or those who they know can never do them any harm.[60]

The Japanese attitude in adversity which favorably impressed Capron was, in Lyman's view, merely a symptom to show that their "feelings are not so deep;" their "lack of deep feeling" enables them to be "cheerful and gay" even "in the most serious predicaments" and even to find it "comparatively easy to part with life itself." Lyman warns that, while their cheerfulness and gaiety of manner are extremely pleasant, such disposition often goes hand in hand with the lack of prudence or neglect of duty.[61]

Lyman's critical view of Japan was mostly due to his bitter experience in Japan, as well as to a large gap he found between his experience and the progressive image of Japan that his contemporary Americans hailed. When the Sino-Japanese war broke out in 1894, Lyman was especially disturbed by the accounts given by American newspapers "blindly in favor of the Japanese side of the war, owing to the absurd prejudice against the Chinese." Lyman sought to warn Americans of Japan's "warlike bent." Speaking in Philadelphia, Lyman predicted the results of Japan's victory ominous both for Japan and for other countries. In order to maintain its "aggressive military character . . . at all hazards, regardless of cost," Japan would have to consume the indemnity "extorted" from China and, in addition, greatly increase taxes at home. Other countries would then have to be on guard against Japan as a potential enemy. "For, though Japan be so much smaller, poorer and weaker than we are, yet with her constant cultivation of the fighting disposition, she might for a time gain as weighty advantages over us as she did . . . over her great, peaceable, industrious, commercial unmilitary, unprepared neighbor."[62]

Cheers for America

Lyman's frustrating experience in Japan seems to have made him an imperialist who supported aggressive American foreign policy at the turn of the century. He came to have firm belief in the superiority of the Anglo-Saxons who had "almost a monopoly of the capacity for successful government" and "could undoubtedly keep the rest of the world in order." He supported not only the U.S. war with Spain but also the annexation of the Philippines, which he regarded as a chance for the United States to "do for [the Philippines] what great Britain has been doing for Egypt, only still better."[63] Unlike Japanese possession of Formosa, where there were many Chinese, "a more vigorous race than [Japanese] and in some respects . . . more advanced," and they as well as numerous aborigines were "not altogether friendly to the Japanese," in the Philippines there were comparatively few Spaniards, and the "imperfectly enlightened" natives were "very friendly to us." The United States could depend upon their "heartiest cooperation" because they should know "great privileges and advantages could never be expected from any other government." but the United States. Lyman even anticipated that if the United States would succeed in the Philippines, "perhaps other countries in that quarter will likewise be desirous of admission."[64]

In 1906-1907, when he visited the Philippines, at the age of seventy-two, to make a survey of coal lands for a New York company, he confirmed correctness of his prediction. He found the city of Manila "improved in the scanty eight years of American occupation to an altogether astonishing degree" and the people showing "in their faces a striking degree of contentment and confidence in Americans, as well as respect for them." Lyman was convinced that "it is a happy thing for the Filipinos that we possess their country, happy for us, and happy for the world."[65]

In spite of his belief in the United States, Lyman's financial situation had been difficult for many years; apart from occasional surveys, he was mostly out of remunerative jobs. What enriched Lyman's life in his declining days was his ties with Japan. While he remained critical of Japanese expansion, he came to cherish the memories of his Japanese experience, which he found were "mellowed as they naturally are with time." In 1902 he was informed that he had been elected an honorary member of the Mining Institute of Japan. Lyman was pleased to see that a large coal company formed in Hokkaido "very kindly makes much of [him] as the father of their industry."[66] Furthermore, his former assistants did not fail to keep in touch with him and sought to cheer him up by sending him letters, money, and Japanese food. Lyman died on January 21, 1920, at the age of eighty-four.

The Case of Edwin Dun

An Unpromising Start

Edwin Dun was born in Springfield, Ohio, on July 19, 1848.[67] His grandfather, an immigrant from Scotland, obtained 15,000 acres of land in Springfield, Ohio, and in the so-called "Dun Plains," Edwin's father and uncles engaged themselves in stock farming, while one of his aunts married Allen G. Thurman, who later became a prominent Senator from Ohio. After quitting Miami College in Oxford, Ohio, at the age of eighteen, Edwin began to learn stock farming on his father's and his uncle's farms. In 1871 he started to engage himself in the livestock business in partnership with his cousin, a son of Senator Thurman's.

The environment in which young Dun grew up seems to have been more characterized by a Southern tradition of chivalry and paternalism than of a Yankee ethic of piety, thrift, and industry. Thus, the life style of Dun Plains could be described as "lordly." In his memory, Dun Plains, during the summer and autumn months, was "the scene of almost daily or nightly festivities," consisting of dinners, dancing and riding parties while the cold winter nights were also "merry with the jingle of sleigh bells and jolly gatherings." Moreover, his father and uncles were concerned with big plans, such as investment, which they amply made, but left routine operations to tenant farmers. They were also kind to those in need. In spite of their hospitality, however, the Dun family was conscious of class distinctions. Dun recalled that "We looked on life and lived it in a different way from the families of neighboring land owners and, although the hospitality of our homes was free to all, and bed and board gladly given to the stranger, our intercourse with them was limited to what kindly feeling and courtesy demanded."[68]

However, this life of self-made aristocracy did not last long. The waste resulting from "lordly" farm management was great and Dun saw thrifty small farmers become steadily more wealthy. Then, depression hit the Duns hard. In May 1873, when Albert B. Capron, Horace Capron's son, came to Dun Plains to purchase cattle for the *Kaitakushi*, the Duns were struggling against hard times. Capron mentioned that the *Kaitakushi* was looking for a man well-experienced both in cattle breeding and practical farming who would be willing accompany the cattle to Japan; the salary was to be $1,500 a year. Capron's proposition interested Dun as it seemeed to him that the depression would continue for another year or more, and that "he would lose nothing by leaving home" at that time. Besides, Dun expected the job would offer "an excellent opportunity to see Japan." So he immediately signed a contract for one year, and left home with the good wishes of his relatives who looked upon his expedition "rather as a joke than a business entreprise."[69]

Commitment to Hokkaido

Dun soon set to taking care of cattle at a *Kaitakushi* farm in Tokyo. He also gave Japanese students instruction in farming as well as in the care of livestock. He found himself "on the best terms" with the students and his relations with the *Kaitakushi* officials "excellent." He especially appreciated the kindness of the two officials who accompanied him, sensing their "evident desire to lessen the loneliness of the stranger so far from his home."[70] When his one-year contract came to an end, Dun decided to stay longer. "I have learned to take a personal interest," Dun explained to Capron, "in the success of the great undertaking which is the object of the department to carry through."[71]

While Dun, who did not think the *Kaitakushi* farm in Tokyo useful for the development of Hokkaido, was eager to go to Hokkaido, only in the spring of 1876 was he allowed to settle in Sapporo.[72] After that he spent six and a half years in Hokkaido, experiencing not only the cool, pleasant summers but also the bitterly cold winters. Dun's life in Hokkaido, with a salary much lower than those of Capron and Lyman ($3,000 at the highest), was a plain one, but was made lively by the presence of his Japanese wife, the daughter of an ex-samurai official at the Nanae *Kaitakushi* Farm, and their little daughter. Dun felt that through his wife he became acquainted with "the most beautiful part of Japan." Dun apparently became a beneficiary of the Japanese tradition that, in his words, "the exclusive mission of woman is to minister to [her husband's] comfort and pleasure, to take proper care of his house and to bear his children," while he never forgets that "he is one of the lords of creation."[73]

Dun devoted himself to the raising of cattle, sheep, and horses, and to the development of dairy industry. For example, when a messenger boy came from the Niikappu Farm, 110 miles away from Sapporo, with news that the best thoroughbred stallion was very ill, Dun set out on a journey in the rainy night. It took him twenty hours, changing horses several times. He later recalled his feelings at that time: "I realized the utter folly of the job I had undertaken but a sense of duty and pride sent me on."[74] While Dun was dedicated to the development of stock-farming in Hokkaido, he at the same time knew that the process would take time in bearing fruit. He wrote Kuroda that he believed that, if his instructions for breeding were followed, the breed of horses of Hokkaido would become as good as that of any country in the world, but he thought it would take 20 years to do it.[75] Dun realized that his efforts would serve only as a stepping-stone for future success.

After the *Kaitakushi* was abolished in December 1881, Dun stayed for another year in Hokkaido with the Department of Agriculture and Commerce. Looking back at his long connection with the *Kaitakushi*, Dun thought: "The ten best years of my life were spent in its service. Little to my personal advantage but I treasure the thought than they were not altogether uselessly wasted in the service of the people of Japan whom I had learned to esteem so highly."[76]

Criticism of American Advisers

Dun's appraisal of the *Kaitakushi* was moderate: "While it accomplished enough to save it from being classed as a failure it left undone so much that might have been accomplished that it cannot be classed as a success."[77] As for the introduction of American methods and techniques of agriculture in Hokkaido, Dun heartily supported it. Through the efforts of the *Kaitakushi*, he was pleased to note, "the superiority of working animals and agricultural machinery over hand labor is becoming generally felt throughout the farming settlements." He believed, "It will induce a more thrifty and comfortable mode of life than is to be found in Hokkaido."[78] At the same time, however, Dun believed that the introduction of American methods and techniques should have been carried out without any great fanfare, but on step-by-step, practical basis and with differences of the climate, soil, and other conditions always in mind.

In this regard, Dun specifically criticized American advisers. For example, he pointed to the case of Edward M. Shelton, a graduate of Michigan Agricultural College, who, although "learned in agricultural chemistry, in botany, in plant life, in all that books can teach in higher agriculture . . . had no practical knowledge whatever."[79] In contrast to Shelton, Dun found his early training at home "invaluable" in offering practical information to the students and officials of the *Kaitakushi*, particularly because they were, as he realized, mostly former *samurai*, or their sons, who were completely new to agriculture and so Dun had to teach them everything from the beginning. Dun was proud that he could "answer [questions] correctly, and almost without thought, in a thousand details, almost any one on which would have stumped the college-bred, book-learned expert." In fact, Dun, showered with all sorts of questions, felt that an agricultural adviser needed to have not only the special knowledge in his field but also to be a "jack of all trades."[80]

Dun also criticized Capron's pet project, the *Kaitakushi* farm in Tokyo. The greater part of the expensive agricultural machinery introduced by Capron struck Dun as being "as useful in Japan as a fifth wheel would be to a wagon." Moreover, Dun thought that the farm in Tokyo was, "owing to difference in climate, soil and almost all other conditions . . . practically of no value in connection with the colonization and development of the natural resources of Hokkaido." Dun knew from his experience of living in Hokkaido that it was far from the promising land Capron had described in his reports. Dun painfully learned this when he experimented in sheep raising, hoping to lay the basis for a wool industry in Hokkaido. While he successfully demonstrated that sheep would thrive in Hokkaido, he found at the same time that, since the ground in Hokkaido was covered with deep snow for half a year, the extra cost of keeping sheep was considerable, resulting in the high cost of wool produced in Hokkaido—three or four times greater than the same article imported from Australia. Besides, 90 percent of the island was unfit for cultivation because of its mountainous character and the extensive sterile soil covered with volcanic ash. Dun had to conclude that the idea of extensive sheep raising in Hokkaido should be abandoned, for arable lands were more urgently needed for the production of food for people than for the growing of grass for sheep.[81]

In the same vein, Dun doubted the value of Sapporo Agricultural College founded on the model of Massachusetts Agricultural College and staffed by Americans. While he admitted that the college had become "a most admirable institution of learning," he could not but notice the difference between the United States and Japan; an agricultural college which offered little practical instruction was important in the United States since most students, coming from farm families, had practical farm experience beforehand; but in Japan, where the sons of farmers rarely went to college, Dun pointed out, a similar institution was "valueless." Moreover, it seemed to Dun that methods of agriculture were so different that the introduction of American methods into Hokkaido "could only be accomplished by practical work in the field." The school Dun considered most helpful for the development of Hokkaido was a small school of technology where classroom work was limited to the winter when it was too cold for work in the field. But Dun knew too well that Japanese were unduly deferential to institutions of higher education. He observed a college was built at a great cost and President Clark was "canonized as a benefactor of Japan generally and Hokkaido in particular," overshadowing Dun and all other American advisers.[82]

A Paean for Traditional Japan

In February 1883 Dun left Japan for Dun Plains, but, while he enjoyed his reunion with the old folks, he soon began to feel that there was no place for him there. "I was not the same man that had left them ten years before. . . . While enjoying their affection I felt that, of my own making, I was a stranger among them."[83] Then, fortunately for Dun, his uncle Thurman managed to get President Arthur to appoint Dun to the newly-created position of Second Secretary of the U.S. Legation in Japan.[84] In the spring of 1884 Dun arrived in Japan to take the post, and was gradually promoted until he was appointed as U.S. Minister to Japan by President Cleveland in 1893. But four years later, under the new Administration, his diplomatic career suddenly came to an end. After having worked as a manager of the International Standard Oil Company established in Niigata and subsequently for a salvage company in Nagasaki, Dun spent his last years in Tokyo.

Around 1919, Dun wrote his memoirs titled *Reminiscences of Nearly a Half Century in Japan*, which presents his views on the value of cultural exchange as well as on his adopted and native countries. While Dun favored the general introduction of Western techniques, he had a strong doubt about the value of transplanting the political, economic, or social institutions of the United States. He thought that, because a culture was by nature unique, the kind of institutions effective in one culture would not necessarily operate well in another. Japanese progress, Dun believed, had to be in tune with Japanese tradition. He wrote that "The Japanese of today was a civilized being three thousand years ago and the teachings, traditions and gradual development of thirty centuries has made him what he is now. He is not a European, American or Chinaman. . . . He must advance as a Japanese." And he was convinced that the Japanese would "in time develop along Japanese lines into a great people and nation."[85]

The predominant features of Japanese society perceived by Dun were its hierarchy, paternalism, and the absence of individualism. Although individual liberty and equality were fully recognized under the law in Japan, "in practice and spirit the feudal system of class distinction" was still fully maintained. The Emperor was endowed with supreme authority, and representatives in the Diet exercised certain functions of government delegated to them by the Emperor. Most of the Japanese did not have voting rights, but they seemed to Dun to be content with their government not only because they had been taught through centuries of discipline to obey the commands of their superiors, but also because the government had always been "benevolent and paternal."[86]

Paternalism seemed to Dun to permeate Japanese society as a whole. He was particularly impressed by the relations between employer and employee in Japan "entirely different from those prevailing in the West." The firm would provide the employee with a sense of security for life, for he would be supported by insurance in case of accident or disease, and by a pension after his retirement; the employee in turn, with the sense of being "part of the firm," would devote himself to it. Dun viewed "a feeling of mutual respect and esteem" as characteristic of Japanese firms.[87]

Individualism was not congenial to such a society, and the Japanese, instead of asserting themselves, behaved with "respect for the feelings of others." Dun noticed it, for example, in their readiness to "go more than half way to secure the good will of foreigners." In adversity it took the form of stoicism. Dun was struck by the way the frequent visitations of pestilence, famine, and fires were "accepted stoically by the people as beyond the power of man to control." Dun observed that the Japanese in fact expressed emotion in front of terror but they soon gave in to resignation, and he attributed this to "centuries of training during which they have been taught to suppress their emotions." Dun however did not think that the Japanese lacked sensibilities. Referring to the *samurai* and the soldier who were ready to take their lives without showing regret or repugnance for their duty or honor, Dun could not but wonder: "If one could read the hearts of these men what a story of suffering might be revealed."[88]

Because he appreciated the Japanese tradition, he was extremely critical of the Japanese "excessive craze for everything foreign" which reached its zenith around 1886. When that craze began to decline, Dun felt relieved to see that "the beauties of their own old customs, ceremonies and dress together with the fitness of old social restraints for the government of Japanese social life began to reassert itself [sic]." Dun however was grieved to discover that Japanese women forever abandoned "the beautiful old court costume" for "the ugly, ever-changing fashions of dress of Europe." Dun regarded the change as "an unforgivable crime against good taste," committed by "young fools who had been sent abroad to study western ways and manners and in the glamour and glitter of what they saw became ashamed of their own country and of whatever it differed from what was considered the proper thing in the West."[89] Probably Dun could not imagine that the Japanese women in western dress would continue to be self-sacrificing and devote themselves to the men.

Dun was also skeptical about other changes which he feared would disrupt the "harmonious working" of Japanese society. He regretted the impact of urbanization, seeing that the Japanese, particularly those living in cities, had "to some degree, broken loose from old restrictions and customs," and that some even "lost all sense of subservience to family restraint." Neither could he support the tendency to organize labor unions which in his view were detrimental to the paternalistic relations between workers and employers. Most of all, Dun could not endorse the demand for universal suffrage, regarding it as "the work of politicians, mischievous agitators and misguided students." He thought that even in the United States universal suffrage did not work well: "In what respect has it improved the ten millions of negroes, two millions of whom have the right to vote? and what benefit have real Americans derived from the privilege granted to ignorant foreigners who value their right to vote only as something they can sell to the highest bidder?" He feared that in Japan universal suffrage would simply "add several millions of ignorant voters to the large number of slightly less ignorant persons" who already had voting rights. Dun argued that "To advocate the abolition of the old feudal life that has been the very spirit of the people of Japan for twenty-five-hundred years for an ideal democracy untried and misunderstood is, to my mind, the height of folly."[90] The fact that universal suffrage for men became a reality within a decade after Dun wrote this might demonstrate that Dun was more attached to the old, passing Japan than were many Japanese.

For all his love of Japan, when Dun said "my country," it was always the United States. Dun wrote on the emotions of a man who left his country: "His love of country may remain unimpaired, his glory in its progress as keen as when he left it. In fact, I believe the exile's interest in his country's wellbeing is, as a rule, keener than that of the resident who accepts whatever comes as a matter of course."[91] Dun's view of America, however, was critical, particularly with regard to the lack of "human brotherhood." He perceived American society as too individualistic and competitive with little regard for those who were too weak to join the race. He wrote that "American democracy has certainly taught individualism, it has inculcated the belief in 'every man for himself and the devil take the hindmost,' but as for the human brotherhood as practiced in Japan for the past two thousand years, the idea is preached in our churches but its practice is left to charitable institutions maintained for the purpose." Dun specifically pointed to the example of a public servant who from age and illness was unable to continue work. "He is ruthlessly cast out as a worn-out shoe is discarded without care or thought for the suffering of one who has spent his life in the service of his country."[92]

Dun was also greatly distressed by American views of Japan. He was chagrined when one Senator mentioned that the Japanese "only fifty years ago were emerging from barbarism." His indignation seems to have carried Dun to emotional polemics:

> That such a colossal fool should live and even be a senator of the United States did not strike me a very extraordinary but that such a foul, brutal insult to a friendly people, whose civilization was far advanced when we had none at all, was not rebuked, was permitted to pass unchallenged by a body of men selected for their ability and enlightenment to form the Senate of the United States caused a feeling of shame for my country that I can never forget.[93]

Dun moreover noticed the gap between what Americans professed as their principles and what they really practiced. One case Dun referred to was the abolition of extraterritoriality in Japan. Dun pointed out that although the United States had practically conceded that the time for its abolition had come, she did not move for more than ten years until Britain and other European powers were prepared to do likewise. While he admitted that the United States had a better record than the rest of the world in this matter, he was disturbed by the idealistic pretense of Americans. He remarked that "But none of the other great powers have, so far as I can remember, pretended to be guided by anything but self interest in their dealings with this country."[94]

Dun called attention to another case—the confiscation of the property of Japanese immigrants. He was mortified to see that Americans "allowed a lot of California gas bags to make endless trouble." Dun hoped that the United States government would rectify such treatment of the helpless immigrants, but was afraid that this might not be the case. If we didn't, he warned following WWI, "Then let this blatant sentimental cant of love of justice, desire to benefit humanity, love of freedom and equality among men, of which we have heard so much during the past few years, cease as it only proclaims us a nation of hypocrites and liars."[95]

Dun agreed with those Japanese who argued that Japan should build up her defenses against the threat from Russia, but he remained optimistic about Japanese-American relations. "An armed conflict between the two countries," Dun thought, "if not impossible, is extremely improbable."[96] Dun died in Tokyo in May 15, 1931, a decade before the improbable became a reality.

*   *   *

Conclusion

For most Americans at home, Japan was veiled in a mist, and, at the news of Capron's mission, they suddenly embraced an almost romantic expectation of obtaining not only the friendship of the Japanese but also an enormous market for American manufactured goods. They regarded Japan as a potentially vast market because they assumed that Japanese would readily absorb or, in the expression of the press, "imitate" the Western civilization as instructed by Capron's party. Americans who chose to go to Japan not only to help Japan but also to help themselves soon found that such American expectations were not grounded in reality. Capron, Lyman, and Dun all invariably recognized the overwhelming alienness of Japanese culture and society. They also experienced the many difficulties involved in working with an alien people. It is noteworthy, however, that their responses were so varied, reflecting in part their different backgrounds and temperament.

The cases of Capron and Lyman more or less represent the predominant American response to an alien culture. While working with the Japanese, they took their own superiority for granted. Their observation of Japanese society sometimes hit the target, and some of their grievances were quite relevant. But at the same time their conviction of the blessings and universality of Western civilization inclined them to take the differences they found in Japan as a mark of inferiority. Moreover, they were especially frustrated to see their freedom of action seriously hampered by the Japanese whose backwardness was so obvious to their eyes. While Capron at times wondered whether material benefits would guarantee happiness, he identified himself so fully with the remarkable agricultural and industrial development of his country in the nineteenth century that in the end he laid aside this question. Lyman, who saw his mission not only as instructing in Western techniques, but also in reforming Japanese values went through the most frustrating and turbulent experience of the three. In spite of his diligent study of the Japanese language, his attitudes, somewhat like those of a good-willed but self-righteous reformer, kept him from understanding Japanese sensibilities.

Dun's attitudes toward the Japanese were, on the other hand, remarkably free of Western prejudices, and instead were characterized by tolerance, patience, and sympathy. He also appreciated Japanese tradition not only in its aesthetic expression, as did many other foreigners, but in its effectiveness in facilitating Japanese development. However, despite the validity of his argument that the progress of Japan should be based upon its history and tradition, it is also true that his preoccupation with the uniqueness of Japanese culture tended to prevent him from perceiving other aspects of Japanese culture which contained receptivity to change, as well as universal values shared by other cultures.

The experiences of the Americans employed by the *Kaitakushi* suggest that we tend to make ethnocentric and normative judgements about them. We should, therefore, try to understand, with sympathy and patience, why an alien people think and feel the way they do, at the same time keeping in mind the fact that every culture has both unique and universal aspects as well as being both enduring and dynamic.

Notes

[1]Capron, memorandum, April 17, 1871, copy, Horace Capron Papers, The Library of Congress (hereafter cited as CLC).

[2]Robeson letter to Capron, July 12, 1871, CLC; Sherman letter to Capron, July 7, 1871, CLC; Henry letter to J. Peter Lesley, May 8, 1871, J. Peter Lesley Collection, American Philosophical Society, Philadelphia, Pennsylvania.

[3]Grant letter to Capron, June 23, 1871, CLC.

[4]The following comments of the press are gathered from *Boston Cultivator*, July 8, 1871; *Chicago Journal*, July 10, 1871; *Massachusetts Ploughman*, July 8, 1871; *New York Farmer*, July 8, 1871; *The New York Times*, July 29, 1871; *Pittsburgh Gazette*, July 8, 1871; and *Prairie Farmer*, July 1871, quoted in Capron's unpublished memoirs, "The Memoirs of Horace Capron," 2 volumes, National Agricultural Library, U.S. Department of Agriculture, Beltsville, Md., microform, 1: p. 170. The press accounts were overlapping, indicating they the same stories were sent to several papers.

[5]Capron's biographical sources are the first volume of "The Memoirs of Horace Capron:"; Merritt Starr, "General Horace Capron, 1804-1885," *Journal of the Illinois State Historical Society*, 18 (1925), pp. 259-349; and various newspaper clippings contained in CLC.

[6]Earle D. Ross, "The United States Department of Agriculture during the Commissionership: A Study in Politics, Administration, and Technology, 1862-1889," *Agricultural History* 20 (1946), p. 134.

[7]*Ibid.*

[8]*Ibid.*, pp. 134, 137-40; Starr, pp. 281-83.

[9]The Memoirs of Horace Capron," 2, p. 9. (The second volume of Capron's memoirs is a journal kept by Capron from the time he met Kuroda in Washington. The date, however, is sometimes unreliable.) Horace Capron Papers at Yale University Library, New Haven, Connecticut. (hereafter cited as CYU), contains records to show that one of Capron's sons constantly informed Capron of the expenses for his younger brother in an asylum for the blind and that Capron regularly sent him money from Japan.

[10]"The Memoirs of Horace Capron," 2, pp. 5, 9.

[11]Capron letter to his son (Albert B. Capron), September 7, October 29, 1871, CLC.

[12]"The Memoirs of Horace Capron," 2, pp. 38-39.

[13]*Ibid.*, 2, pp. 162, 168.

[14]*Ibid.*, 2, pp. 29-32, 52.

[15]Quoted in Starr, p. 313; "The Memoirs of Horace Capron," 2, pp. 18, 38.

[16]"The Memoirs of Horace Capron," 2, pp. 38-40.

[17]*Ibid.*, 2, pp. 50-51, 56, 93-94.

[18]Capron letter to Colonel Warren, February 25, 1872, copy, CYU.

[19]Capron letter to his son September 7, 1871, CLC.

[20]Capron letter to John B. Russel, February 25, 1872, copy, CYU.

[21]Capron, "The First Annual Report,: *Reports and Official Letters to the Kaitakushi by Horace Capron and His Foreign Assistants* (Tokyo, 1875) (hereafter cited as *ROL*), pp. 38-50.

[22]"The Memoirs of Horace Capron," 2, pp. 118, 212.

[23]*Ibid.*, 2, pp. 188-91.

[24]Capron letter to Kuroda, July 8, 1872, in *ROL*, p. 55; Capron letter to Kuroda, June 15, 1873, copy, CYU.

[25]In the case of Capron, there was actually no formal contract: only his memorandum stating his intention "to take charge and direction of the measures for the development of the resources of Hokkaido" upon certain conditions, including an annual salary of $10,000 and the right to select his foreign assistants, and a short notice from Kuroda and Japanese *charge d'affaires* Mori Arinori which accepted his conditions. Capron, memorandum, April 17, 1871, copy, CLC; Mori and Kuroda letter to Capron, May 3, 1871, CLC.

[26]Capron letter to Kuroda, July 18, 1873, copy, CYU.

[27]"The Memoirs of Horace Capron," 2, p. 209.

[28]*Ibid.*, 2, p. 237.

[29]Capron letter to Lyman, July 23, 1874, Benjamin S. Lyman Collection, American Philosophical Society, Philadelphia, Penn. (hereafter cited as LAPS).

[30]"The Memoirs of Horace Capron," 2, pp. 177-78.

[31]*Ibid.*, 2: 208-209; Capron letter to Kuroda, July 18, 1873, copy, CYU.

[32]Capron letter to Kuroda, June 15, 1873, copy CYU.

[33]Capron letter to Russel, June 25, 1873.

[34]Capron letter to Kuroda, June 15, 1873, copy, CYU; "The Memoirs of Horace Capron," 2, p. 241.

[35]Capron, *Japan: Some Remarks in Connection with the Visit of Horace Capron to Japan in 1871-1875* (Philadelphia, 1876), pp. 17-18.

[36]Capron letter to William E. Griffis, February 3, 1876, William E. Griffis Collection, Rutgers University Library, New Brunswick, N. J.; *Japan*, 14; "The Memoirs of Horace Capron," 2, pp. 303-304; Capron's correspondence in the *Japan Mail*, March 10, 1875.

[37]Capron letter to his son, March 18, 1884, CLC.

[38]Lyman Coleman, *Genealogy of the Lyman family in Great Britain and America* (Albany, 1872), p. 35.

[39]Lyman's memorandum, "Edward Hutchinson Robbins Lyman" (July 11, 1887), pp. 1-2, LAPS.

[40]His experience after graduation from college to 1865 is described in his letter to Edwin Hale Abbot, June 23, 1865, Abbot Family Collection, Yale University Library, New Haven, Connecticut.

[41]Lyman letter to Lesley, October 26, 1858, Benjamin S. Lyman

Collection, Forbes Library, Northampton, Massachusetts. (hereafter cited as LFL).

[42]Lyman letter to Joseph Lyman, March 18, 1862, copy, LFL; Lyman letter to Ang. Langel, August 30, 1862, copy, LFL; Lyman letter to Franklin B. Sanborn, September 19, 1862, copy, LFL.

[43]Henry letter to Lesley, May 8, 1871, J. Peter Lesley Collection, American Philosophical Society; Lesley letter to Henry, May 9, 1871, CLC; Lyman letter to Henry, June 9, 1871, CLC.

[44]Lyman letter to Lesley, May 21, June 2, 1872, LFL.

[45]Lesley letter to Henry, May 9, 1871, CLC.

[46]*Ibid.*

[47]Lyman letter to Father, January 22, 1873, copy, LFL; Lyman letter to Aunt [Susan Lesley?], June 8, 1873, copy, LFL; Lyman, "Preliminary Report on the First Season's Work of the Geological Survey of Yesso" [Hokkaido], in *ROL*, pp. 119-120.

[48]Lyman, "Geological Survey of Hokkaido: Report of a Geological Trip Through and Around Yesso" [Hokkaido], in *ROL*, p. 430.

[49]Lyman letter to Kuroda, April 12, 1874, The Correspondence between Employed Foreigners and the *Kaitakushi*, University of Hokkaido Library, Sapporo, Hokkaido (hereafter cited as CEF).

[50]Lyman letter to *Sangi* [Councilor of State], April 16, 1874, draft, LFL. The slightly modified version Lyman wrote the following day is somewhat more reserved in his use of words: Lyman letter to *Sangi*, April 17, 1874, draft, LFL.

[51]Lyman letter to Kuroda, April 17, 1874, copy, LAPS; Lyman letter to Capron, April 27, 1874, CYU.

[52]Lyman letter to Capron, August 26, 1874, CYU; Kuroda letter to Capron, October 31, 1874, CYU; Lyman letter to Capron, November 4, 1874, CEF; Kuroda letter to Capron, November 15, 1874, CYU.

[53]Lyman letter to Capron, January 16, 1875, CEF.

[54]Lyman letter to Capron, February 28, 1875, CEF.

[55]Capron letter to Lyman, February 29, 1875, Benjamin S. Lyman Collection, Historical Society of Pennsylvania, Philadelphia, Penn.; Lyman letter to Capron, March 6, 1875, CYU.

[56]Lyman letter to Otori [Keisuke], September 27, 1876, copy, LAPS.

[57]Lyman letter to J. Poole, April 14, 1879, copy, LFL; Lyman letter to J. Waterhouse, August 15, 1879, copy, LFL; Lyman letter to Lesley, May 28, 1879, LFL.

[58]Lyman, "The Character of the Japanese," *Journal of Speculative Philosophy*, 19 (1885), pp. 134-35, 137-38.

[59]*Ibid.*, pp. 141-43.

[60]*Ibid.*, pp. 146-47, 154-57, 160-61.

61*Ibid.*, pp. 147-49.

62Lyman letter to McCartee, May 25, 1895, copy, LFL; Lyman, *The Future of Japan in its Relations with China and Russia* (Philadelphia, 1897), pp. 5-8.

63Lyman letter to Gilbertson, September 7, 1897, May 13, 1898, copies, LFL.

64Lyman letter to Gilbertson, July 1, 1898, copy, LFL; Lyman letter to Beukema, August 21, 1898, copy, LFL; Lyman letter to Fanny, August 7, 1898, copy, LFL.

65Lyman, *The Philippines*: (Philadelphia, 1907), pp. 7, 20.

66Lyman letter to Yamauchi, April 26, 1896, copy, LFL; Lyman letter to Wynne, July 27, 1905, copy, LAPS.

67Dun's life discussed here relies, unless otherwise mentioned, on his unpublished memoirs, "Reminiscences of Nearly a Half Century in Japan," Copy, University of Hokkaido Library, Sapporo, Japan (hereafter cited as "Reminiscences"); and Takakura Shinichiro, "Edwin Dun shoden [A Brief Biography of Edwin Dun]" in Edwin Dun, *Nihon no okeru hanseiki no kaiso* (Reminiscences of Nearly a Half Century in Japan), translated by Takakura Shinichiro (Sapporo, 1962), pp. 1-30.

68Reminiscences," pp. 2-3.

69*Ibid.*, pp. 6-7.

70*Ibid.*, pp. 14, 17.

71Dun letter to Capron April 5, 1874, CEF.

72Lyman saw Dun "impatient to be authorized to go to Yesso [Hokkaido]...so as to begin his farming operations there in good season." Lyman letter to Murray S. Day, February 16, 1876, copy, LFL.

73"Reminiscences," p. 30.

74*Ibid.*, pp. 41-43.

75Dun letter to Kuroda, December 4, 1875, CEF.

76Reminiscences," p. 62.

77*Ibid.*

78Dun letter to Dzusho Hirotake, January 5, 1879, CEF.

79"Reminiscences," 14; As for Shelton's experience with the *Kaitakushi*, see Herbert H. Gowen, "An American Pioneer in Japan," *Washington Historical Quarterly*, 20 (January 1929), pp. 12-23.

80"Reminiscences," p. 14.

81*Ibid.*, pp. 13-14, 31-32.

82*Ibid.*, pp. 56-57.

83*Ibid.*, p. 63.

84Lucius F. Sinks (great-great grandson of Allen G. Thurman) to the writer, December 4, 1979.

85"Reminiscences," pp. 92-93.

[86]*Ibid.*, pp. 18, 82-83.
[87]*Ibid.*, pp. 87-88.
[88]*Ibid.*, pp. 19-20, 88-89.
[89]*Ibid.*, p. 78.
[90]*Ibid.*, pp. 18, 83-85, 91-92.
[91]*Ibid.*, p. 63.
[92]*Ibid.*, pp. 90-91.
[93]*Ibid.*, p. 89.
[94]*Ibid.*, p. 79.
[95]*Ibid.*, p. 80.
[96]*Ibid.*, p. 93.

7

Westernizing Influences in the Early Modernization of Japanese Women's Education

Dorothy Robins-Mowry

At the elaborate opening ceremonies inaugurating Japan Women's University in 1901, the progressive statesman, Count Okuma Shigenobu hailed its founding as a step toward "setting up a double standard," one that would make Japan "twice as strong." The university would improve the status of women and, thus, provide "effective medicine to radically reform the ideals of family life better to serve the progress of the nation."[1]

In the previous thirty years, a handful of Western missionary educators and their supportive friends had quietly contributed to this modernizing process through their schooling of Japanese girls. Mrs. James Curtis Hepburn, wife of the inventor of romanized Japanese, first took a few boy and girl students into her home in 1863 to teach English and mathematics. Since then, others had educated girls not only in the expected subjects, but also in the extra dimensional qualities of democratic thinking and a humanitarian approach to life. Such inspiration instilled the courage and capacity for creative leadership which enabled a significant number to break through barriers of tradition to trailblaze innovative change in education, in the social freedoms, and in political and economic activities. The modest, but determined and dedicated women missionary educators leavened their girls into becoming thinking women, endowing them with a special persuasiveness of social responsibility.

It remains unclear whether Count Okuma, in praising the "double strength" modernized higher education would build in women, fully realized that this strength was already germinating, almost without notice, in unobtrusive classrooms under the tutelage of earnest Christian women teachers, and that its results would also move outside the realm of family life to challenge the neat, accepted patterns of women's position in society.

This chapter will examine what went into the educational efforts and moral influence of these resolute Western women educators, themselves pioneers in terms of late nineteenth century American society. It will focus on the work and lives of Mary Eddy Kidder, who started the first mission girls' school, Ferris School in Yokohama, and upon Alice Mabel Bacon, associated with both the Peeress School (*Kawoku jogakko*) and Tsuda College. The latter uniquely became a personal link of Western influence in the chain of modernizing educational efforts during the Meiji era.

The Japanese Setting

With the coming of the Black Ships and the opening of Japan to the West in 1857 and the return to power of the Imperial House in 1868, the Meiji era of "civilization and enlightenment," as the young modernist-elite such as Fukuzawa Yukichi and Mori Arinori labeled it, took shape.[2] Pursuit of goals to bring Japan abreast of the Western world's most up-to-date practices making possible modern industrialization gave impetus to social, economic, and political restructuring. Development of a modern public school system, including opportunities for girls, was deemed an essential element in achieving overall advancement.

The Fundamental Code of Education (*Gakusei*) of 1872 initiated this new modern public schooling system. Its preamble established the philosophy of universal education, saying, "While advanced education is left to the ability and means of the individual, a guardian who fails to send a young child, whether a boy or girl, to primary school shall be deemed negligent of his duty."[3] Article two of the Ordinance provided for implementation of the policy, stating definitely that "Education is to be given to women as well as to men."[4] The liberal educators had prevailed. American influence and the personal presence, during the mid 1870s, of David Murray of Rutgers University insured continuing attention to the education of girls in the evolution of the system. Provision for three to four years of equal elementary education began to take shape, and, by the end of the Meiji era, basic schooling extended through six years.

Girls' education had not been completely ignored in the Tokugawa period. It is estimated that some 10 percent of girls by the mid-century attended some kind of elementary school, primarily at the temple or parish *terakoya* schools. About 50 percent of the elite *samurai* women and an even higher percentage of merchant class urban women were literate. However, literacy among the country and lower class women, who represented the largest proportion, was much lower. Confucian concepts, well enunciated in the 1672 *Onna daigaku* (*Greater Learning for Women*) of Kaibara Ekken, dominated the educational principles.

Under Meiji liberalism, elementary education for girls became available on a broader scale. The public, on average, needed convincing of the merit of much "book learning" for girls, who might better attend to babysitting younger brothers and sisters, or help with home and farm chores. Not until the turn of the century did the number of women attending school begin to increase noticeably.[5] Equality of schooling for girls at the middle level found scant application. Tokyo Girls School (*Tokyo jogakko*), set up in 1872, served as a "model school" for women's education. It evolved into Girls' High School, extending education to students up to seventeen years of age. With a curriculum aimed at general education, it was attached in 1882 to Tokyo Women's Normal School, the highest educational institution for women. Higher education for women depended on private efforts until after World War II.

Modifications of official regulations concerning the organization, administration, and curriculum of girls' schools continued at intervals throughout the Meiji period. Curriculum adjusted to the changing tides of liberalism, reversion to new-Confucionist concepts—in measure a reaction to too much Westernization—and the on-going philosophical conflict about the goals of women's education. The Regulation of Girls' High Schools of 1886, *inter alia*, established the principle that subjects of general culture should be balanced with knowledge indispensable for fulfilling duties as wives and mothers. *Ryosai kembo* (good wife and wise mother) thus became the motto of this philosophy which underlay national educational policies into the Taisho and prewar Showa years. The Regulation of Girls High Schools of 1895 clarified the standards. Subsequent regulations were promulgated in 1901 and 1910.

Until the expanding Japanese economy and the home front demands of the wars with China and Russia impelled the government to provide better education for girls needed in the factories and newly-opening white collar jobs, implementation of public middle schools for girls did not keep pace with projections. In 1894 only thirteen middle public schools for about 2,000 girls were operating. For the most part, girls of fourteen years of age who wished to continue their education perforce turned to private secondary schools.[6] The missionary educators were willing and able to fill this vacuum.

One other policy decision of the early Meiji years holds special import for engendering ties with Western educators on behalf of women's education. This is the Charter Oath of 1868 whose tenets were reflected in the constitution prepared later that year. It presented five precepts to guide the new regime. The fifth article assumed particular pertinence for the future development of Japanese women. It encouraged the seeking of knowledge "throughout the world so as to strengthen the foundations of Imperial Rule." Thus, the imprimatur of the most revered authority of the land, the Emperor, proposed and sanctioned a way of learning which, in the case of girls and women, provided, almost inadvertently, the opening which enabled them to step out of the "Confucian box" of traditional education and restraints.

The Iwakura Mission of 1871 to study the West and to negotiate with the United States and other powers, headed by the Prince Iwakura Tomoni, included five girls of good families. History marks it as a landmark response to the opportunity offered women under the fifth precept. Mori Arinori, the Japanese

Consul in Washington, had proposed the inclusion of young women, and the Emperor himself supported the idea. Mori wrote:

> My country is now undergoing a complete change from old to new ideas, which I sincerely desire, and therefore [I] call upon all wise and strong-minded to appear and become good guides to the Government. . . . Females heretofore have had no position socially, because it was considered they were without understanding; but if educated and intelligent, they should have due respect.[7]

Less dramatic, but equally important was the overseas higher education that American and Canadian Christian teachers made possible for specially talented girls and young women attending their missionary schools. Both produced the desired encounter with the West. In time, the results of the two intermeshed.

The story of the five girls who traveled to America aboard the big side-wheeler steamboat is well-known. It is always mentioned as an example of liberal thinking in the early years of the new regime. One modern feminist described the event as the "first time that equal opportunity was opened for Japanese women."[8] The girls, ranging in age from seven to fifteen, were Yoshimasu Ryoko, Ueda Teiko, Yamakawa Sutematsu, Nagai Shigeko, and Tsuda Umeko, the youngest. Empress Haruko honored them with an audience before departure, encouraging them to become "models" for their countrywomen upon the completion of their studies abroad.[9] They faithfully followed this advice.

Twelve-year-old Yamakawa Sutematsu of a *samurai* family of Aidze began her sojourn in the United States in New Haven, Connecticut. The Japanese government paid all of her living and educational expenses. She lived with the family of Dr. Leonard Bacon, minister of New Haven's Center Church-on-the-Green, a professor of theology at Yale University, abolitionist, and the father of fourteen children. The youngest and comparable in age to Sutematsu was Alice. They became like sisters and developed a lifelong friendship. The arrangements for the care and teaching of young "Stamats," as she was called, had been carefully worked out between her brother Kenjiro, then at Yale University, and the Rev. and Mrs. Bacon prior to her arrival in the United States. Rev. Bacon's correspondence reveals that when she came into the Bacon home, he agreed that:

> Mrs. Bacon and the two youngest Bacon daughters would instruct her, she would not go to school at first, she would learn how an American lady keeps house and Nellie Bacon would give her piano lessons if they were desired. In addition, he stressed that she would be treated as a member of the family. This included, as one might expect in a minister's family, attending daily family prayers and church on Sunday.[10]

Upon Sutematsu's graduation from New Haven High School, she went to Vassar College in Poughkeepsie, New York. The "modest," yet fun-loving young woman graduated in 1882, the first Japanese woman to earn a B.A. She achieved academic honors and the admiration of her peers, as seen in her election as class president three years in a row. Despite her personal commitment to "teach Japan about American customs and culture" upon her return home and her assertion that, "There is no probability . . . of my forsaking the noble army of spinsters,"[11] she soon married Japan's Minister of War, Oyama Iwao. Over the years, as we shall see, she exerted leadership, acting in a traditional way from her position as the wife of one of Japan's most powerful men. She became a sponsor of women's patriotic activities, but also continued to support the advancement of women's education and ties with the West.

Nagai Shigeki also advanced from preparatory school to Vassar College where she studied piano and was trained as a music teacher. More easy-going than her co-patriot, she never received a degree. However, she, too, gave of her newly acquired Western knowledge to Japan upon her return. Even after her love marriage to Navy Lieutenant Uryu Solokichi (later Admiral), who had studied at the U.S. Naval Academy in Annapolis, she worked to bring Western music and musical education into the schools.[12]

It is, however, Tsuda Umeko who is most often remembered for her pioneering work in bringing higher education to Japanese women. A child of seven when she set sail across the Pacific, she remained in the United States eleven years. Her father, Tsuda Sen, a retainer of the Sakura clan, had gone to America on a special mission on modern farming in 1867 during the Tokugawa shogunate. Learning of the unusual chance for girls to go with the Iwakura Mission, he acted promptly to get Umeko, his second daughter, included in the group.

Umeko grew up under the care of Mr. and Mrs. Charles Lanman in Washington, D.C. where he was the American Secretary at the Japanese Legation. Through the wide circle of his friends in Washington and in the quiet summer resorts in New England, she met many in literary life and came to have a deep love and appreciation of poetry and literature. She also was converted to Christianity, the only one of the five to take this step. In 1882, she graduated from the Archer Institute, a high school in Washington, and soon thereafter returned to Japan.

Away from Japan during her formative years, she felt herself a "curiosity," a stranger in her own land. She had to re-learn the Japanese language as well as Japanese customs and habits. She received help in this adjustment from her older American "sisters," Stamats and Shige, both of whom, now married, had been through this process. Tsuda's observations on Japanese women, which she subsequently made in a speech, offer a comparative sketch of women's position in Japan and the United States in the early 1890's by someone trained in the attitudes of the West, but born in Japan.

When I returned home after my first visit to America, I was especially struck with the great difference between men and women, and the absolute power which the men held. The women were entirely dependent, having no means of self-support, since no employment or occupation was open to them, except that of teaching, and few were trained for teaching or were capable of it. A woman could hold no property in her own name, and her identity was merged in that of father, husband, or some male relative. Hence there was an utter lack of independent spirit.[134]

Arriving home at a time when feelings were rising against the English language, she taught on a temporary basis in missionary schools. In 1885, the Imperial Household Department established the Peeress School, and she was invited by Ito Hirobumi to teach English, a position she held for fifteen years. Oyama Sutematsu took an active interest in the school, and in 1888, at her urging and that of Tsuda, Alice Mabel Bacon, her foster sister from New Haven, agreed to join the staff for a year.

Tsuda and Bacon became close companions, sharing mutual interests and "liberal" philosophies about women's education. This friendship encouraged Tsuda to take a three-year leave of absence in 1889 to return to the United States to study at Bryn Mawr College. There she studied literature, philosophy, German, and showed exceptional ability in biology and the sciences. Conscious of her goal in life, she also took courses at Oswego (New York) Teacher's College. With the help of Mrs. Wistar Morris, a Philadelphia Quaker whom she had come to know through a missionary friend of her father, Tsuda raised scholarship money to enable other Japanese women to study in the United States. This was the beginning of the Philadelphia-based Japanese Scholarship Committee which continues to the present day. Its grantees include Kawai Michi who helped found Japan's YWCA and who established her own school, Keisen Junior College; Hoshino Ai and Fujita Taki, both Presidents of Tsuda College and the latter, the first Japanese woman to serve on Japan's United Nations Delegation. After her graduation from Bryn Mawr, Tsuda returned to her teaching at the Peeress School, but was restless. She wanted to reach beyond the elegantly gowned high-born girls at the school to teach others who would put their talents and training to more practical uses. During a trip to Europe and the United States in 1898 to represent Japan at the American Association of Women's Clubs, she undertook serious planning with Alice Bacon to establish her own school of higher education. The two of them and Anna Hartshorne, a friend from Tsuda's school days, joined in a fund-raising effort. Their success made possible the founding in 1900 of *Joshi eigaku juku* (Girls' Institute for English Studies).

In a seven-room rented house in Tokyo, set up in a style reminiscent of the old pre-Meiji *terakoya* schools, Tsuda and Bacon, who returned to Japan to help the school get started, launched their educational endeavor with fifteen girls. From this modest beginning Tsuda College grew, with Marchioness Oyama serving as an advisor and trustee. At the quiet opening on September 14, 1900,

Tsuda described her goals. She stressed that buildings and apparatus were not essential, but rather "the zeal, patience and industry of both teachers and pupils, and the spirit in which they pursue their work." She wanted more women to be able to pass the examinations to become teachers. She told them to avoid becoming "narrow" through their specialty in English, but to "keep yourselves informed of general matters and to be in touch with other lines of work." She warned of possible criticism and concluded by encouraging them to a way of etiquette and performance as a "true lady." Her intent was clear, she wanted them to be able to use their training, progressive for the time, in their conservative society.

> So I ask you not in any way to make yourselves conspicuous or to seem forward, but be always gentle, submissive and courteous as have always been our women in the past. This need not in any way interfere with the standard of your studies, for you may as true women endeavor to get the same grasp and hold of knowledge and attain the same standard of study as those of the other sex. To help you in this is my earnest wish.[14]

That Miss Tsuda succeeded is apparent from the roster of graduates who have contributed to their society and to the cause of women's progress. Canadian Caroline MacDonald, who had come to Japan on behalf of the YWCA, but also taught at Tsuda College, wrote to the Philadelphia Committee in the spring of 1909:

> I have no hesitation in saying that I believe Miss Tsuda's school is quite unique in Japan. She is laying the foundation of higher education for women, and no other school in Japan is doing what she is doing and can do if only properly sustained for a few years. . . . Her school also has the advantage of being managed by a Japanese. More and more in Japan, if Christian education is going to count, it must be carried on and controlled by Japanese. They know, as no foreigner ever can, how to adapt ideals in the abstract to the real life of the Japanese girl or boy, and we do well, I think, if we as foreigners can help in whatever way we can. . . .[15]

In conception, creation, and curriculum, Tsuda College linked the energies of mind and spirit of at least two of the five girls of the Iwakura Mission with those of the Western friends and allies who shared their desire for the advancement of Japanese women's educational opportunities. In time, the networking of these Japanese and Westerners intertwined and extended to the YWCA and the building of other important women's organizations, such as the Japanese Association of University Women. The students, over the years, took on challenges of feminism, suffrage, and social freedoms, and, always, appreciation of the values of friendship with the West.

Western Educators and Friends

Japan's reaching out to the West, as it broke with the tradition of Tokugawa isolationism, coincided with an outburst of conscientious Christianity in the West. This unique combination of historical forces, Japanese and Western, served well the cause of the early modernization of Japanese girls' and women's education during the Meiji years.

Western women joined their missionary husbands in teams to go forth in evangelical, medical, and educational endeavors not only to the islands of Japan but throughout Asia. They, as we have seen with Mrs. Hepburn, turned their abundant energies beyond their own family needs to organize classes for girls and activities with women. But primarily, it was the single woman teacher who devoted her life to the girls and young women of Japan. Their names emerge in memoirs and interviews with Japanese women. Miss Sarah C. Smith, a Presbyterian missionary, who started with seven girls in Sapporo and developed Hokusei Girls School, and her colleague Miss Clara Rose are fondly remembered as important influences by Kawai Michi.[16] Nishida Koto, in conversation in her eighty-ninth year, spoke with nostalgic warmth of the Canadian Miss Robertson, teacher at the Methodist girls school in Kofu, who encouraged her, and then took her via small boat and train, to *Toyo Eiwa* in Tokyo to begin her higher education.[17]

These young Americans and Canadians crossed the Pacific to bring Christianity of the Protestant persuasion to those in a far away land where their faith had been proscribed for centuries, and suspicion of its influence lingered. This call to loving service for Christianity fulfilled, in the case of Nannie B. Gaines of the Hiroshima Girls School, an "inexplicable urging."[18]

But they were also educated women who believed in the role of teachers as contributors to the knowledge and well-being of future generations. They became to their shy girl students models of attainment to be followed in the profession of education.

In their own sojourn in a strange culture, remote from home and family, these Western women braved the personal loneliness and cultural and linguistic isolation not unlike those of the young Japanese women who first led the way to Vassar, Wellesley, and Bryn Mawr. Wrote one Kentucky kindergarten teacher, subsequently a well-known writer, from San Francisco as she prepared to sail, "Behold a soldier on the eve of battle! . . . You could cover my courage with a postage stamp."[19] Little Tsuda Umeko wrote in an article two years after arriving in America:

> It was a very beautiful day when the vessel started. How my heart beat as I saw the land falling away! . . . I was very glad to reach the land, although it seemed a great ways from home.[20]

Little wonder that the scattered few, both Japanese and Americans, who ventured into each other's worlds, looked to one another for encouragement and support.

The earliest of this remarkable line of women foreign teachers, whose small beginnings grew into important educational institutions, was Mary Eddy Kidder. Born in 1834 in Vermont, she desired from her school days to undertake missionary work in a foreign country.

When Japan opened its doors to foreigners in 1858, among the first six missionaries to arrive the next year was Samuel R. Brown of the Dutch Reformed Church in America. This church, though small, was eager to spread Christianity in Japan because of the historical and long-time connection between Japan and Holland. Mary Kidder had very much wanted to go with Brown in 1859, but her family opposed her plan. Ten years later, however, her opportunity come. Brown, after his decade of experience, had come to feel strongly the necessity of educating Japanese women. He wrote his Board of Foreign Missions, "Women's education should be accomplished before Japan becomes a Christian country. We need to start immediately."[21] He recommended that Miss Kidder, who was then a high school teacher, undertake this work.

Mary Kidder arrived in Japan in August 1869 and went to Niigata, traveling with Mr. and Mrs. Brown. In the first year, teaching English, she had as one of her students Ueda Teiko who achieved historic significance in her own right as one of the five girls to accompany the Iwakura Mission to the United States. The next year Kidder moved to Yokohama, again accompanying Brown to his new assignment as a teacher of English at *Yokohama shubun-kan*. Within a month, Kidder took over Mrs. Hepburn's private seminar for boys and girls (*Hepburn-juku*),[22] located in a room of Dr. Hepburn's charity hospital, and started to teach English and the Bible. The date was September 21, 1870, since regarded by many as the founding day of the institution which achieved fame as the Ferris School.

Kidder, however, really wanted to devote herself to women's education. The following September she organized a class for girls, called *Kidder san no gakko* (Miss Kidder's School). A year later in 1872, the Governor of Kanagawa Prefecture, Ohe Taku, impressed with her devotion to girls' education, came to her support. Despite the fact that Christianity had not yet been approved by the Japanese Government,[23] he rented space in a government house at Nogeyama (Iseyama) for the Kidder School, and supplied the desks, chairs, and other essentials at his own expense. In another gesture, he offered her a *jinrikisha* so she could get to the school more readily from her home on Yamate Bluff, a restricted area designated for the homes of foreigners. The Governor's wife became one of Kidder's students—some thirty in number at this time—and all of them daughters of prominent figures in Yokohama. Ohe was a politician, well-known for his efforts to relieve the plight of those suffering from discrimination, including women entertainers and *burakumin* (outcastes). His assistance was amazing, but, as the historian of Ferris School opined, characteristic of his forwarding-looking policies and of Yokohama which was the "center of civilization and modernization of Japan."

Ohe's support, officially and financially, as well as his strong endorsement of women's education, is noted here because he represents a very early friend, in a long line of influential Japanese men, who contributed in many important ways to this cause. In the ebb and flow of government policy and public opinion about the merits of Western educational programs for women, the faithful male adherents, such as Mori Arinori, Doi Koka, Nitobe Inzo, and Naruse Jinzo, deserve full recognition and credit.

In 1875, with the completion of a new building at its present location, again with the help of the Governor, Miss Kidder's school was formally established. Named the Isaac Ferris Seminary, it honored the head of the Board of Foreign Missions of the Reformed Church who had originally sent Brown to Japan. His successor, his son John Mason Ferris, who was responsible for Kidder's assignment, actively contributed to the school's growth. He arranged for many of the students to go on to studies in the United States, as well as for other Americans to teach in Japan. The pyramid building was well begun.

Miss Kidder had married Rothsay Miller, a Presbyterian missionary, two years earlier in 1873. In rather unusual fashion for the time, he converted to her church in order to allow her to continue her important endeavors. In 1881, however, she resigned and joined with him in missionary activities in Kochi, Nagano, Hokkaido, and Morioka. She died in Tokyo in 1910, having served the cause of women's education in Japan over forty years.

Miss Kidder, like so many educational missionaries who came later in the century, was deeply influenced by Mary Lyon, the founder of Mount Holyoke Female Seminary. Mount Holyoke's curriculum gave priority to religious education and moral development, followed by home management, teacher training, intellectual enhancement, and artistic cultivation. At Miss Kidder's school, English was used in the morning classes for philosophy, history, math, English, the natural sciences, gymnastics, etc. Japanese teachers took over in the afternoon for calligraphy, Japanese language, history, and literature. The dormitories were Japanese in style as was the food.

Miss Kidder tried to adhere as closely as possible to Japanese customs. As she wrote the Foreign Missions Board in the U.S., "It would not be adequate to educate girls to be unable to live in their own homes, and I think it would be a little dangerous."[24] One is reminded of Miss Tsuda's comparable concerns almost thirty years later.

Her wisdom in dealing with the delicacies of sensitive intercultural situations and intercultural education no doubt contributed to the success of her work. The melding of Japanese cultural qualities with Western studies, especially English, within a framework of Christian ethics and service generated the dynamics of this bicultural education. The joining of Japanese teachers in the mission schools insured a balanced presence of foreigners and Japanese as classroom models.

This attitude of reaching out for Japanese support helped many of the Christian educators and their schools through the rough periods of public antipathy, outright anti-foreign reaction, and official governmental opposition. Said one mayor in a commencement address at a mission school in a small city:

The real significance of your Christian girls' schools is in the fact that when, in the start of woman's education here, our government was discouraged and thought feminine virtue could not stand the temptations accompanying intellectual development, you went ahead and demonstrated that the two were not incompatible.[25]

Nannie B. Gaines of Hiroshima put it most simply. She had learned to wield her influence—and bring survival to her school—by having "ideas, and let[ting] the Japanese carry them out."[26]

Mary Eddy Kidder's story provides a prototype of the foreign Christian missionary teachers who spent many years in Japan living and teaching the Christian faith and expanding the educational horizons of girls and women. In Alice Mabel Bacon, we find a conscientious Christian, not a missionary, but a dedicated advocate of making the world a better place through education. Reliance on the support of Christian faith was axiomatic.

As suggested earlier, Bacon came from a New England household where good works were a way of life. How natural, therefore, to open the family arms to take in young Yamakawa Sutematsu and contribute to a human support system for the pioneering Iwakura girls. Young Alice's ties to Japan were as natural as her ties to the other succoring public service interests of her father and family. Educated at private schools and at home in New Haven, she passed in 1881 the advanced Harvard University achievement examination for women. The Bacon family had, since the American Civil War, worked to found and develop Hampton Normal and Agricultural Institute in Virginia for black freedmen, and Alice, at age twelve, had spent a year there visiting her sister, then assistant principal. In 1883 Alice returned to Hampton to teach, concentrating on the Institute's public elementary school for training student teachers. From then until her death in 1918, Alice Mabel Bacon divided her time and not inconsiderable talents between Hampton Institute and Japanese women's education. Her ten years of sharing Sutematsu as a sister and the logical extension of this friendship to Tsuda Umeko solidified those bonds and the inevitable extension of her capacities to their causes.

Bacon was also an author of note, using this talent to secure support for her work. Her series of articles entitled, "Silhouettes," for the *Southern Workman*, described her activities, often in great detail. She also published "From the Sunrise Kingdom" about her time at the Peeress School in 1888-1889. In addition, she wrote about social customs, life-style, manners, bowing, clothing, the young women at Peeress School and their intellectual capabilities (not the "brightest"), school schedules and curriculum. Commenting about her teaching of *Little Lord Fauntleroy* and *Little Women* she wrote,"It is very pleasant to have the opportunity of showing girls something of the life of children in other parts of the world, and they seem to find it all most interesting."[27]

She expanded her writing to include her observations of the Japanese. In 1891, she published *Japanese Girls and Women*, which she dedicated to "Stematz, the Marchioness Oyama in the name of our girlhood's friendship unchanged and unshaken by the changes and separations of our maturer years."[28] Modest in, as she said, "a field occupied by Griffis, Morse, Greey, Lowell, and Rein," she wrote about an "unexplored corner." Her book dealt with the female half of the population "in the hope that the whole fabric of Japanese social life will be better comprehended."[29] This included material on changes in the lives of women since the end of feudalism, a subject much discussed with Tsuda and her friends in Tokyo during the Peeress School years. In fact, Miss Tsuda collaborated on the book's preparation during her summer holiday while at Bryn Mawr College, and this consultation became the motivation which led her to Tsuda College. The book was well received and, as the only authentic study of this subject, took rank as a standard authority. A second, illustrated edition with a ten-year update, appeared in 1902. Bacon also published *A Japanese Interior* in 1893, based on her letters and diaries.[30]

Bacon had become, in effect, a faithful interpreter of Japan to the West. Her sympathetic treatment of this exotic culture contributed to a broadened knowledge and appreciation of Japan. They undoubtedly assisted her and the American fund-raising friends of the Philadelphia Committee and, subsequently, of Tsuda College in raising the money which helped these causes prosper.

Alice Mabel Bacon was an inspiring human being who brought zest and intelligence to her teaching and to those projects she believed important. Of her teaching at Hampton, it was written, "Her bright and original ways of putting things and her keen sense of humor made her classes a constant delight, and no sleepy or disorderly boy was ever found there."[31] During her two years at Tsuda College, she received no salary. Despite this, she carried a heavy teaching and developmental load, contributing significantly through conduct of morning worship and weekly discussions of current topics. At that time, she also taught at Tokyo Women's Higher Normal School. She met challenges with action as when she raised money to start a hospital at Hampton Institute to provide nurses training for young black women and better health care for the community. It was named Dixie Hospital after her horse, for she cared deeply for animals, even taking her dog, Brucie, to Japan. The challenge offered by Tsuda Umeko's intense desire to break new ground for higher education for women was her kind of challenge, and she threw herself into helping insure its success.

Upon Alice Mabel Bacon's death in 1918, a lifelong friend said of her, "There was nothing small or petty or selfish in her whole make-up; she had a big generosity, a broad love for humanity, and an intense desire to serve."[32]

Other foreign teachers followed at Tsuda College—Anna Hartshorne, who also left her money to the college. They all brought variations on these qualities of generosity and helping others. As recently as the early 1970s, Fujita Taki, then President of Tsuda College, in conversation, queried whether any American women teachers could be recruited to provide once again, by example and by teaching, the kind of experiences she recalled from her own undergraduate years at Tsuda College. These teachers insured, by their very presence at Tsuda, and by their assistance in arranging for Tsuda women to pursue advanced education in America, that a new generation of educated woman would be readied to act upon the needs of progress of women.

Conclusion

In the first thirty years of the Meiji era, the educational and spiritual foundations were laid enabling Japanese women in the next thirty years to take up the cudgels, admittedly in gentle Japanese fashion, on behalf of their social freedoms, economic advancement, and political equality.

The Emperor Meiji and his liberal advisors provided the opportunity; the foreign teachers and missionaries brought the ideas and provided the essential tools needed for women to fulfill their new role in a modernizing society. The numbers of these teachers were few, and they were scattered geographically, but the little pockets of their influence produced disproportionate results of activism. The young lives they touched engaged in creative social engineering with positive domino-effects for Japanese women continuing to the present day.

What are some of the results that can be ascribed to these Western educational influences?

1. An alternative education to that of the Confucian-based "good wife-wise mother" philosophy was introduced. Rather than emphasis on the restraints and rigidity of obedience, the "way of great duty," the Christian teachers encouraged self-development, democratic thinking and action which opened vistas to the values and ways of life of the West. One feisty Japanese has called it, "The humanism of the West that seemed to liberate women of Japan from their inhuman subjugation."[33]

2. These western teachers and schools sponsored the talented, enabling them to continue their education and specialized training overseas, particularly in the United States and Canada. The experience of the girls of the Iwakura Mission has been detailed above. For the others, the experience was equally valuable. Once out of Japan, they saw and learned at first hand that there were other ways of living and getting things done. Having broken out of the classic pattern of education and growing up, they were then emboldened to break through other barriers at home. Wrote Mishima Sumie, "It is we ourselves and no one else that can open and smooth our way. I myself, with my American education, refuse to be a useless woman."[34] Collections of biographies of national and regional women pioneers, issued to commemorate the centenary of the Meiji Restoration, show that more than 50 percent of these women leaders held in common the early experience of having studied, travelled, or lived abroad.[35]

3. The cooperation of Japanese and Americans resulted in spill-over effects in organizational and community activities. The educators, many associated with Tsuda College, moved in and out of positions in the YWCA, for instance, a most important late Meiji organization which promoted continuing education. The Christian-trained within the Women's Christian Temperance Union were active against prostitution. Hiratsuka Raicho, founder of the *Bluestocking Journal (Seito)*, and other early feminists provide further examples of women

whose higher education experiences enabled them to make important social contributions.

In a speech, presented in Denver, in 1898, Tsuda Umeko eloquently expressed the value of the interchange and influence of the Western friends and teachers of Meiji era Japanese women:

> We take your kindness to us, not as a personal matter, but as the reaching out of the women of the West towards the women of the East, the warm welcome of the women of America to the women of Japan. As each nation must learn of other nations, so we too must realize that Japan if she is to advance must join the sisterhood of nations, not only in her diplomatic and commercial relations, but in all things which tend to the progress of her people, not the least in those matters concerning the home and the progress of her women. The present time will mark an era in our advance, and I feel that the day will not be long before our women, too, may take a stand in the foremost part of the strife for the highest and best for women, and in turn, we may, in the future, lend a helping hand and set a bright example to the women of the other lands of the Orient.
>
> Thus from one nation to another will be passed on the work of education and elevation for women, thus, step by step, will women arise, throughout all the world, from the slave and drudge of savage days, from the plaything and doll of later periods, to take her place as true helpmate and equal of man.[36]

Notes

[1] Alice Mabel Bacon, *Japanese Girls and Women* (Boston and New York, 1902), pp. 303-304.

[2] The slogan signified the change from the restrictions of Tokugawa feudalism. See Joseph M. Kitagawa, "Religions and Cultural Ethos of Modern Japan," in *Selected Readings in Modern Japanese Society*, edited by George K. Yamamoto and Ishida Tsuyoshi (Berkeley, 1971), pp. 188-189.

[3] Herbert Passin, *Society and Education in Japan* (New York, 1965), p. 211.

[4] Inoue Hisao, "A Historical Sketch of the Development of the Modern Educational System for Women in Japan," *Education in Japan: A Journal for Overseas* 6 (1971), p. 20.

[5] See, for instance, Yanagida Kunie, *Japanese Manners and Customs in The Meiji Era* (Tokyo, 1956), pp. 251-254.

[6] There is a growing literature on women's education during the Meiji period. Particularly useful are the studies by the Education Research Institute, Japan Women's University, especially *Meiji no joshi kyoiku* [Education of Women in the Meiji Period] (Tokyo, 1967).

[7] Megan Baldridge Murray, "The Girl Thrown Away Forever: Memories of a Princess," *Vassar Quarterly*, (Spring 1983), p. 11.

[8]Kawahara Shizuko, "Awakening of the Meiji Woman," *Asia Scene* (January 1962), p. 45.

[9]Ishimoto Shidzue, *Facing Two Ways: The Story of My Life* (New York, 1935), p. 362.

[10]Bernard Heinz, "First Japanese Student Remembered: Century-Old Friendship Celebrated at Yale," *The New Haven Register* n.d. (Special Collection, Vassar College Library).

[11]Letter from Yamakawa Stematz to Miss Wheeler, Tokyo, December 28, 1882. (Special Collection, Vassar College Library).

[12]"Japanese Vassar Girls: The Home Life in Tokyo of Two College Students," *The Sunday Advertiser,* October 1, 1893. (Special Collection, Vassar College Library). This well-written, illustrated story gives many details of Yamakawa and Nagai at Vassar and, later, in Tokyo.

[13]Yoshikawa Toshikazu, *Tsuda Umeko den* [Biography of Tsuda Umeko] (Tokyo 1956), p. 13.

[14]"The Girls' Home School for English," *Tokyo Magazine for the Study of English.* (Tokyo), n.d. *passim.*

[15]Rebecca Morton, "The History of Tsuda College" (unpublished manuscript. Archives of Bryn Mawr College), p. 15.

[16]See Kawai Michi, *My Lantern* (Tokyo, 1939), pp. 34-58.

[17]Interview with Nishida Koto, July 25, 1972. Nishida subsequently graduated from Miss Madera's School in Washington, D. C. and Vassar College.

[18]Samuel M. Hilburn, *Gaines Sensei: Missionary to Hiroshima* (Kobe, 1936), p. 14.

[19]Frances Little, *The Lady of the Decoration* (New York, 1906), p. 3.

[20]Yoshikawa, p. 112.

[21]*Ferris jyogakuen 110 nen shoshi* [The Short History of the Ferris School's 110 Years] (Yokohama, 1982), pp. 5-6.

[22]Mrs. Hepburn, who opened her school in 1863, taught English and mathematics to both male and female students. This little school, reestablished in 1874 and ultimately evolving into a basic unit of Meiji Gakuin University, included many students who became prominent: Hayashi Tadasu, Foreign Minister; Masuda Takashi, Founder of Mitsui Trading Company; Takahashi Korekiyo, Finance Minister; and Miyake Shigeru, medical doctor.

[23]The ban on Christianity was withdrawn by the Japanese government in February 1873. One of the tasks of the Iwakura Mission had been to observe how important Christianity was in the West and to recommend how Japan should treat the matter.

[24]*Ferris jyogakuen 110 nen shoshi*; p. 15.

[25]Charlotte B. DeForest, "The Devolution of Mission Girls' Schools in Japan," *International Review of Missions,* (1941), p. 422.

[26]Hepburn, p. 120.

[27]Alice Mabel Bacon, "Silhouettes From the Sunrise Kingdom: How We

Go to School in Tokyo," *Southern Workman* (December, 1888), p. 129. (The Hampton University Archives).

[28]Bacon, *Japanese Girls and Women,* Dedication.

[29]*Ibid.,* Preface to first edition, p. vii.

[30]In 1905 Bacon published a third volume, *In the Land of the Gods,* a collection of Japanese folk tales.

[31]"Alice Mabel Bacon," The *Southern Workman* (June 1918), p. 263. (The Hampton University Archives).

[32]*Ibid.,* p. 264.

[33]Mishima Sumie, *My Narrow Isle: The Story of A Modern Woman in Japan* (New York, 1941), p. 240.

[34]*Ibid.,* p. 241.

[35]See *Pioneer Women Educators of Japan: 24 Leaders of the Century* (Tokyo, 1970) and *Michi o kiri hiraita josei ten* [Women Pioneers since the Beginning of the Meiji Era] (Tokyo, 1968). My own interviewing showed the same phenomenon in which Christian heritage or early overseas experience or both became factors in motivating leadership.

[36]Yoshikawa, pp. 217-218.

Photographs

Kuroda Kiyotaka, early 1870s
(photograph in possession of
Hokkaido University Library).

General Horace Capron's party: From left, J. Clark, Capron, Warfield, Antisell,
and Eldridge, ca. 1872 (photograph in possession of Hokkaido University Library).

Kaitakushi main office in Sapporo, 1873 (photograph in possession of Hokkaido University Library).

Benjamin S. Lyman and his assistants, 1880 (photograph in possession of Hokkaido University Library).

Sapporo Agricultural College, 1879 (photograph in possession of Hokkaido University Library).

William S. Clark, ca. 1876 (photograph in possession of Hokkaido University Library).

Tsuda Umeko as a young
woman (used by permission of
Bryn Mawr College Archives).

Mary Eddy Kidder (photograph courtesy of the Archives of The Reformed
Church in America).

Alice Mabel Bacon with dog Brucie (photograph courtesy of Hampton University Archives).

Shinobazu Pond by Antonio Fontanesi (Tokyo National Museum; photograph courtesy of the International Society for Educational Information, Inc.).

Portrait of Professor Edward S. Morse, taken in 1878 in Tokyo (used by permission of Zoological Institute, Faculty of Science, University of Tokyo).

Tokyo Kaisei Gakko, predecessor of Tokyo University, ca. 1870, from "Tokyo Kaisei Gakko Ichiran, in the Year of 1875" (used by permission of Keio University Libraries and Information Centers).

Prof. Edward S. Morse's report "Omori Kaikyo Kobutsu-hen" [Shell mounds of Omori] (used by permission of Zoological Institute, Faculty of Science, University of Tokyo).

Gaimukyo Terashima Munenori's letter of 20 August 1875 to Dajo Daijin Sanjo Sanetomi, suggesting that the government confer the title of Secretaire Honoraire on Frederic Marshall (Archives of the Japanese Ministry of Foreign Affairs, MS. 3-9-3-12, Marshall File, Ritsuan 449).

Frederic Marshall's letter to John Blackwood from Paris, dated 11 August 1872 (The Blackwood Papers at the National Library of Scotland, MS. 4294, ff. 146–7, used by permission of the Trustees of the National Library of Scotland).

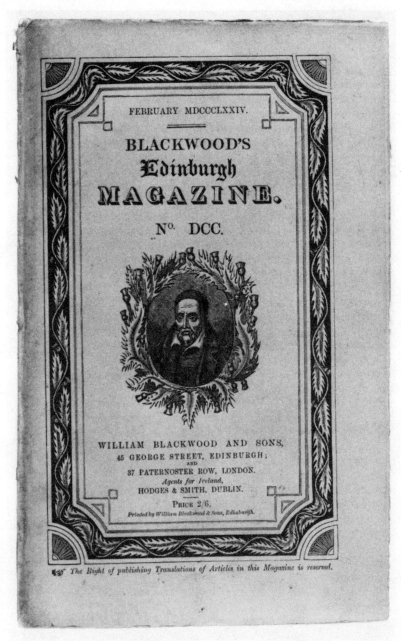

Cover of the February 1874 issue of *Blackwood's Edinburgh Magazine*, in which Marshall's "International Vanities" was printed.

PEABODY MUSEUM,
SALEM, MASSACHUSETTS, U. S. A.
Founded, 1867 (Museum established by East India
Marine Society in 1799).

EDWARD S. MORSE, DIRECTOR.
JOHN H SEARS, CURATOR GEOLOGY AND MINERALOGY
L. W. JENKINS, CURATOR OF ETHNOLOGY
JOHN ROBINSON, KEEPER OF EAST INDIA MARINE SOCIETY RELICS

East India Marine Hall,

Salem, Mass., Oct 27.06

My dear Dr Griffis

My delay in answering your letter
has been due to hunting up the data
you wanted. In some unaccountable
manner the very whirs of the Dai Gakko
annual Rkts I wanted to consult are
missing! The following is a lethal
and possibly completed list from 1877 to

1883. Henry T. Terry
Winfield S. Chaplin   now at Washington Univ.
                                          St Louis
Thomas C. Mendenhall
+ Charles O. Whitman   my successor
Henry M. Paul   now naval Observatory
                                    Washington
William C Houghton   now Bowdoin College
                                       Brunswick Me.
Ernest F. Fenollosa
J. A L. Waddell

I wish I could give you more. there
certainly were many men, whose names
for the life of me I cannot recall

Edward S. Morse's letter to William Elliot Griffis, dated 27 October 1906
(used by permission of Special Collections and Archives, Rutgers University
Libraries).

PEABODY MUSEUM,

SALEM, MASSACHUSETTS, U. S. A.

Founded, 1867 (Museum established by East India
Marine Society in 1799).

EDWARD S. MORSE, DIRECTOR.
JOHN H SEARS, CURATOR GEOLOGY AND MINERALOGY
L. W. JENKINS, CURATOR OF ETHNOLOGY
JOHN ROBINSON, KEEPER OF EAST INDIA MARINE SOCIETY RELICS

East India Marine Hall,

Salem, Mass.,

Dr Veeder and Rev Dr. Syles. and a
teacher in English in the Preparatory School
who became afterwards Librarian in
San Francisco. also Mr Jewett a fine
fellow who went to the Sandwich Islands.
Would it not be a good idea to write
direct to the Imperial University and
ask for a list of American teachers
within the dates you want. most of
them you would probably find in Who's Who
As soon as gap occurs in my work I will
tell you my own work there.

Your Mikados Empire is still a
prominent book in the maze of books since
published on that fascinating country
If you are ever this way I would like you
to see the final Ethnological Collection Japan
that I am building up here. Faithfully

Edw S Morse

Benjamin Smith Lyman (used by permission of Special Collections and Archives, Rutgers University Libraries).

8

Principles and Pragmatism: The *Yatoi* in the Field of Art

Ellen P. Conant

> Histories of art are themselves part of history, far from immune to the
> artistic temper of their age.
>
> Edgar Wind, *Art and Anarchy*

The "discovery" of Japanese art followed close on the heels of the
"reopening" of Japan in 1854. As Westerners were once again able to set foot
in that long-secluded realm, they were fascinated anew by the expressiveness,
humor, ingenuity and technical virtuosity of Japanese arts and handicrafts.
First-hand acquaintance gradually enabled them to distinguish what was
Japanese from amidst the mass of Orientalia that had reached Europe during
Japan's more than two centuries of seclusion. The diverse assemblage of
artifacts long prized for their ethnological values that had been brought back by
members of the Dutch East India Company—the only Europeans with direct
entree to Japan during that period of self-imposed isolation—now assumed new
significance.[1] The accounts of members of the Perry Expedition and other early
voyagers whetted the curiosity and acquisitive instincts of Western collectors,
which were further augmented by the writings of such early diplomats as Sir
Rutherford Alcock and Aimé Humbert.[2] This burgeoning interest in Japanese
culture meshed, moreover, with the reciprocal desire of the Japanese to expand
the export market for their traditional arts, which along with silk and tea were
then the principal sources of foreign currency sorely needed by the Japanese
authorities to finance their military and industrial development.

There was, however, a fundamental ambivalence inherent in what should
have been a mutually beneficial area of supply and demand. During the course
of the Edo period, the Japanese had become adept at producing artifacts for the
export market and they thus had no difficulty accommodating to Occidental
preference for those aspects of Japanese art that had already absorbed elements of
Western art. Meiji officials were surprised, therefore, when this blossoming

trade soon elicited the criticism of commentators and journalists—self-styled connoisseurs—who decried Japan's willingness to pander to the exotic cravings of the export trade by readily adopting Western forms and imagery, as well as the overly intricate designs and excessive manipulation of rich materials so dear to Victorian taste. Even the enthusiasts of *Japonisme*, unaware of their own complicity, were soon bemoaning what they assumed to be the decline of Japanese art as a whole. Early Meiji officials and entrepreneurs were puzzled by these contradictory reactions and found it difficult to reconcile their sensitivity to such criticism with their desire to expand their markets and to garner awards at international expositions. They were no less astonished to find that all manner of foreigners, be they diplomats, legation personnel, teachers, travellers, traders, missionaries, and technicians, spouses included, had pronounced views regarding Japanese art—past, present and future. In no other field of endeavor were the Japanese the recipients of so much unsolicited and gratuitous advice.

Japan had an ancient, mature and sophisticated art tradition that had already absorbed and integrated, over the centuries, elements of Western, Near Eastern, Indian, Chinese and Korean art. Despite difficulties adapting to the sweeping political, economic and social changes instituted by the Meiji government, the traditional artists and craftsmen, for the most part, were able to weather the restoration because their work continued to be highly admired and broadly patronized. Such dislocations as did occur tended to receive prompt attention because of the government's urgent need to expand foreign trade and domestic markets. Immediate steps were taken by local officials to aid the weaving, dyeing and pottery industries of Kyoto, the kilns at Arita and Kanazawa, and numerous other craft centers throughout the country. The shift of the capital and court to Tokyo necessitated the services of countless artists and craftsmen to build, repair, refurbish and otherwise meet the needs of the Imperial Court and the nobles who were now required to reside in Tokyo. Imperial mausoleums and major Shinto shrines had to be renovated and refurbished; carpenters and craftsmen were needed to provide accommodations in Tokyo for a new government bureaucracy; traditional artists, engravers and printers were hired to produce paper currency, legal documents, maps, school text books and many other official papers. Much additional information could be adduced to refute the general assumption that the traditional arts suffered a precipitate decline during the *bakumatsu* and early Meiji. This notion, based upon artists' and artisans' recollections of their difficulties adjusting to a new era, compounded by nostalgia for by-gone days, gained credence in late Meiji, when Fujioka Sakutaro and other scholars published the first histories of modern Japanese art.[3]

The situation in the field of art during the *bakumatsu* and early Meiji was very different, therefore, from those fields wherein Japan frankly recognized the need to master Western technology. Institutions for Western studies were quickly established and some Japanese students were sent abroad, at first surreptitiously, to observe and report on Western mining, shipbuilding, arms manufacture and various other industrial processes. The waning Tokugawa regime invited the French to build a naval base and drydock, to erect a spinning mill, and to send a military training mission. These tentative efforts were vastly expanded by the new Meiji government whose credo was embodied in the slogan *fukoku kyohei,* "enrich the country and strengthen its arms." A surprisingly large portion of the national budget was spent to send students abroad to study and to invite foreign experts to help import new technologies and train the Japanese to operate them.[4] Comparatively few *yatoi* were needed in the field of art and they were primarily concerned with assisting the Japanese to master those aspects of Western art thought essential to achieving these goals. This chapter will therefore confine itself to the limited number of *yatoi* who were employed full-time in the field of art to teach Western architecture, painting, sculpture, drawing, drafting and printing, as distinguished from those in other fields whose advice was solicited, on a supplemental basis, regarding new materials and methods for improving craft production, establishing such new institutions as art schools and museums and facilitating Japan's participation in international expositions.

I

Even if the imperative for reform in the field of art was less pressing, it was no less compelling. The Japanese quickly realized the need to master mechanical drawing, drafting and other aspects of Western art. A year after the establishment of the *Bansho Shirabesho* (Institute for Barbarian Studies) in 1856, a scholar of Dutch studies trained in the traditional schools of painting, Kawakami Togai, was instructed to investigate Western methods of drawing and painting.[5] Based on his study of Dutch and English elementary self-teaching manuals and utilizing painstakingly improvised materials, he began in 1861 to teach his newly-acquired knowledge to a number of samurai and scholars, as well as some artists reared in the traditions of the Kano school, such as Takahashi Yuichi and Kano Tomonobu. After the Restoration, this school became part of the Kaiseijo (later incorporated into Tokyo University), and here Togai taught numerous pupils eager to receive training that would qualify them for employment with the government and newly established companies as draftsmen, cartographers, illustrators, teachers, etc. The importance attached to these skills was such that pencil drawing was included in the curriculum of the nationwide system of elementary schools established in 1872 by the newly-formed Ministry of Education.[6]

One of the two books by Togai that were adopted as texts was published by the Military Affairs Ministry which in 1874 employed a French architect and artist, Abel Guerineau, to help Togai organize and teach a special course in drawing and painting for the personnel of the Military Academy.[7] Virtually nothing is known about Guerineau, who seems to have been the first *oyatoi* engaged to teach a *bona fide* art course. According to an advertisement that he placed in *The Japan Weekly Mail* of May 23, 1874,[8] soon after his arrival, he was a graduate of the Ecole des Beaux Arts in Paris and wanted employment as an architect and civil engineer. This reveals the effort of some *oyatoi* to solicit private work of which comparatively little is known. He may have come to Japan with the French Military Mission and records show that he remained in official employ until June 1880, working as an architect and drawing architectural plans.[9]

Among the first to be employed as an "architect" was another Frenchman, Edmond Auguste Bastien in 1839.[10] He was born in Cherbourg and was working as a shipwright at the docks there when he was engaged, in 1866, to come to Japan to help erect a naval depot at Yokosuka. He was granted temporary leave in 1871 to build the Tomioka Spinning Mill according to plans provided by Paul Brunat.[11] After the completion of the Yokosuka project in 1875, he worked as an architect and inspector of the Building Department of the Ministry of Public Works until 1880, when like Guerineau, he dropped from sight. What became of him thereafter is uncertain, other than that he died in Yokohama in 1888 and is buried in the foreign cemetery on the Bluff.

Another French architect, C. de Boinville, whose work is relevant because of his association with the Imperial College of Engineering, came to Japan in 1872 and worked as a surveyor, architect and teacher for the Ministry of Public Works but once again virtually nothing is known of his antecedents.[12] He erected a new building for the Printing Bureau, completed in 1876, that was based upon the design by an English architect, T. J. Waters, and is thought to have added the decorative details that derive from French Renaissance architecture. In 1877 he built, in a similar style, the auditorium building of the Imperial College of Engineering. He was principally responsible for the design and construction of the Ministry of Foreign Affairs, which was finished in 1881, with the assistance of Giovanni Vincenzo Cappelletti, whose activities are detailed below. It is not certain what other projects, of an official or private nature, he may have been involved with nor what became of him after 1881. Architectural historians have assiduously sought to document the work of numerous other foreign architects and/or engineers, particularly two major figures who arrived soon after the restoration, an Englishman, T. J. Waters, and an American, R. F. Bridgens, but apart from studying the numerous buildings they are known to have erected, scholars have yet to trace their background, chart the full range of their activities in Japan, and determine what became of them thereafter, an important factor in tracing the reverse flow of Japanese influence on Western art.[13]

Architects were the first *oyatoi* to be engaged in the field of art because Meiji officials were determined to become technically competitive and self-reliant as soon as possible. Since Japanese architecture offered no suitable precedents for factories, mints, railroad stations and the like, the Japanese pragmatically began importing Western technology *in toto*, buildings and all. When the many vacant *yashiki* in Tokyo utilized by the government in early Meiji proved ill-suited to the requirements of foreign institutions, Western architecture was also adopted for schools, post offices, banks, public buildings and government offices. The Ministry of Public Works, created in 1870 to develop communications, transportation, mining and heavy industry, also advocated the use of Western architecture because of its greater utility and resistance to fire and earthquakes. In 1873 this ministry was put in charge of all government building. Architecture accordingly was added to the curriculum of the Imperial College of Engineering that was founded in 1874 by the prime minister, Ito Hirobumi. He hired Henry Dyer and a group of promising young engineers and scientists to set up a school, modeled upon the most advanced in Europe, to train engineers, mechanics, architects and technicians.[14]

When the first students entered the advanced class in 1876, the Ministry engaged Josiah Conder to teach architecture.[15] The choice of an Englishman was not indicative of architectural preference but in keeping with the preponderance of Britishers in the Ministry as a whole and on the staff of the Imperial College of Engineering. Conder was born in London in 1852, attended the Bedford Commercial School and in 1868 entered the office of T. Roger Smith, Professor of Architecture and Building Construction at University College, London, and was twice president of the Architectural Association. Smith is known for his many large undistinguished institutional buildings. Conder also studied architecture at the South Kensington Art School and attended the Slade Life Classes at University College. In 1874 he became architectural assistant to the noted medievalist, William Burges, who was amongst the first in England to collect Japanese prints and to extoll, along with A. E. Godwin, James Whistler, Sir Rutherford Alcock, John Leighton and others, the virtues of Japanese art.[16] In 1876 Conder was awarded the Soane Medallion for the design of a country house in French Gothic style. It was a signal honor for a young architect. Undoubtedly due to the influence of Burges, he was recruited by the Japanese later that year and, after a brief tour of Europe, arrived in Tokyo in January 1877, where he began to teach the first systematic course in architecture at the Imperial College of Engineering and to serve as consulting architect to the Ministry of Public Works.

Conder was a model *oyatoi*. He was an extremely methodical teacher who trained and nurtured the ablest of the first generation of Japanese to master Western architecture, among them Tatsuno Kingo, Katayama Tokuma and Sone Tatsuzo, while at the same time producing a steady stream of buildings, both official and private, too numerous to list. His letters and drawings reveal his painstaking efforts, precise planning, proposals for the use of new materials, inventive structural solutions and innovative scientific tests.[17] He was keenly aware of the circumscribed role of an *oyatoi* yet did not hesitate to express his views nor vent his pique when he was not heeded nor kept apprised of developments.[18] When the Imperial College of Engineering was absorbed by the Engineering Department of Tokyo Imperial University in 1886, he graciously made way for his pupils and willingly collaborated with them on several important commissions.

Some four years after his arrival, he formally married Maeha Kumeko. He thus had more direct entree to Japanese circles then most *oyatoi*, but at the same time retained a firm footing in the British community, maintaining close relations with academic, diplomatic and business circles and actively participating in amateur theatrics. Through his brother, Roger T. Conder, who was also an architect and recipient of the Soane Medallion, he was able to remain informed of professional developments in England and beyond. He was an accomplished draftsman and competent watercolorist, as can be seen from his extensive architectural drawings and paintings of the many noted sites he visited.[19] He was quick to appreciate the talent and originality of the eccentric artist, Kawanabe Gyosai, and collected many of his works which he later published.[20] He also studied ink painting with Gyosai and became proficient enough to exhibit his work. Conder's keen appreciation of Japanese art encompassed both the stark simplicity of its domestic architecture and the elaborate decoration and rich coloring of the Toshogu in Nikko. His views were set forth in a series of articles on Japanese architecture, theaters, gardens, costume and flower arrangement.[21]

At the beginning of his career, when he was strongly under the influence of Burges, he tried to incorporate Oriental decorative details into his eclectically derived European structures. His most notable early building, the National Museum in Ueno Park, completed in 1881, has distinctive Venetian features, as well as mouldings and finials of Saracenic derivation that recall Burges' design for the Bombay School of Art.[22] Indeed the relevance of ideas advanced by British architects as suitable for India and the possible influence of the Western style buildings they erected there merits further study.[23] Conder helped design the audience chambers of the Imperial Palace in Tokyo and the Imperial Household Building, as well as royal residences for Prince Arisugawa and Prince Kitashirakawa. He also built the German, Austro-Hungarian and Italian embassies, as well as numerous clubs and churches, but no one structure was more completely the embodiment of the Meiji era than his *Rokumeikan*.[24] Because of his extensive activity as a builder and the painstaking attention he gave to interior decor, including furniture, he trained a far wider range of people than those who attended his architectural courses. His expertise, uncompromising principles and high standards directly contributed to Japan's present international eminence in the field of architecture.

With the passage of time, he had increasingly grave reservations about the wisdom of combining Eastern and Western architectural motives. In a paper on "The Condition of Architecture in Japan" that was read at the World's Congress of Architects, held at the Centennial Exposition in Chicago in 1893, he forcibly declared that:

> To design a civil building in masonry having all the characteristics of
> the classical styles of Europe, and to crown it with fantastic lanterns,
> roofs and turrets of timber in imitation of portions of Japanese religious
> constructions, is not adapting the national style to modern purposes—it
> is to create a bizarre and hybrid ensemble as revolting to Japanese taste
> and common sense as it is wanting in *the permanent and fire-resisting
> qualities which are the first conditions of the programme imposed*
> (author's own italics).[25]

These views coincided with those of his principal private clients, members of the prominent Iwasaki family. Due to extensive travel and residence abroad, they wanted the luxurious residences and villas that he built for them to be purely Western in style and comparable to the mansions then being built in Europe and America. He continued, however, to make sensitive use of Japanese decorative elements and design concepts, primarily for interior decor, and had no compunctions about including, where required, some purely Japanese rooms. Indeed his own home in Azabu, out of deference to his wife, was part Japanese. He also built for the Iwasaki's corporate entity, Mitsubishi, a block of commercial buildings that were a dominant feature of the Marunouchi district of Tokyo until they were torn down in 1970.

By the late 1890s, official architecture was tending in a somewhat different direction. As Fujioka Hiroyasu perceptively notes:

> The period around the turn of the century was one of extremely mixed emotions for Japanese. Half a century had passed since the country had been opened to the world, and its people—architects included—had learned a great deal about the West. The task of catching up still far from complete, however, they suffered a constant sense of inferiority. On the other hand, the Japanese people were well aware of the fascination with "things Japanese" amongst Westerners and this stirred the national pride. Victory in both the Sino-Japanese (1894-1895) and Russo-Japanese wars (1904-1905), too, fueled nationalist sentiment, and the pendulum began to swing back from total adulation of the West. The ground was steadily being laid for acceptance of architecture with a distinctively Japanese flair.[26]

Early Meiji officials had wanted "bona-fide Western-style architecture that would express the dignity of the state and convince Europe and the United States that Japan was a 'civilized nation' deserving of respect and equal treatment," and hence they rejected the revised plans submitted by Hermann Ende, following his trip to Japan in 1887, for the Imperial Diet building that featured a Japanese-style roof with projecting eaves and other traditional elements superimposed on a new-Baroque building.[27] Yet a decade later, Kaneko Kentaro, briefly Minister of Agriculture and Commerce in the third Ito cabinet, invited the American architect, Ralph Adam Cram, to submit a design for a new Diet Building that was a pastiche of Japanese traditional architecture reminiscent of the Gion Shrine erected in Kyoto in 1895.[28] The project fortunately floundered with the fall of the cabinet in July 1898. Conder's opposition to this type of sterile eclecticism does not seem to have impaired his career, but it may explain why he was posthumously less renowned than his contemporary, Ernest Fenollosa (1853-1908), who had from the outset espoused such eclecticism. But, in view of the foregoing, would Fenollosa's eclecticism have appealed to Meiji officials during the 1880s when he theoretically was most influential?

Conder and his wife died within a few days of each other in June 1920 and are buried in Zoshigaya Cemetery in Tokyo. He received the fourth-class Order of the Rising Sun in 1884 and the third-class Order of the Sacred Treasure in 1894. A bronze statue of Conder by Shinkai Taketaro (1868-1927)[29] was erected in the courtyard of the College of Engineering at Tokyo University in 1913 and Shirataki Ikunosuke was commissioned to paint his portrait for presentation at the fifteenth anniversary of the reorganization of the Institute of Japanese Architects in 1920.[30] Despite these numerous honors, scholars have been laggard in addressing the issues. There is still no comprehensive Western language monograph on Condor[31] and Japanese sources have not adequately explored his manifold contributions to the development of Meiji art nor his significant role as a *oyatoi.*

II

In conjunction with the addition of architecture to the curriculum of the Imperial College of Engineering, an adjunct art school, known as the Technical Art School,[32] was established in 1876 to train students in painting, sculpture and a wide range of related arts that were an integral part of the Beaux Arts tradition and nineteenth century architectural eclecticism. To achieve the parity they sought, the Ministry decided to engage experienced men capable of training the Japanese to design and execute the wide range of skills requisite for the interior and exterior decoration of the "historic" styles of architecture then in vogue that Ito Hirobumi had observed during the course of his travels with the Iwakura Mission. Since Italians were considered the most expert at stone carving, fresco and mural painting, stucco, mosaic, intarsia, ormulu and other related crafts, he turned to the Italian Minister, Comte Alessandro de Fei, for help in securing the services of a painter, sculptor and architectural draftsman to teach the principles and practice of Western art.[33]

Italy had every reason to be cooperative. The Italians had been too preoccupied with their own struggle for unification to join the five other Western powers that signed formal treaties with Japan in 1858. They nevertheless were pioneer students of Japanese language and literature and by 1863 had appointed Antelmo Severini Professor of Far Eastern Languages at the Royal Institute of Higher Studies in Florence.[34] Similar courses were established during the 1870s in Rome, Venice and Naples. The major imperative, as in France, was the dire need of the Italian silk industry to obtain a new strain of silkworms to replenish native cocoons that had been ravaged by disease in the early 1860s.[35] This impelled the Italian government to dispatch the corvette "Magenta," under the leadership of Vittorio Armijon, to sign a trade agreement with Japan in August 1866.[36] The first Italian Minister, Comte Vittorio Sallier de la Tour, arrived in May 1867, and in his wake came officials, merchants, technicians and travellers whose early interest in Japanese art has still to be studied.

It is remarkable that so accomplished and well-known a painter as Antonio Fontanesi[37] should have responded to the Ministerial Circular of August 4, 1875, soliciting applications for the positions at the Technical Art School and accompanying instructions from the Italian Legation in Tokyo. Although Fontanesi would appear to have been an unlikely candidate, he proved an exceptional one. Born in Reggio Emilia to a family of modest means, he was only seven when his father died. At fourteen he entered the local school of fine arts and studied painting under Prospero Minghetti[38] who was skilled at portraiture and religious painting. Family circumstances compelled him, three years later, to accept work as a decorator and fresco painter, but he spent his leisure hours at a cafe frequented by local patriots. His mother's death in 1847 left him free to take part in the first campaign for the independence of Italy in March 1848. He battled Austrian troops in Luciano Manara's battalion and then fought with Garibaldi on the shores of Lake Maggiore. He found refuge that September with other Italian exiles in Lugano, where he supported himself by giving painting lessons.

In December 1850 Fontanesi settled in Geneva, set up an atelier and began anew his career as a painter. Surrounded by Alpine peaks and genial views of Lake Geneva, he turned to landscape. He became friends with Francois Diday and Alexander Calame, two of the leading local artists noted for their pictures of Alpine scenery.[39] The influence of Calame is apparent in his early watercolors and prints. Two series of lithographs that he issued in 1854 gained him recognition as one of the major artists in Geneva.[40] He also worked with a group of French artists clustered about Francois-Auguste Ravier (1814-1895)[41] at Cremieu and later Morestel in the Dauphine. He frequently visited Italy where he regularly exhibited. He attended the International Exposition held in Paris in 1855, when the critical debates over Courbet's realism took place, and was drawn to the work of Corot, Rousseau, Daubigny and other artists of the Barbizon school. During 1856-1857 he travelled throughout Liguria and, after taking part in the second war of independence in 1859, returned to Geneva. In 1861 he exhibited in Paris and later in Florence, where he first encountered the Macchiaioli but they evidently had no impact on his work.[42] He was particularly attracted at that time to the paintings of Ravier, Corot and Troyon and also showed a marked interest in the work of Rembrandt. While in London during 1865 to 1866, he produced a fine series of heliographs of the noted sights[43] and was influenced, meanwhile, by the works of Turner and Constable. He then went to Florence and rented the studio of Cristiano Banti which he occupied until the spring of 1868, when he went to teach at the art school in Lucca. Early in 1869 he was offered the position of landscape painter at the Academy Albertine in Turin which, apart from his sojourn in Japan, he retained until his death in 1882.

Thus Fontanesi was the best informed Italian painter about artistic development in the rest of Europe.[44] Annie Paule Quinsac notes that:

> He does not belong to any school. His approach to nature is a very personal one, conveyed by means of chiaroscuro and design. His color is

applied by heavy flat texture which has an enamel-like quality.
Sometimes the paint is scratched with the palette knife which conveys a
fascinating and unusual effect. All those technical experiments were used
to express a certain mood of melancholy and restraint which was in the
tradition of Romanticism. His subjects are animals or peasants in a
natural setting, or the landscape itself with studies of trees.[45]

In Italy, according to Quinsac, "The coming of Romanticism corresponds to a
nationalist claim, a new theory according to which Italy had to find in its own
past the strength to assert its own autonomy."[46] She aptly conveys the essence
of his mature style when she writes, relative to a painting formerly in the
possession of Arturo Toscanini, that "The landscape is a synthesis between a
direct and continuous observation of nature and the expression of a keen
emotion, which is almost pantheistic. In spite of the concise rendition of
reality, the scenery remains suggested more than described."[47] She observes in
his work the lasting impact of Ravier and the Lyons School of Landscape, as
does Marco Valsecchi who further notes that Fontanesi was "an outstanding
example to the Piedmont artists who came after him because his landscape
paintings were international in tone."[48] A more recent study by Gianfranco
Bruno[49] observes his influence on the painters of Liguria as well, and the
current critical reevaluation of Ottocento painting continues to enhance the
reputation of Fontanesi.

A sense of failing health and growing despondency seems to have
heightened rather than impaired his creative powers and tempted him to consider
venturing abroad once again. Fontanesi apparently had no particular interest in
Japan per se,[50] but simply wanted to get away from Turin for a while because
he felt that the staff and particularly the director of the Academy Albertine,
Count Panissera di Veglio, were undermining his efforts and that Turin art
circles did not fully appreciate his talents. His current income was not adequate
to meet outstanding debts and debilitating attacks of gout and rheumatism made
him anxious about providing for his old age. He had no family ties binding
him to Italy and, having already lived abroad for two decades, the thought of a
foreign assignment seemed challenging, particularly when the salary and
emoluments were generous enough to permit him to save a tidy sum. He duly
submitted his application to the Minister of Education in November 1875 and
after receiving confirmation of his appointment, spent the ensuing months
making arrangements and preparing necessary teaching materials. After bidding
farewell to friends and pupils in Turin, he spent some time in Rome and then
proceeded to Naples, where he met up with Vincenzo Ragusa and Giovanni
Vincenzo Cappelletti. Together they set sail for Japan on July 18, 1876.

Because of his age and ill health, Fontanesi felt slighted by his companions.
Ragusa was not only twenty-three years his junior, but a Sicilian, born in
Partanna Mondello near Palermo in 1841 and from childhood displayed a
marked interest in art.[51] He studied first with a local artist of religious
paintings by the name of Patricolo and also frequented the workshop of a local
ivory carver. He often visited the home of a family friend who was interested

in the decorative arts. Since his family was opposed to his becoming an artist, he worked for a while at a tax office in Palermo. When Sicily rebelled against the Bourbons in 1860, Ragusa joined the forces of Garibaldi and while in service was able to visit numerous art centers and attend the Pan-Italian Art Exhibition held in Florence in 1861, as did Fontanesi. He then returned to Palermo and, despite continuing parental objections, enrolled in the sculpture course conducted by Nunzio Morello, a drawing class based on casts of ancient sculpture given by a well-known Palermo painter, Salvatore Lo Forte, and in the evening attended life classes at a local academy. In 1867 he took part in an art competition held in Palermo and won a travel grant that enabled him to attend a major exhibition held in Parma and to visit other major cities. The prize awarded him at the exhibition held in Milan in 1872 for a plaster cast of a *Decorative Stove* brought him to the attention of Conte Wonderwies, who commissioned him to execute it in marble for his villa in Lugano. He then settled in Milan where he received numerous other commissions. Ragusa entered a competition, in 1875, to select a teacher of sculpture for the new art school in Tokyo. Although Ragusa had no teaching experience, and would have lacked formal qualifications had not the Academia del Brera accomodatingly awarded him a diploma, he was appointed to train the Japanese in the hitherto unknown field of Western sculpture.

By contrast, virtually nothing is known about Cappelletti prior to his departure for Japan, nor even how he was recruited. He is thought to have been an experienced architect of about forty to fifty years of age who was engaged to teach Japanese students the fundamentals of Western art such as geometry, perspective, chiaroscuro, design and other basic requirements.[52]

Fontanesi was not well by the time they arrived in Japan in late August, and although frequently ill during the first six months, managed to perform his duties. He was spurred by the possibilities for shaping a new academy of art and developing the promising potentials of students, some of whom had already received initial training in Western art from Kawakami Togai, Takahashi Yuichi and other early *yoga* painters, and from foreigners such as Guerineau, Charles Wirgman, an English artist resident in Yokohama who was correspondent for the *London Illustrated News*, and Mrs. Raphael Schoyer, an amateur artist who was the wife of an American newspaper editor.[53] Although he had difficulty communicating with his Japanese pupils, they instinctively recognized his talents and were eager to receive his instruction. Even established artists such as Takahashi Yuichi sought him out and tried to benefit by his knowledge.

What also attracted these students, as well as trained artists, was the remarkable selection of books, plaster casts of ancient sculpture, reproductions of masterpieces of European art from antiquity to the present, numerous other teaching aids and hitherto unavailable art supplies such as canvas, paper, brushes, oil pigments, pencils, charcoal, pastels, watercolors, etc., that these teachers brought with them. Fontanesi even published a hitherto unknown work entitled *Elements of Theoretical and Practical Perspective*.[54] Ozaki Takafumi found many of these resources still preserved at the College of

Engineering of Tokyo University. A selection of this material, along with drawings and sketches by the pupils of Fontanesi, Cappelletti and San Giovanni, was exhibited at Tokyo University of Fine Arts in the fall of 1985.[55] It is readily apparent that, in terms of available resources, curriculum requirements, level of instruction, type of assignments and student achievement, the Technical Art School was not inferior to comparable European schools.

Fontanesi was busy that first year getting settled, organizing his classes and instructing "some forty pupils to whom I had to teach geometry, plane and solid, drawing and painting figures and from landscapes! And all of this through an interpreter who knows only a little French and makes me say what I have not said." He further informed his pupil, Carlo Strata, that he scarcely had any time for his own work, nor could he have sold them:

> . . . as it is quite exceptional for the Japanese to buy pictures and such exceptions are very rare. Anyhow the country is very beautiful, life is easy, and one could be quite happy here if one knew the language, which is amazingly difficult, and if one were not obsessed by those artistic aspirations that can only be satisfied in the great art centres, such as Paris. . . . In short, Japan is a very beautiful country, the climate differs little from ours; the habits and customs of the people are, of course, quite different, but they do not strike one too unpleasantly, except the clothing of the very poor, who display rather too much of what our European women perhaps hide too carefully in the streets.[56]

But his health was deteriorating. By mid-year he was confined to bed for some time with a severe case of dropsy. After the rainy season and summer of 1877, the exceedingly humid climate of Tokyo brought on increasingly acute attacks of malaria to which he was prone. He was also disappointed to learn that plans to erect a new building for the art school, which he had planned to help design and to decorate with his pupils, was postponed because of financial burdens arising from the Satsuma Rebellion. He became so ill and dejected that he asked to be released from his contract. Recently discovered records reveal that he wrote to an Italian artist then working in Calcutta, Prospero Ferretti, and offered to pay his passage to Japan if he would agree to fulfill the final year of his contract for him.[57] His acquiescence enabled Fontanesi to resign on September 30, 1878 and to leave Japan some two weeks later for Turin.

Fontanesi resumed his position at the Academy Albertine, comforted to be back among old friends and faithful pupils. During the last four years of his life, he produced some of his most profound paintings which curiously show no trace of Japanese influence, an influence that is, at most, only occasionally discernible in his late drawings. Therefore, what was for Fontanesi but a sad interlude, was for his Japanese students a mighty leap towards mastery of the technical means essential for creative expression.

It is unfortunate that Francesco Paolo Michetti (1851-1929) was unsuccessful in his attempt to succeed Fontanesi because he had a genuine interest in Japan. He is one of the artists cited by Ernest Chesneau in 1878 as having assimilated the art of Japan while maintaining his own individual identity.[58] It is interesting to speculate what effect his appointment might have had upon himself and the pupils of the Technical Art School. Fontanesi's departure had saddled the school with Ferretti, who was so inferior that the students in the painting section asked that he be replaced. When their request went unheeded, many of the ablest withdrew, amongst them Asai Chu, Koyama Shotaro, Matsuoka Hisashi, Nakamura Seijuro, Yamamoto Hosui, Goseda Yoshimatsu, Takahashi Genkichi, Tanaka Miyogi, Hikita Keizo, Morizumi Yugyo and Ichikawa Rikizo.[59] This was a testament to Fontanesi's accomplishments and the determination of these young men to pursue their artistic training as best they could.

It is essential to bear in mind, however, that training painters per se was not the primary goal of the Technical Art School. This is evident from the fact that Cappelletti, although nominally in charge of the school, was transferred to the Architectural Bureau of the Ministry on completion of his three year contract in August 1879, and worked thereafter as an architect. His two principal buildings, completed in 1881, were the General Staff Office and the Army Memorial Hall, a military museum adjacent the Yasukuni Shrine; both were destroyed in the earthquake of 1923.[60] He remained active in Japan as an architect and artist until his departure for America in January 1885. He is reported to have found employment as an architect in the San Francisco area but soon became ill and moved to the Napa valley, where he died, possibly in 1887.

The painting section for the art school limped along under Ferretti until the end of January 1880 when the government hired in his stead Acchile San Giovanni, who is believed to have come from Naples, but whose background and activities are otherwise unknown.[61] San Giovanni taught the remaining students in the painting course according to the program established by Fontanesi and also took over the preparatory courses that had been taught by Cappelletti. As the students in the oil painting class became more proficient, he subdivided them into figure painting and landscape painting. Early in 1881 he invited scholars from Tokyo University to lecture on anatomy and physiology and arranged for his students to observe the human dissections at the Medical Department. He was also very clever at teaching his students how to use more varied and brighter pigments. His own paintings and those of his students were greatly admired when they were exhibited at the Second National Industrial Exposition held in Tokyo in 1881. San Giovanni remained with the school until it was formally closed on January 23, 1883, when diplomas were awarded to the remaining fifteen students. His official duties completed, he evidently returned to Europe where he is known to have exhibited in Paris in 1885 the pictures he had painted in Japan, but no one knows what became of him thereafter. His achievements can best be judged by the work of his many prominent pupils, particularly Soyama Yukihiko, Matsumuro Jugo, Horie Masaaki, Fuji Masazo and Uesugi Kumamatsu.[62]

Of the approximately sixty students (including six women) who entered the art school in the fall of 1876, barely twenty could be persuaded to enroll in the sculpture course, and then only with the assurance of a liberal scholarship. The social background and aspiration of the students did not incline them towards a profession associated with the artisan class. By late Edo, most carvers were craftsmen producing small scale decorative items for private consumption or export trade. Traditional sculptors, employed by temples or shrines to restore existing works or to make new ones, were for the most part so constrained by iconographic requirements and artistic conventions as to leave little scope for creative expression. Furthermore, their livelihood was threatened by Meiji edicts requiring the separation of Buddhism and Shintoism. Unlike Western-style painting, the principles and techniques of Western sculpture were virtually unknown, and career options seemed limited.

Ragusa's contract obligated him to teach his pupils "how to mould and engrave the flowers, plants, animals and human figures used in architecture."[63] Since these students had no prior training in sculpture, they were obliged to take the preparatory courses taught by Cappelletti. Ragusa relied primarily on practice rather than theory, and hence was less impeded by language barriers. Students were first expected to make a careful drawing of a plaster cast in charcoal or pencil, and then to make a three dimensional copy of it in modeling clay, a medium previously unknown in Japan. Ragusa then would point out errors or himself corrected them. In the afternoon, while he was occupied with his own work, the students were expected to attempt new themes based on their observation of live models who were then being employed for the first time. He taught them how to cast their work in plaster and how to make multiple copies of plaster casts. Then they were taught to execute their work in marble. For that purpose, a skilled stone carver by the name of Tommaso Gariardo was engaged in July 1879 to serve as his assistant for one year.[64] Because Ragusa considered anatomy even more essential for sculpture than for painting, a member of the Medical Department of Tokyo University was invited early in 1881 to lecture twice a week on anatomy.

Upon the termination of Ragusa's second three-year contract, the sculpture course was discontinued and on June 28, 1882, the twenty remaining students were awarded first, second and third class diplomas depending upon their period of study and proficiency.[65] His pupils—Okuma Ujihiro, Fujita Bunzo, Kikuchi Chutaro, Sano Akira, Ogura Sojiro, Terauchi Shin'ichiro, Nakamura Keitaro, Kondo Yuichi, Naito Yozo, and Kobayashi Eijiro—laid the foundations of Western sculpture in Japan, but there are as many more whose subsequent careers were varied and difficult to trace. The majority found employment with the government, a fact too often overlooked in biographical accounts of even such well-known figures as Okuma Ujihiro and Sano Akira.

Ragusa produced numerous works of his own while in Japan, some of which remained behind to influence later students. He also became keenly interested in Japanese art and began to collect with a view towards establishing an industrial art school in his native Palermo where he wished to introduce Japanese methods of painting, lacquer, embroidery and other crafts. An attractive young Japanese woman artist, Kiyohara Otama, who modelled for him in 1878, agreed to help him collect suitable samples and to make watercolor reproductions of his principal objects, in return for instruction in Western art.[66] She also accompanied him in 1880 on a study tour of artistic monuments in Hakone, Kyoto and Nara. When Ragusa left Yokohama on August 11, 1882, he was accompanied by Otama, her sister Ochiyo, a skilled embroiderer, and Ochiyo's husband, Kiyohara Einosuke, a lacquer artist.

Back in Palermo, Ragusa found the Italian government reluctant to fund his school and he, therefore, tried to arouse local interest by exhibiting his collection. He managed to establish a private school which subsequently became part of the Higher School of Applied Arts. In 1889 Ochiyo and her husband returned to Japan and Otama, at long last, married Ragusa and assumed the name Eleanora Ragusa.[67] She meanwhile had been diligently studying oil painting and also taught women pupils at the local art school. She exhibited widely in Italy and abroad, including the international expositions held in Chicago in 1893 and in St. Louis in 1904. After Ragusa's death in 1928, she felt isolated until discovered by Kimura Ki, who made her the heroine of a novel.[68] Otama returned to Japan in 1933, and after an absence of half a century, she was a curiosity to her own countrymen. She continued to paint and exhibit until her death in 1939. Although she received many awards and important commissions, she remained a curiously limited artist, whose figure paintings are strangely saccharine, but because of her singular role abroad and current interest in women artists, she has been the subject of numerous exhibitions, publications and a major television program.[69] It is not yet possible to assess Ragusa's efforts to introduce Japanese art to his native Palermo nor to judge the quality of his collection, because a major portion was sold following his death and the remnants, which now repose in the Museo Luigi Pigorini in Rome, have not been opened. Judging by Otama's drawings, he had numerous bronzes of the type that were so appealing to foreigners during the Meiji era. Otama also brought back many of the works that Ragusa had made in Japan which she bequeathed to the School of Fine Arts in Tokyo.[70]

In addition to those who taught at the Technical Art School, the Japanese engaged still another Italian artist, Edoardo Chiossone,[71] who contributed greatly to the development of Japanese art. He preceded the other Italians, having come to Japan in January 1875 to work for the Printing Bureau of the Ministry of Finance and remained until his death in 1898, never once returning to his native land. In length of service, cordiality of relations with his employers and associates, standing within the Italian community, breadth of interests and level of achievement, he is the *yatoi* who comes closest in the field of art to approximating the accomplishments of Conder, but he is more difficult to study because of a significant difference. Whereas Conder openly avowed his marriage to a Japanese, and the identity of his daughter and grandchildren is known, Chiossone took care to conceal his private life. He left a will bequesting his extensive collection of Oriental art to the Accademia ligustica di belle arti of his native Genoa. His executor was a close friend, Luigi Casati, who served as interpreter for the Italian Legation in Tokyo from

1881 to 1906.[72] Casati did such a thorough job of sifting the bequest that virtually nothing of a personal nature can be found at the Edoardo Chiossone Museum of Oriental Art. We likewise do not know what became of his private possessions. Casati may have wished to withhold knowledge of what some scholars believe was Chiossone's marriage to a Japanese.[73] Such marriages were not uncommon in Meiji Japan, but it was all too customary, until recently, to conceal them. Inasmuch as the director of the Chiossone Museum, Giuliano Frabetti, has been unable to trace family heirs or the descendants of former friends in Italy, Chiossone remains a curiously remote figure.

Frabetti has confirmed that Chiossone was born in 1832 at Arenzano, in the environs of Genoa and that his early activity as an engraver has been confused with that of his cousin, Domenico Chiossone, who was also an engraver.[74] He attended a local primary school and from 1847 to 1855 studied engraving under Raffaele Granara at the Accademia Ligustica.[75] He appears to have also spent some time in Florence making engravings of Renaissance paintings by Fra Angelico, Andrea del Sarto and Fra Bartolomeo for a lavishly illustrated book on Italian art.[76] On his return to Genoa, he produced numerous engravings of popular works by contemporary artists.[77] In 1858 he made an engraving of Domenico Induno's painting, *Pane e lacrime*, that he exhibited in Florence in 1861 and at the London Exposition of 1862. He also participated in the Paris Exposition of 1867 and received numerous awards. Having established himself as one of the leading Italian engravers of the works of contemporary artists, he was made a member in 1862 of the Accademici di Merito of the Accademia Ligustica[78] and was commissioned in 1867 to design and engrave a new first class medal for the school.

Chiossone astutely realized that new developments in the field of steel engraving, lithography and photo-engraving could be applied to the production of a superior quality of paper currency. Hence he was appointed to oversee the printing of a new issue of currency that the National Bank of Italy had just ordered from the Dondorf Company in Frankfurt, Germany. The Italian bank subsequently rejected his recommendations and so Chiossone departed for England where he spent some time investigating the newest developments in the field of printing. While working in Frankfort, he had met the Japanese mission that had placed a large currency order with the Dondorf Company in 1870 and again in 1873.[79] A member of the delegation sought him out in London in 1874 and offered him a three-year contract to supervise the production of paper currency for the Printing Bureau of the Ministry of Finance. They also engaged two technicians from the Dondorf Company, Karl Anton Bruck and Bruno Liebers, to assist him. The fact that Chiossone was paid more than twice as much as Fontanesi and the other Italians is further proof that pragmatic goals and not aesthetic considerations were the primary determinant of value.

Tokuno Ryosuke had decided, upon becoming head of the Printing Bureau in 1874, that he would make Japan independent of foreign sources. Thus he was instrumental in engaging Chiossone and did all he could to facilitate his work. Chiossone, in turn, helped Tokuno order new equipment, build a new paper plant, develop the manufacture of inks and other supplies, and train personnel, including numerous artists.[80] Because of the interdependence of the Printing Bureau and private printing companies in early Meiji, Chiossone's influence extended far beyond his official role. Not until the complex developments in the field of printing during early Meiji are more thoroughly integrated with the study of Meiji art as a whole will it be possible to determine the extent of his influence.[81]

During the close to seventeen years that Chiossone spent in the employ of the bureau, he introduced many new printing techniques to produce a succession of licenses, stamps, currency, bank notes, bonds, deeds, official awards and decorations, and all manner of other official papers. He appears to have kept proofs of everything he printed and the museum in Genoa has a complete set.[82] Although the format and technique was Western, he made increasing use of Japanese motifs and in effect created new imagery, as when he depicted the legendary Empress Jingu on the one yen note he designed in 1878.[83]

In the course of formulating such imagery, he became avidly interested in Japanese art and therefore may have been instrumental in encouraging Tokuno to undertake a four-and-a-half month research trip in the spring of 1878 to record, by means of photography and drawing, the major monuments and art objects of earlier periods which were an integral part of the nation's cultural heritage. The 510 photographs and 200 drawings gathered by the group were then reproduced by means of colored lithography and other new processes to produce a series of albums of excellent quality. One album was devoted to the Ise Shrine; another illustrated a selection of rare objects from the Shosoin; numerous other volumes depicted temple treasures that Fenollosa would have us believe the Japanese had ceased to value.[84] Chiossone also produced a superbly illustrated album on *Ancient Japanese Coinage* that may have been prompted by Heinrich von Siebold's interest in this subject.[85] These publications led to the development of techniques that facilitated the production of illustrated art books and journals, such as *Kokka*, that helped to engender a greater appreciation of Japanese art at home and abroad.

Chiossone was also called upon to draw portraits of the Meiji leaders. Working mostly from photographs, he produced, by means of lithography, engraving, mezzotint, and other processes, portraits of such notables as Iwakura Tomomi, Okubo Toshimichi, Kido Koin, Sanjo Sanetami, Saigo Tsugumichi, Saigo Takamori, Oyama Iwao and his wife, the former Yamakawa Sutematsu, as well as the Crown Prince Higashi-no-miya, Prince Arisugawa and Prince Kitashirakawa.[86] In 1888 he had the single honor of being selected to make a mature, seated portrait of the Meiji Emperor which was photographically reproduced for distribution to schools and public offices throughout Japan, as well as a companion portrait of the Empress; he also drew a standing portrait of the Emperor in 1893 which was printed by means of steel-engraving.[87] He also produced engravings of his colleague, Tokuno Ryosuke, and the noted Japanologist, Philipp Franz von Siebold. All these works had a decided

influence on the development of Meiji portraiture.[88] Even after he retired from
the Printing Bureau in 1891, he continued to receive commissions from them,
while at the same time working with private industry, an aspect of his career
that is little known.

Chiossone contributed to the appreciation of Japanese art in Italy by
bequeathing his collection to his native Genoa. After its arrival in 1899,
lengthy negotiation and considerable local funding were required before the
collection could be sorted and displayed in galleries on the ground floor of the
Accademia ligustica. The Museo Chiossone was formally opened to the public
on November 8, 1905, and remained on view until 1940.[89] Jurisdiction then
passed to the city government which stored it during the war. In 1971 the
collection was reorganized and handsomely installed in a new building designed
by Mario Labo set on the slope of a attractive park known as the Villetta di
Negro.[90] It contains some 15,000 objects that span most periods and media,
but the preponderance of works are Japanese and date from late Edo to the time
of his death. Even though it boasts one of the major collections of Japanese art
in Italy, the museum remains relatively unknown because it is off the main
tourist routes and because of limited interest, apart from *ukiyo-e*, in late
Edo and Meiji art. The current shift in taste and the publication of its fine
collection of prints is bound to gain the museum a wider audience.[91] Museo
Chiossone has the further distinction of being the only documented collection
of Japanese art abroad, assembled during the Meiji era, that has been maintained
intact.

Finally, it is important to bear in mind that the Technical Art School was a
pilot program that was duly closed early in 1883, when the last Italian artist
had completed his contract and an adequate number of Japanese had been trained
to meet the needs of the Ministry of Public Works. The ministry likewise
disposed of its other projects prior to its own dissolution in 1886, at which
time the Imperial College of Engineering became part of the College of
Engineering of Tokyo Imperial University. By strict adherence to foreign
tutelage for a relatively short period of time, supplemented by practical
experience working for the ministry and some additional training abroad, these
officials and their *oyatoi* staff had reared, in the course of barely two decades,
a corps of Japanese engineers, architects and artists capable of constructing
a wide range of Western architecture of competitive quality, independent
of reliance on foreign expertise. Having mastered the essentials, they then
were free to produce Western-style architecture with a Japanese accent.
Notwithstanding complaints about the narrow focus of the curriculum,
even those who aspired to be painters, and were drawn to the school only
because it provided access to foreign teachers and vital materials otherwise
unavailable, received invaluable training. Indeed most of the first generation of
Western-style painters also worked for the government in various capacities
because it was difficult, in early Meiji, to sustain a viable career as an
independent *yoga* artist. Ito Hirobumi and his colleagues had certainly achieved
their goal.

III

Most art historians, nonetheless, persist in believing that the Technical Art School was an outgrowth of the indiscriminate Westernization of early Meiji that was fortunately arrested by the timely warnings of Ernest F. Fenollosa and the resurgent nationalism of the 1880s. Despite the publication of new documentation concerning the Technical Art School, these scholars still fail to grasp the ancillary nature of the school, its limited goals and the thrust of government policy. They tend to fault the school for its stress on technical skill at the expense of theoretical and aesthetic principles, and even infer that the officials who organized the school were not cognizant of what constituted "art" in Japan, let alone the West.[92] The diaries of Kido Koin reveal, however, that the role of Meiji "modernizer" did not preclude an appreciation of the traditional arts,[93] and many prominent officials such as Inoue Kaoru and Matsukata Masayoshi are known to have been avid collectors of Japanese art, including Kano school printings. Recent scholarship notwithstanding, scholars[94] still subscribe to the views expressed by Uyeno Naoteru in his pioneering work on Meiji arts and crafts:

> It was to Ernest Fenollosa (1853-1908) that credit must go for the first foreign sparking of a widespread re-interest in the traditional forms of Japanese art. . . . Although the full details of Fenollosa's activities in Japan are difficult to determine, his influence on early Meiji connoisseurship and art appreciation was a decisive one. His lectures— often adaptations of Hegelian theory—threw new light on the nature and importance of Japanese art, and opened Japanese eyes to the necessity of reexamining and revaluing their heritage. Fenollosa, carried away by his enthusiasm, even went so far as to argue the superiority of Japanese painting over Western oil painting, and these arguments, doubtless aimed specifically at the Government-sponsored Art School, were to be instrumental . . . in its abolishment.[95]

Ernest F. Fenollosa is one of five *oyatoi* singled out for special commendation in Japanese elementary school texts and hence his name is familiar to most Japanese.[96] It is not surprising, therefore, that the literature on Fenollosa exceeds that of all other *oyatoi* in the field of art.[97] Unlike those heretofore discussed in this chapter, Fenollosa came to Japan in 1878 to teach philosophy and political economy at Tokyo University. His art activities prior to 1886 were essentially of a private nature, roughly comparable to that of Edward Sylvester Morse, Sir Rutherford Alcock, Dr. William Anderson and Dr. Erwin Baelz.[98] From 1886 to 1890, he was "engaged by the Department of Education to participate in their works relating to Fine Arts," and to perform the same services for the Department of the Imperial Household.[99] In this capacity, he can be likened to Gottfried Wagener, Alexander and Heinrich von Siebold, Leon Dury, Capt. Frank Brinkley and Charles Lanman, who also served as art advisors for periods of varying duration.[100] It seems appropriate, therefore, to reserve consideration of Fenollosa for a subsequent article on these other important contributors to the development and appreciation of Japanese art, but his putative role in bringing about the foreclosure of the Technical Art School and the denigration of yoga merit brief attention.

The Italian *yatoi* on limited contracts and life-time residents like Conder and Chiossone, confident of official and private commissions, were content to impart their practical and technical skills. Even Conder's writings were meant to acquaint a Western audience with those aspects of Japanese art that fell within his expertise or interests. The successive renewal of Fenollosa's contract with the University of Tokyo, on the other hand, grew increasingly precarious as foreign members of the Department of Literature were replaced by Japanese returning from study abroad. Fenollosa had no prior employment in the United States and no certain profession to which he could return, since he had obtained no advanced degree in philosophy before abandoning that field, had only limited training and skill as an artist, no known instruction in art history and, in the early 1880s, no acquaintance with the masterpieces of Western art in European collections. Desirous of remaining in Japan and needing therefore, to establish his credentials as an art expert and to facilitate his activities as a art collector and advisor as such to resident and visiting Americans, Fenollosa grasped and indeed promoted every opportunity to air his often controversial views on Western, Chinese and Japanese art to audiences consisting largely of government bureaucrats and in the case of Kanga-kai, an art organization that he helped to found, disaffected artists seeking some measure of recognition and assistance. To what extent his views concurred or were altered to conform to those of the faction in the Ministry of Education headed by Kuki Ryuichi,[101] with which he aligned himself, bears investigation, but his bread with Takehashi Yuichi and his reevaluation of ukiyo-e suggests that he was not immune to such influence.

The famous speech that Fenollosa delivered in 1882, later published under the title *Bijutsu shinsetsu,* as well as Okakura Kakuzo's differences with Koyama Shotaro over the merits of calligraphy, were salvos in a behind the scenes struggle waged by Kuki, who was then Vice Minister of Education, and his cohorts to postpone the establishment of a permanent art school offering training in both Japanese and Western style art to replace the Technical Art School because they feared it would be dominated by the proponents of Western art. In 1889 they finally succeeded in establishing a school devoted exclusively to the traditional arts. The Tokyo Art School was supposedly the embodiment of Fenollosa's ideals and dictums and he expected to play a dominant role, along with Okakura, in its management and that of the National Museum, only to find the following year that the Ministry of Education would not renew his contract, thereby prompting his return to the United States.

His further failure to grasp the objectives of the Meiji government is best conveyed by a letter from Ito Hirobumi, dated September 15, 1886, tactfully informing Fenollosa that, contrary to his recommendations, the purpose of the exhibition planned for 1890 is industrial, intended to stimulate native industries, "art per se being a mere adjunct" and that the establishment of a museum must await improved economic conditions.[102] Clearly it was not aesthetic principles, artistic preferences, or even the relative merits of the traditional arts as compared to Western art, but the thrust of government policy and the political prowess of the protagonists that shaped the institutional development of Japanese art during the Meiji era and this was bound to influence the *course*, if not the actual *character* of modern Japanese art. Only by disregarding officials such as Kuki, Machida Hisanari, Yamataka Nobuakira, Sano Tsunetami, Kawase Shuji, Makimura Masanao, Nakazawa Iwata, and numerous others who determined policy, authorized and funded institutions, awarded grants for study abroad, managed domestic and international expositions, dominated art organizations and controlled juries, can scholars maintain that ardent romantics such as Fenollosa and Okakura played the decisive roles attributed to them.

IV

There is a political dimension as well to the literature on these *oyatoi* that should not be overlooked even if it can only be briefly alluded to in this study. After the departure of the Italian artists and the demise of Chiossone, they were, except for the occasional recollections of former pupils, virtually forgotten, until Kimura Ki encountered Kiyohara Tama and began in 1930 publishing articles on her and Ragusa. Kiyohara's return to Japan in 1933 stimulated further interest in these artists of a bygone era. The appointment that same year of Giacinto Auriti, who served until 1940 as Italian Ambassador to Japan, fostered closer cultural relations between the two countries. Auriti's friendship with Yashiro Yukio,[103] who had spent many years studying Renaissance art in Italy and had published a book on Botticelli, greatly facilitated Auriti's study of Japanese art and his ability to form a collection, principally of bronzes that he later bequeathed to the Museo Nazionale d'Arte Orientale in Rome.[104] By 1937, Auriti had begun to publish articles on Japanese art and later wrote a comprehensive history of Japanese art.[105] But it was against the background of Japanese efforts in 1938-1939 to strengthen relations with Germany and Italy that culminated in the Tripartite Pact, signed in September 1940, that Muto's article on Italo-Japanese cultural relations first appeared.[106] Kumamoto Kenjiro, who had been assigned to study *yoga* when he entered the Art Research Institute in 1932 immediately following his graduation from Tokyo University, may have been officially encouraged to pursue his pioneer study of the Italian *oyatoi*, which he first published in the institute's official organ, *Bijutsu kenkyu*, a journal that usually did not evince much interest in Meiji art, particularly *yoga*. Kumamoto clearly had access to relevant Italian sources that may have been provided by the Italian Embassy or the Istituto Italo-Giapponese in Tokyo which awarded him in 1939 the Leonardo da Vinci Prize for these articles that they published in book form in December 1940.[107] Kumamoto continued to reprint these seminal articles, with but minor modifications, in his subsequent publications and they constitute five of the six chapters of his posthumous volume on *Art* in the *Oyatoi gaikokujin* series. In the aftermath of World War II, neither country had the means to encourage further study and Kumamoto was never able to research the subject in Italy. Apart from Iseki Masaaki,[108] a Japanese diplomat long resident in Italy, these *oyatoi* received little scholarly study, partly because Kumamoto dominated the field but also because Meiji period *yoga* held little interest for foreign scholars in the post-war period. It is in large measure due to the exhibitions mounted by the Italian Cultural Center in Tokyo, at the instigation of Lia Beretta, that renewed interest in these figures has begun to emerge and the important research undertaken in recent years by the Meiji Art Society helps to place these figures in a wider and more meaningful context.

The sole remaining chapter in Kumamoto's book on the *oyatoi* in the field of art is devoted to Ernest F. Fenollosa. He concludes with the observation that "As Alexander the Great bridged the East and the West, and as Columbus discovered America, so was Fenollosa a bridge for cultural interchange between East and West and the prophet of a new era."[109] It comes as no surprise that the first major study of Fenollosa likewise appeared in *Bijutsu kenkyu* in the spring of 1941,[110] when Japan's militarists were reprinting Okakura's propitious view that "Asia is One," and that "Japan is the real repository of the truest of Asiatic thought and culture."[111] It was written by Odakane Taro, who was assigned to study *nihonga* at the Art Research Institute directly upon graduating from Tokyo University in 1933. His article provided the basic delineation that subsequent authors have sought to elaborate. On the other hand, Conder's signal contributions to the development of modern Japanese architecture could expect no plaudits from a militarist government bent on extolling nationalistic tendencies. Only by putting aside the tangled threads of nationalism, chauvinism, escapism, exoticism and ethnocentricity that has colored the literature on these men can we arrive at a truer understanding of these *oyatoi* and a juster evaluation of their relative contribution to the development of modern Japanese art.

Notes

[1] Engelbert Kaempfer's collection was purchased by the British Museum in 1753; Karl Peter Thunberg's collection is now in the Etnografiska Museet in Stockholm; Isaac Titsingh's material, following his death in 1812, was auctioned in Paris in 1812, 1814, 1820, and 1840; the extensive holdings of J. F. van Overmeer Fisscher and Phillipp Franz von Siebold were eventually acquired by the Ethnological Museum in Leiden. Their activities are ably surveyed by Donald Keene, *The Japanese Discovery of Europe, 1720-1830*, revised edition (Stanford, 1969). See also Friedrich von Wenckstern, *A Bibliography of the Japanese Empire* (Leiden, 1895).

[2] Matthew Calbraith Perry, *Narrative of the Expedition of an American Squadron to the China Seas and Japan, performed in the years 1852, 1853, and 1854, under the command of Commodore M. C. Perry, United States Navy, by*

order of the Government of the United States (Washington, 1856); Kinahan Cornwallis, *Two Journeys to Japan*, 1856-7 (London, 1859); Baron Charles de Chassiron, *Notes sur le Japon, la Chine, et l'Inde. 1859-1859-1860* (Paris, 1861); Robert Fortune, *Yedo and Peking, A Narrative of a Journey to the Capitals of Japan and China* (London, 1863). More extensive coverage, based upon actual residence, is provided by Sir Rutherford Alcock, *The Capital of the Tycoon: A Narrative of a Three Years' Residence in Japan* (London, 1863) and Aimé Humbert, *Le Japon illustre* (Paris, 1870). For additional sources, see John Ashmead Jr., "The Idea of Japan 1853-1895: Japan as Described by American and Other Travellers from the West" (unpublished Ph. D. dissertation, Harvard University, 1951) and Toshio Yokoyama, *Japan in the Victorian Mind* (London, 1987).

[3]Fujioka Sakutaro, *Kinsei kaiga shi* [A History of Modern Painting], (Tokyo, 1903).

[4]Hazel J. Jones, *Live Machines: Hired Foreigners and Meiji Japan* (Vancouver, 1980); Umetani Noboru, *Oyatoi gaikokujin, I Gaisetsu* [Foreign Employees, 1. General Introduction] (Tokyo, 1968); Ishizuki Minoru, *Kindai Nihon no kaigai ryugaku shi* [A History of Modern Japan's Overseas Students] (Kyoto, 1972).

[5]John M. Rosenfield, "Western Style Painting in the Early Meiji Period and Its Critics, " Edited by Donald H. Shively, *Tradition and Modernization in Japanese Culture* (Princeton, 1971), pp. 184-201.

[6]Yamagata Hiroshi, ed., *Nihon bijutsu kyoiku shi* [History of Japanese Art Education] (Tokyo, 1967), pp. 20-59.

[7]Yunesuko Higashi Ajia Bunka Kenkyu Senta, *Shiryo oyatoi gaikokujin* [Documents Concerning Foreign Employees] (Tokyo, 1975), p. 272, (hereafter *Shiryo*). He does not appear in Takeuchi Hiroshi, *Rainichi seiyo jinmei jiten* [Biographical Dictionary of Western Visitors to Japan] (Tokyo, 1983), (hereafter *Rainichi*), a convenient source of biographical and bibliographical information about foreigners who visited or worked in Japan, nor do many other early architects. There is only brief reference to him in Kumamoto Kenjiro, *Kindai Nihon bijutsu no kenkyu* [Studies of Modern Japanese Art], (Tokyo, 1961), pp. 24, 52, 204-205 (hereafter *KNBK*) and his *Oyatoi gaikokujin, 16. Bijutsu* [Foreign Employees, 16 Art], (Tokyo, 1976), pp. 3-4 (hereafter *Oyatoi, 16*).

[8]p. 420. Qualifications for and distinctions between builder, engineer and architect were not precisely defined and it was common for an individual to function in various capacities. Another important feature noted by Richard Henry Brunton, "The Japan Lights," *Minutes of Proceedings of the Institute of Civil Engineers, 47*, Part 1 (Sessions 1876-1877), pp. 19-20, is that the Japanese staff were supervised by commissioners who "are supposed to work in concert with the chief Europeans in office but are actually vested with supreme control and the Europeans have little or no authority. . . . The Europeans are specially directed to be attentive instructing . . . and rewards are held out to those who succeed in training the most efficient men."

[9]*Shiryo*: p. 272.

[10]*Rainichi*, p. 276; *Shiryo*, p. 348.

[11]Yoshida Mitsukuni, *Oyatoi gaikokujin, II Sangyo* [Foreign Employees, 2 Industry], (Tokyo, 1968), pp. 60, 64.

[12]*Shiryo*, p. 337; Muramatsu Teijiro, *Oyatoi gaikokujin, 15 Kenchiku, doboku* (Foreign Employees, 15 Architecture and Engineering) (Tokyo, 1976), pp. 21-24, 31, 34. Although invariably identified as French, Prof. Toshio Watanabe, Chelsea Art School, London, informs me that de Boinville is Scottish, and this, in turn, may lead to more ample identification..

[13]See Muramatsu Teijiro, *Nihon kindai kenchiku no rekishi* [History of Modern Japanese Architecture] (Tokyo, 1977), Koshino Takeshi, *Kaika no katachi* (Nihon no kenchiku: Meiji, Taisho, Showa) (Forms of Enlightenment, Japanese Architecture: Meiji, Taisho Showa Eras) 1 (Tokyo 1979), and other sources provide little information concerning these early foreign architects..

[14]Henry Dyer, *Dai Nippon: The Britain of the East, A Study in National Evolution* (London, 1904), pp. 1-13. For Japanese records concerning the school, see Kyu Kobu Daigakko Shiryo Hensankai, *Kyu kobu daigakko shiryo* [Documents of the Former Imperial College of Engineering] (Tokyo, 1931); Kita Masami, *Kokusai Nihon o hiraita hitobito* (Tokyo, 1984), pp. 93-172.

[15]*Rainichi*, p. 151. For official British account, see "Obituary, Josiah Conder ," *Journal of Royal Institute of British Architects* 27, 3rd series (1920), p. 459 (hereafter R.I.B.A.) and Walter Millard, "The Late Dr. Conder," *ibid*. p. 474. Japanese colleagues issued Condoru Hakase Kinen Hyoshokai, *Conderu hakase isakushu* [Collection of the Posthumous Works of Dr. Conder] (Tokyo, 1931). For additional information, see Onogi Shigekatsu, *Yoshiki no ishizue* [Foundations of Western Style] (Tokyo 1979), pp. 94-166, and Kato Yoshi-yuki, editor, *Josaia Kondoru kenchiku zumen shu* [Collection of the Architectural Plans of Josiah Conder] I (Tokyo, 1981), pp. 6-12. Muramatsu, *Oyatoi gaikokujin, 15 Kenchiku, doboku*, pp. 24-50, discusses his role as an *yatoi*.

[16]J. Mordaunt Crook, *William Burges and the High Victorian Dream* (London, 1981), pp. 80-82. This book also provides much valuable background material. Elizabeth Aslin, "E. W. Godwin and the Japanese Taste," *Apollo* 76, 10, n.s. (December, 1962), pp. 781, was the first to note that Burges, in the 1850s, was one of the pioneer collectors of Japanese prints in England.

[17]See Kawahigashi, *Josaia Kondoru kenchiku zumen shu*, 3 volumes, see also series of detailed articles by Onogi Shigekatsu, "Keikaku no keii to sekkei an: Konderu no ekkenjo keikaku, I" [Design and Details of the Plan: Palace Plans of Conder, I], " *Nihon Kenchiku Gakkai ronbun hokokushu*, 166 (December, 1969), pp. 75-82; 170 (April, 1970), pp. 99-106; 172 (June, 1970), pp. 59-65; "Ueno hakubutsukan no sekkei oyobi kensetsu jijo: Kondoru sekkei Ueno Hakubutsukan ni kansuru kosatsu, 1 [Plans for the Ueno Museum and Building Circumstances: Consideration of Conder's Design of the Ueno Museum]," *ibid*, 179 (January, 1971), pp. 87-94; 181 (March, 1971), pp. 67-73; 184 (April, 1971), pp. 113-120; 185 (May, 1971), pp. 79-85.

[18]*Ibid*., 166, pp. 77-78.

[19]A representative selection of such works are illustrated in *Konderu hakase isakushu*.

[20]Josiah Conder, *Paintings and Studies by Kawanabe Gyosai* (Tokyo, 1911).

[21]For want of a convenient source, the following publications of Josiah Conder are listed: "Notes on Japanese Architecture," *Sessional Papers of the R.I.B.A.* [Royal Institute of British Architecture] (1877-1878), pp. 179-192, 209-212; "Theaters in Japan," *The Builder* 37 (1879), pp. 368-376; "Letter to Editor: Japanese Pagodas and their Construction," *Building News* (April 20, 1883), p. 529; "Further Notes on Japanese Architecture," *Journal of Proceedings of R.I.B.A.* 2, n.s. (1886), pp. 249-256; "Domestic Architecture in Japan," *ibid.* 3, n.s. (1887), pp. 103-127;"An Architect's Notes on the Great Earthquake of October 1891," *Seismological Journal of Japan,* 2 (1893), pp. 1-92; "The Condition of Architecture in Japan," *Proceedings of the Twenty-seventh Annual Convention of the American Institute of Architects held at Chicago, July 31-August 1, 1893,* edited by Alfred Stone (Chicago, 1893), pp. 365-381; "The History of Japanese Costume, I. Court Dress," *Transactions of the Asiatic Society of Japan,* 8 (1880), pp. 333-368; "The History of Japanese Costume, 2. Armour," *ibid,* 9, pt. 3 (1881), pp. 254-280; *The Flowers of Japan and the Art of Floral Arrangement* (Tokyo, 1891); "The Art of Landscape Gardening in Japan," *Transactions of the Asiatic Society of Japan,* 14, pt. 2 (1886), pp. 119-175; and *Landscape Gardening in Japan* (Tokyo, 1893).

[22]Crooks, *William Burges,* pp. 48, 82, 209, 241-2, pl.; William Burges, "Proposed School of Art at Bombay, " *Sessions of the R.I.B.A.* (1867-1868), pp. 83-85. Although this project was never realized, the pupil that Burges sent to India in 1866 to implement it, Sir William Emerson (1843-1925), became, in effect, architect to the Raj. He translated Burgesian Gothic into Indian and created Anglo-Indian Gothic. His work was purely eclectic and some of it looked, in the opinion of one writer, as if it had walked out of the pages of Voillet le Duc. Conder maintained close relations with Burges and his pupils and would certainly have been familiar with Emerson's work in India.

[23]Roger Smith, "On Building for European Occupation in Tropical Climates, Especially India," *ibid.,* pp. 197-208. He concludes, on p. 208, that an architect should produce "not merely a work of skill, but also a work of art....that the solution lies first in the adoption of a type essentially European; and, secondly, in the retention, and blending with it of such admissible features as are to be found in the best styles of architecture that have been elaborated already in tropical climates;" and that these are to be found in the most perfect manner in "the best of the Mahommedan buildings, which mark, as I should like ours to do, the residence in India of a conquering race—a race, alas, far more artistic than we, and whose works are nobler monuments of art, than it can be hoped ours may be."

[24]Fascination with the Rokumeikan, which has figured prominently in literature, prints and film, does not seem to have extended to Conder. He is not even mentioned in a popular book about the foreigners in Japan in early Meiji by Pat Barr, whose title, *The Deer Cry Pavilion* (New York, 1969), is the English translation of *Rokumeikan.*

[25]p. 367.

[26]"The Search for 'Japanesese Architecture' in Modern Ages," *The Japan Foundation Newsletter,* 15, (December, 1987), p. 4, but I question whether there had ever been "total adulation of the West."

[27]*Ibid.,* p. 2.

[28]Ralph Adams Cram, *Impressions of Japanese Architecture and the Allied Arts* (Boston, 1930), pp. 19-21, pl. LIII; see also his, *My Life in Architecture* (Boston, 1936), pp. 98-100. Robert Muccigrosso, *American Gothic: The Mind and Art of Ralph Adams Cram* (Washington, D.C., 1979), pp. 79-80, correctly notes that Cram was encouraged to undertake this project by the Reverend Arthur May Knapp, whom he identifies as "a Unitarian minister living in Japan and father of one of Cram's friends." Knapp returned to Japan in a private capacity in 1897 and his ensuing relationship with Kaneko, for whom he was instrumental in obtaining an honorary degree from Harvard University, has still to be explored.

[29]Laurence P. Roberts, *A Dictionary of Japanese Artists* (Tokyo, 1976), p. 149.

[30]*Ibid.,* p. 149.

[31]David Newman, a London art dealer, is working on a biographical study of Conder.

[32]Although Kobusho, Kobu Daigakko and Kobu bijutsu Gakko all employ the same characters for kobu, *The Japan Directory* (1879), pp. 78-79, following official usage, translates them respectively as Ministry of Public Works, Imperial College of Engineering and School of Fine Arts. Since this is not sufficient to distinguish the last mentioned from the School of Fine Arts, founded in Tokyo in 1889, it seems preferable to use the term Technical art School adopted by Takashina Shuji, "Eastern and Western Dynamics in the Development of Western-style Oil Painting during the Meiji Era," Washington University Gallery of Art, *Paris in Japan: The Japanese Encounter with European Painting* (St. Louis, October 2-November 22, 1987), p. 22. However his rendering of the first two terms as Ministry of Industry and Technology and Imperial College of Technology seems arbitrary and ultimately confusing to those who have frequent recourse to Meiji era Western language publications.

[33]Henry Dyer, *Dai Nippon,* p. 207, betrays how unaware he was of what went on beyond his narrow sphere and how dependent he was in writing his book on material subsequently furnished him by the Japanese when he states that: The Italians thought that their special sphere was that of art, and they were anxious that there should be a School of Art in which they could impart the methods and ideals of European art. To please them the Government established such a school, which was, for convenience, connected with the Engineering College.

It is worth noting that the members of the Iwakura Mission had independently observed that: Although the fashions of France were the shining example for all of Europe, England was the first to break away and create out of its traditions the crafts and customs appropriate to itself. England had gradually stimulated other nations to produce what they can do best. At present, the crafts of Europe vie in beauty with each other. . . . These were our thoughts after seeing the Kensington Exposition. Those who read this record should reflect upon the lesson to be drawn for Japan . . . cited by Marlene J. Mayo, "Rationality in the Restoration," in *Modern Japanese Leadership: Transition and Change*. Edited by Bernard S. Silberman and Harry D. Harootunian (Tuscon, 1966), pp. 357-358. Also see Note 77.

[34]Marcello Mucciolo, "Japanese Studies in Italy," *East and West*, 2 (April, 1951), pp. 9-10; Adolfo Tamburello, "Japanese Studies in Italy," *The Japan Foundation Newsletter*, 4, 4 (October, 1976), pp. 3-4.

[35]G. A. Baffo, *Dell' arte di allevare i bachi da seta del Giappone* (Venezia, 1865). See also Ellen P. Conant, "The French Connection: Emile Guimet's Mission to Japan," *Japan in Transition: Thought and Action in the Meiji Era, 1868-1911*. Edited by Hilary Conroy, et al.(Rutherford, N. J., 1984), pp. 114-117.

[36]Yoshiura Morizumi, *Nichi-I bunka shiko* [Thoughts on Japanese-Italian Cultural History], (Tokyo, 1968) pp. 145-156.

[37]Iseki Masaaki, *Gaka Fontaneji* [Painter Fontanesi], (Tokyo, 1984), is a major monograph with extensive bibliography; see also *Rainichi*, pp. 330-331. Apart from Koyama Shotaro, "Fontaneji," *Bijutsu seiron* 1, 1 (January, 1912), the first evidence of renewed interest in these Italian *oyatoi* is Muto Tomoo, "Wagakuni no bunka to Itaria no kyoryoku [The Cooperation of Italian and Our Culture]," *Chuo koron* 53, 5 (May, 1938) (hereafter *Wagakuni*), followed by the pioneer work of Kumamoto Kenjiro, "Antonio Fontaneji ni tsuite [Concerning Antonio Fontanesi]," *Bijutsu kenkyu*, 94 (October, 1939), pp. 3-53, which also appeared in his *Meiji shoki raicho Itaria bijutsuka no kenkyu* [Studies on Italian Artists in Early Meiji Japan], (Tokyo, 1940), pp. 5-51, 143-155, and 1-41 (hereafter *Meiji shoki*); *KNBK*, 121-141, pls. 104-120, and *Oyatoi*, 16, pp. 43-77.

[38]Giulio Bolaffi ed., *Dizionario enciclopedico Bolaffi dei pittori e degli incisori italiani*, 7 (Torino, 1975), pp. 401.

[39]Alfred Schreiber-Favre, *Francois Diday 1802-1877, Fondateur de l'Ecole Suisse de Paysage* (Geneve, 1942) p. 39 and his *Alexandre Calame: Peintre paysagiste, graveur et lithographe* (Geneve, 1934) p. 31, lists Fontanesi as one of the many pupils of Calame. See also his *La lithographie artistique en Suisse au XIXe siecle: Alexandre Calame, La paysage* (Neuchatel, 1966). Florens Deuchler, Marcel Roethlisberger, Hans Luthy, *Swiss Painting* (Geneva, 1976), pp. 141, 152-3, and 160 furnishes a more recent appraisal of their role in the development of Swiss painting.

[40]Antonio Fontanesi, *Beaulieu-Villa Eynard, au bord du lac de Geneve* (Geneve, 1854) and his *Promenades pittoresques a l'interieur de Geneve* (Geneve, 1854), each consisting of twenty lithographs, were published by Pilet et Cougnard. Some of these prints were included in the exhibition of the graphic works of Fontanesi organized by the Istituto Italiano di Cultura in Tokyo, see Itaria Bunka Kaikan, *Antonio Fontaneji hanga ten* [L'opera grafica di Antonio Fontanese], (Tokyo, 6 ott.-27 nov., 1977), Nos. 12-43. This was held in conjunction with another exhibition, Kokuritsu Kindai Bijutsukan, *Fontaneji, Raguza to Meiji zenki no bijutsu* [Fontanesi, Ragusa e

l'arte giapponese nel primo periodo Meiji] (Tokyo, October 10-November 27, 1977).

[41]Monique Faux, *August Ravier 1814-1895,* Musee de Reims (Reims, 17 October-13 December 1964).

[42]Annie Paule Quinsac, *Ottocento Painting.* Columbia (S. C.) Museum of Art (Columbia, 1972), p. 72. Scholars have begun to explore the influence of Japanese art on the Macchiaioli. See Nancy Gray Troyer, "Telemaco Signorini and Macchiaioli *Giapponismo:* A Report on Research in Progress, " *The Art Bulletin,* 66, 1 (March 1984), pp. 136-145.

[43]*Antonio Fontaneji hanga ten,* Nos. 100-109.

[44]Marco Valsecchi, *Landscape Painting of the Nineteenth Century* (Greenwich, 1969), p. 344. This book is particularly pertinent because it places these Italian artists in a wider context.

[45]Quinsac, *Ottocento Painting,* p. 72.

[46]*Ibid.,* p. 13.

[47]*Ibid.,* p. 73.

[48]Valsecchi, *Landscape Painting,* p. 344.

[49]Gianfranco Bruno, *La pittura in Liguria dal 1850 divisionismo* (Genova, 1982): p. 39. See also Mario Monteverdi, *Storia della pittura italiana dell'Ottocento* (2nd ed.) 2 volumes (Busto Arsizio, 1983) for an account of Fontanesi's wider influence.

[50]Marziano Bernardi, "Antonio Fontanesi in Japan," *East and West* 4 (July 1953), p. 110.

[51]*Rainichi,* pp. 472-473. Information concerning Ragusa first appeared in Japanese articles on Kiyohara Otama, cf. Note 62. The first article to feature Ragusa was Muto, *Wagakuni,* followed soon thereafter by Kumamoto Kenjiro, "Binchenzo Raguza no kaiko [Vincenzo Ragusa Retrospective], *Kaizo* 21, 5 (May 1939), which then appeared in *Meiji shoki raicho,* pp. 75-103, pls. 46-71; *KNBK,* pp. 105-120, pls. 83-103, and *Oyatoi* 16, pp. 102-129. See also Mario Oliveri, *Un Artefice del Marmo* (Palermo, 1929).

[52]*Rainichi,* o. 79; *Shiryo,* p. 246. Apart from Goseda Horyu, "Kaperetchi sonota [Cappelletti and Others]," *Junsei bijutsu* (August, 1921), he is first featured in Muto, *Wagakunii;* Kumamoto's initial article, "Kapperuretti oyobi San Jovanni ni tsuite [Concerning Cappelletti and San Giovanni]," *Bijutsu kenkyu,* 8, 12 (December, 1939), was included in *Meiji shoki* pp. 65-74, pls. 43-45; *KNBK,* pp. 142-147, pls 123-126; *Oyatoi,* 16, pp. 94-99.

[53]As is apparent from *Rainichi,* pp. 523-524, there is as yet no major study, in Japanese or Western languages, on Wirgman, whose name appears frequently in accounts of the development of Western style painting in Japan. His depiction of Japanese events for the *Illustrated London News,* his role as editor of *Japan Punch* and his partnership with Felix Beato in a commercial photographic establishment in Yokohama helped shape the image of Japan, not only of foreign residents, but of a much wider Western audience. None of the brief accounts of the American business man, Raphael Schoyer (1800-1865), who came to Japan in 1859 and founded a commercial newspaper, *Japan*

Express, in 1862, contain any information concerning the background and training of his wife or what became of her after his sudden death and interment in the Foreign Cemetery in Yokohama.

[54]The author is indebted to Ozaki Takafumi for information concerning this book, which was printed by G. Bruno of Turin in May 1876 with English and French text on facing pages. It bears the following dedication:

To his Excellency, the Minister of the Public Works in Tokio:
Excellency,
 I take the liberty to offer and dedicate you this little book, which has been written for the only purpose to facilitate to the young students who are to be my pupils the conscientious study of Perspective. I have not had the ambition to publish some theorems of my own invention; but I have had in view to render myself useful to the School that will be confided to my care, by uniting some theoretical and practical lessons of my former studies for, the long experience that I have acquired, has always shown me that theory alone, or practice alone, are either too much or too little for those who are in want of clear, sure and right notions of that science which Leonardo do Vinci has called the logic of painting.
 If I could hope to attain, by this book, the end that I have proposed to myself, I should be most happy, and should be more so, because my efforts could deserve your approval.
 Of your Excellency,

Most Obedient Servant
A. Fontanesi

[55]Ozaki Takafumi, "Kobu Bijutsu Gakko shi kohon [Manuscript History of the Technical Art School], an unpublished paper presented at the symposium *Continuity and Change in Modern Japanese Art*, held at Dunwalke, Princeton University, April 5-8, 1987; Tokyo Geijutsu Daigaku Geijutsu Shriyokan, *Kobu Bijutsu Gakko seito shuga sakuhin ten* [Exhibition of Exercise Drawings by Students of the Technical Art School] (November 18-December 24, 1985).

[56]Bernardi, "Antonio Fontanesi in Japan," p. 112.

[57]Records of Ferretti's suit to recover travel costs from Fontanesi, recently discovered in the archives of the Istituto Italiano de Cultura in Tokyo, provide the first information that Ferretti had come from Calcutta at Fontanesi's instigation. The author is indebted to the assistant director, Lia Beretta, for bringing this material to her attention. See also *Shiryo*, p. 370.

[58]Ernest Chesneau, "Le Japon a Paris," *Gazette des beaux-arts*, 18 (1878): p. 396. For biographical information, see Giulio Bolaffi ed., *Catalogo Bolaffi della pittura italiana dell'800* (Torino, 1974), pp. 264-266.

[59]See *NKBK*, passim, for information concerning these eleven artists and the organization known as Juichikai which they established.

[60]*Ibid.*, pp. 145-147, pls. 125-126.

[61]*Rainichi*, pp. 161-162; see Note 52 for list of articles by Kumamoto. Beppu Kan'ichiro, an aged Japanese artist long resident in Venice, maintains

that San Giovanni came from Naples and his descendants still reside there. Ozaki, *Kobu Bijutsu Gakko*, n.p., has found evidence that another Italian named Guiseppe Perorio (sp.?) arrived a week after San Giovanni and taught the preparatory course from February 19 - July 31, 1880.

[62]For a complete list of his pupils, see *ibid.*, n.p.; *Meiji shoki* pp. 69-73; *KNBK*; and Roberts, *A Dictionary of Japanese Artists*, provide some biographical data.

[63]*Meiji shoki*, p. 81.

[64]It has not been possible to obtain any information concerning Gariardo.

[65]*Ibid.*, pp. 83-85.

[66]These drawings, now kept in the Archives Division, Tokyo University of Fine Arts, are reproduced in Marunouchi Garo, *Ragusa Otama ten* [Exhibition of Ragusa Otama], (Tokyo, May 10-28, 1983), figs. 1-22, and Odakyu Shinjuku ten, *Tama Eleanora Ragusa* (Tokyo, October 4-November 3, 1986), pls. 1-11.

[67]This signature appears prominently in two portraits of Ragusa that she painted in 1920, see *ibid.*, pls. 40-41.

[68]Kimura wrote an article, "Shoki Meiji yoga shi kara mita Ragusa Otama fujin [History of Early Meiji Western-style Painting as Viewed by Ragusa Otama]," Kaizo 15, 12 (December, 1930) prior to publishing his book, *Ragusa Otama* (Tokyo, 1931); he also edited *Ragusa Otama jijoden* [The Autobiography of Ragusa Otama], (Tokyo, 1980). For additional sources, see *Tama Eleanora Ragusa*, pp. 132-133.

[69]*Ibid.*, pls. 33-38, 47-48; for recent exhibitions, see Note 65; and Kaji Etsuko, *Ragusa Tama, joryu yogaka dai ichigo no shogai* [Ragusa Tama, The Career of the Leading Female Western-style Painter], (Tokyo, 1984), which was published by NHK.

[70]*Meiji shoki*, pl. 67.

[71]Giuliano Frabetti, "Edoardo Chiossone," *Dizionario biographico degli Italiani* 25 (Roma, 1981), pp. 25-28; see also *Rainichi*, pp. 97-98; *Shiryo*, p. 253. These sources fail to include an article by Iseki Masaaki, "Edoardo Chiossone—His Achievements and Doings in Japan," *Annuario dell'Istituto Giapponese di Cultura di Roma* 1 (1963-1964), pp. 199-209.

[72]Casati first appears in the *Japan Directory* (Yokohama, 1881), p. 2. According to information furnished by Lia Beretta, he was born at Torre Ratti, a village near Novi Ligure in the province of Alessandria, approximately 25 miles north of Genoa, on September 29, 1850 and died in Seoul on December 11, 1909. He apparently was absent during 1894-1895, returned to Tokyo in 1896, and remained in the same post until 1906, see *Japan Directory* (Yokohama, 1906), p. 676.

[73]Yoshida, *Oyatoi gaikokujin, II, Sangyo* p. 177. Yoshida recently informed the author that he obtained this information from Kumamoto Kenjiro.

[74]Thieme-Becker, *Allgemeines Lexikon der Bildenden Kunstler*, 6 (Leipzig, 1912), pp. 511-512; Luigi Servolini, *Dizionario illustrato degli incisori italiani moderni e contemporanei* (Milano, 1955), p. 198.

[75]Thieme-Becker, 14, p. 502; *Dizionario enciclopedico Bolaffi* 6 (Torino, 1974), pp. 137-138. Granara was noted for his engravings of the paintings of Raphael and other Renaissance masters. For further information about Chiossone and the course in engraving, see A. Merli, *Delle arti del disegno e dei principali artisti in Liguria* (Genova, 1862), pp. 43-46, and his *Appendice al sunto storico della arti del disegno e dei principali artisti in Liguria* (Genova, 1866), pp. 84-90.

[76]Domenico e David Chiossone, *Italia artistica o galleria di capolavori italiana, designati ed incisi dai quadrei originali esistenti nelle varie citta della pensiola publicata fer cura dell'artista Domenico Chiossone, illustrata da brevi cenni storica e da biografie di piu celebri pittori pu David Chiossone* (Firenze, 1860). See also C. Meldolesi, "David Chiossone," *Dizionario biografie degli italiani*, 25, pp. 22-25.

[77]Itaria bunka kaikan, *Oyatoi gaikokujin Edoarudo Kiyosone to sono jidai ten* [Un artista italiano al servizio del governo giapponese dal 1875 al 1893] (Tokyo, 4-24 ott. 1976), pl. 14.

[78]Marcello Staglieno, *Memorie e documenti sulla Accademia Ligustica di a Belle Arti* (Genova, 1862), p. 229.

[79]*Meiji shoki*, p. 107-109.

[80]Watanabe Morihiro, *Tokuno Ryosuke den* [Biography of Tokuno Ryosuke] (Tokyo, 1921) provides the most immediate account of Chiossone's close relations with his superior. See also Okurasho, *Insatsukyoku hyakunen shi* [Centennial History of the Printing Bureau] I (Tokyo, 1971).

[81]Ono Tadashige, *Nihon no sekihanga* [Japanese Lithography], 2nd edition (Tokyo, 1976) ably surveys developments in this field during early Meiji; see also his, *Meiji no sekihanga* [Meiji Lithography] (Tokyo, 1978) and Tokyo-to Bijutsukan, *Nihon doganga shi ten* [Exhibition of the History of Japanese Copper Engravings] (Tokyo, October 1-November 28, 1982) which provide convenient summaries and good illustrations.

[82]This valuable material is not listed in any of the catalogues of the museum. Other specimens of early currency and official papers produced during Chiossone's tenure can be seen at the Memorial Museum of the Printing Bureau in Ichigaya, Tokyo, which was established in 1971, and in the Currency Museum of the Bank of Otemachi, Tokyo. For a brief, well-illustrated account of this currency, see Asahi shashin bukku, *Nihon no shihei* [Japanese Paper Currency] 94 (Tokyo, 1959).

[83]*KNBK*, pl. 143.

[84]Copies of these albums are in the possession of the Chiossone Museum and the Memorial Museum of the Printing Bureau. See *ibid.*, pp. 159-161. Another early attempt at art reproduction by means of lithography is the original publication of Ninagawa Noritane, *Kanko zusetsu*, 5 volumes, see Ono, *Nihon no sekihanga*, pp. 75-76.

[85]Chiossone Museum, Acquisition No. LI 2605, *Kahei seizu* [Collection of Coinage] printed in September, 1878. For information concerning von Siebold's activities as a coin collector, see Josef Kreiner, "Heinrich Freiherr von Siebold, ein Beitrag zur geschichte der japanischen Volkerkunde und

Urgeschichte," *Beitrage zur japanischen Ethnogeneses: 100 Jahr nach Heinrich von Siebold* (Bonn, 1980), pp. 152-156.

[86]Itaria bunka kaikan, *Oyatoi gaikokujin Edoarudo Kiyosone to sono jidai ten*, pp. 29-32, pls. 1-12. For additional information on Sutematsu, see Dorothy Robins-Mowry, Chapter 8 of this volume, "Westernizing Influences in the early Modernization of Japanese Women's Education."

[87]*Ibid.*, pls. 1-3; see also Taki Koji, "Tenno no shozo—Zuzo no seijigaku e no kokoromi, Meiji zenpan ni okeru [Portrait of the Emperor, An Attempt at Official Portraiture in the First Phase of Meiji]," *Shiso* No. 740 (February, 1986), pp. 2-27.

[88]With regard to portraiture in the Meiji era, see Doris Croissant, "Meiji shoki yoga no shozoga riarisumu—Takahashi Yuichi o chushin ni [The Realistic Portraiture of Early Meiji Western-style Painting, and particularly that of Takahashi Yuichi]," *Jinbun gakuho*, 53 (March, 1982), pp. 157-187.

[89]It is possible to trace the evolution of the museum through records kept in the archives of the Accademia ligustica and the various catalogues of the museum; see Frabetti, *Edoardo Chiossone*, p. 28, for bibliography.

[90]Guiliano Frabetti, "Il nuovo Museo 'Chiossone' [The New 'Chiossone' Museum]," *La Casana* 14, 2 (Aprile-Giugno 1972), pp. 10-17.

[91]L. Bernabo Brea and Eiko Kondo, *Ukiyo-e Prints and Paintings from the Early Masters to Shunsho*, Edoardo Chiossone Civic Museum of Oriental Art Genoa (Genoa, 1980) and forthcoming Muneshige Narazaki ed. *Ukiyo-e Masterpieces in European Collections*, 10-11, Museo d'Arte Orientale I-II, scheduled to appear in the fall of 1990.

[92]Takashina, "Eastern and Western Dynamics," p. 23.

[93]Kido Takayoshi, *The Diary of Kido Takayoshi*. Translated by Sidney Devere Brown and Akiko Hirota (Tokyo, 1983), passim.

[94]Takashina, "Eastern and Western Dynamics," p. 24, states that: "The utilitarian, art-as-technology approach of Japan's first official art school . . . made it difficult for yoga to achieve artistic independence and maturity, which in turn hindered the development of supporting aesthetic principles. As a consequence, when the American Ernest Fenollosa came wielding his own brand of aesthetics, and delivered a blistering attack on yoga in the late 1870s, the Technical Art School, with its grounding in utilitarian values, could muster neither the aesthetic principles nor the artistic concepts to withstand the onslaught and crumpled under the assault."

[95]Uyeno Naoteru ed., *Japanese Arts and Crafts in the Meiji Era*, English adaptation by Richard Lane (Centenary Culture Council Series) (Tokyo, 1958), pp. 16, 18. It was originally published in Japanese in 1956.

[96]Ishimori Nobuo, *Shogaku shinkokugo* [New Japanese Language Text for Elementary School Students] (Tokyo, 1971), pp. 90-105, was designed for elementary school sixth grade students.

[97]*Rainichi*, p. 324-326, and many more articles have appeared in the five years since its publication.

[98]While teaching zoology at Tokyo University from 1878-1879, Edward S.

Morse contributed to the development of Japanese paleontology and archaeology with his publication on the Shell-Mounds at Omori, and began assembling a major collection of Japanese pottery that was acquired by the Museum of Fine Arts in Boston in 1892. He published a detailed catalogue of these works in 1901. Sir Rutherford Alcock, the first British Minister to Japan, displayed his collection of Japanese artifacts at the International Exhibition held in London in 1862 and published one of the first books on the subject, *Art and Art Industries in Japan* (London, 1878). Dr. William Anderson, who taught at the Naval Medical College while serving as medical officer in the British Legation from 1873-1880, collected Japanese painting and published the first major article on the subject, "A History of Japanese Art," *Transactions of the Asiatic Society of Japan*, 7, 4 (1879), pp. 339-373. During his thirty years residence in Japan, Dr. Erwin Baelz taught medicine at Tokyo University, served as personal physician to the Meiji Emperor and acquired a collection of Japanese art, part of which is now in the possession of Ruprecht-Karls-Universitat, Heidelberg.

[99]Original English version of "Articles of Agreement between H. E. Tsuji Shinji, Vice-Minister and Director of the Bureau of General Supervision, in the Department of Education, the part of the first part and Mr. Ernest F. Fenollosa of the United States of America, the part of the second part." Signed August 1, 1886. Article I. Document in the possession of the Imperial Household Ministry, Tokyo.

[100]Gottfried Wagener was a German chemist who, in addition to intermittently teaching chemistry at various government schools, served as a principal advisor to the Japanese commissioners to the international expositions held in Vienna in 1873 and in Philadelphia in 1876. He was also responsible for introducing new designs, materials and methods for manufacturing ceramics, cloisonne, glass and other artifacts. Alexander von Siebold, the elder son of noted Japanologist, Phillip Franz von Siebold, spent some seventeen years in the employ of the Ministries of Public Works, Finance and Foreign Affairs, during which he was involved in Japan's participation in the international expositions held in Paris in 1867 and 1878 and in Vienna in 1873. His younger brother, Heinrich, also accompanied the Japanese delegations to the Paris exposition of 1867 and the Vienna exposition of 1873. During the close to thirty years that Heinrich spent in the service of the Austro-Hungarian Legation in Tokyo, he formed numerous collections of Japanese archaeological, numismatic and art objects for major European museums. The French physician, Dr. Leon Dury, taught in Kyoto and Tokyo in the early 1870s and also assisted Kyoto authorities in improving their textile and ceramic industries. He helped Emile Guimet during his visit to Japan and subsequent establishment of a museum in Lyon. Captain Frank Brinkely was a British military officer who worked in Japan as a teacher and journalist from 1867 until his death in 1912. In addition to assembling an important collection of Japanese prints and pottery, he wrote or translated many of the art catalogues and other official publications that the Japanese government issued in conjunction with the exhibits they sent to international expositions. Charles

Lanman was the principal foreign employee at the Japanese Legation in Washington from 1871-1882. Although it is well known that Tsuda Umeko and some of the other young women who came to America with the Iwakura Mission lived at his home while studying in Washington, Japanese sources fail to note that he was also an important American artist whose influence and activities in this field, as relates to Japan, has not yet been explored.

[101]There is as yet no adequate study of this influential figure; for basic data, see Nakaya Kazumasa, *Danshaku Kuki Ryuichi den* [Biography of Baron Kuki Ryuichi] (Osaka, 1966). Now that his son, Kuki Shuzo, has died and Matsumoto Seicho at long last has disclosed Okakura's liaison with Kuki's wife and her subsequent confinement in a mental institution, it should be possible for confinement in a mental institution, it should be possible for scholars to undertake a more objective account of Kuki's life and career.

[102]This rare evidence of direct Japanese response to Fenollosa's proposals is now in the possession of Houghton Library, Harvard University, b MS Am 1759.3 (5).

[103]Tamburello, "Japanese Studies in Italy," p. 5. See also the chapter on Auriti in Yashiro Yukio, *Nihon bijutsu no onjintachi* [The Benefactors of Japanese Art] (Tokyo, 1961). Although Yashiro was trained in Western art, it is interesting to note that his quixotic selection of "benefactors" is confined to those who in some manner extolled Japan's traditional culture but excludes Conder, the Italians and many other *yatoi* whose knowledge of Western art and technology contributed so greatly to the development of modern Japanese art.

[104]Lionello Lanciotti, "La donazione Auriti al Museo Nazionale d'Arte Orientale," *Il Giappone* 2 (1962). The catalogue of the collection was published by Alexander C. Soper, *Chinese, Korean and Japanese Bronzes—A Catalogue of the Auriti Collection donated to IsMEO and preserved in the Museo Nazionale d'Arte Orientale in Rome* (Rome, 1966); an Italian edition was issued at the same time.

[105]Giacinto Auriti, *Compendio di storia della cultura giapponese della eta arcaica alla Restaurazione Meiji* (Roma, 1948). For a list of articles by Auriti, see *East and West*, 20 (1970), pp. 255-256. He also taught Japanese culture at the University of Rome for a number of years.

[106]See Note 36.

[107]*Meiji shoki*, p. 2-3. It is interesting to note the accompanying preface by Dan Ino, who figures conspicuously in the career of Fenollosa.

[108]Iseki Masaaki (1928-) is head of the Italian Legation in Rome and director of the Istituto Giapponese di Cultura di Roma. His two relevant publications are cited in Note 36 and Note 70.

[109]*Oyatoi*, 16, p. 178.

[110]Odakane Taro, "Anesuto F. Fenorosa no bijutsu undo [The Art Movement of Ernest F. Fenollosa]," *Bijutsu kenkyu* 110-112, (February-April, 1941), pp. 48-62, 82-94, 112-121.

[111]Okakura Kakuzo, *The Ideals of the East*. Reprint (Tokyo, 1970), pp. 1, 5.

9

Edward Warren Clark and the Formation of the Shizuoka and Koishikawa Christian Bands (1871-1879)

A. Hamish Ion

In the decade following the Meiji Restoration, a great many Western ideas were imported into Japan. Foreign employees provided one significant conduit through which these ideas were introduced. However, the *yatoi's* role in the subsequent permeation of Western ideas into wider circles of the Japanese population is less clear. Indeed, it can be assumed that the process of change and adaptation necessary to allow foreign ideas to penetrate into the broad society lay within the prerogative of Japanese intellectuals and not of Westerners. The crucial part played by Japanese opinion leaders is underlined by this study of the way in which Protestantism was transmitted across cultural barriers and came to be accepted by those *sabakuha* [supporter of the Tokugawa shogunate] who made up the Shizuoka and Koishikawa Christian Bands. Nevertheless, in looking at the three Westerners, Edward Warren Clark (1849-1907), Davidson McDonald (1837-1904), and George Cochran (1833-1900), who were associated with the creation of these two groups, it is clear that their perception of Western ideas usually ran parallel with the perception of the Japanese. In saying that, this study shows that two "streams" of Western ideas were at work in the case of the formation of the Shizuoka and Koishikawa Christian Bands. One was an indigenous Japanese knowledge of things Western derived from Dutch Studies, translations of foreign books and the overseas experiences of those Japanese who had studied or visited abroad. The other "stream" was Western ideas as understood by the three Westerners.

These two streams of Western ideas were directed toward different ends, and the potential for misunderstanding, argument and disappointment between the exponents of each was great. In the hands of intellectuals like those associated with the *Meirokusha*[1] (Meiji Six Society), among whose members were most of the leading Japanese Western studies specialists), Japanese knowledge of Western ideas was being exploited to yield different Japanese theories of civilization (which in this Victorian context means modernization). The purpose was to assuage the feelings of disorientation and anxiety within Japanese society which had accompanied the beginnings of Meiji modernization. These problems were caused by the Government's indiscriminate and opportunistic introduction of the material aspects of Western civilization without due concern for their effect on the life of the general population. By constructing their own Japanese theories of civilization, Fukuzawa Yukichi, Nakamura Masanao and others sought to show Japanese people what civilization truly was and how they could attain it in Japan. They were concerned with synthesizing, adapting and indigenizing Western ideas in order to help transform traditional society so that Japan could achieve specific national goals. Nakamura Masanao's (Keiu, 1832-1891) intimate connection with the members of both the Shizuoka and Koishikawa groups brought his ideas, at least, of civilization down to the grass roots.

In propagating Christianity, Clark, McDonald and Cochran also wanted to change the traditional outlook of the Japanese people. However, they already possessed a theory of civilization—a Western one in which Christianity loomed large. As it was superior to all others in their opinion, they saw no need to adapt their theory to Japanese needs. Moreover, while the three Westerners were genuinely concerned about improving the physical and material well-being of the Japanese, their primary goal was not helping Japan achieve modernization, but rather the "saving of souls." It so happened that Nakamura Masanao's Japanese theory of civilization had Christianity as an integral part of it. Certainly, Clark and the other two Westerners agreed with Nakamura on the central question of the relationship of Christianity to Western civilization. That is, they all saw Christianity as the essence of Western civilization. Indeed, such was the apparent parallelism in their thinking that it would appear that the role of the three was not in the introduction of completely new ideas *per se* but lay in reinforcing the validity of certain of those ideas that the Japanese already held. In other words, Clark, McDonald and Cochran were merely catalysts for Japanese intellectual activity and enquiry. However, it still has to be remembered that both Westerners and Japanese were creatures of their own cultural backgrounds. Underneath the surface of seeming unity of thought were great differences in perception and understanding. This was evident even in such a vital matter as their understanding of what religion was. In the West, the supernatural and transcendental aspects of religion were stressed. In Japan, religion placed emphasis on the human side. To many Japanese inquirers Christianity was seen as being a moral code superior to that of Neo-Confucianism. This was far from what the three Westerners perceived as being the most important.

Having said that, however, many other factors contributed to the formation of the Shizuoka and Koishikawa Bands other than a clear understanding of the meaning of Christianity. Christian ideas were disseminated along skeins of acquaintances. As a result, the acceptance of Christian values reflected a sensitive response of the individual to nuances of social relationships and hierarchical positions among friends, family members, schoolmates and teachers. As well as that, becoming a Christian had often no more to it than an initial desire to learn English. It has to be remembered that the majority of converts were young students who were being taught Western studies. Being young, they, undoubtedly, were easily swayed in their opinions. Yet what is noticeable about many of those who remained Christian was their intense loyalty to the first Westerners that they had known.

The link between the webs of individuals who formed the two Christian groups was Edward Warren Clark, a young American layman who taught at the *Gakumonjo* in Shizuoka (1871-73), and later at the *Kaisei Gakko* in Tokyo (1874-75). His former pupils formed the core of the Shizuoka Band. The Koishikawa Band in Tokyo was centered in the *Dojinsha* school, which had been founded by Nakamura Masanao, Clark's closest Japanese friend while in Shizuoka. Clark's evangelistic endeavours in Shizuoka and Tokyo were continued by McDonald and Cochran, the two pioneer missionaries of the (Wesleyan) Methodist Church of Canada,[2] who baptized the members of the two Bands. As a result of the continuity provided by the Canadians, it is possible to follow the course of the development of the two groups from the time of Clark's arrival in Japan in 1871 until the departure of McDonald from Shizuoka in 1878 and Cochran from Tokyo in 1879. In doing so, the Christian activities of three Western employees and the small groups of Japanese most intimately connected to them during a highly dramatic era of change will be illuminated.

Clark in Shizuoka

E. W. Clark is recognized as an important interpreter of Japan to the West,[3] and is also known for having been a close friend of W. E. Griffis both at Rutgers and in Japan.[4] Clark, like his friend Griffis, first became interested in Japan as a result of his contact with Japanese students, who were studying at Rutgers College or the New Brunswick Grammar School. The notion of going to Japan had, according to Clark, both for Griffis and himself "so lit our imagination, at the outset, and caused our dreams to run wild in fairy-land, and our poetic fancies to soar to marvellous heights."[5] The exotic and romantic appeal of Japan gradually wore off once Clark was on Japanese soil, but life there still remained an adventure for him.

Clark left the United States for Japan in the late summer of 1871 without any job awaiting him there. On his way out, however, he learnt that Griffis had made an arrangement with Katsu Kaishu (Awa Rintaro) that he take up a teaching post in Shizuoka.[6] As he already had letters of introduction to Katsu Kaishu, Clark was pleased to accept this appointment. Nevertheless, after his arrival in Yokohama, he delayed the signing of his contract because he found that the Japanese Foreign Affairs Department, which ratified all contracts with foreigners, had included a clause which prevented him from teaching Christianity. Clark refused to sign unless he was allowed to teach the Bible. He felt that it was impossible for "a Christian man to bind himself to go for three years among a heathen people, and yet hold his tongue on the Christian religion."[7] This was an unprecedented stand for Clark to take, as Griffis and other Western teachers had never contested the ban on their teaching Christianity.[8] Despite this, Clark had the support of Katsu behind his insistence that the offending article be removed from his contract.[9] It was, nonetheless, a *Gaimusho* matter. In this, Clark was fortunate that he had an entree to Iwakura Tomomi, the Foreign Minister, as a result of his friendship with Iwakura's son who had studied at Rutgers. Indeed, when the clause was deleted from his contract, Clark thought that "the influence of my good friend *Ewa-ku-ra* had not a little to do with it."[10] He was right.[11] Thus, in the middle of October 1871 Clark arrived in Shizuoka as the first Westerner free to teach Christianity outside the treaty concessions.

In the early 1870s Shizuoka was by no means simply a provincial town in a Prefecture well-known for its mandarin oranges and tea. Shizuoka was the ancestral home of the Tokugawa Shoguns, and it was to there that Tokugawa Yoshinobu, the last Shogun, retired following the Meiji Restoration. Many of his former retainers followed him there into semi-exile, and approximately 6,000 ex-Tokugawa samurai were living in Shizuoka and its vicinity in late 1871.

Even though it had lost political power as a result of the Meiji Restoration, the Tokugawa family initially hoped that it might regain its former control of Japan. For this reason the Tokugawa family, in the autumn of 1868, established the Military Academy at Numazu, some 30 miles from Shizuoka, with the leading Western studies scholar, Nishi Amane, as its first headmaster.[12] With less overtly militaristic aims in mind, the Tokugawa authorities also founded, in late 1868, the *Gakumonjo* in Shizuoka. By 1871 this Shizuoka school was the "higher education" center of a network of 8 or 9 junior schools which the Tokugawa family had established in Shizuoka Prefecture.[13] Prior to 1868, the Tokugawa Government had been at the forefront of the introduction of Western studies in Japan and their continued sponsorship of Western studies in Shizuoka Prefecture after 1868 was consistent with this.

Nevertheless, more important factors were involved. The purpose of the *Gakumonjo* was to help provide education in Western studies for the sons of ex-Tokugawa samurai.[14] Entry to the school was restricted to those of the samurai class and, importantly, tuition was free.[15] Among the followers of the ex-Shogun there was naturally very considerable resentment against the new Meiji Government, for the majority of *declasse* samurai were living in conditions of great hardship and suffering.[16] It was thought by Katsu Kaishu and other Tokugawa elders that by educating the sons of ex-samurai in Western science, at least some of the former Tokugawa influence in Japan could be regained. Moreover, as the demand for experts in Western studies increased, these would be employment opportunities for these young men. In recognizing the future need for Western studies specialists, the progressive spirit of the Tokugawa exiles was clear.

Since the founding of the *Gakumonjo*, the Tokugawa authorities had wanted to hire a Western teacher.[17] After all, the school had been established to teach Western subjects—English, French, German and Dutch languages, mathematics and Western science—as well as traditional Chinese studies. The need for a Western professor became increasingly acute as the *Gakumonjo* expanded. Indeed, by November 1871, it had grown to such an extent that it had been divided into four different schools—the *Shogakujo*, the *Denshujo*, the *Shugakujo* and the Shizuoka *Honko* (the old *Gakumonjo*). What these divisions meant in practical terms was that Western subjects were now being offered from primary school to the highest academic level, and to students ranging from young boys to mature men in their thirties. Compounding educational problems posed by expansion was the simple reality that English had replaced Dutch as the major language of Western studies. The shortage of English language teachers was clearly illustrated in the fact that the Tokugawa authorities sent Sugiyama Magoroku, the son of Sugiyama Sanhachi, a Dutch scholar who was a key figure in Western studies at the *Gakumonjo*, in 1871 to learn English in Yokohama instead of continuing his Dutch studies.[18] As well as learning English, Sugiyama Magoroku was converted to Christianity as an early member of the Yokohama Band, the first Japanese Protestant group in Japan.

Among other members of the *Gakumonjo* faculty who understood the need for a Western teacher was Nakamura Masanao, who was in charge of Chinese studies. Nakamura had recent experience of living abroad having been in England between 1866 and early 1868 as one of the supervisors of a group of 12 students sent there by the Tokugawa Government. Nakamura, together with Hitomi Fujitaro, an influential Tokugawa bureaucrat, was particularly important in the successful lobbying of Katsu Kaishu to hire a foreign professor for Shizuoka.[19] Later, both Nakamura and Hitomi were in Yokohama, while Clark waited for his contract to be changed, and accompanied him to Shizuoka.[20]

Clark described Nakamura at their first meeting in Yokohama as "one of the officers sent from the province where I was going, and although he was the most noted scholar of Chinese literature in Japan, he was as simple as a child, and quite amusing in his use of broken English."[21] However, Nakamura, for his part, was much taken by Clark. Indeed, he declined an invitation to join the Iwakura Mission which was going to the United States because he wished to study Christianity with Clark.[22] When he learnt that Clark had succeeded in having the religious clause removed from his contract, he had reportedly told Clark that "you have conquered, and have broken down a strong Japanese wall. Now you can also teach us the Bible and Christianity."[23] While he had lived in London, Nakamura had been struck by the high moral standards of English people which he felt had been fostered by Christianity.[24] Such was his admiration of Christianity, that Nakamura had undergone baptism while in England.[25] The impact of the Christianity that he had seen in England is evident in an article (*Keitenaijinsetsu,* "Revere God and Love Man") which he had published in 1868.[26] Likewise, his translation of Samuel Smile's *Self-Help* which was published in Shizuoka in 1871 under the title of *Saikokurishihen* (Stories of Success in the West) would also appear to attribute the ultimate cause of people's success to Christianity.[27] In making that point, however, it has to be stressed that the appeal of Christianity was not its spiritual tenets but principally due to its moral code.

Shortly after meeting Clark, Nakamura wrote a memorial addressed to the Emperor urging the toleration of Christianity. In it he stated that "the industry, patience and perseverance in their arts, inventions, and machinery, all have their origin in the faith, hope and charity of their religion, and religion is the root and foundation on which their prosperity depends."[28] Nakamura even went as far as advocating that the Emperor himself should be baptized as that act would help improve relations with the West.[29] Nakamura's advocacy of freedom of worship for Christianity was set against a background of Clark's evangelistic activities in Shizuoka.

The first Sunday that he was in Shizuoka, Clark had conducted a Bible class with Nakamura acting as interpreter. At the end of the class attended by "as earnest and intelligent body of young men as it was ever my privilege to address,"[30] he handed out copies of the Scriptures which he had brought with him from Yokohama. After a time, the Japanese organized them-selves into their own Bible classes. Clark was not prevented from propagating the Gospel by his contract, and he was also fortunate in being on good terms with the authorities in Shizuoka. Okubo Ichio, who was Governor of Shizuoka when Clark arrived, became a close friend, and his ten year old son lived with Clark.[31] Okubo's friendship with Clark is significant, as he became Lord Mayor of Tokyo in 1872 during the time when missionaries first began to proselytize there. As W. E. Griffis noted in *The Mikado's Empire* in describing a visit to Shizuoka at the beginning of February 1872, "Clark is extremely fortunate in having so many cultivated gentlemen, famous characters and educated, intelligent helpers."[32] He, likewise, noted that Nakamura was Clark's right-hand man who was at that time printing his famous translation of J. S. Mill's *On Liberty.* Clark would write the preface to this translation. It is clear that Nakamura and Clark mutually helped each other; Clark helping Nakamura with his translations, and in return receiving help with his Bible classes and teaching. The very positive and supportive atmosphere in which Clark found himself in early 1872 obviously aided the success of his Bible classes.

For the young students in Shizuoka, Clark's Bible classes offered another opportunity to hear English. Such an opportunity, given the nature of the school, was important for those serious about mastering English. Concerning his teaching in Shizuoka, Clark later wrote about the *Gakumonjo* as it appeared to him in early 1872 :

> with an institution of nearly one thousand students, under the supervision of a single foreigner with fifty Japanese assistants to direct and instruct; with classes in various scientific departments, both theoretical and practical; with interpreters to be drilled, regulations to be made and enforced, experiments prepared, and lectures given through the three-fold medium of English, French and Japanese you may believe I had my hands full.[33]

Certainly, Clark was busy with classes,[34] and as a result student access to him was undoubtedly difficult. Henry Satoh (Sato Shigemichi), then a ten-year old student, noted about his own academic progress :

> English was a very favorite subject. My attention was practically concentrated on learning the English language, to the neglect of other subjects. I soon made myself objectionable to my Japanese teacher in English. I began to ask questions which were soon found to be too much for my teacher. The manner which he removed this objectionable boy continually worrying him with questions was to send him up to a higher class with his certificate for the boy's competency. In this way I ran up three classes in one year. I then found my classmates seven to ten years my senior in age. In the class taught by Mr.Clark I managed to learn enough to act as the interpreter of the class.[35]

Satoh's rapid promotion to Clark's English course does suggest that the standard of English language teaching was not very high outside of those classes given by the Western teacher himself. Indeed, Satoh does allude to a very different kind of school than the disciplined institution which Clark described. By late 1872, Clark himself had become increasingly disillusioned about the school. He lamented in a letter to Griffis that:

> things are getting pretty lonely here now-a-days, for I have no friends now and no company, nor diversions of any kind. But I never get 'homesick', and in fact scarcely know what the thing is. The chaotic, or rather the 'Japonic' state, which are synonymous terms in which the school has been for a long time past, has made me quite disgusted with everything, and I don't think hereafter I shall work quite so hard if all my zeal goes for nothing.[36]

One reason for Clark's loneliness was that Nakamura in late 1872 had to live in Tokyo where he proceeded to establish his own private school, the *Dojinsha*, in Koishikawa ward. In leaving Shizuoka, Nakamura was merely joining the "brain drain" to Tokyo where there were better employment opportunities. Part of the reason for the exodus to Tokyo was that major changes in the nature of regional government had meant the end of direct Tokugawa rule in Shizuoka. As one element in the administrative changes that the Meiji Government was making, educational reforms were inaugurated in which it was decided to centralize advanced Western studies in Tokyo at the expense of the provincial centers. While the Meiji Government had tolerated in 1868 the creation of the Military Academy at Numazu and the *Gakumonjo* in Shizuoka, it now forced their closure. As early as 1871, the Military Academy was moved to Tokyo where it was absorbed into the national military college system. The *Gakumonjo* was allowed to suffer a lingering demise. Clark had the unpleasant experience of having to teach through a period which saw a once fine institution "reach utter ruin."[37] While he realized the intention of the Meiji Government's educational policy and thoroughly disapproved of it, the authorities in Shizuoka had not told him that they were prepared to allow the school to deteriorate. In June 1873 when the state of what was now a private school was close to being, in Clark's opinion, beyond repair, he was asked to take over direction of the school.[38] This he reluctantly did, but it was clear that he was eager to leave Shizuoka. By the middle of 1873, it was clear that the attempt by the Tokugawa family to continue to retain influence through the training of experts in Western studies had been largely frustrated by the educational reforms of the Meiji Government.

Despite this, there remained a desire among those in Shizuoka to continue to make some provision for Western studies education in the city, even though it would not be on the scale of the *Gakumonjo*. In October 1873, when it was known that Clark was leaving Shizuoka to take up a teaching post at the *Kaisei Gakko* in Tokyo, Hitomi Fujitaro approached George Cochran, a Canadian Methodist missionary recently arrived in Japan who happened to make a short visit to Shizuoka at that time, if he would replace Clark as the Western teacher in Shizuoka. Family reasons prevented Cochran himself from accepting, but he did arrange that his colleague, Davidson McDonald M.D., to take up the offer. Clark left Shizuoka permanently in December 1873 for Tokyo.

McDonald in Shizuoka

After delays caused by the slowness of the Government to approve his contract, McDonald and his wife arrived in Shizuoka in April 1874. McDonald was different in personality from Clark. He was a mature man in his late thirties, and he was a medical doctor as well as an ordained minister with considerable pastoral experience. McDonald was, Henry Satoh wrote, "a gentleman very widely admired on account of his high character and of his Christian virtues of doing good for others."[39] He was representative of the finest ministers in the Methodist Church of Canada, and because he was such had been asked by the Church authorities to become one of the two pioneer missionaries that they sent out to Japan in the summer of 1873.

McDonald would need all his strength of personality. For the circumstances in Shizuoka were very different in the spring of 1874 from what they had been less than three years before when Clark had first come there. The *Shizuhatasha* (*Shizuhatanoya*) founded by Hitomi Fujitaro after the closure of the *Gakumonjo* had only ten students, most of them former pupils of Clark, when McDonald began teaching there. The school was conducted in McDonald's home (Clark's former residence), a comfortable Western-style stone house within the confines of the old Shizuoka Castle. The classes that McDonald taught included physics, chemistry, natural history and language study. For English classes he made use of Ontario school primers.[40] Although teaching was somewhat hampered owing to language difficulties the curriculum, like that of the *Gakumonjo* before it, revealed that a surprisingly high level of educational sophistication was expected of the pupils. Three of the students, Yamanaka Emi, Tsuyuki Seiichi and Tsuchiya Hikoroku (all former Clark students), served as interpreters for McDonald, who was still learning Japanese.[41] McDonald's wife also became involved in teaching quite separately from her husband, for she was drawn into giving instruction in English, knitting and music to classes of women. For the McDonalds, however, teaching was merely the excuse used to gain permission to live outside the treaty ports. Their primary aim remained to propagate the Gospel.

Soon after his arrival, McDonald held his first Bible class, which consisted of a reading of the Lord's Prayer and was attended by 17 people.[42] The majority of those present were McDonald's students at the *Shizuhatasha*, but most crucial was the presence of Sugiyama Magoroku as interpreter. Just as Nakamura's presence had drawn students to Clark's early Bible classes, so too did Sugiyama's role in McDonald's prove vitally important. Sugiyama came from a well-known, high-ranking samurai family. Both he and his father had taught at the *Gakumonjo*. He had also been much involved in the process of getting McDonald to come to Shizuoka. Sugiyama was already a Christian, having been baptized some two years before by James Ballagh in Yokohama.[43] His younger brother, Tsuchiya Hikoroku, was one of McDonald's students who later became a leading figure in the Canadian Methodist Church in Shizuoka. Three other present at this first Bible class, Yamanaka Emi, Tsuyuki Seiichi and Muramatsu Ichi, all of them *Shizuhatasha* students, had been former pupils of Sugiyama at the *Gakumonjo*. They all eventually became ministers or leading laymen in the Church.

McDonald's Bible class was a continuation of a process which had been begun by Clark in his days in Shizuoka. It became a part of the intellectual activity of the *Shizuhatasha* students, an accepted extra-curricular lesson. It was part and parcel of the heady eclectic desire of the Japanese youngsters at the school to learn as much as possible of things Western and also to transmit their knowledge to a broader audience. It was not the only out-of-class pursuit, for as well as attending Bible classes, Clark's former students had been involved in publishing pamphlets on geometry and other things of scientific interest. Yet, behind the interest in Christianity was the view held by Sugiyama and

Nakamura that characterized Christianity as "the religion of civilization."[44] Extending this line of argument, if these young men were to understand Western studies, then they would have to know something of Christianity. It was the acceptance of this idea, which is perfectly understandable as it was one held by their Japanese mentors, that resulted in the young students being open to Christian influence.

While it is doubtful whether McDonald was fully aware of the complex and subtle motives behind their conversion to Christianity, he was quickly able to convert his students. On September 27, 1874, McDonald baptized 11 young men, all of them his students at the *Shizuhatasha*.[45] Before their baptism, he had given them special instruction concerning the nature and obligations of Christian life, the doctrines of Christianity and the Christian church. He had also discussed with them the condition of their country, the possibility of opposition to their baptism and even of persecution. Only one of the 11 had any fears concerning being baptized.[46] They became Christians entirely of their own free choice, as it is evident that McDonald did not put pressure on any of them to convert. It is important, however, to remember that the majority of them had been attending Bible classes since Clark's time. Further, in Sugiyama Magoroku they also possessed a person who could answer many of their questions out of his own experience of conversion. There, indeed, might well have been an element of wanting to please Sugiyama, an older and more senior person, by following his example and becoming a Christian. Be that as it may, it is clear that the first converts' acquisition of Christian knowledge was not solely restricted to their ability to comprehend McDonald's English (although most of them had now been studying English for a number of years).

After the baptismal service, a Christian Church was organized in accordance with Canadian Methodist discipline. In creating a Japanese-led Methodist Class, McDonald wanted to ensure that there were some Japanese, had he to leave Shizuoka unexpectedly, who were accustomed to holding meetings and even to speaking to the people about the truth of the Bible.[47] McDonald need not have worried that his work would prove unsuccessful. By March 1875 he had baptized some 27 people, and had begun to hold regular services on Sunday morning and in the evening, with a Bible class conducted by one of the Japanese converts on Wednesday evenings.[48] The Methodist Class members were also very keen to help in evangelistic work themselves. Many of them like Henry Satoh were able to assist McDonald as interpreters and also capable of going out independently into the city and the surrounding villages.[49] This Christian activity was very much in keeping with their general desire to communicate their knowledge of Western things to the broader society.

While the initial interest in Christianity had been largely restricted to McDonald's students at the *Shizuhatasha*, by 1876 Christianity had gained a certain popularity in Shizuoka among the townspeople. At one Sunday service, McDonald reported that as many as 380 pairs of geta were checked.[50] In July 1876, Amenomori Nobushige, a student at the *Kaisei Gakko* in Tokyo, wrote to his American professor, W. E. Griffis, about the state of affairs in Shizuoka, stating that "about five hundred of the people are gathered together on Sunday evening to receive the 'Bread of Life' sent down from heaven."[51] Attendance was not always that high, but it does indicate that McDonald's services were attracting local attention, even if part of it was due to just plain curiosity. Yet the number of converts increased quite steadily. By 1877 McDonald had baptized over 120 people. Of these, some 65 maintained a connection with the Church in Shizuoka.[52] A major reason why the number of Church members was only just half the number baptized was simply that many moved away from Shizuoka to Tokyo in search of work. Despite this migration, by 1877 McDonald found it necessary, because of the growth of the Church, to discontinue using his house as a meeting place and to rent a hall in the city. The average attendance at the regular services held in the rented hall was 35.[53]

Although the growing interest in Christianity brought criticism against him from Buddhist and Shinto priests in Shizuoka, one reason why the Church in Shizuoka continued to grow was that McDonald began to undertake medical work as well as teaching. In 1875 McDonald reported that during the year he had "dispensed medicines freely in and out of season."[54] While he admitted that medical work was taking an increasing amount of his time and energy, it was also gaining him friends. In December 1876 the Shizuoka authorities opened a hospital in which McDonald was appointed a doctor.[55] This was the first Western-style hospital in the Prefecture. However, McDonald's medical practice was not simply restricted to treating patients at the hospital, for as his medical work became better known he was frequently asked to visit sick people outside of Shizuoka itself. Indeed, he was often called out to attend cases as far away as Numazu and Shimada. Naturally, he took the opportunity offered by his medical work to engage in Christian work outside of Shizuoka. As a result of this, the growth of the Church was sustained and developed beyond being solely restricted to the students at the *Shizuhatasha*.

As McDonald's reputation increased throughout the Prefecture, new opportunities for missionary work appeared. During 1875 McDonald was approached by Ebara Soroku, the headmaster of a private school in Numazu, to see if it could be arranged that a missionary like McDonald could come to teach in Numazu. In September 1876 George M. Meacham arrived to teach in Ebara's school. With Meacham happily working in Numazu, McDonald applied for leave to attend the Ophthalmical Institution in New York for further study. In early 1878, he was given permission to leave Shizuoka and return to North America. McDonald and his wife had been in Shizuoka for four years, and their departure meant the end of almost seven years of continuous Christian evangelism by resident Westerners.

By the time that McDonald left, three or four Japanese had been trained as Canadian Methodist evangelists by George Cochran in Tokyo. Among these were Tsuchiya Hikoroku and Yamanaka Emi from Shizuoka. As a result, when McDonald left Shizuoka, his place was taken by Yamanaka, already a qualified evangelist. Although McDonald returned to Japan in 1880, he took up permanent residence in Tsukiji, Tokyo, where he worked for the next 24 years as a doctor with most of his patients coming from the Western community. From 1880 onwards, his missionary work was largely concerned with administration rather than evangelism or teaching. As far as Shizuoka was concerned, it was not until 1886 that another Canadian Methodist missionary, F. A. Cassidy, took up permanent residence there.

McDonald, as the first clerical missionary and Western physician in Shizuoka, left a mark on the history of the city and prefecture which transcends the narrow confines of his Christian work. As a living Western encyclopedia in Shizuoka, he and his Ontario school primers helped lay the foundations for English language education, contributed to the development of Western-style medical practice, aided in stimulating interest in female education as well as influenced a generation of Christians in the city.

Certainly, the leading members of the Shizuoka Band proved that they were quite capable of continuing the Church after McDonald's departure. The acquisition of Western learning opened new horizons for these men as English teachers, journalists and pastors. While it has to be pointed out that very few of them gained national prominence in Japan, either in the Christian or secular spheres, they did have a significant local impact. Among those who were converted to Christianity, in the early 1880s, was Yamaji Aizan who was one of the few members of the Shizuoka Band to gain a national reputation. Yet, the process of the creation of the Band had begun with Clark. If Clark played an important role in Shizuoka, the same was equally true of the Koishikawa Band in Tokyo.

Clark, Cochran, and the Koishikawa Band

Cochran's meeting with E. W. Clark in Shizuoka in October 1873 had led to McDonald going to Shizuoka, it was equally responsible for Cochran becoming a contract teacher at Nakamura Masanao's *Dojinsha* school in the Koishikawa district of Tokyo. In a real sense, the Koishikawa Band was made up of the "Clarkites" who had left Shizuoka to go to Tokyo. The Christian group at the *Dojinsha* that Cochran nurtured belonged to the same group of individuals who made up the core of the Shizuoka Band. The difference was that they (when the *Gakumonjo* had collapsed) had moved on to seek new opportunities in Tokyo. Added to this "Shizuoka" center were some of Clark's students at the *Kaisei Gakko*, the Government College where Clark had begun to teach in early 1874. Once his students had expressed an interest in Christianity, Clark would direct them to Cochran's Bible class which the Canadian had begun at the *Dojinsha*, near the *Kaisei Gakko*, in the early spring of 1874. Prior to Cochran, Clark himself and W. E. Griffis had been helping with Bible instruction at the *Dojinsha*. According to Hiraiwa Yoshiyasu, one of Clark's students at the *Kaisei Gakko*, Clark was an inspiring teacher when it came to science, but was disappointing when it came to explaining Christianity.[56] Indeed, it was the organ music which Clark played during his Bible classes that initially attracted Hiraiwa to them. In contrast to the young Clark, the mature, dignified and erudite Cochran not only possessed an imposing figure which bespoke respect but also was a man of deep learning. Like his colleague, McDonald, Cochran was an outstanding minister in the Canadian Methodist Church, and had been pastor of the Metropolitan Church in Toronto, the largest Canadian Methodist Church, before becoming a missionary.

It was Clark who introduced Cochran to Nakamura Masanao. Clark and his Japanese friend had travelled down from Tokyo to Yokohama for a visit in January 1874, and had heard Cochran give a sermon at the Union Church. The sermon was on "The Person and Work of the Holy Spirit," and marked part of the founding exercises of the Evangelical Alliance in Japan.[57] Cochran was the corresponding secretary of the newly founded Japan Chapter. Nakamura had been impressed with Cochran's sermon and asked him for a copy of it. Not long after their introduction, Nakamura invited Cochran to visit him in Tokyo. It is obvious that Nakamura already knew of Cochran before their meeting, not only because of the latter's growing prominence among the missionary group in Yokohama as revealed by his official post in the new Evangelical Alliance, but also because of Sugiyama Magoroku, who had wanted him to come to teach in Shizuoka.[58]

Cochran knew Nakamura was the "Chinese translator" to the Meiji Government, and was, in addition, the translator of Samuel Smile's *Self-Help* and J. S. Mill's *On Liberty*. Further, he knew that Nakamura was the writer of a memorial in 1871 asking the Government to tolerate Christianity. Cochran also knew that Nakamura had read the Bible in English as well as in Chinese and was very interested in the Christian religion.[59] What he did not realize initially was that Nakamura also ran a school. This was the *Dojinsha* which Nakamura had started in 1873 in order to educate young men belonging to the families of his personal friends. In other words, it catered to the needs of the children of Tokugawa ex-samurai. When Cochran first visited the school in January 1874, it had 100 pupils. In 1874 the *Dojinsha* together with Fukuzawa Yukichi's *Keio Gijuku* and Kondo Makoto's *Koshusha* were regarded as the best three private schools in Tokyo specializing in Western studies.[60]

In mid-January, when Cochran gave his first Bible class at the *Dojinsha*, he was astonished to find over 30 young men assembled to hear him. Many of them had Bibles in their hands, and were able to understand an English sermon when it was delivered slowly and distinctly in simple sentences. At Nakamura's request, Cochran preached on "Man's sinful state, and the need of a Saviour," definitely not the easiest of subjects. The student group listened, however, with apparent attention, and at the end asked some intelligent questions.

The fact that the student group at the *Dojinsha* already knew something of Christianity is clear from a visit to the school in February 1874 by S. R.

Brown, an American Dutch Reformed Church missionary.[61] Brown attended a class presided over by Clark. Like Cochran, Brown was very much impressed, both with Nakamura, whom he considered if not already one of Christ's disciples someone not far from the "kingdom of heaven," and with the Bible class.[62] Among the audience, Brown recognized a former pupil of his from the Government School in Yokohama who was a Christian and now worked as an assistant teacher at the *Dojinsha* (who this was is not known, but it might well have been Sugiyama). This is another indication of the inter-relationship between the Yokohama Band and the groups in Shizuoka and in Koishikawa. The room in which Brown gave his lecture was well-furnished with English Bibles and the walls were decorated with numerous large illuminated Biblical texts.[63] From what Brown wrote, it is clear that the inspiration for, and indeed knowledge of, Christianity came from the Japanese themselves and specifically from Nakamura. Although there was as yet no Japanese translation of the Bible, Japanese could use W. A. P. Martin's *Tendo Sakugen*, either in Japanese or Chinese translation.

From January 1874 Cochran began to come up to the *Dojinsha* from Yokohama every Saturday and returned home to his family on Monday. Sometimes he stayed with Nakamura who provided him with a comfortable Japanese bed and excellent Western-style meals, and at other times he stayed with Clark who lived close by with W. E. Griffis and his sister Margaret Clark Griffis. When he stayed with Clark, Cochran would help with Clark's Bible class of *Kaisei Gakko* students on Sunday evenings. For Cochran, this contact with *Kaisei Gakko* students offered a new channel for potential converts.

Cochran was also introduced to some, at least, of Nakamura's Japanese friends. Shortly after Cochran agreed to come and live with his family at the *Dojinsha*, the Canadian was a guest at a party given by Nakamura "to meet a large company of his friends distinguished sinologues, and persons of rank."[64] Among them was Okubo Ichio, who had been closely associated with the establishment of the *Gakumonjo* in Shizuoka and since 1872 had been Lord Mayor of Tokyo. It was at this same party that Cochran learnt that "Mr. Katsu, the present Admiral of the Navy in Japan, advised the people of Shizuoka to secure, if possible, the services of a Missionary to take charge of their school; and this was the chief reason of their overture to Dr. McDonald."[65] The crucial point to be made is that in McDonald's and Cochran's cases their appointments had the blessing of the highest authorities among ex-Tokugawa advisers and that without this approval it would have been unlikely that they would have obtained their teaching positions. Regardless of what subsequently happened in Shizuoka or at the *Dojinsha*, the personal influence of Okubo or Katsu Kaishu obviously could have cut short any Christian activity, and those who later converted did so realizing that these two senior men did not openly disapprove. Like most things connected with the beginning of Canadian Methodist evangelistic work, the Canadians owed a debt to Clark who was a friend of both Okubo Ichio and Katsu Kaishu. Clark's example obviously had helped in convincing them to approve of hiring missionaries for schools catering to ex-Tokugawa supporters.

In April 1874 Cochran and his family moved from Yokohama to take up residence in a Western style house built for them on the *Dojinsha* campus. At the school, Cochran taught English for one or two hours daily, but his main work was religious. He held a morning and afternoon service every Sunday, with an average attendance at each service of between 35 and 50. Five nights a week he gave Bible classes. As in the initial stage at Shizuoka, when Sugiyama translated for McDonald, Nakamura interpreted for Cochran, which was obviously important in stimulating interest among the students. Given the intensity of the Christian activity, it was not long before converts were made. Nakamura was the first to ask for baptism. His baptism took place at ten o'clock on Christmas morning 1874. The service was held in the parlor of Cochran's home and was witnessed by both students and friends. Among those present were General Viscount Saigo Tsugumichi's wife and daughter, who made a magnificent floral presentation.[66] What is striking is the presence of the intellectual and political elite at this ceremony.

Nakamura's conversion to Christianity and his baptism were a signal for others to make a public confession of their faith. In March 1875 four teachers at the school were baptized. Interesting is the hierarchial nature of the baptismal process, the Principal being followed by the teachers. In May, Nakamura's wife and other members of the family were baptized. In August 1875 two more teachers, together with members of their families, became Christian. The group had filled out along family lines. In keeping with seniority, the next to be baptized were two students from the *Kaisei Gakko* of whom one, Hiraiwa Yoshiyasu, would become the leading pastor in the Canadian Methodist mission and an influential Japanese Christian leader.

As the number of converts increased, Cochran decided, like McDonald had done in Shizuoka, to form a Methodist Class. This he did in December 1875, with Nakamura as Class Leader. This original class numbered 18. As part of his aim to encourage self-reliance among the converts, Cochran gave the members of the group in Koishikawa the chance to preach. Like their counterparts in Shizuoka, the young converts proved very eager to proselytize. Charles Eby, a Canadian Methodist missionary who arrived in September 1876 noted about the Koishikawa Band that "nearly a score are already local preachers, and more are coming on. Most of them, if the way was open, would become evangelists and preachers of the most promising class," and he further added that "they are nearly all graduates or undergraduates of the Imperial University (*Kaisei Gakko*), and some of them, of eminent scholarly attainments. They are thoroughly versed in Chinese classics and Confucian philosophy, but they are babes in Christian theology."[67] Prominent among them was Hiraiwa Yoshiyasu. Among Hiraiwa's friends at the *Kaisei Gakko* whom Cochran baptized in August 1876 were Yokoi Tokio and Yamazaki Tamenori, both of whom belonged to the famed Kumamoto Christian Band and who were now briefly at the *Kaisei Gakko*. Although Yokoi and Yamazaki left

Tokyo a month after their baptism to join their friends at the *Doshisha* in Kyoto, it was the young members of the Koishikawa Band drawing their friends and their families to Christianity which expanded the group.

In June 1876 Mrs. Cochran's ill-health caused the Cochrans to move from their home on the *Dojinsha* campus to first a house in the Surugadai district, and then in 1877 to Tsukiji, the treaty concession in Tokyo. Finally, in early 1879 continued concern over his wife's health caused Cochran to return home to Canada. Shortly before his departure, the first Canadian Methodist Church building in Tokyo had been dedicated in Ushigome ward. Nakamura delivered the dedication address. The total membership of the Tokyo Church at that time stood at 49.

Cochran's return to Canada (although he would come back to Japan in 1882) marked the end of that era of Christian development which had begun with Clark in 1871. The Koishikawa Band was made up of Nakamura's disciples. In a real sense, his prestige protected and justified the conversion of the others. In terms of the Shizuoka Band, it is notable that their Christian endeavour was only one aspect of the activities of the group. The same, of course, is true of their counterparts in Tokyo. As a group identified with Nakamura, the Koishikawa Band also played a part in the educational and intellectual endeavours that are associated with his name from 1874 until 1879. These activities are seen not only in his writings in the *Meiroku Zasshi*, but also, and more importantly, in the establishment of the *Dojinsha* Girls' School in 1875 (where Mrs. Cochran taught), in his interest in kindergartens, and in the publication of the *Dojinsha Bungaku Zasshi*. In other words, Christian conversion took place for Nakamura and the others during a period of hectic activity.

Cochran saw his own role within the context of evangelistic effort, but in the overall activity of Nakamura and the Koishikawa Band he was only a necessary accessory. For them, Cochran was essential in two ways: first, as a Christian authority who reinforced their Christian ideas; and second, as a living reference book of things Western. However, it is not superfluous to note that the educational interests of Nakamura, as seen in his concern about female and children's education, were precisely the fields in which missionaries were interested. It is in this similarity of interest that the influence of Cochran and before him Clark can be seen. It was Clark, who had returned to the United States in 1875 to become a clergyman, who served to link all the individuals together. It was Clark's example in Shizuoka, his friendship with Nakamura, Okubo Ichio and Katsu Kaishu that paved the way for the two Canadians to continue his Christian work in shizuoka and Tokyo. Without the help of E. W. Clark, the course of the development of the Canadian Methodist mission in Japan would have been very different. Indeed, it is a strange twist of history that a young American should have played so great a part in the beginnings of cultural contact between Canada and Japan.

Notes

[1]For the *Meirokusha*, see Okubo Toshiaki, *Meirokusha Kangae* [Thought of the Meiji Six Society] (Tokyo, 1976).

[2]For the Japan Mission of the Methodist Church of Canada, see Kuranaga Takashi, *Kanada Mesojisuto Nippon dendo gaishi* [A Short History of the Evangelistic Work of the Canadian Methodist Mission] (Tokyo, 1937).

[3]Ardath W. Burks, editor, "The Legacy: Products and By-Products of Cultural Exchange," in his *The Modernizers: Overseas Students, Foreign Employees, and Meiji Japan.* (Boulder, 1985), p. 365.

[4]See Edward R. Beauchamp, *An American Teacher in Early Meiji Japan* (Honolulu, 1976).

[5]E. W. Clark to W. E. Griffis, October 17, 1871. William Elliot Griffis Collection in the Rutgers University Library (hereafter cited as GCRUL).

[6]*Ibid.*

[7]E. W. Clark to W. E. Griffis, November 27, 1871, *ibid.*

[8]Griffis wrote of his own contract that "nothing was said concerning religion in any reference whatever, but perfect freedom from all duties whatsoever was guaranteed me on Sunday; and I had absolute liberty to speak, teach, or do as I pleased in my own house." W. E. Griffis, *The Mikado's Empire* (New York, 1899), p. 402.

[9]Yamamoto Yukinori, "Shizuoka han oyatoi gaikokujin kyoshi: E. W. Kuraku, Shizuoka Bando seiritsu no haikei" [Shizuoka Han Foreign Employee Teacher: E. W. Clark and the Background to the Establishment of the Shizuoka Band], in *Kirisutokyo Shakai Mondai Kenkyu* [Studies in Christianity and Sopcial Problems] 29, 3 (1981), p. 130.

[10]E. W. Clark to W. E. Griffis, November 27, 1871, GCRUL.

[11]Yamamoto, p. 130.

[12]Thomas R. H. Havens, *Nishi Amane and Modern Japanese Thought* (Princeton: 1970), p. 72.

[13]Yamamoto, pp. 135-36.

[14]Iida Hiroshi, *Shizuoka Ken Eigakushi* [A History of the Study of English in Shizuoka Prefecture] (Tokyo, 1967), p. 11.

[15]Henry Satoh, *My Boyhood: A Reminiscence* (Tokyo, 1921), 2nd edition, p. 76.

[16]Ota Aito, *Meiji Kirisutokyo no ryuiki: Shizuoka Bando to Bakushintachi* [The Course of Meiji Christianity: The Shizuoka Band and Vassals of the Shogun] (Tokyo, 1979), p. 12.

[17]Yamamoto, p. 122.

[18]Ota, p. 18.

[19]Yamamoto, pp. 121-123.

[20]*Ibid.*, p. 131.

21E. W. Clark, *Life and Adventure in Japan* (New York, 1878), p. 13.

22Takahashi Masao, *Nakamura Keiu* [Nakamura Keiu] (Tokyo, 1967), p. 94.

23E. W. Clark, p. 12.

24Ogihara Takashi, *Nakamura Keiu to Meiji Keimo shiso* [Nakamura Keiu and the Thought of the Meiji Enlightenment] (Tokyo, 1984), p. 214.

25Kuranaga Takashi, *Hiraiwa Yoshiyasu den* [The Biography of Hiraiwa Yoshiyasu] (Tokyo, 1937), p. 260.

26Ogihara, p. 215.

27See A. Hamish Ion, "Edward Warren Clark and Early Meiji Japan: A Case Study of Cultural Contact," *Modern Asian Studies*, 11, 4 (1977), pp. 564-565.

28Otis Cary, *A History of Christianity in Japan* (New York, 1909), Volume II, p. 25.

29Ogihara, p. 149.

30E. W. Clark, pp. 36-37.

31E. W. Clark, *Katz Awa: The Bismarck of Japan* (New York, 1904), pp. 14-15.

32W. E. Griffis, p. 548.

33E. W. Clark, *Life and Adventure in Japan*, pp. 41-42.

34Yamamoto, p. 134.

35Henry Satoh, p. 77.

36E. W. Clark to W. E. Griffis (October 26, 1872), GCRUL.

37E. W. Clark to W. E. Griffis (June 9, 1873), *ibid.*

38*Ibid.*

39Henry Satoh, p. 79.

40Ota Aito, p. 95.

41*Ibid.*, p. 97.

42John W. Saunby, *The New Chivalry in Japan: Methodist Golden Jubilee* (Toronto, 1923), p. 63.

43Ota Aito, p. 63.

44Matsuzawa Hiroaki, "Kirisutokyo to Chishikijin" [Christianity and Intellectuals] in *Iwanami Koza Nihon Rekishi* [Iwanami Lectures on Japanese History], 16, kindai 3 (Tokyo, 1976), pp. 282-320, passim.

45Ota Aito, p. 97,

46*Missionary Notices*, Third Series, IV, August 1876, letter from Davidson McDonald October 1, 1874, p. 7.

47*Ibid.*, p. 8.

48Ota Aito, p. 103.

49Iida Hiroshi, p. 53.

50*Missionary Notices*, Third Series, IV, August 1876, letter from Davidson McDonald (April 7 1876), p. 150.

51Amenomori Nobushige to W. E. Griffis, (July 23, 1876), GCRUL.

[52]Yamamoto Yukinori, "Yamaji Aizan to Kirisutokyo: Meiji niji nendai o chushin to shite" [Yamaji Aizan and Christianity, with a Particular Emphasis on the Period of the Meiji 20s], in *Kirisutokyo shakai Mondai Kenkyu* [Studies in Christianity and Social Problems] 26 (December 1977), pp. 102-162, p. 109.

[53]*Fifty-Fourth Annual Report of the Missionary Society of the Methodist Church of Canada*, p. xxxi.

[54]*Missionary Notices*, Third Series, 111 (June 1875), p. 46.

[55]Iida Hiroshi, p. 31.

[56]Kuranaga Takashi, pp. 22-23.

[57]Takahashi Masao, p. 128.

[58]*Wesleyan Missionary Notices*, XXIV, August 1874, letter from G. Cochran, April 22, 1874, p. 377.

[59]*Ibid.*

[60]Takahashi Masao, pp. 136-137.

[61]S. R. Brown to J. M. Ferris (February 19, 1874), Box 747.4N in the Archives of the Japan Mission of the Reformed Church of America, Gardiner Sage Library, New Brunswick Theological Seminary, New Brunswick, New Jersey.

[62]*Ibid.*

[63]*Ibid.*

[64]*Wesleyan Missionary Notices*, XXIV, August 1874, p. 379.

[65]*Ibid.*, p. 380.

[66]M. Kosaka (compiler and editor), *Japanese Thought in the Meiji Era*, (translated and adapted by David Abosch) (Tokyo, 1958), pp. 64-65.

[67]*Missionary Notices*, Third Series, IV, January 1877, letter from Charles S. Eby (October 24, 1877), p. 175.

PART THREE

CASE STUDIES: JAPANESE VIEWS

10

Contributions of Edward S. Morse to Developing Young Japan

Isono Naohide

Introduction

In June 1877, an American zoologist, Edward Sylvester Morse (1838-1925) visited Japan to collect and study various species of brachiopods.[1] Unexpectedly, he was offered the Professorship of Zoology at the recently established University of Tokyo[2] which he accepted, and taught at until August 1879.

Although his stay in Japan was rather short, he worked actively in diverse fields; he founded the Zoological Institute and the Museum of the Science Department at the University of Tokyo; he opened a Marine biological laboratory at Enoshima; he discovered and excavated the Omori shell mounds; he introduced Darwin's theory of evolution; and he organized the Biological Society, etc. Among the *yatoi* teachers of the Meiji period, only a few persons exerted as wide and deep an influence as Morse did upon the developing young Japan.

As the first step to a detailed study of his contributions, this author, together with Professor Sahara Makoto (Nara National Cultural Properties Research Institute) and Dr. Shiina Noritaka (National Science Museum), have been tracing Morse's daily activities through Japanese and English newspapers and journals of the period, annual publications of the University of Tokyo, documents of the Ministries of Education and Foreign Affairs, and the diaries of several contemporary Japanese. We have obtained a number of new findings, and corrected several mistakes and ambiguous descriptions found in Morse's *Japan Day by Day*[3] as well as in memoirs written by his students.[4]

Agreement Between Morse and the University of Tokyo

A few years ago, Professor Yoshida Tadashi, of Tohoku University, kindly offered the author use of copies of several letters addressed to Morse from Kato Hiroyuki, President of the University of Tokyo, which had been preserved in the Peabody Museum in Salem, Massachusetts. Among them were found the original agreement between Morse and the University of Tokyo, plus an additional agreement.[5] The full text is as follows:

Articles of Agreement between Mr. Hiroyuki Kato Sori of the Departments of Law, Science and Literature in Tokyo Daigaku [university] the party of the first part and Mr. Edward S. Morse of the United States of America.

Article 1—The said Mr. Morse is hereby appointed Professor of Zoology and Physiology in the Department of Science of Tokyo Daigaku for the term of two years, to wit, from the twelfth day of the seventh month of the tenth year of Meiji (July 12, 1877) to the eleventh day of the seventh month of the twelfth year of Meiji (July 11, 1879).

Article 2—The said Mr. Morse shall receive a salary of three hundred and fifty (350) Yen per month payable monthly in Japanese coin or its equivalent.

Article 3—The said Mr. Morse shall be provided with an unfurnished house and stable, free of rent, or at the option of the party of the first part shall receive the sum of thirty (30) Yen per month in Japanese currency in lease thereof.

N.B. It shall be understood that if a house is provided for the said Mr. Morse it shall be kept in proper repair by the party of the first part, but neither changes in the interior structure of any part of the house now any addition to it shall be made at the request of the said Mr. Morse.

Article 4—The power to fix hours and order of instruction to be given in the University shall rest with the party of the first part, but the said Mr. Morse shall in no case be required to teach more than four hours a day nor to teach on Sunday.

Article 5—The said Mr. Morse shall have the privilege of submitting his opinions in reference to matters connected with his Department of instruction at all times to the party of the first part, with whom the right of final decision shall remain.

Article 6—If the said Mr. Morse shall willfully neglect the proper duties of his position or shall be guilty of immoral conduct or shall refuse to comply with the regulations of the institution, this engagement may be annulled and from the day of such annulling no more salary shall be due or be paid.

Article 7—If the said Mr. Morse shall by reason of sickness be unable to perform his duties for a period of twenty consecutive days, then during the remainder of such sickness he shall receive only one third of his salary, and if after a period of sixty days from the beginning of such sickness he be still unable to resume his duties this engagement may be annulled and from the day of such annulling no more salary shall be due or be paid.

Article 8—If for reason of his own the said Mr. Morse shall at his request be released from this engagement, then his salary shall cease from the day of such release.

Article 9—If for reason of its own the party of the first part shall desire to discontinue the services of the said Mr. Morse before the term of this engagement has expired, it shall have the right to do so by paying him his salary for one half the unexpired term.

Article 10—The said Mr. Morse at the end of his services under the contract unless his service shall be continued and also when his services come to an end under the article 7 or 9 of the said contract shall receive the sum of four hundred and fifty Yen for travelling expenses of his return journey, but when his services come to an end under any other articles the said Mr. Morse shall have no right to receive the said travelling expenses.

Article 11—For reason of his own the said Mr. Morse shall during the term of his services be allowed to return to his own country and stay there during five months from the first day of November of this year to the thirty first day of March of next year, and during which time the said Mr. Morse shall not receive any salary.

N.B. The said Mr. Morse shall, while in America collect zoological specimens for the institution and on that account he shall receive a salary for three months and the expenses for transporting the specimens from America to Japan shall be paid by the party of the first part.

Dated at Tokyo this 16th day of the 7th month of the 10th year of Meiji (July 16, 1877)
Hiroyuki Kato
Sori of the Departments of Law, Science and Literature, Tokyo Daigaku
Edward S. Morse
Citizen of the United States of America

Additional Article

It is hereby agreed between Mr. Hiroyuki Kato, the Sori and Mr. Morse the Professor to renew the foregoing contract for the term of one month and twenty days, i.e. from the 12th day of the 7th month of the 12th year of Meiji to the 31st day of the 8th month of the same year under the same conditions as mentioned in the same contract with exception of the following alteration in the article 2.

Article 2—The said Mr. Morse shall receive a salary of three hundred and seventy (370) Yen per month in Japanese Bo-yeki-ichi-yen-gin (trade one yen), or its equivalent the same to be paid at the end of each month.

Dated at Tokyo this 12th day of the 7th month of the 12th year of
Meiji.

Kato Hiroyuki
Edward S. Morse

The above agreement seems to be a typical example in the employment of
yatoi teachers in the University, except for Article 11, which enabled Morse to
go back home so that he could fulfill his contract to present winter lectures,
and bring his family back to Japan.

His salary, $350 a month, was not extraordinary among the foreign
professors in the Departments of Law, Science and Literature. In the academic
year 1877, Professors H. Terry (law), W.E. Grigsby (law), P.V. Veeder
(physics), W.S. Chaplin (civil engineering), E. Naumann (geology) and C.A.
Netto (mining) received $350, respectively; W.E. Parson (mathematics) $335,
and F.F. Jewett (chemistry) $300.[6]

Zoology

Zoological Institute. The modern school of zoology in Japan dates from the
appointment of Morse to the professorship at the University of Tokyo.
Although F.M. Hilgendorf, a German zoologist, had been teaching natural
history at the Tokyo Medical School (predecessor of the Medical Department of
the University of Tokyo) from 1873 to 1876, he had no great influence on
biology in Japan, for he worked only in its preparatory course, and therefore
had no special students of zoology.[7]

As the first professor of zoology, Morse started from nothing. He had to
begin his lectures from the most basic elements of zoology, to train his
students to use plankton-nets, to dredge marine forms, to dissect them, and to
prepare zoological specimens. The Zoological Institute had only a few reference
books, little equipment and few specimens necessary for teaching zoology. In
short, he faced all kinds troubles. Through his tireless efforts, however, a sound
foundation was finally established for the Institute. Morse's students rapidly
attained a level that enabled them to study specialized subjects under the
guidance of Professor C.O. Whitman, Morse's successor in Japan.

Morse had five special students in the Zoological Institute—Matsura
Sayonhiko, Sasaki Chujiro, Iijima Isao, Iwakawa Tomotaro and Ishikawa
Chiyomatsu. Unfortunately, Matsura died of typhoid fever in 1878, but the
remaining four all became leaders of zoology in Japan. Morse exerted a
profound influence on these young students.[8]

Marine laboratories. In July 1877, Morse opened a seaside laboratory at
Enoshima, near Kamakura, and studied marine fauna until the end of August.[9]
Although small and temporary, it was the first marine biological station in
Japan. Morse later used similar facilities at Hakodate and Nagasaki. It was
noted by Whitman in his article, *Zoology in the University of Tokyo*,[10] that
Morse had also suggested to the University the establishment of a permanent
marine station. This suggestion was not realized at the time, but may have

been influential in the establishment of the Misaki Marine Biological Station in 1886.[11]

Biological Society. The establishment of the Biological Society of the University of Tokyo was also one of Morse's contributions.[12] Though its members numbered only twelve at first, its regular meetings were always greatly stimulating to students of biology. Records of the meetings were published in the *Tokyo Times.* In the course of time, this society developed into the present Zoological Society of Japan.

Invitation of Charles Whitman. Another of Morse's contributions was the invitation of Charles Otis Whitman (1842-1910) as his successor. Morse recognized that biologists of the next generation should master microscopical techniques (fixation of samples, microtome section cutting, staining of tissues, etc.) which had recently been developed in Europe. With this in mind, Morse recommended Whitman, since he had studied zoology in Germany and Italy for several years and had thoroughly learned these new methods.[13] Morse's choice was the correct one as Whitman carefully trained his students until they were competent in their field.

When Whitman left Japan in 1881, his name was scarcely known in the scientific community, but he later became an eminent zoologist, and is now remembered as the first Director of the Marine Biological Laboratory at Woods Hole, Massachusetts, and the founder of *Journal of Morphology.*

Table 1. List of publications appearing in *Memoirs*, 1879-1885.

Title of Journal	Vol./No.	Author/Title of Article Year of Publication
MSUT	Vol.1-Pt.1	E. S. Morse "Shell mounds of Omori" (1879)
MSUT	Vol. 2	C. A. Netto "On mining and mines in Japan" (1879)
MSUT	Vol. 3-Pt. 1	T. C. Mendenhall "Report on the meteorology of Tokyo for the year 2539 (1879)" (1880)
MSTD	No. 4	D. Brauns "Geology of the environs of Tokyo" (1881)
MSTD	No. 5	T. C. Mendenhall "Measurements of the force of gravity at Tokyo and on the summit of Fujinoyama" (1881)
MSTD	No. 6	R. W. Atkinson "The chemistry of Sake-brewing" (1881)
MSTD	No. 7	T. C. Mendenhall "Report on the meteorology of Tokyo for the year 2540 (1880)" (1881) The following two related reports are included. W. C. Chaplin "The height of Fujinoyama" and K. Yamagawa "Fires in Tokyo"
MSTD	No. 8	T. C. Mendenhall "The wave-length of some of the principal Fraunhofer lines of the solar spectrum" (1881)

MSTD	No. 9	J. A. Ewing "Earthquake measurement" (1883)
ATD	No. 10	J. F. Eykman "Phytochemische Notizen ueber einige Japanische Pflanzen" (1883)
MTD	No. 11	J. A. Waddell "A system of iron railroad bridges for Japan" (Text vol. + Plate-Table vol.) (1885)
ATD	No. 12	D. Kitao "Leukoscop, seine Anwendung und seine Theorie" (1885)
MSTD	Vol. 1-Pt. 1	I. Iijima & C. Sasaki "Okadaira shell mound at
	AP	Hitachi" (1885)
MSTD	No. 5 AP	A. Tanakadate, R. Fujisawa & S. Tanaka "Measurement of the force of gravity at Sapporo (Yesso)" (1882)
MTD	No. 5 AP	A. Sakai & E. Yamaguchi "Measurement of the force of gravity at Naha (Okinawa) and Kagoshima" (1884) The following related report is included. E. Yamaguchi "Observations of magnetic elements"
MTD	No. 5 AP	A. Tanakadate "Measurement of the force of gravity and magnetic constants at Ogasawarajima (Bonin Island)" (1885)

Abbreviations used: MSUT		*Memoirs of the Science Department, University of Tokyo, Japan*
	MSTD	*Memoirs of the Science Department, Tokyo Daigaku (University of Tokyo)*
	MTD	*Memoirs of the Tokyo Daigaku (University of Tokyo)*
	ATD	*Abhandlungen des Tokyo Daigaku (Universitat zu Tokyo)*
	AP	Appendix

Table 2. List of publications of the *Rika Kaisui*

No. (Chitsu)	Author (Translator)/Title of Article Date of Publication*
1-jo satsu	E. S. Morse (R. Yatabe) "Omori kaikyo kobutsuhen" (December 1879) (Translation of *Memoirs*, Vol. 1-Pt.1)
2	C. A. Netto (I. Imai & K. Ando) "Nihon kozanhen" (July 1880) (Translation of *Memoirs*, Vol. 2)
3-1 satsu	T. C. Mendenhall (K. Yamagawa) "Tokyo kishohen (1879)" (December 1880) (Translation of *Memoirs*, Vol. 3-Pt. 1)
3-2 satsu	T. C. Mendenhall (K. Yamagawa) "Tokyo kishohen (1880)" (September/October 1882**) (Translation of *Memoirs*, No. 7) The following two related reports are included.

	W. S. Chaplin (K. Yamagawa) "Fujisan no kodo"
	K. Yamagawa "Tokyo-fuka kasairoku"
4	D. Brauns (M. Nishi) "Tokyo kinbo chishitsuhen"(June 1882) (Translation of *Memoirs*, No. 4)
4-furoku	T. Kochibe "Gaisoku Johoku chishitsuhen" (October 1883***)
5	R. W. Atkinson (I. Nakazawa & T. Ishido) "Nihon joshuhen" (June 1882***) (Translation of *Memoirs*, No. 6)

*	Date of publication on the front cover, unless otherwise noted.
**	According to *Shuppan Shomoku Geppo*.
***	According to *Mombusho Shuppan Shomoku*.

The University of Tokyo

Morse's contributions to the University of Tokyo were not confined to the area of zoology.

Publication of science journals. In the autumn of 1877, Morse advised the officers of the University to publish an academic science journal, and to exchange it for the publications of American and European universities or scientific institutions.[14] His advice was accepted, and the Science Department began to publish two kinds of journals in 1879; one was *Memoirs of the Science Department, University of Tokyo, Japan* published in English, and the other was the *Rika Kaisui*, the Japanese version of the former. The first issue of the *Memoirs* was Morse's "Shell mounds of Omori," and that of the latter was its translation, "Omori Kaikyo Kobutsuhen." It is uncertain, however, if it was also Morse's idea to publish both English and Japanese language editions.

In August 1877, the University founded the *Gakugei Shirin*, a monthly Japanese journal, that was a kind of popular magazine. Accordingly, the *Memoirs* and the *Rika Kaisui* were the first academic science journals in Japan. Tables 1 and 2 contain a complete list of articles appearing in them.[15] As is evident from these tables, most of the contributors were *yatoi* professors.

The title of the *Memoirs* was modified in 1881 to *Memoirs of the Science Department, Tokyo Daigaku (University of Tokyo)*; in 1884, its title was again altered to *Memoirs of the Tokyo Daigaku (University of Tokyo)* for the English language edition, and to *Abhandlungen des Tokyo Daigaku (Universitat zu Tokyo)* for the German language edition. Sixteen issues including four supplements were published in all, before this journal was succeeded by *Journal of the College of Science, Imperial University, Japan*, after the name of the University had been changed in 1886 to the Imperial University.

Only seven issues of the *Rika Kaisui* were published between 1879 and 1883, and six of them were the translations from the English version, and the other an original article written by a Japanese student. It is unclear why the University ceased to publish the Japanese version.

Museum. Morse had been working both in the Museum of Comparative Zoology at Harvard University, and in the Peabody Academy of Science at

Salem (he later served as its director from 1880 to 1916). Accordingly, he recognized the importance of museums to natural science, and made a constant effort to develop them in Japan. He set up a zoological museum (specimen-room) in the Zoological Institute as soon as he started to teach zoology at the University of Tokyo.[16] In addition, he participated in the work of the Education Museum at Ueno from 1877 to 1879.[17]

The establishment in 1879 of the Museum of the University of Tokyo (*Hakubutsujo*) was also a result of his influence, and its two-storied building was designed by Morse himself.[18] Initially the University authorities were enthusiastic about developing this Museum, but several years later they lost their interest in it. As a result, the Museum was closed down in 1885 when the Science Department moved to a new campus at Hongo.

Unfortunately, this loss of enthusiasm also affected the Education Museum at Ueno which was discontinued in 1889. In the Museum of the Department of Agriculture and Commerce (the predecessor of the Imperial Museum), its natural history section declined with the passage of time. In short, Morse's expectation was not fulfilled. Even today, except for small and local ones, we have no real museum of natural history.

Library. Morse also contributed to the University Library. When he returned to America on a leave of absence in 1877-1878, he collected 2,500 books and pamphlets, as well as 3,000 zoological specimens, and brought them back to the University of Tokyo.[19] Even after leaving the chair of zoology, he worked to strengthen the University and, when he left Japan in 1879, Kato Hiroyuki, President of the University, asked Morse to carry to America a number of copies of *Shell Mounds of Omori,* together with duplicates of the specimens he had collected in order to exchange them for American journals and specimens useful for the University.[20] Morse agreed to this proposal and fulfilled the request.

Half a century later, he again made a major contribution to the University Library. On September 1, 1923, Tokyo was severely damaged by the Great Kanto Earthquake, and the Main Library of the Tokyo Imperial University (successor of the University of Tokyo) was completely destroyed by fire. Learning of this news, Morse bequeathed his entire scientific library, amounting to 12,000 volumes, to enable the library to reopen.[21]

On the recommendation of Morse, three American professors, Thomas C. Mendenhall (physics), Ernest F. Fenollosa (philosophy), and Charles Otis Whitman (zoology) were invited to take up positions at the University of Tokyo. They were all excellent teachers, and contributed greatly to the development of their respective fields in Japan.

Later, Morse's lectures on Japan at the Lowell Institute, in Massachusetts, fascinated a member of the audience, Percival Lowell, and he visited Japan in the summer of 1883. After remaining in Japan and Korea for several years, he published *The Soul of the Far East,* in 1888. It is often suggested that his book made a deep impression on Lafcadio Hearn, and may have influenced him to sail for Japan. Thus, on a number of levels, Morse seems to have played a significant role in cultural exchange between the United States and Japan.

Archaeology and Anthropology

In 1877, Morse's first scientific investigation of kitchen-middens in Japan resulted in his discovery and excavation of the famous Omari shell mounds. In addition, he unearthed a number of ancient pottery, bone tools and stone implements. Later he briefly examined shell heaps and other ancient remains at the Koishikawa Botanical Garden, Nishigahara and Tokyo as well as at Otaru, Hakodate, Kumamoto, Osaka and Kabutoyama.

As mentioned previously, the results of his investigation of the Omori shell mounds were published as the first issue of the *Memoirs*.[22] Even today, this report is valued highly, and shows much originality, accurate drawings, the classification of pottery according to its uses, and evolutionary studies on the shells obtained from the mounds.[23]

Morse claimed in this and other articles, that the shell mounds found in Japan had been produced by inhabitants living in Japan before the Ainu arrived, and that these early people were cannibal, as judged from the human bone fragments obtained in the mounds.

Both Morse's achievements and claims became widely known through his lectures, as well as through newspapers and magazines in other parts of the world. Many Japanese took great interest in his work and a large numbers of them examined ancient heaps and other remains for themselves. Although an interest in ancient implements and pottery had existed during the late Tokugawa period, it was generally pursued as a mere hobby. It was only as a result of Morse's Omori excavations that modern archaeology and anthropology emerged as scientific disciplines in Japan.

Among those with an interest in ancient remains were two of Morse's students, Sasaki Chujiro and Iijima Isao. In July 1879, the former discovered several shell heaps in Ibaraki Prefecture. He and Iijima excavated one of them at Okadaira in the following autumn and winter, and published their reports in 1880 and 1883.[24] This was the first independent excavation carried out by Japanese, and the reports were the first scientific archaeological publications prepared by Japanese scholars. However, both of these men later concentrated on zoology, and abandoned archeology.

Tsuboi Shogoro, whose interest was aroused by Morse's achievements, founded the modern fields of archeology and anthropology in Japan. Tsuboi, however, was not able to match Morse's accurate drawing, quantitative analysis, and functional classification of pottery, and a critic once suggested that Tsuboi's lack of skill delayed the development of these sciences in Japan.[25]

Darwinism

Introduction of evolutionary theory. It was Morse who introduced Darwin's theory of evolution into Japan. On September 24, 1877, he first referred to the problem of evolution in his lecture before a class in the Preparatory School of the University. One of his pupils, Tanakadate Aikitsu wrote in his journal, "A lecture on the Evolution Theory by Dr. Morse, very forcibly delivered."[26] In the following month, Morse gave a series of three lectures on evolution at the main hall of the University.[27] Although this series was opened to the public, the audience seems to have been limited mainly to professors and students, for his lectures were delivered with an interpreter.

On the other hand, in 1878 and 1879, Morse often made with the help of an interpreter, public lectures on Darwinism. It was through these lectures that the theory of evolution became widespread in Japan. The most popular of Morse's public appearances was a series of four lectures held at the Ibumuraro tea house (tea houses were often used as a public hall in those days) in the autumn of 1878.[28] An outline of these lectures was published in the weekly magazine, *Geijutsu Soshi*,[29] and was sold out as soon as they appeared in book-stores.

Another series of nine special lectures, delivered by Morse at the Main Hall of the University from March 5 to April 30, 1879 is also well known.[30] This series was delivered at the request of his pupils in the Preparatory School. One of them, Ishikawa Chiyomatsu, later translated Morse's lectures notes into Japanese, and published them in 1883 under the title, *Dobutsu Shinkaron* [The Theory of Animal Evolution].[31] This was the first Japanese book on evolution to be published.

Social Darwinism. It has been charged that Morse's lectures on evolution were of poor quality and led the public to an inadequate understanding of evolutionary theory. These critics also contend that Morse often inadequately applied Darwinian ideas to mankind, and was responsible for popularizing the concept of "Social Darwinism" (an idea applying the concepts of the "survival of the fittest" directly to human society), and these concepts were used by military circles for the oppression of democratic movements, as well as providing a justification for aggression upon Korea and China.

However, so far as judged from his book *Dobutsu Shinkaron* and the lecture summary appearing in the *Geijutsu Soshi*, the above criticism does not appear to be a valid one.

The great majority of Morse's audiences, including professors and students, were quite unfamiliar with modern biology. It was then not surprising that Morse's lectures were not academic, but popular. This does not necessarily mean, however, that his lectures were of poor quality. On the contrary, they were well-planned for beginners, containing most of the knowledge necessary for understanding Darwinism, and illustrating many good examples of evolution and natural selection. It is true that he often referred to mankind, but most of the examples cited seem to be appropriate ones. In *Dobutsu Shinkaron*, the only reference to Social Darwinism was a brief one, which reads:

In old times, when races fought with each other, the survivor was always the one having a stronger fighting instinct. This instinct is necessary also for civilization and for modern wars. . . .

One of the influential leaders of the Social Darwinists was Herbert Spencer, who claimed that the struggle for existence led to the evolution of human society. Some of his writings had already been known among Japan's intellectual community *before* Darwinism itself was introduced by Morse, although Spencer's evolutionary ideas did not achieve popularity at this time.[32]

During the 1880s, however, Spencer's philosophy spread rapidly in Japan. Interestingly enough, his publications were utilized not only by conservatives but also by liberals, for his ideas were so broad that they could be interpreted in various ways. During the period from 1877 to 1886, as many as twenty of Spencer's writings were translated into Japanese.[33] On the other hand, only three translations were published on Darwinian theory during the same period. Two of them were partial translations that did not include the central ideas of evolutionary theory. Morse's *Dobutsu Shinkaron* was the only book available on evolutionary theory.

Examined in this context, it is unlikely that Morse's lectures led to the introduction of Spencer's theory. On the contrary, it is highly likely that they were rather intentionally utilized for the authorization of the latter.

Attack on missionaries. Darwinian evolutionary thought is inconsistent with the Christian conception of man and nature as described in the Bible. Although twenty years had passed since the publication of Darwin's *Origin of Species*, many missionaries living in Japan still refused to admit that living things were the products of evolution, and that man and ape were the descendants from a common ancestor. Morse, an ardent advocate of Darwinism, always sharply criticized these attitudes of the missionaries in his lectures. This criticism posed a danger to the missionaries; therefore, they launched a vigorous campaign against Morse's arguments. It was, however, far from being persuasive and they failed in their efforts to refute Darwinism.[34]

Acceptance of evolutionary theory. Unlike Americans or Europeans, the Japanese accepted the theory of evolution without strong objections. What, then, was the difference between the Western world and Japan?

Naturally the first is the difference in religious backgrounds. Buddhism postulates that everything is constantly changing in the Universe. In other words, "change" is not abnormal, but normal. To people living in such a world, the concept of evolution was nothing particularly new or strange, in contrast to those grown up in the Christian world.

Second, apes do not inhabit Europe and the United States, whereas they have been one of the most familiar animals in Japan. Even today, Japanese apes can be seen not only in remote areas, but also in the neighborhood of villages or even towns. They often appear in folk stories, and sometimes were worshipped as gods or dogs' emissaries. Every Japanese well knows that apes bear close resemblances to men in both appearance and behavior. Accordingly, when Morse stated that man and ape had a common origin, most of the audience would have accepted this view without hesitation.

Third, during the time when Morse visited Japan, everything had been changing rapidly in the midst of *Bunmei Kaika* (civilization and enlightenment); it was an age of "evolution." The struggle for existence and the survival of the fittest were daily events in the Japan of the latter half of the nineteenth century. It was no wonder that most Japanese found Darwinian ideas compatible with the spirit of their age.

Finally, when a new paradigm emerged with the publication of *The Origin of Species*, several eminent Western biologists vehemently rejected Darwinian ideas (e.g., Louis Agassiz). A long, heated controversy ensued in America and Europe, preventing the rapid spread of Darwin's theory. However, in Japan, modern biology had not yet been established, so the old paradigm did not exist. Naturally, no objection was offered from biologists, and Darwinism spread as soon as it was introduced.

Biological studies on evolution. Morse studied brachiopods in order to make their origins clear. He also worked on the bones of birds to ascertain the relationship between birds and reptiles. In America and Europe, studies along similar lines had been actively carried out in systematics, morphology, embryology, ecology, physiology, and biochemistry. But, in Japan, such an approach had been generally ignored. This curious situation seems to result mainly from Japan's neglect of her natural history.

In Europe, modern natural history was born in the middle of the sixteenth century, and a vast amount of knowledge was accumulated about animals and plants during the subsequent years. It was this accumulation that led to an emergence of Darwin's theory and to further developments in studies of evolution. Today's evolutionary ecology, one of the newest fields in biological research, is also built upon the structure of natural history.

Natural history, thus, occupies an important position in biology. Japanese biologists, however, have not fully recognized its importance until recently. This is reflected by the lack of natural history museums as described previously. Natural history was regarded by some as an obsolete science, and this attitude was a major reason why studies on evolution developed poorly in Japan.

On the other hand, when evolutionary theory was introduced in Japan, there was no opposition defending the traditional views. In addition, Western biologists in early Meiji Japan, including Morse and Whitman, were convinced Darwinians. Naturally, Darwin's theory of evolution was easily accepted by these scientists, but owing to a lack of controversy the chance to strengthen biological studies on evolution was lost.

Morse expected that the evolutionary approach would be fully developed in Japan, but this has not occured. The situation today is unsatisfactory with many Japanese biologists claiming that biology in Japan needs to be reconstructed.[35]

Public Lectures

It was in the mid-1870s that public lectures became popular in Japan, but they rarely took up scientific subjects. The one exception was the Egi Gakko Kodankai (Egi Lecture School), a public lecture association established by Egi Takato, Professor at the Preparatory School of the University of Tokyo.[36]

Upon returning from study in America in 1876, Egi began to organize public lectures, including one on June 30, 1878, in which Morse delivered a lecture on the Omori shell mounds.

On September 21, 1878, Egi formally established the Egi Gakko Kodankai.[37] This association had regular bi-monthly meetings at the Ibumurauo tea house which was used as a public hall in those days. A number of distinguished scholars joined the association as regular lecturers. Among them were Egi Takato, Kato Hiroyuki (President of the University of Tokyo), Toyama Masakazu (Professor of Philosophy), Kikuchi Dairoku (Professor of Mathematics), Fukuzawa Yukichi (founder of Keio University), as well as foreigners like Ernest S. Fenollosa and Thomas C. Mendenhall. This association continued until March 1881.

Morse and Mendenhall lectured at least thirteen times, and their lectures were always crowded with an audience of several hundred people. The most famous was a series of four lectures on evolution delivered by Morse. In addition, he lectured on such diverse subjects as insect life, spiders, glaciers, the principles of animal growth, and the arts of illustration.

Mendenhall lectured primarily on scientific instruments such as the telegraph, the telephone, the phonograph, the magnet and compass, often demonstrating the apparatus during the meeting.[38] People were greatly interested in those novel electrical products, and the apparatus which most astonished them was the telephone, invented only a few years earlier. Mendenhall also gave a talk on the moon, using lantern slides, which attracted a large audience, for slide projections were still uncommon in Japan.

In the early Meiji era when people had few occasions to learn about scientific matters, these lectures contributed greatly to the popularization of science. Unfortunately, the significance of the Egi Gakko Kodankai has been ignored in the history of Japanese science.

Morse and Today's Japan

Morse left two great legacies. One is his collection of Japanese pottery and ethnological articles which he began to collect while in Japan between 1877 and 1879. His interest in these things, however, seems to have increased upon his return to the United States, and he visited Japan again in 1882-1883 solely for the purpose of adding to his collections. His Japanese pottery collection is now preserved in the Boston Museum of Fine Arts and his ethnological materials in the Peabody Museum of Salem (formerly the Peabody Academy of Science).

An important characteristic of both collections is that they include not only artistically important materials, but also many common articles used by people in their daily lives during the late Tokugawa and early Meiji periods. The latter makes the collection especially valuable for at least two reasons. First, such articles were seldom collected and rarely preserved so that man can see how his predecessors lived. Second, much of what did exist were destroyed in the great Kanto Earthquake of 1923, and during the World War II bombing raids on Japan.

While Morse left many "specimens" of the articles used by the Meiji Japanese in his collections, he also made a detailed "description" of their daily life in two publications, *Japanese Homes and Their Surroundings* (1886)[39] and *Japan Day by Day* (1917).[40] In the former book, we find hundreds of accurate sketches of houses and household furniture, together with precise descriptions of them, all of which are rarely available elsewhere. It differs sharply from similar books in that its major subject is neither shrines nor temples, but the houses of middle-class families, and is so detailed that he even describes lavatories and privies. Furthermore, he tried hard to see things, insofar as a human being can, through unbiased eyes. This attitude contributed to making the book one of the best ethnological reports on Japanese life.[41]

The second book, *Japan Day by Day*, is a record of his residence in Japan, and includes interesting and valuable information on the Japanese of the time. He described their daily life in detail including customs, feelings, morals, strengths and weaknesses, without religious or cultural bias. He informs the reader of many things that otherwise would have been lost during the past century.

Much is owed to Edward S. Morse. Not only did he contribute to the economic development of Japan, but he also enables people of today to gain a better understanding of life in an age that has receded into the mists of history.

Appendix

Morse in Japan, 1877-1879 and 1882-1883. Morse visited Japan three times: the first, from June 17 to November 5, 1877; the second, from April 23, 1878 to September 3, 1879; the third, from June 4, 1882 to February 14, 1883.* Events during these three visits are summarized below.**

1877

April 28	The *Tokyo Times* reported that Morse would visit Japan before long.
June 17	Arrived at Yokohama at midnight (the date may have been June 18.)
June 19	On his way to Tokyo by train, he discovered the Omori shell mounds. When he met Dr. David Murray and Professor

	Toyama Masakazu at the Ministry of Education, the latter offered Morse the Professorship of Zoology at the University of Tokyo.
June 26	Delivered a special lecture at the University, at Professor Toyama's request.
June 29	Left Tokyo for Nikko, with Dr. David Murray (returned on July 8).
July 16	Signed a two-year contract (from June 12, 1877 to June 11, 1879) to teach at Tokyo University.
July 17	Visited Enoshima with Yatabe Ryokichi, Professor of Botany, and rented a cottage to use as a temporary marine laboratory. He studied there from July 21 to August 29.
September 12	Started lectures at Tokyo University.
September 16	Excavated the Omori shell mounds for the first time.
September 26	Lectured on the theory of evolution before a class in the Preparatory School, University of Tokyo.
October 6	Started a course of three lectures on Darwinism at the University.
	The October 6 issue of the *Tokyo Times* first reported Morse's discovery of the Omori shell mounds—"Professor E. S. Morse has made an important discovery in the study of ancient man in this part of the world, lighting on evidence of the remains of pre-historic inhabitants of Nippon who apparently must have antedated even the Ainos [Ainn]. The eyes of this distinguished scholar, possessing as they do the rare quality of seeing, observed, while he was on his first trip to the capital from Yokohama, one of those significant shell-heaps which have been found in many countries and prove the high antiquity of the human race. This particular *kjokkenmoedding* is situated near Omori, on the line of the railroad, and is rich in evidence of a rude people that dwelt in Japan at a very early age. . . . This heap, which is about ten feet in thickness at its greatest diameter, under a loam deposit of six feet, and half a mile from the present shore of third bay, exhibited all the peculiarities of its type, containing bone, both in fragment and rudely fashioned into implements, and characteristic pottery. Some of the earthen ware is curious enough, and is thoroughly representative of a development of the race coinciding with that of the ancient savages of America and Europe. . . ."
October 13	Delivered a lecture on the Omori shell mounds before the Asiatic Society of Japan.
November 5	Sailed from Yokohama for America. During his absence, the excavations were carried out by his special students, Matsura Sayonhiko and Sasaki Chujiro.

1878

April 23	Arrived at Yokohama, with his family and Takamine Hikeo (later to become Assistant Professor of Zoology).
May 11	A public lecture on the glacial age at the University of Tokyo.
June 2	A lecture on archaeology and the Omori shell mounds before a native archaeological club.
June 8	An open lecture under the title "Arts of illustration" at Tokyo University.
June 30	An open lecture on the Omori shell mounds, through an interpreter, at the Ibumuraro tea house. It was virtually his first lecture before the general public.
July 5	His special student, Mausura Sayohiko, died of typhoid.
July 13	Sailed from Yokohama for Hakodate, on an expedition to Hokkaido, together with Yatabe, Takamine, Sasaki and others. Morse opened a temporary marine laboratory at Hakodate.
August 18	Morse and Yatabe started a land trip from Aomori to Tokyo (arrived on August 27).
September 21	Attended the opening ceremony of the Egi Gakko Kodankai (a public lecture association).
October 20	The first meeting of the Biological Society of the Tokyo Dai Gaku (now the Zoological Society of Japan), which was founded under the leadership of Morse.
October 27	Started a course of four lectures on Darwinism before the Egi Gakko Kodankai.
	Morse began to collect Japanese pottery during autumn 1878.
December 3	Examined a shell heap in the Koishikawa Botanical Garden, University of Tokyo.
December 18	Fukuzawa Yukichi, founder of Keio Gijuku, recommended Morse for membership of the Tokyo Gakushi Kaiin (the Academy of Tokyo), but this recommendation was not accepted.

1879

January 25	Began a series of three lectures on Darwinism at the Ministry of Education.
March 5	Began a series of nine lectures on Darwinism at the University, by the request of his students.
March 21	Examined a shell heap at Nishigahara, Tokyo.
May 7	Sailed from Yokohama on an expedition to western Japan. At Nagasaki, he opened a marine laboratory during his stay. After visiting Kagoshima and Kumamoto, he went to Osaka, and examined the ancient dolmens in its neighborhood. He sailed from Kobe, and arrived at Tokyo on June 19.

July 12	His contract with the University was extended till August 31.
July 20	Began a series of four lectures before an audience of high society and nobles, at the Kazoku Kaikan hall. Late in July, Sasaki Chujiro discovered several shell heaps in Ibaragi Prefecture, and asked Morse's advice for the excavations.
August 10	Left Tokyo to visit the ancient tombs at Kabutoyama.
September 3	Left Yokohama with his family for America. Morse's report, "Shell mounds of Omori" in *Memoirs of the Science Department, University of Tokyo, Japan* seems to have been published just before his departure. Its Japanese version, *Omori Kaikyo Kobutsuhen* was published somewhat later in the *Rika Kaisui*.

1882

June 4	Morse and William S. Bigelow arrived at Yokohama.
June 30	Lectured on the theory of evolution at the Meiji Kaido Hall under the sponsorship of the Biological Society.
July 5	Lectured on the fish culture in America and Europe, before the Fisheries Society of Great Japan.
July 26	Left Tokyo by *jinrikisha* for the Kansai region to collect Japanese pottery and folk articles, together with Bigelow and E. F. Fenollosa. They visited Kyoto, Osaka, Hiroshima, Iwakuni, Wakayama and Nara. Morse returned to Tokyo on September 11.
October 6	Left Tokyo to visit the ancient tombs at Kabutoyama again.
October 18	Lectured at the *Gakushuin* (the Peer's School).

1883

January 11	Lectured on the origin of man at the Tokyo Semmon Gakko (now Waseda University).
January 12	Lectured on the reptilian nature of birds at the University of Tokyo.
February 14	Left Japan for China. After visiting China and other Asian countries, he went to Europe, and after staying France and England, he arrived at New York on June 5.

* *Japan Weekly Mail*, June 23, 1877; November 10, 1877; April 23, 1878; September 6, 1879; June 10, 1882. Also, *Japan Gazette Fortnightly Review*, February 23, 1883.

** References to each item are shown in Isono Naohide, "Edowado Shiruvesuta Mosu" (see note 1); Isono Naohide, *Mosu Sonohi Sonohi* (Yokohama: Yurindo, in press); Isono Naohide, "Mosu nenpyo," in *Mosu to Nihon*. Edited by Moriya Takeshi (Tokyo: Shogakukan, in press).

Notes

[1]Morse's life and his activities in Japan are described in: D. G. Wayman, *Edward Sylvester Morse: A Biography* (Cambridge, 1942); Watanabe Masao, "E. S. Mosu," in *Oyatoi Beikokugin Kagaku Kyoshi* (Tokyo, 1976), pp. 197-273; Isono Naohide, "Edowado Shiruvesuta Mosu," *Keio Gijiku Daigaku Hiyoshi Ronbunshu, Shizen Kagakuhen*, No. 18 (1894), pp. 48-113.

[2]Although Tokyo was spelled Tokio during the Meiji period, this chapter uses the spelling Tokyo throughout.

[3]E. S. Morse, *Japan Day by Day* (Boston, 1917).

[4]Iwakawa Tomotaro, "Onshi Morusu sensei o omou," *Toyo Gakugei Zasshi*, 42 (1926), pp. 125-127; Iwakawa Tomotaro, "Morusu sensei o tuisosu," *Dobutsugaku Zasshi*, 38 (1926), pp. 204-210, 316-319; Sasaki Chujiro, "Nihon dobutsugaku no onjin, Morusu sensei," *Jinruigaku Zasshi*, 41 (1926), pp. 43-48; Sasaki Chujiro, "Nihon dobutsugaku n sigen," *Dobutsugaku Zasshi*, 41 (1929), pp. 361-362; Ishikawa Chiyomatsu, "50 nen mae no nihon no dobutsugaku," *Dobutsugaku Zasshi*, 41 (1929), pp. 349-358; Ishikawa Chiyomatsu, *Ro Kagakusha no Shuki* (Tokyo, 1936).

[5]Isono Naohide, "Edowado S. Mosu no keiyakusho," *Keio Gijuku Daigaku Hiyoshi Kiyo, Shizen Kagaku*, No. 1 (1985), pp. 63-68.

[6]*Monbusho Daigo Nenpo, Furoku*, pp. 5-6.

[7]Isono Naohide, "Oyatoi doitsujin hakubutsugaku kyoshi," *Keio Gijuku Daigaku Hiyoshi Kiyo, Shizen Kagaku*, No. 2 (1986), pp. 24-47.

[8]Ishikawa Chiyomatsu, "Onshi Morusu sensei," *Toyo Gakugei Zasshi*, 42 (1926), pp. 121-125; Sasaki Chujiro, "Ko Morusu sensei no itsuji," *Dobutsugaku Zasshi*, 38 (1926), pp. 84-86; see also literature cited in note 4.

[9]Morse, *Japan Day by Day*, Vol. 1, pp. 138-245.

[10]C. O. Whitman, *Zoology in the University of Tokyo* (Yokohama, 1881), p. 29.

[11]Isono Naohide, "Tokyo Daigaku Misaki Rinkai Jikkenjo shi, I," *Keio Gijuku Daigaku Hiyoshi Ronbunshu, Shizen Kagakuhen* No. 19 (1985), pp. 42-74; Isono Naohide, "Tokyo Daigaku Misaki Rinkai Jikkenjo shi, II," *Keio Gijuku Daigaku Hiyoshi Kiyo, Shizen Kagaku*, No. 1 (1985), pp. 42-62.

[12]*Dobutsugaku Zasshi*, 23 (1911), pp. 532-534; Isono Naohide, "Edowado S. Mosu."

[13]E. S. Morse, "Biographical memoir of Charles Otis Whitman, 1842-1910," *National Academy of Sciences, Biographical Memoirs*, 7 (1912), pp. 269-288.

[14]Morse, *Japan Day by Day*, Vol. I, p. 311.

[15]Isono Naohide, "Honpo saisho no daigaku kiyo," *Keio Gijuku Daigaku Hiyoshi Kiyo, Shizen Kagaku*, No. 2 (1986), pp. 48-56.

[16]Morse, *Japan Day by Day*, Vol. I, p. 319.

[17]Shiina Noritaka, "E. E. Mosu to hakubutsukan," *Kokogaku Kenkyu*, 24: 3/4 (1977), pp. 70-76.

[18]Morse, *Japan Day by Day*, Vol. II, p. 211.

[19]Ibid., Vol. I, p. 139; E. S. Morse, "Dobutsugaku kyoju Edowarudo Esu Morusu shi shinpo," *Tokyo Daigaku Ho-ri-bungakubu Dairoku Nenpo*, pp. 64-77.

[20]The letter from Kato Hiroyuki to Morse, August 30, 1879 (Peabody Museum of Salem).

[21]Wayman, *Edward Sylvester Morse*, p. 432.

[22]E. S. Morse, "Shell mounds of Omori," *Memoirs of the Science Department, University of Tokyo, Japan*, Vol. 1-Part 1 (1879); Sahara Makoto, "Omori kaizuka hyakunen," *Kokogaku Kenkyu*, 24: 3/4 (1977), pp. 19-48.

[23]Kondo Shiro and Sahara Makoto, "Kaisetsu" in E. S. Morse's *Omori Kaizuka* (New translation of "Shell mounds").

[24]Sasaki Chujiro and Iijima Isao, "Jo-shu Okadaira kaikyo hokoku," *Gakugei Shirin*, 6 (1880), pp. 91-110; Iijima Isao and Sasaki Chujiro, "Okadaira shell mound at Hitachi," *Memoirs of the science Department, Tokyo Daigaku (University of Tokyo)*, Appendix to Vol. 1-Part 1 (1883).

[25]Kondo and Sahara, "Kaisetsu," p. 213.

[26]Tanakadate Aikitsu's journal, September 24, 1877 (preserved in National Science Museum, Tokyo).

[27]Morse, *Japan Day by Day*, Vol. I, pp. 339-340.

[28]Isono Naohide, "Shinkaron no nihon eno donyu to Mosu," *Saiensu*, 15: 4 (1985), pp. 96-107.

[29]*Geijutsu Soshi*, Nos. 20-25 (1878).

[30]Isono, "Shinkaron no nihon eno donyu to Mosu."

[31]E. S. Morse (translated by Ishikawa Chiyomatsu), *Dobutsu Shinkaron* (Bankan Shoro zohan, 1883).

[32]Spencer's name began to appear in editorials or correspondences of Japanese newspapers around 1876. For example, see *Yubin Hochi Shimbun*, July 15, 1876; December 21, 1876; *Tokyo Nichi Nichi Shimbun*, December 28, 1876; January 24, 1877; April 25, 1877. The Ministry of Education started to translate Spencer's *Education* in the spring of 1877, *Tokyo Nichi Nichi Shimbun* (April 2, 1877).

[33]Yamashita Shigekazu, *Supensa to Nihon Kindai* (Tokyo, 1983), pp. 4-7.

[34]Honda Yoichi, "Kirisutokyo" in *Kaikoku Gojunenshi* (Edited by Okuma Shigenobu, Kaikoku gojunensi Hakkojo, 1908), Vol. 2, pp. 109-110. [*Fifty Years of New Japan*, Vol. II (London, 1910), p. 88].

[35]E. S. Morse, "What American zoologists have done for evolution," *Proceedings of the American Association for the Advancement of Science*, 25 (1876), pp. 137-176.

[36]Isono Naohide, "Egi Gakko Kodankai to Mosu no kagaku koen," *Shinagawa Rekishikan Kiyo*, No. 2 (1987), pp. 35-50.

[37]*Yubin Hochi Shimbun*, September 18, 20, 24, 1878; Fujita Mokichi, "Kodankai" (editorial), *ibid.* (September 24, 1878).

[38]*Yubin Hochi Shimbun*, January 13, 16, 1878; *Tokyo Nichi Nichi Shimbun*, January 15, 1878; Richard Rubinger, "A Scientist Views Early Meiji Japan: The Autobiographical Notes of Thomas C. Mendenhall," chapter

5 of this volume. See also, Rubinger's, *An American Scientist in Early Modern Japan: The Autobiographical Notes of Thomas C. Mendenhall* (Honolulu, 1989).

[39]E. S. Morse, *Japanese Homes and Their Surroundings* (Boston, 1886).

[40]See Note 3.

[41]Saito Shoji, "Kaisetsu" in E. S. Morse's *Nihonjin no Sumai* (Translation of *Japanese Homes and Their Surroundings* by Saito Shoji & Fujimoto Shuichi: Tokyo, 1979), pp. 165-203.

11

Margaret C. Griffis and the Education of Women in Early Meiji Japan

Usui Chizuko

Introduction

An American Teacher in Early Meiji Japan, by Edward Beauchamp, provides a full account of the reasons behind the decision of Margaret Clark Griffis (1838-1913) to journey to Japan in August, 1872. Beauchamp suggests that William Elliot Griffis urged his sister Margaret (more often called Maggie), to join him in Japan because of his yearning for female companionship following the death of his mother and his rejection by the young woman he loved in the United States. A second reason for Maggie's decision to go to Japan was the opportunity to secure a teaching position.[1]

In any event, Maggie arrived in Japan in the autumn of 1872 and remained with her brother for two years. During this period she worked as an English teacher, for a year and four months, at Tokyo Jogakko, Japan's first government school for girls.

Studies of William Elliot Griffis refer to Maggie as a good helper though, naturally, she is depicted as a secondary figure. Furthermore, few works on the history of women's education in Japan mention her, partly because of her relatively short stay in Japan and partly because of a scarcity of materials concerning her.

Tokyo Jogakko, established in February 1872 and closed in February 1877 as a result of governmental budget cuts, still enjoys a good reputation in the

The author wishes to thank Mr. Clark Beck, of the Rutgers University Library, for his help in providing materials upon which this study is based.

history of women's education in Japan. The school reflected the enlightened, progressive and innovative character of the early Meiji government in supporting female education.[2]

Maggie Griffis was one of the original group of foreign women employed by the government and her journals and letters, as well as the English essays written by her students, provide valuable data for reconstructing the early history of Tokyo Jogakko. They included details on student-teacher relations and the family backgrounds of her students.[3]

Reference Materials About Margaret Griffis in Japan

(1) Government Documents

There is an official record containing basic information on Maggie's employment in Japan. It lists her age as 28 years in 1873, and records her starting salary as 50 yen per month from March 1, 1873. This was raised to 110 yen per month starting in September 1, 1873 and to 150 yen per month from April, 1874. She is described as the "elder sister of W. E. Griffis; teaches three hours a day, which was increased to 6 hours a day from September 1, 1873; awarded bonus of 50 yen for fulfilling the period of employment."[4] It is interesting to note that, in 1873, Maggie was actually 35 years old and not 28 as listed in this document.

(2) A Glimpse of Maggie in the Autobiography of Takahashi Koreikiyo

Takahashi Koreikiyo, a renowned Japanese politician in the 1920s, assisted Maggie's brother William Elliot Griffis, during the former's student days at Kaisei Gakko, translating Japanese classical literature. While the two men worked, Maggie sat listening to their conversation until they sent her from the room whenever some obscene words had to be translated.[5] Clearly, Maggie shared her brother William's interest in Japanese culture.

(3) Opinion of Hatoyama Haruko About Maggie

Hatoyama Haruko, a prominent female educator and a graduate of Tokyo Jogakko, describes in her autobiography how Maggie was quite indulgent to those of her pupils who did not study hard.[6]

(4) Annual Reports of the Ministry of Education

The annual reports of the Ministry of Education for 1872 and 1873 describe the Tokyo Jogakko opening at an elementary educational level in February 1872. English was taught by foreign teachers and the best students would serve as interpreters. One of these interpreters, Akai Yone, proved to be Maggie's best pupil and friend.

The Ministry of Education's report for 1873 made it clear that the Tokyo Jogakko was not an ordinary elementary school for girls, but was a training school for female teachers and interpreters. The 1874 report stated that the school offered an elementary course including English and handicrafts. The number of pupils enrolled increased from 18 in 1873 to 78 the following year, but the number of teachers remained constant—six Japanese and one foreigner. The pupils' ages ranged from 8 to 15 years.

In 1875, however, the school was transformed into a secondary school and the age span of pupils was increased to ages 14-17. Clearly the school was an interesting mixture of elementary and secondary levels during the period in which Maggie taught at Tokyo Jogakko. Among the textbooks used by Maggie were the *Wilson Reader* and the *Wilson Speller*.

Maggie's Life Prior to Japan

According to Rosemary Carroll, Maggie was born the daughter of a socially prominent and prosperous businessman, engaged in the coal business in Philadelphia, and his pious Dutch Reformed wife in 1838.[7] Young Maggie was educated in a school for young ladies operated by a Reverend and Mrs. Patton, where she was taught music, sewing and reading. Serious and melancholy by nature, Maggie liked to study and particularly enjoyed music and foreign languages. She acquired a familiarity with French, German and Latin while reading widely in the works of Plutarch, Friedrich Schiller, Sir Walter Scott, James Fenimore Cooper, Washington Irving, Harriet Beecher Stowe and Henry James.[8]

The Panic of 1857 destroyed the economic foundation of the Griffis family forcing William to drop out of Central High School and Maggie to take a job as a governess in Tennessee. This began her teaching career which is outlined below:[9]

1857–October, 1858: Governess of the children of William B. Isler on the Meriwether Plantation, Meriwether Landing, near Tiptonville, Tennessee.

November, 1859–March, 1860: Governess to the Robinson family, Benville (near Centreville), Virginia).

January–April, 1861: Governess of the five children of the Augustus Addison family at "Sunnyside," near Washington, D. C.

November, 1864–September, 1865: Governess to the Solis family (location unknown).

November, 1865–1868: Governess to Mitchell family (location unknown).

June–September, 1869: European trip with brother William.

1871–1872: Tutoring Sei Yehi Tejima, a Lafayette College student boarding with the Griffis family.

August, 1872–July, 1874: English teacher at Tokyo Jogakko.

1876–1898: Teacher in Miss R. E. Judkin's School for Girls, Philadelphia.

As this brief chronology suggests, Maggie began her teaching when she was 19 years old because of the decline of the economic fortunes of the Griffis family. Thus she had already toiled for 15 years as a teacher when she came to Japan in 1872, and she spent 24 more years teaching after leaving Japan in 1874.

Maggie's educational background consisted of what she had received at Reverend and Mrs. Patton's School for Girls, and the type of education that in those days was referred to as "accomplishments" for the better class of young women. Due to Maggie's proclivity for study and her constant striving for an intelligent family atmosphere, however, she was essentially self-taught. Though without a formal college education, Maggie possessed a broad intelligence which served her well.

Life at Tokyo Jogakko

Upon arriving in Japan, Maggie kept house for her brother William and helped him with his work. She was, however, unemployed during the autumn of 1872, and in a letter to her sisters she made it clear that "I want to be working for myself. I don't like dependence on anybody, and then I want to be helping you. I know you have just as much as I have, but I would like to send you presents of money."[10]

She became friends with the wives of two well-known members of the foreign community, Mrs. Guido Verbeck and Mrs. Peter Veeder.

Mrs. Verbeck has just made me a call and we have arranged for a horseback ride tomorrow. I have had a long talk with her about school, [and] she says that the mania for female education seems to have died out and the Japs expect to get taught for nothing. I wanted to establish a private school, but I cannot get any scholars so I must try to and stay contented without any teaching.[11]

Mrs. Veeder had been teaching at Tokyo Jogakko since its founding in February, 1872, and was sympathetic to Maggie's plight. "Mrs. Veeder," Maggie wrote, "is very kind and would do anything in the world for me."[12] It came as no surprise, therefore, that she asked Maggie to substitute teach for her on occasion.

I have been teaching school two days a week for Mrs. Veeder, who has gone to Yokohama. It is just like Martha's teaching, the girls are of all ages from 7 to 17, some spell only, some read simple, easy books—and she teaches through an interpreter. She has about 50 pupils. The school is both English and Japanese. 1/2 study Japanese in the morning, while the other half are at English, then they exchange. There are not purely English schools yet, the Japs don't like their language neglected. the girls are very interesting, and as good as boys, no trouble in teaching in regard to discipline.[13]

The above makes it clear that Maggie had some teaching experience at Tokyo Jogakko prior to becoming a full-time teacher at the school in February, 1873. At that time she wrote that:

Mr. [Marion M.] Scott here last evening, and Mr. Verbeck called to offer me a position in Mrs. Veeder's school to teach 2 and 1/2 hours per day at 50 yen a month. I am to give an answer today. The government intended to give up the school, but have finally decided to keep it up with two English teachers, each teaching 2 and 1/2 hours.[14]

Thus, it appears that Mrs. Veeder shared her teaching job with Maggie, and when her contract expired in August, 1873, Maggie's teaching hours more than doubled to six hours a day and her salary increased to 110 yen monthly. that the government considered abolishing Tokyo Jogakko as early as February 1873 suggests possible frictions over the desirability of female education within progressive and conservative groups close to the ruling circle.

Maggie as a Teacher

Although Maggie's contract was dated March 1, 1873, she did not begin her teaching until March 3. Mrs. Veeder taught morning classes while Maggie taught afternoons. She had two classes with 16 pupils in one and six in the other and felt that her teaching "got on very nicely." Earlier in the year she had written about the girls to her cousin Hattie: "The girls that attend the government school are of the higher classes, they ride back and forth attended by a servant. They are very pretty and very interesting and extremely polite. I often visit Mrs. Veeder's school to see them.[15]

On July 12, 1873, Maggie describes a visit to Tokyo Jogakko by the recently arrived David Murray, another Rutgers' man who served as National Superintendent of Education from 1873 to 1878. Maggie dined with Murray and his companion Iwakura Tomosada.[16]

Beginning in September, Maggie's teaching became more intensive and on September 4 she recorded in her diary: "Have been busy teaching five hours a day this week."[17]

On September 26 she wrote:

Last Sunday did not go to church as it rained, . . . it rained also on Monday, [and] on Tuesday it still rained very hard. I went to school but found only seven little girls. I left in two hours and the storm increased until we had a typhoon, blowing down the compound fences, the plaster off the new school roof, washing away bridges, stopping the trains.[18]

On November 14, the wife of David Murray and a young woman named Crosby, from Yokohama Kyoritsu Jogakko, visited Maggie's school.[19] Miss Crosby, along with two other women missionaries, a Mrs. Pruyn and a Mrs. Pearson, opened the American Mission House in Yokohama during 1871. Maggie later visited that institution and was strongly impressed by its religious atmosphere.

The following day, two more visitors arrived at Tokyo Jogakko, Mr. Mori Arinori, a future Minister of Education, and Mr. James Ballagh, a prominent missionary of the day.[20] Mori is said to have planned the establishment of a girls' secondary school and often visited such schools.[21]

November 29, 1873 was a momentous day for the school and for Maggie. Maggie recorded the visit of the Empress to Tokyo Jogakko in these words.

> This morning the Empress visited. . . . All the girls were dressed elegantly and elaborately. Professor Murray [and a number of Japanese officials] were in attendance. The Empress wore a scarlet *hakama* [a kind of trousers], a long outside dress of red heavily embroidered, her hair hung down her back in the usual style. She wore foreign shoes as did her four maids of honor. . . . The Empress looked and acted very stiffly, looking neither to the right nor to the left. . . . The girls read in English and Japanese and also wrote. We received many compliments from all. . . . About ten of the best scholars were presented to the Empress and she gave them a prize. . . . All the girls were outside to bid her farewell [and] everything passed off beautifully.[22]

The following day the local newspapers announced the names of the girls who received prizes.[23] From this description we can trace their family backgrounds; eight of the fifteen young women who received an honor from the Empress later wrote assays on the "History of My Family," for Maggie's class. Years later, the biographer of one of these girls, Shibusawa Uta, daughter of the well-known businessman and government official Shibusawa Eiichi, reported that when the Empress visited her school, she distributed copies of a Japanese translation of Samuel Smiles' famous *Self-Help* to all the girls, and English dictionaries to those more advanced. Young Uta was presented to the Empress and made a recitation in her honor.[24]

The use of Smiles' *Self-Help*, along with Fukuzawa Yukichi's *An Encouragement of Learning* as textbooks in the Tokyo Jogakko illustrates the progressive dimension of education in the school.

Several diary entries suggest that Maggie was able to build a close relationship with many of her pupils and, in fact, they often became so close that Maggie experienced pangs of sorrow when she left her pupils. For example, on January 4, 1874, she recorded in her diary that:

On Saturday all my little girls came to see me. I gave them some refreshments, a book each, [and] they brought me a handsome piece of blue crape [sic], one of red and elegantly embroidered sofa pillow cover. They played battledore and shuttlecock and enjoyed themselves for several hours. They looked lovely.[25]

In a letter to her sisters in Philadelphia, dated January 11, 1874, Maggie described the visit of her pupils.

I had my scholars here on Saturday. There were 35 of them and they looked lovely in their crape [sic] dresses, elegantly embroidered [with] their different styles of head-dress. They brought me a piece of blue crape[sic], a piece of scarlet crape [sic] and a handsomely embroidered sofa cushion, a box of sewing silk and pieces of blue silk.[26]

On April 11 she confided to her diary that she "gave an entertainment to my little girls. Mr. [Edward Warren] Clark showed them sterioptican [slides] and they all enjoyed it very much.[27]

When the time for her return to the United States drew closer, Maggie clearly had some second thoughts. David Murray attempted to persuade her to remain in Japan abut she told her diary that "I cannot."[28] The following day she wrote:

Have been thinking all day about staying here. The school is to be enlarged, a new building erected and the pupils are to be brought from all parts of the country as boarding pupils. In connection [with this school] is to be a normal school and a number of classes. Over this I am to be placed, to reside in the building and have one or two assistants. An increased salary and advantages, but I must leave it all. I cannot stay out here without Willie [her brother who, as the result of a contractual dispute was determined to return home], and after two years' absence from all I hold dear, my heart is yearning for home too strongly to consent to stay two years longer. Had my brother stayed I should have rejoiced in the work, and tried to be happy, but I am too dependent on home ties to keep them so long broken. Prof. Murray and the Director [Kosugi Kotaro] both are greatly disappointed that I cannot remain.[29]

On June 11, she wrote, "We are preparing to go home and every day I feel regret at leaving my dear little pupils,"[30] and a few days later she wrote, "The Director would very much like to have me take some . . . advanced pupils to America with me, but it is doubtful whether the Mombusho [Ministry of Education] will consent to send them."[31]

After what must have been an emotional evening, Maggie confided to her diary that "all my pupils spent the evening and each brought me a parting gift, some elegant and costly, others pretty only. They enjoyed an hour or two, then we parted, not without tears from many."[32]

220   *Margaret C. Griffis and the Education of Women*

Maggie's Friendship with Akai Yone

Akai Yone (1855-1947) is the most often mentioned pupil in Maggie's diary. Yone was older than most of the other girls in her class and served as an interpreter for both Mrs. Veeder and Maggie. In many ways Yone was more of a friend than Maggie's pupil. In early fall of 1872, Maggie began to tutor Yone's ten-year-old brother, Yu, "to have a little occupation."[33] In the course of instructing Yu, Maggie met Yone, a pupil in Mrs. Veeder's class. On December 10, 1872 she describes the formation of a Sunday school class in which Yone was a member.[34] Soon afterward her diary records how Yone had dinner at Maggie's home, and she began to accompany Maggie on several outings in Tokyo.[35]

In March, 1873, Maggie tells how Yone, "My friend and assistant pupil," is to be "married next week to a Mr. Yoshiwara" whom she had seen only once. "[A]ll the necessary arrangements have been made by a go-between. . . . She is now getting her trousseau made and will not see the gentleman until she is taken to his house by her father."[36] Less than fortnight after Yone's marriage, Maggie writes that:

Yesterday [April 17] spent the afternoon with Yone, she lives opposite the Gaimusho [Ministry of Foreign Affairs]. The house has a parlor furnished in foreign style, then Japanese parlor. In the *tokonama* [alcove] was a wooden stand on which was a pine tree, a plum tree in blossom and some other kind of tree. On each side were two *tsuru*, or storks, which are supposed to live a thousand years [and] at the foot of the tree were two large and two small tortoises with fringed tails, also long-lived. In the branches of the tree was a nest of silk cotton containing the stork's young. . . . When the bride arrived at her new house she sat before this *tokonama* and drank sake; she takes the cup and drinks first, and the husband and so on, for nine times. Then the mother made her appearance and the same drinking of innumerable small cups of sake, then Mr. Yoshiwara's brother came in, and the ceremony was repeated. This constitutes a Japanese marriage ceremony. I spent an hour or two looking at Yone's wardrobe, her sashes of elaborately embroidered and brocaded silk. . . . The whole of the Japanese wardrobe and dressing room I saw for the first time.[37]

Akai Yone was 17 years old when she met Maggie Griffis and their friendship continued for two years until she was married at the age of 19. According to Shimamoto Hisae, Yone's ancestors were Confucianists from Takamatsu han in Shikoku.[38] The name of Akai Tokai is found in the *Who's Who of the Tokugawa Period*.[39] Akai Tokai remained a Confucian for life, although he did become interested in western studies through the influence of such men as Takano Choei, Sugita Genzui, Ogata Koan and James Hepburn.[40]

Maggie's Pupil, Aoki Koto, and Edward H. House

Maggie wrote in her diary that Aoki Koto was a most intelligent and thoughtful student. She also often wrote of Edward H. House with friendly feelings. House adopted Aoki as his daughter and spent the rest of his life with her. House was teaching English at one of the institutions that was amalgamated into Tokyo Imperial University and enjoyed a close friendship with both Willie and Maggie Griffis. On February 18, 1873, Maggie confided to her diary that "Mr. House spent the evening on Sunday at McCartee and we stayed until late enjoying his fascinating conversation."[41] A year later Maggie recounted how "One of my pupils, Aoki, is to be married tomorrow night."[42] The marriage was not a success and when Aoki was on the verge of suicide she fortuitously met House again. He had been a substitute teacher at Tokyo Jogakko and had known her as a student.[43] Upon hearing of her travail, he offered to adopt her as his daughter and they went home to Boston in 1880. This happened several years after Maggie returned to Philadelphia, but one of her English essays exists in which she told how much she was impressed with the teaching of Maggie at Tokyo Jogakko.[44]

House later published a novel, *A Child of Japan, or the Story of Yone Santo* in which the story is modelled after the experience of Aoki Koto and House depicted Tokyo Jogakko in these words.

> ...while universal culture was undoubtedly a consummation earnestly to be desired, the transition from ignorance to enlightenment could not be accomplished without great hardship and suffering in many, not to say the majority of instances; and by way of partial illustration, I related circumstances in the life of a young girl of unusual intelligence, who, after rapidly passing through such courses of instruction as were supplied by the best government school in the capital, and becoming at least theoretically familiar with the gentler conditions of society in other lands, had been thrown back into the narrow grooves of existence which was no longer suited to her, and in which happiness must be forever denied her.[45]

The following is a fictionalized account of how Santo Yone (or Aoki Koto) gained access to Tokyo Jogakko. House created a fictional Doctor Charwell who in the course of his summer holiday had occasion to meet Santo Yone. Upon his return to Tokyo he visited her to ask about her education prospects.

They were dim, because education was costly, under the most moderate teachers, unless one could enter a government college; Charwell managed to get permission for Yone to enter the best national schools for her sex, an establishment recently opened for the study of the English language [Tokyo Jogakko], a knowledge which might lead, in various ways, to future advancement. Her father was gratified at the opportunity thus opened, while her aunts and her grandmother were not happy at the news,

from the domestic economy of the former and by a blind hostility to
alien ideas for the latter. Not long after her admission to the school, the
last remaining female servant was dismissed.

Yone pledged herself to perform all the household work. She rose
long before dawn, set the house in order for the day prepared the morning
meal for all, and so on. There was no warmth or affection for her among
the women who reared her, which might have been the reason for her
yearning for a career to which she could attach herself with undivided
devotion. Her high standing in the school, of which she speedily became
one of the most promising pupils, alone saved her from harsher rebuke
for being late for school. In the interval between the morning and
afternoon sessions she stole away into seclusion, unwilling that her
companions should see the insufficient quantity and dubious quality of
the food that she was permitted to bring for her luncheon, and also
anxious to gain a few extra moments for study. Her teacher, a foreign
lady [Maggie Griffis] told Yone to take care of her personal neatness,
particularly her red disfigured hands...but she offered no excuse or
explanation. She did not confess the cold attitude of her family members
to her father.

The only happiness she knew was in her studies, but the formidable
rebellion in the western provinces imposed upon the government the
need of sudden retrenchment, and by imperial edict, the foreign schools
for girls were indefinitely suspended. Yone's study was brought to an
abrupt end, for she had passed beyond the stage where native or
missionary teachers could benefit her.[46]

This depiction of Santo Yone's family background and school life at Tokyo
Jogakko is helpful in providing today's readers with a "feel" for the realities of
that period. Diaries, student essays, novels such as Edward House's *A Child of
Japan* help to shed more light on the education of females in early Meiji Japan.
The model for Santo Yone, Aoki Koto, lived in Boston with Edward House and
pursued her interests in horseback riding and oil painting as well as becoming a
close friend of the Mark Twains.[47] Aoki and House returned to Japan in 1893
where House died in 1901.

Maggie's Activities Upon Returning to the United States

Although her brother was a prolific author of books and articles
about Japan, Maggie produced a single article on the topic. It was titled
"Little Kine" and was published in March 1885 by the magazine, *St.
Nicholas*. She expressed her pleasure upon receiving a check for $15.00 on
September 25, 1874 but for unknown reasons the article did not appear in print
until eleven years later. When it finally did appear, Maggie wrote that "My
article 'Little Kine' appears in *St. Nicholas* beautifully illustrated this
month."[48]

The contents of her article dealing with the education of women were, of course, badly out-of-date, but it is still a useful description of the education of women in early Meiji. In her article, Maggie attempted to introduce American youngsters to how a Japanese girl was raised, cared for and disciplined at home and school The girl in the article is modelled on one of her pupils, Sakamoto Kine, presumably Akai Yone's cousin. Maggie clearly loved this young girl and referred to her as "Little Kine" in her diary. For example, "Little Kine and Nakamura Sen came to church yesterday and dined with me."[49] In the following excerpt from her article she describes her pupil's education.

The home of little Kine is just outside the great wall and moat of the castle of Yedo in Tokyo. Kine is a little girl of about eleven years of age, timid and shy, but very amiable and lovely, as nearly all Japanese girls are. Just now she is busy getting an education, both in Japanese and English. At six years of age, Kine's education was to begin.

First, she must go to writing school, where with other children, she sat down on the floor, and with a brush made of camel's hair, instead of a pen and ink, made by rubbing a thick cake of India ink with a little water on a stone, she took her first lessons. Besides reading and writing, Kine learned to play on the *samisen* [a Japanese lute] . . .

When the music lessons were over, dancing was learned. Until she was ten years of age, Kine learned writing and reading, dancing and guitar-playing [sic]. At ten years of age Kine began to go regularly to school, to have books, and to learn to read in her own and a foreign tongue. Kine gets her books, ties them up in a large square piece of silk crape [sic], takes her umbrella, which is made of oiled paper, steps out the door on her high wooden clogs, slipping her toe into the loop by which she holds them on her feet, and making a low bow to her parents, starts for school, accompanied by her servant carrying her books. The girdle is so tight around the hips that all freedom is prevented, and the high wooden shoes make the gait of a Japanese girl or woman exceedingly awkward. Arriving at school, Kine leaves her shoes outside the door and steps into the room. In the school-room she spends three hours with the Japanese teachers and three with her English teacher. She still studies the Chinese characters, and in her native tongue recites lessons in history and geography. This is not done in a quiet, ordinary tone, but shouted out at the top of her voice in a sing-song way that sounds very funny to foreign ears. When the Japanese lessons are over, she spends three hours in learning to read in English and translates what she reads into Japanese. She learns arithmetic in foreign style, which is totally different from the old system of her native land.[50]

We find that Kine has attended *terakoya* before entering Tokyo Jogakko. Before a national system of compulsory education was adopted in 1872, this was a popular educational institution for the common people, often held in a local Buddhist temple. Learning to play the *samisen* and perform Japanese dances were popular accomplishments for middle class girls.

Sakamoto Kine was married to Sakamoto Sannosuke, a high government official who served as Governor of Fukui Prefecture. She died in 1902 at the relatively young age of 39.[51]

Assistance to Mission Schools in Japan

Maggie was very close to the three American women (Mrs. Pruyn, Mrs. Pearson and Miss Crosby) involved with the American Mission House (later Yokohama Kyoritsu Jogakko) in Yokohama. On September 21, 1873, she described a visit to this institution.

> On Sunday, Willie and I went to Yokohama…[and] went up to Mrs. Pruyn's…[and] enjoyed the visit very much, for they have a lovely home. There are sixteen children there now, all well and looking happy. We had prayers in the school house on Sunday morning, all uniting in reading the Bible, prayers and singing, first in English and then in Japanese.[52]

Six months later she wrote to her sisters to ask about financial aid from a Philadelphia church.

> I wish you would ask Mrs. Rudolph if the Monthly Missionary Society of Mr. Chamber's church still donate their monthly sums. . . . If so, perhaps she might get me a donation for the "Home" as Mrs. Pruyn's house is called. . . .
> There are plenty of places to use the money where it is greatly needed, $10 a month will support a child in the Mission Homes.[53]

It is not known whether a donation was forthcoming, but Maggie retained her interest in helping missionary schools in Japan. Thirteen years after leaving Japan, her diary contains the following entry:

> Our school gave a supper, prepared by our Cooking Class . . . in aid of three charities, the Aged Couples' Home . . . , the Ferris Seminary in Yokohama, and Woman's Christian Association of our city.[54]

Conclusion

Thanks to Maggie's proclivity for keeping a diary, her many letters and the essays of her Japanese students, it is possible to gain some insight into the education of women. It is clear from these materials that Maggie loved her students and that her affection was returned by her young charges. One must remember that Maggie went to Japan at a time when hostile sentiment toward foreigners was still common. One of her young pupils tells how uneasy many were at the prospect of being taught by a foreign teacher. One of the students describes this phenomenon and although her English is not very good, her sincerity makes up for that shortcoming.

> When I saw Mrs. Vider [Veeder], then I was very afraid because she was a foreign woman, and I first time can not do ABC. After one year, then you [Maggie] came to this school, and you are a very good and kind teacher, when you will go back to America, I am very sorry.[55]

The institutional and administrative aspects of Meiji women's education can be found in Ministry of Education reports of the time, but the human dimensions can best be found in the letters and diaries of teachers like Margaret C. Griffis as well as in the essays of her pupils. Fortunately, some of the priceless documents still exist.

Notes

[1]Edward R. Beauchamp, *An American Teacher in Early Meiji Japan* (Honolulu, 1976), pp. 82-83.

[2]Aoyama Nao, *Meiji Jogakko no Kenkyo* [*Meiji Women's Education*] (Tokyo, 1972), pp. 537-556.

[3]Maggie had her pupils write English essays on the subject of the "History of My Life" in June 1874. These are preserved in the William Elliot Griffis Collection, housed at Rutgers University, in New Brunswick, N. J. (hereafter GCRUL). From these essays we can identify the names of about thirty of Maggie's pupils. See also Usui Chizuko, "The Fundamental Study on Kanritsu Tokyo Jogakko—Follow Up Investigation of Student Essays," *Tokai-Gakuen-Joshi-Tanki-Daigaku*, 9 (1984), pp. 1-17. This article analyzes the essays and traces the family backgrounds as well as the lives of the pupils following graduation.

[4]Unesco, *Shiryo Oyatoi Gaikokujin* [*Materials on Foreign Employees*] (Tokyo, 1975), p. 264.

[5]Takahashi Korekiyo, Takahashi Korekiyo Jiden [*Diary of Takahashi Korekiyo*], I (Tokyo, 1976), p. 126.

[6]Hatoyama Haruko, *Ji-Ju-Den* [*Legend of Ji-Ju*] (Tokyo, 1981), pp. 358-359.

[7]Rosemary F. Carroll, "Margaret Clark Griffis: Plantation Teacher," *Tennessee Historical Quarterly* 3 (Fall, 1967), pp. 295-303.

[8]Carroll, p. 296.

[9]Donald A. Sinclair (compiler), *A Guide to Manuscript Diaries and Journals in the Special Collections Department, Rutgers University* (New Brunswick, N. J.), pp. 160-161.

[10]Letter, MCG to Sisters (November 17, 1872), GCRUL.

[11]Letter, MCG to Sisters (November 18, 1872), GCRUL.
[12]Letter, MCG to Sisters (November 18, 1872), GCRUL.
[13]Letter, MCG to Sisters (October 30, 1872), GCRUL.
[14]Diary, MCG (February 18, 1873), GCRUL.
[15]Letter, MCG to Hattie (January 4, 1873), GCRUL.
[16]Diary, MCG (July 12, 1873), GCRUL.
[17]Diary, MCG (September 4, 1873), GCRUL.
[18]Diary, MCG (September 26, 1873), GCRUL.
[19]Diary, MCG (November 14, 1873), GCRUL.
[20]Diary, MCG (November 15, 1873), GCRUL.
[21]Kondo Tomie, *Roku Mei Kan Ko* (Tokyo, 1983), p. 55.
[22]Diary, MCG (November 29, 1873), GCRUL.
[23]The names of the honored girls were Shida Kiku, Aoki Koto, Mituhashi Shiho, Tsuda Kuni, Honda Sen of the upper class; and in the lower class Kobayashi Ei, Kusakabe Machio, Sugi Yo, Itakura Tane, Sakamoto Kine, Nakamura Sen, Mashima Sachi, Nakamura Fumi, Shibusawa Uta, Hosono Kon.
[24]Ashitani Shigetune, *Hozumi Utako* (Tokyo, 1934), p. 62.
[25]Diary, MCG (January 4, 1874), GCRUL.
[26]Letter, MCG to Sisters (January 11, 1874), GCRUL.
[27]Diary, MCG (April 11, 1874), GCRUL.
[28]Diary, MCG (May 18, 1874), GCRUL.
[29]Diary, MCG (May 19, 1874), GCRUL.
[30]Diary, MCG (June 11, 1874),, GCRUL.
[31]Diary, MCG (June 17, 1874), GCRUL.
[32]Diary, MCG (July 16, 1874), GCRUL.
[33]Letter, MCG to Sisters (October 2, 1872), GCRUL.
[34]Diary, MCG (December 10, 1872) GCRUL.
[35]Diary, MCG (November 29, 1873; March 16 and 19, 1874), GCRUL.
[36]Diary, MCG (March 26, 1874), GCRUL.
[37]Diary, MCG (April 18, 1874), GCRUL.
[38]Shimamoto Hisae, *Meiji no Joseitachi Misuzu* (Tokyo, 1966), p. 245.
[39]Mori Senzo, *et al.* (eds.), *Kin Sei Jinmei Roku Shuusei* II, (Tokyo, 1976), p. 48.
[40]Nagai Isaburo, *Fuuju no Nenrin* , II (Tokyo, 1976), p. 60.
[41]Diary, MCG (February 18, 1873), GCRUL.
[42]Diary, MCG (March 5, 1874), GCRUL.
[43]"E. H. House," *Kindai Bungaku Kenkyu Sousho* [*Modern Literature Resource Materials*] V, (Tokyo, 1957), p. 392.
[44]Aoki Koto's "Student Essay" (June 20, 1874), GCRUL.
[45]Edward H. House, *A Child of Japan, or the Story of Yone Santo* (Boston, 1888) p. 5.
[46]Ibid., summary of pp. 6-70.

[47]Kuroda Hatuko, *Hahatachi no Sedai* [*Mother's Reign*] (Tokyo, 1981), p. 175.

[48]Diary, MCG (March 7, 1885), GCRUL.

[49]Diary, MCG (February 9, 1874), GCRUL.

[50]Margaret C. Griffis, "Little Kine," *St. Nicholas* (March 1885), pp. 327-331.

[51]Mr. Sakamoto Takehiko, grandson of Sakamoto Kine owns a scroll in which a picture of Kine is drawn and a short statement of her background is presented. "Kine was the first daughter of Sakamoto Seikin, a high official of the Gen-Rou-Tu. She was born on February 22, 1864. Seikin had no sons, therefore, Kine became heiress and married Sakamoto Sannouske, who is now serving as Governor of Fukui Prefecture. His wife, Kine, was bright and entered Shihan Gakko where she graduated from the English course. She proved to be a virtuous woman and died on March 17, 1902 at the age of 39."

[52]Diary, MCG (September 21, 1873), GCRUL.

[53]Letter, MCG to Sisters (March 29, 1874), GCRUL.

[54]Diary, MCG (April 17, 1887), GCRUL.

[55]Student Essay, Sergi Yo (1874), GCRUL.

12

American Professors in the Development of Hokkaido: The Case of the Sapporo Agricultural College (SAC)

Akizuki Toshiyuki

Dual Role of Yatoi *in Hokkaido*

Foreigners employed by the Hokkaido Colonization Commission (*Kaitakushi*) during the early Meiji period were generally called *oyatoi kyoshi*, or "foreign teachers." This suggests that they were expected to play a dual role as teachers, in addition to fulfilling their duties as technical specialists assisting in development work. There were, in fact, many instances where these men taught in schools established by the *Kaitakushi*. Thomas Antisel, for example, a geologist, simultaneously served as vice-principal of the Provisional School (*Kaitakushi karigakko*), and James Wasson, a surveyor, also taught mathematics, drawing and English at this school. Stuart Eldridge, a physician at the Hakodate Hospital, also trained medical students at the nearby Igakko Medical School which had been erected at his suggestion. Benjamin S. Lyman, a geologist, who with the assistance of Japanese students surveyed mineral deposits in Hokkaido and drew the first geological maps of Hokkaido, can also be described as a teacher. A similar judgement can be made in the case of Edwin Dun[1] who provided young farmers with practical training at government farms.

This dual role of the *yatoi* employed by the *Kaitakushi* resulted from the pressure from the Japanese authorities to develop Hokkaido as quickly as possible. In the 1870s, Hokkaido was the only uncultivated land left in Japan, and as Sakhalin was already under the joint authority of Russia and Japan, the Japanese feared that Hokkaido would undergo a similar fate. When in 1871, the *Kaitakushi* invited foreign specialists to assist in the rapid development of Hokkaido, they encouraged the dual role of technical assistant and teacher.

Of the seventy-eight foreigners employed by the *Kaitakushi* between 1871 and 1882, forty-eight, or 61.5 percent of the total number hired, were

Americans. This suggests that the Japanese authorities were well aware of the resemblances between Hokkaido and the American frontier.

In March, 1875 Horace Capron,[2] chief officer of the *yatoi* employed by the *Kaitakushi*, presented to his employers a voluminous report, titled *Report and Official Letters to the Kaitakushi by Horace Capron, Commissioner and Advisor, and his Foreign Assistants*. This report included a summary of the major reports submitted by various *yatoi* since 1871, and also indicated the actual state of attainment in a number of fields, including topographical survey, geological research, road construction, agriculture, and stock farming.[3] Several months later, however, Capron returned to the United States and most of the other *yatoi* employed by the *Kaitakushi* also left its employ. With the establishment of the Sapporo Agricultural College (SAC) in August 1876, a total of thirty-seven hired foreigners had left, leaving only sixteen still in place.[4]

Following the departure of the foreigners, almost all work was carried out by the Japanese, but the existing pool of Japanese technical experts was so small that it was impossible to assign them to every branch of the *Kaitakushi*. Moreover, the office's "Ten Year Plan" (1872-1881) had not reached the halfway mark; the real work of colonization was about to begin.

American Professors and the Opening of SAC

Kuroda Kiyotaka (1840-1900), the Governor of the *Kaitakushi*, was eager to improve the education of young people. As his office was in need of Japanese specialists to assist in the future development of Hokkaido, he arranged to send thirty-three students abroad during 1871-1872. Among them were five young women, including Tsuda Umeko, founder of Tsuda College. Among the other students receiving financial support from the *Kaitakushi* were Yamakawa Kenjiro (President of Tokyo University), and Niijima Jo (founder of Doshisha University), who had been in the United States after illegally "escaping" from Japan in 1862.

At the same time, the *Kaitakushi* hurried to establish a college of agriculture, mining and engineering in Hokkaido. A provisional school (*Kaitakushi kari-gakko*), to prepare students to enter college, was opened in Tokyo in 1872. Soon afterwards, a girls' school was added to it which became one of the earliest women's educational institutions in Sapporo and served as a preparatory school for the Sapporo Agricultural College after it was founded in 1876.

The original plan for this college was scaled back to be merely an agricultural college when it was discovered that including mining and engineering departments would require several additional foreign professors. The Sapporo Agricultural College was modeled on the Massachusetts Agricultural College (now the Amherst campus of the University of Massachusetts), primarily because this institution was well-known in Japan, and two *Kaitakushi* officials had studied there.

Now that the proposed college's character was determined, the problem was to find a capable man who, in addition to having experience in agricultural education, possessed the administrative skills and the vision needed to found the first agricultural college in Japan. Governor Kuroda requested the Japanese Minister in Washington, Yoshida Kiyonari, to search for this man. Through his earnest efforts, and with the recommendation of B. C. Northrop (Commissioner of Education for the state of Connecticut), Yoshida found his man. He was William Smith Clark (1826-1888), the then President of the Massachusetts Agricultural College.

In March 1876, Clark signed a contract with Yoshida to serve as the first president of Sapporo Agricultural College (the precursor of Hokkaido University). Clark, in turn, chose two graduates of his institution, William Wheeler and David P. Penhallow, as the first foreign professors for Sapporo Agricultural College. They were later joined by William P. Brooks.[5] The first SAC students were chosen from the *Kaitakushi*'s preparatory school (Sapporo Gakko) and the Tokyo English School (the preparatory school for Tokyo University). The total number of entrants totalled twenty-four.[6]

As mentioned above, when the American professors arrived in Sapporo in late June, 1876, the first half of the *Kaitakushi*'s Ten Year Plan had ended, and most of the *yatoi* had left for other jobs. Thus, the *Kaitakushi* was forced to promptly engage other foreign specialists in fields such as railway construction, mining, harbor works, canning, etc. Since the terms of the new foreign specialists' contracts were usually quite short, and their duties carefully spelled out and clearly limited to specific jobs, the authorities could not reasonably expect professional advice on matters falling outside the scope of these contracts.

With the opening of SAC at about this time, however, Sapporo was the site of the head office of the *Kaitakushi*. The SAC professors were from the Massachusetts Agricultural College which was oriented toward the best agricultural technology of the day. It was natural, therefore, that they would be asked for advice or technical assistance whenever the need arose.

It must, however, be pointed out that the primary duty of these American professors was that of a college teacher and did not include development work as technical specialists. According to their contracts, they were only required to teach SAC students in specific fields of knowledge. Although one of the clauses in their contracts provided that they must obey the orders of the *Kaitakushi*, it did not obligate them to perform tasks beyond those spelled out in their contracts. This was a general condition which also applied in the contracts of such foreign language teachers as P. F. Fuque (French teacher at the preparatory school), and Russian, V. L. Sartov (Russian teacher at Hakodate Ro-gakko).

Activities of American Professors Beyond Their Contractual Duties

It is well known that Clark and Kuroda had a disagreement over the proper moral education of Japanese students, while sailing from Tokyo to Sapporo aboard the *Genbu-maru*. It is also quite likely that the two men exchanged opinions on the development of Hokkaido during the voyage. In any event, several days after their arrival in Sapporo, Clark accompanied Kuroda on an inspection of the Sorachi coal mine. During Kuroda's brief stay in Sapporo, we know that Clark gave him various suggestions and recommendations on a wide range of subjects.[7] Clark's advice not only covered college affairs, but ranged as far afield as colonial policy in general. Clark proposed, for example, improving Japanese food, clothing and housing customs so as to be better suited for the cold northern climate.[8] He was also pleased with Kuroda's idea to invite American colonists to Hokkaido to serve as models for Japanese farmers. In fact, Clark presented Kuroda with a plan along these lines.[9]

With the opening of SAC, Clark was busy making college rules and recitation schedules, planning the establishment of a college farm, a chemistry laboratory and the like. During this busy period, however, the *Kaitakushi* authorities flooded Clark with requests for advice over such matters as the production of turpentine oil, maple syrup, and salted beef; the examination of silk threads by a *Kaitakushi* factory; and even asked him to undertake an inspection of neighboring areas. Clark also agreed to guide local officials in farm management, and he replied to an inquiry about forest administration. He also promised to report on the situation for canned fish production in the United States, and suggested that the Japanese plant sugar beets and import seeds from the United States.

Clark appears to have willingly and graciously responded to these and similar requests. He clearly seems to have been extremely interested in participating fully in the development work of the *Kaitakushi* in Hokkaido. His earnest concern for Hokkaido's development was reflected in his stated intention of transforming the college farm into a central experimental station for introducing scientific agriculture and modern farm management to the region. Clark planned the construction of a barn, known as the "model barn," on the college farm. When completed it became the symbol for modern agriculture in Hokkaido.

Clark left Sapporo in April, 1877. After only eight months in Japan, Clark had laid the foundation for SAC and made such a profound impression on his students that he is remembered today in Hokkaido.[10] On his way to the port of Hakodate, Clark made a side trip to the village of Date, where a feudal lord and virtually all of his vassals had migrated after being defeated during the civil war which accompanied the Meiji Restoration of 1868. There he met Tamura Akimasa, the former chief retainer, and advised him to cultivate sugar beets.[11] Thus, it is not surprising that the government chose Date as the site of the first sugar beet factory in Japan a few years later.

Clark also stopped at the government farm at Nanae at the request of its director, Sadamoto Yuichi, one of his students in America, to give advice on building a barn.[12] It was during this visit that he wrote his opinion concerning the future construction of highways in Hokkaido to Zushi Hirotake, his direct superior in Sapporo.[13]

The above suggests that Clark appears to have regarded himself as an advisor, like Capron, to the *Kaitakushi*. When he was asked if he would return to Hokkaido, he made it a condition that he be given a position of responsibility for the development in general, or for the sugar beet industry in particular.[14] Upon his return to the United States, Clark carried out a survey of the canned fish, fish oil, and fish fertilizer industries. He also purchased machines of public works and agriculture in compliance with a request from the *Kaitakushi*. In addition, on his own initiative, he made several recommendations for measures promoting fisheries in Hokkaido, and he also sent several samples of wood pulp to the authorities.[15] Upon his retirement from the presidency of the Massachusetts Agricultural College, in April 1880, Clark expressed an interest in being reemployed by the *Kaitakushi* in a letter to Kuroda.[16] Although nothing came of this wish, it clearly suggests that Clark nourished an unfulfilled dream of Hokkaido's development.

William Wheeler, a mathematician and civil engineer, had pursued a successful career as a civil engineer in Boston. While under consideration for a position with the *Kaitakushi*, the famous American poet and philosopher, Ralph Waldo Emerson, wrote a letter of recommendation to the Japanese minister in Washington D. C. for his fellow native of Concord.[17]

Upon his arrival in Sapporo, Wheeler soon began to pursue a number of voluntary activities. Foremost among these was his taking meteorological observations, using the system of the Smithsonian Institution. Quickly recognizing its importance, the *Kaitakushi* asked him to continue these on a regular basis. Wheeler was a very valuable man to the Japanese, as the *Kaitakushi* had no office of civil engineering in those days.[18] In fact, during the winter vacation in 1876, at the eager request of the authorities, Wheeler looked into the possibility of building a new canal between Sapporo and the Ishikari River.[19] Following that he set out to make a survey of a projected carriage or railway route from Sapporo to the port of Otaru. He subsequently submitted a cost estimate to complete this project.

In April, 1877 Wheeler took over Clark's duties as acting president, but this appears not to have diminished the Kaitakushi's expectations of him as a civil engineer. In response to their requests, he reported on the transportation costs of coal by railway in the United States, designed and supervised the construction of a new bridge on the Toyohira River in Sapporo, and made the sketch and directions for the famous Sapporo building and landmark, now called the "Clock Tower," (*Tokei-dai*).[20] He spent the following summer vacation with his students, surveying the proposed route for new roads in the southern part of Hokkaido. While engaged in this activity, Wheeler examined several water sources at the request of the local Hakodate office, and he also gave advice on the construction of a wharf at Mori. Wheeler wrote of this type of voluntary work:

> In the midst of the pressing duties which have regularly fallen to the officers of instruction, by virtue of their limited number, they have given freely of their time and strength to the promotion of any and all objects of interest of the Colonial Department to which their consideration has been called; and such calls have not been infrequent.[21]

Wheeler's contributions greatly exceeded those of an ordinary college professor, and were indispensable to the *Kaitakushi*. In recognition of his contribution, Wheeler was given the additional title of "Engineer of the *Kaitakushi*," in April, 1879. Probably more appreciated, however, was that his teaching duties were taken over by C. H. Peabody, a graduate of the Massachusetts Agricultural College and the Massachusetts Institute of Technology.

David Penhallow, a Professor of Chemistry and Botany, submitted a design for a chemical laboratory to the *Kaitakushi* upon his arrival in Sapporo. When completed, both the laboratory and the expert chemist were found to be essential to the Kaitakushi's work. There was a great need for chemical analysis and experimentation, and whenever such an occasion arose, Penhallow was asked to make a qualitative or quantitative analysis of mineral ores, soils, plants and the like. He was sometimes consulted on the manufacture of coke, soap, candles, fish oil and other products. The following is a list of chemical analyses and other work which Penhallow performed during the period of October-November, 1878.[22]

> Composition of the grain and straw of wheat (Oct. 7), Composition of corn/maize (Oct. 8), A statement of the general process of whisky manufacture (Oct. 8), Examination of Yezo coal oil (Oct. 18), Examination of stone from Horoizumi supposed to contain silver (Oct. 22), Determination of the actual cause for winter killing mulberry trees (from Oct. 22 through the winter), Examination of the oil extracted from *kuromoji* (spice bush) wood (Oct. 29), Examination of hops regarding the portion soluble in water (Nov. 2), Examination of the resinous substance found on the beach near Jenibako (Nov. 13), Opinion upon two samples of barley for their value in the manufacture of beer (Nov. 13), Examination of the malt in the brewery of the *Kaitakushi* (Nov. 15), Test of fish bones for the capability of extracting phosphorous (Nov. 26).

In 1877 and 1878, Penhallow made analyses of sugar beets imported from various countries on behalf of the *Kaitakushi*, and reported on the potential value of this plant for the production of sugar in Hokkaido. His well-known scientific expedition during the summer vacation of 1878 was also prepared at the special request of the *Kaitakushi*, the result of which appeared as

"Contributions to the Natural History of Hokkaido."[23] Penhallow carried out numerous investigations, but the focus of his efforts was on collecting specimens for the Museum of Natural History, and in this he received the vigorous assistance of his students. Acting President Wheeler wrote in his report to the *Kaitakushi*: "Perhaps no part of his (Penhallow's) work outside the lecture room has quite equalled in importance that devoted to the collection and preparation of specimens for the Museum."[24]

William P. Brooks, a professor of agriculture and botany, succeeded Clark as the director of the college farm in 1877. As the farm was intended to become a model of modern agriculture, Brooks imported domestic animals, crops and grass seed, and agricultural tools and machines from America. Inevitably he had to experiment with the imported crops and select those best fit for the climate and soils of Hokkaido. Such crops as onions, cabbages, corn, flax and sugar beets that he recommended later became important products of Hokkaido.[25] He also instructed the students and employees of the college farm in breeding of animals and handling of foreign tools and machines.

Brooks' field of activity was not limited to the classroom or the college farm. During winter, when the nearby farmers were free, Brooks gave them practical talks on cultivating new crops, the care and training of animals and general agriculture.[26] It was on his suggestion that the students of SAC issued a monthly journal, titled *Nogyo Sodan (Agricultural Miscellany)* in order to promote the spread of agricultural knowledge among farmers. He also recommended and subsequently organized the first agricultural exposition in Sapporo in 1878, expecting it to foster crop improvements by stimulating the efforts of farmers.[27]

At Brooks' request several large buildings were erected on the college farm for the storage of hay, fodder and other crops. For accommodating horses, cattle and hogs a "model barn" was built according to specifications of Professor Wheeler. These buildings were all in the American style and seemed to the Japanese of the period to be symbols of the scientific agriculture and modern management that W. S. Clark eagerly wanted to introduce to Hokkaido.[28]

American Contributions to the Development of Hokkaido

The above is a rough sketch of the work carried out by American professors at Sapporo Agricultural College for the development of Hokkaido in its early years. The circumstances under which their technical assistance became indispensable to the *Kaitakushi* has been described earlier. In his two reports to the *Kaitakushi* in 1872 and 1873, Horace Capron had listed a number of works essential to the development of Hokkaido.[29] A careful examination suggests that a considerable number of those works were accomplished by the American professors at SAC. For example, meteorological observations were started by Wheeler, and the constructions plans for a road (between Sapporo and Otaru) and a canal (between Sapporo and Shinoro) were also investigated by him.

Wheeler eventually rejected the idea of the construction of the canal as "ignorant and wasteful," but recommended the construction of a railway between Sapporo and Muroran. The foundation of an agricultural college with an experimental farm and chemical laboratory was successfully achieved by Clark. In addition, the chemical laboratory was well managed by Penhallow, who also organized a museum of natural history. Brooks carried out his task even more successfully than Capron had expected: "The establishment of model farms on both these islands on a scale sufficiently extensive to experiment in the production of all the food plants of Europe and America, as well as for the introduction of improved breeds of horses, sheep, cattle and swine; also for the introduction of the most improved kinds of farm implements and machinery and the instruction of the people of Japan in their uses."[30]

In a word, the services they rendered to the *Kaitakushi* were those of technical specialists and went well beyond their duties as college professors. For all these efforts they were not rewarded with extra money. We cannot, however, find any evidence that they deemed it a breach of contract. On the contrary, it is apparent that they carried out such work willingly. W. S. Clark wrote in the "First Annual Report of Sapporo Agricultural College, 1877" as follows:

". . . In addition to their regular prescribed duties in the recitation rooms the officers of the College have very cheerfully done whatever they could to advance the interests of the Department [*Kaitakushi*]."[31]

In every annual report of SAC their contributions to the *Kaitakushi* were recorded with a sense of pride. For these services the *Kaitakushi* sometimes presented them with silk fabrics, lacquer ware, and ceramics, as tokens of its appreciation. In return the professors sent polite letters of thanks every time they received such gifts. From the western point of view, it would not seem unnatural that they demand equitable rewards for their extra work, but that never occured. William Brooks even paid some of his students for their practical exercise on the college farm in order to make them recognize the value of labor. James Summers, a professor of English literature at SAC, complained that according to his contract he had no obligation to instruct at the preparatory course, and succeeded in getting a salary increase to do so.[32] Why then did the American professors not raise similar objections?

Their unselfish cooperation in the development work of Hokkaido can be partly explained by their already high salaries in comparison with those of language teachers.[33] Even so, their generous assistance far exceeded the expectations of the *Kaitakushi*, which described them as "the most trustworthy persons among the *yatoi* employed up to this time."[34] They were also excellent teachers who earnestly taught students in the lecture room, laboratories and on training excursions. We know this from the reports of each instructional department's statement of activities, contained in the annual reports of SAC, as well as in recollections of their students. To cite one instance, they took it on themselves to carefully and critically examine and correct their students' notebooks.[35]

Judging from all the evidence, they were very diligent men who went well beyond their contractual obligations. The could also be said of other American professors who followed them. For example, J. C. Cutter (Professor of Physiology and Anatomy) served as a physician at the Sapporo Hospital, H. E. Stockbridge (Professor of Chemistry and Geology) took the additional title of Engineer of the Hokkaido Prefectural Government, and Arthur Brigham (Professor of Agriculture and the Director of the College Farm) made every effort to improve agriculture in Hokkaido. These men were also from Massachusetts, and their contributions were equal to that of their predecessors; both in fulfilling college duties as well as work outside the college.[36] We can see in all of them the active frontier spirit of a young America in a period of rising capitalism. Their diligence seems to have originated from their faith, namely New England Protestantism and the spirit of Benjamin Franklin.[37] In his inauguration speech in 1876 President W. S. Clark demanded that the freshmen "control their appetites and passions, cultivate habits of obedience and diligence." As for the faculty, he promised that "We will by our example and our teachings endeavor to develop in the young men who may become our pupils those qualities of mind and heart which will best fit them for usefulness in life."[38] Under the influence of these American professors, Sapporo Agricultural College produced many "conspicuous figures,"[39] and Sapporo City became one of the cradles of Protestantism in Japan.

Notes

[1]Edwin Dun became the U.S. Minister to Japan from 1890-1897. See pp. 107-113 above.

[2]Horace Capron was the commissioner of the Department of Agriculture of the United States when he accepted the offer of the position from the *Kaitakushi* in 1871. See pp. 89-99 above.

[3]This report also included a summary of a report by W. P. Blake who had been employed by the Hakodate Magistrate of the Tokugawa Shogunate (*bakufu*) during 1862 and 1863.

[4]Those remaining included W. Corwine (English teacher at Sapporo-gakko), L. Boehmer (horticulturist), E. Dun (stock farmer), C. and J. Schmidt brothers (Captain and Chief Engineer of a government ship, plus eleven Chinese farmers).

[5]Watanabe Masao. *Oyatoi beikokujin kagaku kyoshi [Science across the Pacific: American Science Teachers in Meiji Japan]*, (Tokyo, 1976). See Chapter 5 above.

[6]At that time it was called Kaisei Gakko and was renamed Tokyo daigaku (Tokyo University) the next year.

[7]Governor Kuroda remained at the branch office in Tokyo, as he was also a cabinet member in the Japanese government.

[8]Letter, Clark to Kuroda, Sept. 8, 1876 (Clark Letters in Hokkaido University Library [hereafter HUL]).

[9]Letter, Clark to Kuroda, Sept. 12, 1876 (Clark Letters, HUL). The idea of inviting American colonists to Hokkaido was first suggested by Capron to Kuroda in his "First Report" of 1872.

[10]Clark's name is known throughout Japan for his farewell words "Boys, be ambitious!"

[11]*Date-cho shi* [*A History of the Town of Date*] (Date, 1949), p. 168.

[12]Letter, Clark to Hori, March 22, 1877 (Clark Letters, HUL).

[13]Letter, Clark to Zusho, Apr. 22, 1877 (Clark Letters, HUL).

[14]*Hokudai hyakunen-shi. Sapporo Nogakko shiryo* [*A Centennial History of Hokkaido University*] SAC documents Vol. 1 (Sapporo, 1981), p. 288.

[15]Clark Letters, HUL.

[16]Letter, Clark to Kuroda, Apr. 1, 1880 (HUL).

[17]*Osaka Shingo: Clark-sensei shoden* [*Memoir of Dr. W. S. Clark*], 2nd ed. (Sapporo, 1965), pp. 246-247.

[18]Letter, Zusho to Wheeler, Oct. 13, 1876 (Wheeler Letters, HUL).

[19]William Wheeler, "Report on Transportation Routes Between Sapporo and [the] Tide-Water." *First Annual Report of the Sapporo Agriculture College, 1877.* (Sapporo, 1877), p. 89-125.

[20]The *Tokei-dai*, built as the military-hall of SAC in 1878, is one of the most famous buildings in Sapporo and is a national cultural property.

[21]*The Second Annual Report of Sapporo Agricultural College, 1878.* (Sapporo: Sapporo Agricultural College, 1878), p. 15.

[22]Penhallow Letters (HUL).

[23]*Second Annual Report of the Sapporo Agriculture College* (Sapporo, 1878), p. 145-171.

[24]*Ibid.*, p. 16.

[25]*Kaitaku no gunzo* [*The Colonial Pioneers*] vol. I (Sapporo, 1969), p. 202.

[26]*Ibid.*, p. 204.

[27]Letter, Brooks to Zusho, Oct. 4, 1878 (Brooks Letters, HUL).

[28]These buildings were also designated as national cultural properties in 1969.

[29]*Report and Official Letters to the Kaitakushi by Horace Capron, Commissioner and Adviser, and his Foreign Assistants* (Tokyo, 1875), pp. 37, 50, 95, and 109.

[30]*Ibid.*, p. 99.

[31]*First Annual Report of the Sapporo Agricultural College* (Sapporo, 1877), p. 35.

[32]*A Centennial History of Hokkaido University.* SAC Materials, Vol. 1 (Sapporo, 1981), p. 536-538.

[33]Clark, Wheeler, Penhallow and Brooks received an annual salary of ¥7,200, ¥4,800, ¥3,600 and ¥3,600 respectively, while Summers was paid

¥2,400. As the yen and the dollar were nearly equivalent in value in those days, Clark's salary in Sapporo was 75 percent more than $4,000 he received in Massachusetts. See John Maki *Clark; sono eiko to zasetsu* [William Smith Clark; a Yankee in Hokkaido] (Sapporo, 1976) p. 160.

[34]A Central History of Hokkaido University, SAC Document, Vol. 1, p. 288. In a letter dated Jan. 23, 1877, Wheeler wrote to his mother as follows: "Gov. Hori remarked the other night when speaking of renewing contracts, that the *Kaitakushi* had employed many foreigners before, but never any like the last three [Clark, Wheeler and Penhallow. Brooks had not yet arrived in Sapporo— A. K.]. He had said about the same before to Pres. C." [The original letter is held in the University of Massachusetts Library].

[35]*First Annual Report of the Sapporo Agricultural College* (Sapporo, 1877), p. 47; *Second Annual Report of the Sapporo Agricultural College* (Sapporo, 1878), p. 40.

[36]*Oyatoi Gaikokujin* [*Foreign Employees*] (Sapporo, 1981); also *Kaitaku no gunzo* [*The Colonial Pioneers*] (Sapporo, 1969), 3 volumes.

[37]Max Weber called it "the Spirit of Capitalism."

[38]*Sapporo Nogakko Gakukei-kai* [Sapporo Agricultural College Student Association] (Sapporo, 1898), Volume IV.

[39]Katayama Sen, one of the prominent socialists in Japan, wrote in 1898 as follows: "It is the only college in Japan that has the so-called college spirit which has been moulding the character of students ever since the distinctive impression made upon the college by the first Pres. W. S. Clark. The college is noted for making men though she has not neglected making scholars. Sons of the college are *conspicuous figures* everywhere throughout the Empire." *Labor World,* no. 20, English column (Sept. 15, 1898).

13

Engineering and Technical *Yatoi* in the Public Works Department of Meiji Japan

Imatsu Kenji

The Public Works Department

The Industrial Revolution of the eighteenth and nineteenth centuries spread throughout Europe. Initially impacting on Great Britain, this revolution ushered in an age of steam that revolutionized both land and sea transportation. The development of steamships, resulting in the improvement of transportation services was a particularly powerful spur to industrialization in many parts of the world. By 1853, Japan, one of the last nations of the world to be included in world shipping routes, was compelled to open her doors to the "black ships" of Commodore Matthew C. Perry. The United States was anxious to establish regular service across the Pacific from California which was, at the time, swept by gold fever. Indeed, with the opening of Japan a truly worldwide network of transportation and communication had been established.[1]

At the same time, Great Britain and other European powers also wanted commercial intercourse with Japan. The British demand was supported by both strong, steam-powered naval and merchant fleets. Under the circumstances Japan had little choice but to enter the world economy that was being developed by modern technology. This required a complete change in Japanese thinking—the abandonment of her two-and-a-half century old policy of isolation, and to reestablish her national policy on the basis of commerce. This also meant a sharp break with existing feudal ideas and the creation of a modern society under a single political authority.

Following the Meiji Restoration of 1868, the new government was confronted with the urgent task of providing requisite harbor facilities needed for the opening of regular steamship service. Even prior to the creation of the new government, however, regular steamship service was offered in Japan by the world's leading shipping companies, and serious proposals had been made to lay telegraph cables and to construct railways, coal supply depots and repair docks. Faced with a threat of possible colonization, the new government hurried the construction of various facilities needed for the opening of regular service. For this purpose, therefore, a Department of Public Works (*Kobusho*) was established in 1870.[2]

Improvements in regularizing service closely followed developments in the technology of maritime engines and heavy machinery. It was, however, necessary to complete such facilities as coal supply depots, repair docks, lighthouses and berths for ships and a submarine cable network before regular service could prove its value to the newly emerging industrial society in Japan. Since these facilities, especially coal deposit depots and repair docks, were essential, shipping firms exerted strenuous efforts to construct these facilities prior to opening regular steamship routes. The experience of constructing these elements exactly paralleled the growth of regular steam service. The same was true of the construction of submarine cables; no shipping company would operate unless it had a worldwide cable network.[3]

The construction of these enterprises in Japan were, in large measure, dependent upon advanced technology available only in the West. Japan had no choice but to import this technology, and was completely dependent upon foreign technicians to construct and operate the facilities she needed for economic development. The introduction of virtually everything from installing telecommunication lines to learning new techniques of coal mining were carried out under the guidance of foreign engineers.

The Department of Public Works, between 1870 and 1885, employed a large proportion, about 750, of the foreigners employed by the Japanese government in early Meiji. Furthermore, about 75% of these foreigners (580) were engineers.[4] The Japanese administrators within the Public Works Department nominally supervised the work carried out by the foreign engineers, but at the time lacked the expertise needed to carry out the practical work. They did, however, gradually acquire technical knowledge as a result of their experience working with the foreign engineers. In addition, they learned foreign languages and often were sent abroad for further study.[5]

It was at the Imperial College of Engineering (*Kogakuryo*) that, in 1873, the systematic organization of engineering education started in Japan. The first teachers were Henry Dyer (1848-1918) and others from Glasgow University. The first Japanese engineering graduates of the Kogakuryo, in 1879, were employed by the Department of Public Works, replacing many of the foreign engineers.[6] Table 1 shows the numbers of foreign (*yatoi*) and Japanese engineers employed annually by the Department of Public Works.

Table 1:

Number of the Foreign and Japanese Engineers in the Public Works Department

BUREAU	RAILWAY		TELEGRAPH		LIGHT-HOUSE		MINING		MACHINERY	
YEAR	Foreign	Japan	Foreign	Japan	Foreign	Japan	Foreign	Japan	Foreign	Japan
1871	54 94.7%	3	11 14.9%	63	23 40.4%	34	5 100.0%	0	4 80.0%	1
1872	79 84.9	14	25 26.6	69	28 41.8	39	15 34.1	29	9 29.0	22
1873	103 65.0	60	24 22.0	85	30 42.9	40	25 32.9	51	11 25.6	32
1874	115 63.9	65	31 22.6	106	25 45.3	29	27 30.0	63	10 33.3	20
1875	111 63.5	64	31 20.7	119	21 41.2	30	24 29.6	57	12 50.0	12
1876	104 72.2	40	31 21.1	116	16 36.4	28	24 41.4	58	8 40.0	12
1877	72 62.6	43	28 23.0	94	12 42.9	16	20 35.1	37	9 30.0	21
1878	58 66.7	29	27 18.5	119	10 45.5	12	12 35.3	22	9 27.3	24
1879	45 55.6	36	20 11.8	150	9 45.0	11	15 34.9	28	11 36.7	19
1880	35 49.3	35	15 7.8	177	3 17.6	14	13 21.3	48	10 20.0	40
1881	25 44.6	31	6 3.6	161	0 0.0	13	18 24.3	56	12 23.5	39
1882	22 39.3	34	5 2.9	170	0 0.0	14	11 14.9	63	10 21.7	36
1883	18 31.0	40	5 2.4	206	0 0.0	14	5 7.4	63	6 23.1	20
1884	7 28.3	43	5 2.3	200	0 0.0	13	2 2.9	67	4 18.2	18
1885	6 20.0	64	4 3.8	101	0 0.0	15	0 0.0	40	0 0.0	13

Source: *History of the Public Works Department (Kobusho Enkaku Hokoku, Tokyo, 1889).*

Growth in Number of Japanese Engineers

Japan, unlike Great Britain, was faced with the problem of consolidating a newly emerging modern society on an already existing technology that was characterized by the steamship. Great Britain's experience, on the other hand, was a gradual one in which she first experienced the mechanization of her textile industry in the early days of the Industrial Revolution. This was followed by the development of the steam engine and, later, by a transportation revolution fueled by steamships and locomotives. Japan, therefore, would have to leapfrog in order to compete as a modern country in the world economy of the day.

With the development of modern facilities, centering on telecommunications and transportation, Japan was on her way to becoming a modern state. This development was reinforced by the abolition of fiefs and the creation of prefectures, as well as land reforms, the unification of currency, the lifting of restrictions on domestic travel, the reorganization of a modern military force, and a reform of the educational system.

Thus, it is important to note that now the nation's principal cities were linked to each other with a new and powerful steam-generated transportation system, including a telecommunication network and postal service that depended on steamships. Telecommunications and regular postal services, developed in the middle of the nineteenth century, had important and wide ranging effects on communication, and it is often pointed out that these made a great contribution to the development of world trade and subsequent cultural exchanges.[7]

The fact that a modern communications network was established at the time Japan began to modernize appears to have deeply influenced economic exchange between Japan and other nations. Among today's leading industrial nations, Japan is the only one to have had a complete communications network at the beginning of her modernization process. Although foreign engineers played a major role in the construction of the first Japanese railways and the installation of modern communications within the nation, they were soon replaced by Japanese engineers who had formerly worked for the Department of Public Works.

In the 1880s, many of the government-owned facilities were sold to the private sector and played an important role in the development of many industries, especially mining and shipbuilding. At the time, government-operated industries were plagued by management problems, but once in private hands the problems were resolved.[8] In fact, it is not an overstatement to suggest that the two major pre-World War II *zaibatsu* (financial groups), Mitsui and Mitsubishi, used the shipping and trading businesses to secure a firm foundation for their economic success.

In addition, engineers working for these giant combines had often served as technical officers in the Department of Public Works. At least in part, their technical expertise was a result of the foreign engineers with whom they worked, and from whom they learned much about technology. These Japanese engineers soon replaced their western "teachers." Thus, a new profession, that of the engineer, was founded in Japan by foreign employees.

Road to Industrialization

The role of the Japanese government in the development of transportation and communications was vital to the nation's industrialization. The government maintained an aggressive policy in fostering industrial development, and not only carefully promoted each industry but protected it as well. It also worked hard to promote industrial education to provide a skilled workforce. What was especially characteristic of this period, aside from the positive role played by government, was the emergence of a spirit of entrepreneurship among industrialists. Thus, one can argue that the initiatives displayed by the private sector took over the industrialization process and carried it to fruition.[9] One of the most important features of Japan's modernization was the key role played by non-governmental economic interests after the initial governmental domination.

The case of Japan, in this writer's opinion, is one in which the government deserves credit. This credit, however, is not primarily for its role as a vehicle for industrialization, but rather for getting the process started and encouraging ambitious industrialists in the private sector to carry it through to a successful conclusion.

One cannot, however, underestimate the contributions to Japan's industrialization that was made by foreign employees who introduced the most advanced technology of the day into Japanese society. This technological flow has continued to enter Japan, with the exception of the war years, and has played an important role in Japanese development. We must also recognize the role played by the newly trained Japanese engineers who transformed this technology to better fit the often unique circumstances found in Japan. As a result of all of these factors Japan was rapidly transformed from a backward agricultural society to one that is among the most highly industrialized in the world. Japan is now not only an importer of technology, but also an important exporter as well. One can truly describe the foreign engineer, or *yatoi*, as the first minister of modern technology in Japan.

Notes

[1]Imatsu Kenji, "Modern Technology and Japanese Electrical Engineers," in Okochi Akira & Uchida Hiroshi (eds). *Development and Diffusion of Technology* (Tokyo, 1980).

[2]Grace Fox, *Britain and Japan: 1855-1883* (London, 1969), pp. 370-377.

[3] C. Ernest Fayle, *A Short History of the World's Shipping Industry* (London, 1933).

[4]*Kobusho Enkaku Hokoku* [The History of the Public Work Department] (Tokyo, 1889). Also see, Yoshida Mitsukuni, *Sangyo—yatoi 2* (Tokyo, 1968).

[5]Imatsu Kenji, "Miike Tanko to *yatoi*—Eijin F. A. Potter" [The Miike Colliery and *yatoi*—R. A. Potter], in Sakata Noduo and Yoshida Sadanobu. *Sekaishi no nakano Meiji-Ishin* [The Meiji Restoration in World History] (Kyoto, 1973).

[6]Miyoshi Nobuyoshi, *Nippon Kogyo-Kyoiku-Seiritsu-Shi no kenkyu* [The Study of the Formation of Engineering Education in Japan] (Tokyo: Kazama-shobo, 1979). See also, Kita Masami, *Kokusai Nippon o hiraita hitobito* [Men Opening the Door to Japan for the World] (Tokyo, 1984).

[7]Imatsu Kenji, "Meiji-Zenki no Kancho-Shuppan-butsu to Fuken" [The Publications of Government and Local Prefectures in the Early Meiji Period], in Sakata Nobuo and Yoshida Sadanobu. *19-seiki Nippon no Joho to Shakai-Hendo* [The Information and Social Movements in 19-century Japan] (Kyoto, 1985).

[8]Kobayashi Masaaki, *Nippon no Kogyoka to Kangyo-Haraisage* [The Japanese Industrialization and Disposal of Government Enterprise] (Tokyo, 1977).

[9]Johannes Hirschmeier, *The Origins of Entrepreneurship in Meiji Japan* (Cambridge, 1964).

14

William Elliot Griffis'
Lecture Notes on Chemistry

Uchida Takane, Oki Hisaya,
Sakan Fujio, Isa Kimio,
and Nakata Ryuji

Introduction

As was specified in his contract with the local Fukui authorities, William Elliot Griffis (1843-1928) resided in Fukui from May, 1871 to January, 1872.[1] During this period, he primarily taught chemistry and natural philosophy at the so-called *Meishinkan*.[2] His accomplishments in Fukui have been fairly well documented through a number of studies and translations of his books, diaries and numerous letters.[3] Little attention, however, has been paid to the details of the chemistry and natural philosophy which he taught in Fukui, with the exception of some references to the existence of his lecture notes and some of the reference books he used in his teaching.

Some of Griffis' chemistry notebooks are included in his papers that the Griffis Collection in the Alexander Library of Rutgers University. Copies of these materials have been acquired by the Fukui University Library as the result of an agreement establishing scholarly relations between Rutgers University and Fukui University in 1981.[4] Scholars at Fukui University have been extremely interested in these materials, as well as in Griffis' chemistry lectures. Although in poor condition, Griffis' notebooks have been intensely scrutinized to better understand the details of his chemistry instruction in Fukui.[5]

In this chapter, the authors detail the contents of a portion of Griffis' chemistry lecture notes, written in Fukui, and compare these contents with those of standard chemistry reference books of the time.

Outline of the Lecture Notes

This chapter deals primarily with the following notebooks:[6]

I.   "Chemistry and Natural Philosophy—An Outline of the Science of Chemistry."
II. "Chemistry—Qualitative Analysis."

These two notebooks were certainly written by Griffis, but parts are fragmentary and difficult to read. We have, therefore, made typescripts of them, as well as added notes in order to clarify their meaning, after which we have analyzed their details.

Notebook I is a printed diary (19.5 x 12.0 cm. in size) which has the inscription, "Letts' Diary," and the dates from 1870 on the upper part of each page. On the first page, "Chemical and Natural Philosophy," is written in large letters. Notebook I was undoubtedly written for Griffis' class in Fukui because he commented in it, "Hence more rain in Fukoui [Fukui] than at Yedo [Tokyo]."[7] This notebook is thought to be the manuscript for a proposed chemistry textbook mentioned in his diary (March 11, 1871).

The notebook is divided into the following sections, or chapters:

Introduction		
Chapter	2	The Air, Oxygen, Hydrogen, Nitrogen
Chapter	8	Compounds of Nitrogen and Oxygen
Chapter	9	Compounds of Nitrogen and Hydrogen
Chapter	10	Carbon
Chapter	11	Chlorine

If it is assumed that the Introduction and Chapter 1 correspond, then Chapters 3-7 have probably been lost, or at least not yet found. Complete versions of Chapters 8-11 may have also been lost because, in the notebook, they only exist in short versions. Furthermore, the Introduction and Chapter 2 appear to resemble memoranda more than a well-organized chapter in a textbook manuscript. It seems likely, therefore, that Griffis organized this outline for a projected chemistry textbook, and probably used these notes for his teaching in Fukui.

The first part of Notebook II (14.3 x 9.2 cm. in size) was used as a laboratory notebook for experiments in qualitative analysis. This can be confirmed by comparing the dates listed in the notebook with those of a perpetual calendar. The first part of the notebook was written over the period of one year, beginning in October 1869. Unfortunately, however, this section is too fragmentary and incoherent to decipher. The authors could not understand the nature of the experiments undertaken, and so have not included it in the subjects investigated in this chapter.

At the end of Notebook II there are short, simple explanations of the following eight elements: oxygen, silicon, boron, arsenic, phosphorous, zinc, magnesium and cadmium. Griffis, inscribed such handwritten comments as "It is found in Japan," "Many Japanese minerals contain magnesium," etc. which suggests that these comments were written as lecture notes to be used with his Japanese pupils. These and other comments found in the notebook are so simple and short that they appear to be notes for simple English conversation. These notes, however, effectively comprise a simple, introductory textbook of basic chemistry. It is, therefore, likely that this notebook is the "Chem. Conversation book" prepared for his interpreter, Iwabuchi, which Griffis cited in his diary (September 9, 17, 27, 28, 1871). Although we cannot know exactly how these notes were used in his classes, one can imagine that they must have been extremely helpful to pupils beginning the study of chemistry or English conversation.

In a diary entry for September 2, 1871, Griffis wrote that he had completed sections on iron, silver, etc. Although he undoubtedly made other chemistry notebooks, these sections have not been found in other notebooks, except for some memoranda on chemical experiments concerning the production of matches, soap, and sugar found in Notebook II.[8]

Chemistry Books Consulted by Griffis and his Pupils

In order to analyze the contents of Griffis' notebooks, it is necessary to know which chemistry textbooks he and his pupils used in Fukui. After examining the titles and authors of chemistry textbooks noted in his diary and letters, we have found the following volumes noted by Griffis in the City Library of Fukui:

1. H. L. Roscoe, *Lessons in Elements of Chemistry: Inorganic and Organic* (New York, 1868).
2. W. A. Miller, *Elements of Chemistry: Theoretical and Practical.* 4th edition (London, 1867).
3. J. E. Bowman, *An Introduction to Practical Chemistry, Including Analysis.* 5th edition (London, 1866).

An entry in Griffis' diary, dated July 12, 1871, provides evidence that Griffis and his pupils read, or were familiar with Roscoe's book. It is interesting to note that this volume also contains the hand-written notes of Kusakabe Taro, a Fukui native who attended Rutgers during the late 1860s. Unfortunately, however, young Kusakabe died while at Rutgers, and is buried in New Brunswick. When Griffis came to Japan shortly thereafter, he brought with him Kusakabe's personal effects. It seems likely, therefore, that Kusakabe probably purchased this book during his college days in New Brunswick, and that it was subsequently brought to Fukui by Griffis, and eventually added to the library of the *Meishinkan*. From this brief history of Roscoe's book, it is reasonable to assume that this volume was read by Griffis and his Fukui pupils.

Subsequent editions of *Lessons in Elements of Chemistry* have been found throughout the world, and it was translated into Japanese by the future Japanese chemists who studied under Griffis at the Tokyo *Kaisei Gakko*,[9] after he left Fukui. This volume was used widely as a textbook at many middle schools, as well as teacher training institutions in Japan. There are, for example, records indicating its use in the Meishin Middle School in 1878, and the Fukui Prefectural Teachers' School in 1882.[10] This suggests the kind of influence that Griffis and his Japanese students exerted on the development of chemistry in Japan.

The name of W. A. Miller, author of *Elements of Chemistry*, is mentioned in Griffis' diary entry for September 4, 1871. An examination of Griffis' copy of this book reveals some of his handwritten notes on experimental apparatus, on the endpaper of Part II of this book. Although they were written in pencil and are unclear, we have concluded that they are probably his notes for laboratory equipment.

Two copies of J. E. Bowman's *An Introduction to Practical Chemistry* (1866) were signed by "Owiwa" and "Karl," whom we know were Japanese pupils of Griffis in Fukui. Karl is identified in Griffis' diary as Carl, or Kasahara (in Japanese) in entries dated July 1 and September 4, 1871. In a diary entry for October 23, 1871, Griffis relates that he and his students read Bowman's book. Both the Miller and Bowman volumes belonged to the *Meishinkan*, so it is reasonable to conclude that they were probably used by other students as well.

There also exists in the City Library of Fukui, a book by C. W. Eliot and F. H. Storer, *A Manual of Inorganic Chemistry, Arranged to Facilitate the Experimental Demonstration of the Facts and Principles of the Science.* (New York, 1871). One of the interesting things about this book is that it contains the book stamp of the "Awusa Prefectural School,"[11] and on the first page is a handwritten note: "Begun from 15th Oct. 1873," and signed N. Amenomori. Thus, it appears probable that one of Griffis' best students, Amenomori Nobushige, studied from it.

Griffis and Chemical Education in Fukui

On the basis of Griffis' diary and letters it has been concluded that he taught chemistry in a conscientious manner. He not only presented well-prepared lectures, but he also ensured that a modern laboratory, experimental apparatus and tools were available to his pupils. Furthermore, he regularly conducted experiments in his classes as well as analyzing a number of samples he had obtained in Japan.[12] In order to understand the total of Griffis' contribution to the spread of chemistry in Japan, it is necessary to examine the details of his lectures and experimental work in Fukui. Thus, we now turn to a discussion of his work based on a comparison of Notebooks I and II with widely used chemistry textbooks of the period.

As mentioned earlier, part of Notebook I is thought to be a preliminary manuscript for an elementary chemistry textbook because, among other things, a memorandum at the beginning indicating the size of print type to be used, as well as the figures to be included in each section, an experimental section at the end of the book, and a table of technical terms.

In the Introduction, Griffis outlines some of his views on chemistry as follows: (1) "Chemistry treats of the constitution of characteristic bodies, and the specific properties of matter;" (2) "The modern European definition of chemistry includes more than the Chinese character expresses. The latter means only simply the science of analysis, whereas, this is but half of chemistry, which also includes the idea of synthesis;" (3) "Chemistry is both a science and an art, that is, it is both a collection of principles and knowledge, and treats also of the practical applications of those principles and knowledge to the uses of common life;" (4) "Chemistry, is a science, two branches of it are organic and inorganic;" (5) "The practical study of chemistry divides itself into a knowledge of the principles & facts of the science, and manipulation of the apparatus necessary for research and demonstration;" (6) Organic chemistry treats those substances which are produced by the various processes of life, whether mineral or animal, such as growth, decay, and destruction;" (7) Inorganic chemistry treats of those substances which have not been formed by life;" (8) "Method of study—deductive, actual examination—modern modes of investigation. Stores of knowledge in books—proof by experiment: definition of experiment. Chemistry—not a science of reasoning, such as mathematics, where we can reason from certain propositions—but a science of experiment;" (9) "An element is a simple body. All substances are either elements or compounds. Whatever can be split into more than one element is a compound."

It has been documented that Griffis knew that there were 65 elements in all, and that 52 of them were metals and 13 non-metals. These elements will be discussed later. Griffis also referred to the five elements in traditional Chinese thought and the four elements of the ancient European philosophy, but explained that they are not "real" elements, but compounds or properties giving character to the body. He also discussed the differences between physical and chemical changes.

To sum up, Griffis knew that natural science in Japan (or Fukui) was regulated by the five elements derived from the Chinese tradition, but he was confident that he would demonstrate the superiority of European natural science. Moreover, in an important philosophical point, Griffis argued that chemistry was not only concerned with *analysis* but also *synthesis*, and that the object of chemistry was the application of chemical knowledge in real life. The principles undergirding his view of chemistry are close to today's understanding of the field, so it is fair to conclude that Griffis was on the cutting edge of chemistry education in his time.

As suggested above, Griffis' Introduction appears to be Chapter 1, and the "Map of the Elements" (see Appendix I) may well have been intended as the frontpiece for Chapter 1. This figure has not been found in any of the textbooks of the time, and probably indicates a distribution ratio of the elements with the framework. On the following page, Griffis lists such items as a table of elements with their Latin names, combining weights, etc. Although the origin of these data has not been clarified, an explanation of the elements was surely intended in the following pages. In the last part of this section, the four characteristics of acids, the characteristics of bases, and the nomenclature of acids and bases, along with metals and non-metals are discussed.

At the beginning of Chapter 2, a figure, labeled "Atmospheric Column" appears followed by a treatment of air, oxygen and nitrogen. A part of the data is on the composition of atmosphere (see Appendix II). As these data contain more significant figures than the values given in either the Roscoe or the Eliot volumes, they probably were derived from other sources.

In the first section of text in Chapter 2, a discussion of air takes two pages. Griffis' description of a liter of air weighing 1.2932 grams, and atmospheric pressure corresponding to 10.33 meters height of a water column, or 76 centimeters of a mercury column are consistent with data found in Eliot. In addition, there is a brief note in Griffis' manuscript: "Eliot & Storer" strongly suggesting that he was referring to that text.

Griffis' notes contain the following: "The air [is] an ocean—fills space of life, cells, etc. Trim enough to hold bird's wings two mighty forces, gravity, and heat—perfect balance. Relation of air to light, colors. Diffusion of sun's rays—benefits atmosphere [and] distributes sun's heat, trade winds." Appendix III is used to illustrate the principle that water is the major component in both animal and plant life, and that water in the air results in both animal and plant life, and that water in the air results in the formation of clouds and rain. In particular, his note "Hence more rain in Foukui than at Yedo" is interesting as an example.

Oxygen is dealt with in the next section. Griffis discusses "Com. pro. 16" (abbreviation for combining proportion), accompanied by its atomic weight. The first part of this term is used in Roscoe's text, and the latter in Eliot's. This suggests that Griffis used both Roscoe and Eliot in his preparing his notes.

Griffis' treatment of oxygen covers four pages, but is so fragmentary that it is often too ambiguous to decipher clear meanings. However, we wish to take note of the following matters. First, the reaction between potassium chlorate and manganese dioxide is shown as a method to generate oxygen. However, Griffis' description of oxygen as "No heavier than air" does not correspond with today's knowledge. Finally, some descriptions regarding the combination with oxygen, that is, combustion, dissolution in water, respiration of animals, the existence of ozone and the components of rock are provided. For example, ozone is described as follows:

Theory—elements in combination & free state—act differently—molecules & atoms—HH, NN, etc.

+ O- O = O; Ozone & anozone = 0

Atom of O = O

Molecule of O = $\left. \begin{array}{c} O \\ O \end{array} \right\}$

Griffis' treatment of hydrogen occupies two pages. To his comment that hydrogen is generated by adding hydrochloric acid to zinc, Griffis cautioned, "Beware of fire in the Exp."

The reaction formula "$2HC_1 + Z = ZnCL_2 + 2H$" attracted our attention to the confusion between hydrogen molecule (HH) and atom (H).[13] This formula and data with ratios of hydrogen to various substances, such as air, water, mercury, in weight appear to have been derived from Eliot's text. In this section the very light and diffusable qualities of hydrogen are emphasized. This suggests that Griffis probably utilized several experiments designed to illustrate that hydrogen is lighter than other gases, that balloons or soap bubbles filled with hydrogen rise, and that hydrogen readily mixes with air.

Griffis also taught his students that the flame of hydrogen is extremely hot compared with that of other substances; that hydrogen reacts with oxygen explosively with the sound of a shot (he called it a "gas pistol"), and that the resulting product is water.

The last part of Chapter 2 consists of two pages of material on nitrogen. This section relies heavily on summaries of material from Eliot's text. Following a description of the preparation and physical properties of nitrogen, Griffis concludes that nitrogen is an inert, suffocative gas and a major component of air, found only in coal and saltpeter which does not easily decompose.

Following Chapter 2, there are two blank pages, followed by Chapters 8 and 9 which consist of four pages of short questions about several elements and compounds. It is not clear which part these problems correspond with in the text, or to their specific purpose. The form and content are, however, very similar to those contained in Roscoe and, indeed, some of the language is virtually identical. Appendix 4 illustrates the resemblance with Roscoe's text.

Griffis' notebook also contains additional problems which are simpler than those contained in Roscoe. The latter contains arithmetic problems while Griffis provides problems dealing with such things as symbols and equivalent weights (including so-called "combining weight") of elements. Thus, it is likely that Griffis prepared these problems as exercises for his pupils to carry out in class. Of particular interest to the authors is the following problem:

Two volumes of H and one of O from two volumes of steam. How many volumes of gas are condensed into H_2O? (Chapter 8, Number 8).

Did Griffis intend to teach Avogadro's molecular hypothesis that hydrogen or oxygen is a diatomic molecule? The answer is undoubtedly no, because the hypothesis had not yet been included in either Roscoe or Eliot's texts. The question therefore, probably reflected the conventional wisdom that water (steam) occupies two-fold volumes of atoms such as hydrogen and oxygen.

It has already been mentioned that Notebook II is a planned manuscript for an "English Conversation Book in Chemistry," including details on the eight elements, written specifically for Japanese pupils. Interestingly, the level of its language is almost identical with that used in first year English conversation classes in Japanese junior high schools today. Given Griffis' sensitivity to the linguistic needs of his pupils, it seems virtually certain that he used these notes to explain chemical terms, chemical substances and chemical knowledge in addition to using many experiments. Although we have not been able to ascertain whether contemporary textbooks took the same form as Notebook II, we conclude that this notebook is the creation of Griffis himself since its contents would have been familiar to beginners in both chemistry and basic English. Thus, we suggest that Notebook II is a valuable contribution to chemical education in Japan during the early Meiji era.

This notebook treats these elements: oxygen, silicon, boron, arsenic, phosphorous, zinc, magnesium and cadmium. The number "1" is written in form of the first element, oxygen, while the others are unnumbered. Perhaps, Griffis intended to number the other elements. Oxygen and silicon are listed in the same order as the "Map of Elements" described above, but the logic of the order of the remaining six elements is not clear. We assume that Griffis had physical possession of these eight elements in his laboratory, and could and did use them in his classroom experiments.

Griffis gave 65 as the number of elements in both Notebooks I and II, but the content of these elements is not found in his notes. On the other hand, it is well known in the history of chemistry that Mendeleev published a periodic law table of 63 elements between 1869 and 1871, predicting the existence of further undiscovered elements.[14] Hence in Roscoe's book 63 elements were identified while 65 were listed in Eliot's work. Thus, it seems safe to assume that Griffis drew upon the latter in his notes. He also described, at the end of the notebook, 14 non-metal elements; O, H, N, Cl, B, BR, C, I, P, SE, S, and TE. Roscoe, on the other hand, also includes Si as a non-metal element, and As was added to this list in the second edition of the Japanese version that was published in 1885. At the time a good many studies of the history of recognition and discovery of the elements had already been completed.

The structure of Notebook II is an interesting one. The first part contains 177 simple and short sentences pertaining to oxygen. Griffis makes a point of explaining that, along with gold and silver, oxygen is one of the 65 elements and has "O" as its chemical symbol, and an atomic weight of 16. When combined with hydrogen it forms water, and it is tasteless, odorless and colorless. Further, it is generated by heating HgO (red), KC_1O_3, or a mixture of KC_1O_3 and MNO_2. It is slightly soluble in water; the combination of sulfur gives SO_2 which is a strong acid with an irritant odor. The burning of carbon and phosphorous bears CO_2 and P_2O_5, respectively; the white hot of iron wire with sulfur falls in sparks and forms Fe_3O_4, and others.

This notebook contains many important experiments and, if Griffis actually demonstrated them to his classes, the chemical education of his pupils would have been a remarkably good one for the place and time.

The following section consists of 69 sentences about silicon. In them Griffis documents that silicon contains allotropes, such as oxygen, and when silicon combines with oxygen it forms a plentiful and beautiful quartz or very hard flint. SiO_2 is soluble in water, and a combination of SiO_2 and sodium forms a water soluble compound, into which the addition of hydrochloric acid results in a white, jelly-like solution that is transformed into a white powder upon drying.

The next 56 sentences explain boron. Griffis notes that boron is a green powder produced from boracic acid in Italy, China, the United States and Peru. A solution of borax in alcohol burns green, and the residue is acidic. It combines with chlorine, fluorine, sulfur and nitrogen.

In the following 86 sentences arsenic is described as a strong poison, found in pyrites. It is like a metal and when burnt smells like garlic. It combines with hydrogen to produce AsH_3, a colorless poisonous gas, and is water soluble. Arsenic forms two oxides, chloride and sulfide.

The section on phosphorous contains 186 sentences. It seems that Griffis had two allotropic forms of phosphorous for use in his experiments. He described yellow phosphorous as wax-like in appearance, and a poison that burns with white smoke, and is used to make matches. Thus, he continued, it must be saved in water. It is also soluble in carbon disulfide, and a paper soaked in the solution smokes.

Red phosphorous is described as odorless, tasteless, non-poisonous and insoluble in carbon disulfide. It burns and is used on the side of boxes of safety matches. When a mixture of phosphorous and potassium nitrate is struck by a hammer on an anvil, it makes a loud noise. Heating a flask containing phosphorous and potassium hydroxide on a sand bath, causes bubbles to rise and take fire. Further, phosphorous oxide, phosphoric acid, phosphorous tri- and penta-chloride are also mentioned in this section.

The following two sections describe zinc in 149 sentences. The first discusses the generation of hydrogen gas and hydrogen experiments. The second focuses on the characteristics of zinc and its compounds.

Extrapolation suggests that a section on strontium is missing from the notebook because Griffis writes, "We have studied strontium: today we shall study zinc."

Presumably, Griffis had acquired both granulated zinc and its sheet and generated hydrogen gas by adding hydrogen chloride to the granulated zinc, to demonstrate the fast diffusion and combustion of hydrogen. There are also further descriptions of vaporization of zinc, the existence of oxides and sulfides, the alloys of zinc with lead and copper, and the formation of salts through the reaction of zinc with acid and alkali.

The next 40 sentences concern magnesium produced from magnesium chloride found in seawater. Griffis describes how magnesium chloride makes seawater bitter; how magnesium is as white as tin and burns with a dazzling light before turning to a white powder; and the use of sulfonate, carbonate, silicate and citrate in medicines.

The final section consists of 10 sentences about cadmium. He describes it as a white and ductile metal, distilled like zinc. The sulfide is used as yellow point and the iodide in photography.

As mentioned earlier, Notebook II is also incomplete, but other research indicates that Griffis conscientiously taught his eager students well. Considering the difficulty of obtaining chemical reagents and apparatus in Japan during the early 1870s, Griffis' approach to chemical education, especially his many experiments, was admirable, and certainly at least the equal of similar attempts in Osaka, Kanazawa and Shizuoka.

Appendix I. Map of Elements

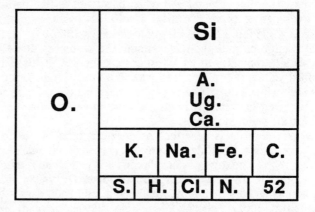

Appendix II. Atmospheric Column

Element	Fraction (%)	Present Data
O	20.61	20.93 (O_2)
N	77.95	78.10 (N_2)
CO_2	0.04	0.03
H_2O	1.4	
NO_2		
NH_4	Trace	(Ar 0.9325)
C_2H_4		

Appendix III. Principle of Rainfall

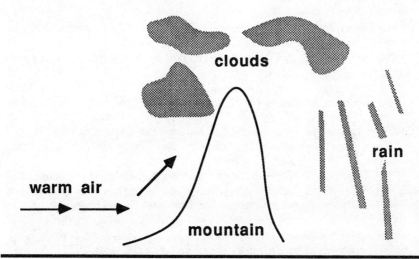

Appendix IV. Comparisons of titles of Chapters and numbers of the problems
between Griffis' notebook (2) and Roscoe's book (4).

	Griffis (2)			Roscoe (4)	
	Superscription	Number		Superscription	Number
VIII	Compounds of Nitrogen and Oxygen	24	VI	Nitric Acid and Oxides of Nitrogen	10
IX	Compounds of Nitrogen and Hydrogen	14	VII	Oxides of Nitrogen and Ammonia	10
X	Carbon	32	VIII	Carbon and Carbonic Acid	10
XI	Chlorine	13	X	Chlorine	12

Notes

The authors wish to thank Professor Shimada Tadashi (former Dean of the Faculty of Education, Fukui University) for his invaluable encouragement. Our gratitude is also extended to Mr. Hiraizumi Hiroyuki (Fukui University) and Mr. Fujita Hideo (Kyoto University both for their loans of valuable materials and many helpful suggestions. Thanks are also due to Mrs. Aoyama Kinuyo, Miss Kumagai Yasuko, and Miss Okuda Sayuri for their painstaking typing of the manuscript. Finally, we wish to acknowledge the generous support of the Faculty of Education, Fukui University, which enabled us to carry out this project. A Japanese version of this paper was published in *The Journal of the Japanese Society for the History of Chemistry*, 32 (1986). It was translated into English by Uchida Takane, Oki Hisaya, Isa Kimio and Nakata Ryuji.

[1]For further details, see The Board of Education of Fukui Prefecture, *The Century History of Education in Fukui Prefecture* (Fukui, 1970).

[2]The "Meishinkan" was the central school of the Fukui clan and had earlier been known as the *Meidokan.*

[3]See Watanabe Masao, "American Science Teachers in the Early Meiji Period," *Japanese Studies in the History of Science,* 15 (1976), pp. 127-144; Yamashita Eiichi, *Griffis in Fukui* (Fukui, 1979); Edward R. Beauchamp, "Griffis in Japan: The Fukui Interlude," *Monumenta Nipponica,* 30, 4 (Winter 1975), pp. 423-452; and his *An American Teacher in Early Meiji Japan* (Honolulu, 1976), especially Chapter 3.

[4]The Kusakabe-Griffis Foundation for Academic-Cultural Exchange, *The List of Griffis' Notes* (Fukui, 1984). See also, "Agreement for Establishing Scholarly Relations Between Rutgers University and Fukui University, October 7, 1981."

[5]Uchida Takane, Oki Hisaya, Sakan Fujio, Isa Kimio and Nakata Ryuji, *Griffis' Lecture Notes on Chemistry (Texts and Notes)* (Fukui, 1987).

[6]*The List of Griffis' Notes.* Notebook I (Ref. No. MI-82 and MI-83) and Notebook II (Ref. No. MI-85, and MI-86 and MI-87).

[7]Yedo (or Edo) is the former name for Tokyo.

[8]Griffis' diary entry of January 13, 1872 describes the chemical composition of a matche, and his teaching a student named Honda to make one.

[9]Okuna Hiroshi, *Chemistry at the Edo Period* (Tanagawa, 1980)..

[10]M. Millar, I.T. Millar, and E.G. Walaschewski, *Journal of Chemical Education,* 62 (1985), p. 275.

[11]Fukui was incorporated into Asuwa Prefecture, but was later re-named Fukui Prefecture.

[12]See his diary for December 21, 1871 and January 5, 1872.

[13]Z should be Zn; CL should be Cl.

[14]M. E. Weeks, "Discovery of the Elements," *Journal of Chemical Education* (1956), n.p.

15

Frederic Marshall as an Employee of the Japanese Legation in Paris

Yokoyama Toshio

A New Perspective on the Late Nineteenth Century

The impact of the development of global transportation and communication networks on human societies in the last three decades of the nineteenth century has been insufficiently studied. Modes of contact between peoples changed dramatically with technological advances during this period. Among the most important developments were the completion of the Transcontinental Railroad in the United States, the opening of telegraphic communications between London and Shanghai, the establishment of regularly scheduled trans-Pacific passenger service and the opening of the Suez Canal, which significantly shortened travel time between Europe and Asia. Intercultural contact, which had previously been slow and inhibited by social factors (for example, contacts between medieval Europe and the Islamic world) became rapid, large-scale, and inevitable. The new technological environment made high-speed global interconnectedness possible, and was largely responsible for the growth of "grand tours" to the West by more than five hundred Japanese students during the first half of the 1870s, as well as the participation of about the same number

The following institutions and corporations have kindly given the author formal permission to reproduce quotations from or photographic copies of documents either in their custody or whose copyright they own: the Trustees of the National Library of Scotland and Messrs. William Blackwood & Sons; the Archives of the Japanese Ministry of Foreign Affairs; and the British Library. I would also like to thank Ms. Marguerite Wells for her stylistic advice on this chapter.

of western specialists in numerous Japanese governmental enterprises during
the same period. To attribute these phenomena mainly to technological
advances, however, overlooks the fact (pointed out by many historians) that
advances are most often the result of conscious human activities. For example,
the modernization of the Japanese military system has often been attributed to
"the unique imitative characteristic of the Japanese."[1] The range of influences
exerted on local Japanese communities by those embodying the new
technologies went far beyond what one might have expected. Some examples of
such people were evangelical missionaries, adventurous merchants, foreign
specialists, and Japanese students returning from the West. Radical changes
were not confined to the Japanese side, but were often on the other side.

To date, most studies of the *oyatoi* have treated them as representatives of
superior western cultures impacting upon a less developed Japanese society
when, in truth, many of these foreigners were profoundly influenced by close
encounters with their Japanese hosts. This chapter will, therefore, focus on one
example which illustrates this historical reality. It is hoped that this approach
will help modify the inaccurate, but persistent view that the West represented
the center of civilization and merely acted upon Japan rather than the more
accurate and complex view of reciprocal influences.

Frederic Marshall's Encounter with Sameshima

The protagonist in the story which follows is Frederic Marshall, a British
barrister who is virtually unknown to historians, and whose biography is yet to
be written. The highly fragmented documents on his life cannot but make any
biographer shrink from such an undertaking. Marshall was born in 1839, lived
in Paris from the latter half of the 1840s until 1880, before moving to
Brighton in South England where he died in 1905.

It was Marshall who was primarily instrumental in establishing effective
Japanese diplomatic agencies in Europe. He was employed in Paris, in 1871,
by Sameshima Naonobu (1845-1880), the first Japanese resident diplomat in
Europe. During the next 17 years, Marshall made great efforts on behalf of
Japan to revise Japan's "unequal treaties" with European countries. Why then
has he been forgotten in Japan? It is probably because his first Japanese
employer and close friend Sameshima passed away in Paris at the early age of
35 years.

The Archives of the Japanese Ministry of Foreign Affairs (Gaimusho)
possesses two groups of documents relating to Marshall. The first, "Zaigai
kokan gaikokujin koyo kankei zakken" and the other, "Eijin Furederikku
Masharu seikyo hokuku zassan" provide useful information about his work on
behalf of the Japanese government. One of the files in the first group tells of
Marshall's employment, during August-September 1871, by the newly-
established Japanese Legation in Paris on a part-time (half-day) basis with a
salary of 50 pounds a month. In the autumn of 1872, when the Iwakura
Mission was staying in Britain, Marshall was given a full-time post at the
Legation, and his monthly salary was raised to 80 pounds. In 1875, he was

made *Shokikan Kaku* (honorary secretary) of the Embassy, and in 1878 was invested with *Kun Yonto Kyokujitsu Sho* (the 4th class of the Order of the Rising Sun). He was promoted to *Komon Kaku* (Honorary Counselor) in the summer of 1881. In 1883, Marshall was awarded a bonus of 10,000 francs, but was abruptly dismissed in June 1888 when Japanese diplomatic establishments abroad were told to cut their expenses. Upon his separation, Marshall received a lump sum of 1,500 francs, and the 3rd class of the Order of the Rising Sun.

It appears, however, that the Japanese government considered that Marshall, a foreigner, had been too deeply involved in Japanese diplomacy, sharing much intelligence about Japan's state secrets, so he simply had to be cut off from the source of sensitive information. In order to put the best face on this action, it was decided to pay him an annual pension of 1,500 yen, and to receive from him "Reports on European Affairs" which he would consider to be useful for Japan. For these services, Marshall would receive an additional payment of 1,500 yen, financed from the secret funds of the Paris Legation. After 1891, Marshall was given a five year contract and his remuneration was changed to a monthly salary of 97 yen from the Legation's regular budget. Marshall managed to get renewals of this employment until his death in 1905.

The second group of documents consists of three files of most of Marshall's "reports" sent to the Japanese Ministry of Foreign Affairs after 1888. It is, however, virtually impossible to ascertain from these files anything of Marshall's actual activities in the service of the Japanese government.

In the late 1970s, however, the author found, in the National Library of Scotland in Edinburgh, numerous of Marshall's letters in the archives of the Edinburgh publishers, William Blackwood and Sons. The letters, mostly from France, provide details of Marshall's life as an indispensable guide to Sameshima.

Blackwood's Edinburgh Magazine, a monthly published without interruption for more than a century and a half until December 1980, was one of the most influential magazines in Great Britain. In addition to being a conservative organ for the often not highly educated landed gentry of the British establishment,[2] the magazine provided a notable forum for many Scottish and English officials and merchants active on the frontiers of the British empire.

In July 1871, shortly before Marshall became employed by Sameshima, Marshall's first article appeared in this magazine under the title, "History of the Commune of Paris." This was one of the early critical and detailed accounts of the Commune which were written for British readers by British residents in Paris, and was, according to the editor of the magazine, "by far the clearest narrative that has appeared [on the subject], and the best warning to [the British gentry] against similar dangers at home."[3] The magazine's editor, John Blackwood (1818-1879), was an able judge of literary talent, and is best known in the history of English literature for his discovery of George Eliot and for his friendship with such figures as de Quincey, Thackery and Trollope.

With Blackwood's encouragement, Marshall began writing an eight-part series on French home life for the magazine in the autumn of 1871.[4] Drawing upon his experience of living in France for more than twenty years, Marshall discussed various aspects of traditional French urban family life. To his readers, Marshall's topics were fresh and attractive, as each was presented in a comparative framework with their British equivalents. Among his topics were the French servants' friendly attitudes to their masters, French mothers' strong, (sometimes too strong) influence on their children's education, the recent growth of "vain" gaudy taste in furniture and its moral effects, or the carefully maintained economy and elegance of their cooking.

When this series was about to be completed in the summer of 1872, Marshall suddenly requested the editor to substitute a paper on Japan for the final piece of the series. Marshall's request was made because Sameshima, whom Marshall called "my Japanese master," wanted to make the British public aware of the current situation in Japan, as the Iwakura Mission was about to arrive in Britain. When the mission had left Japan at the end of 1871, it had hoped to negotiate an end to her unequal treaties with the Western powers. During a stay of about seven months in the United States, however, they came to realize that their desire for early treaty revisions was not a realistic one. When the Mission left the United States for Europe, they were determined to learn the characteristics of European civilization by visiting various public institutions and military and industrial sites, rather than publicly condemning the unfair nature of the treaties. Sameshima, however, had no chance of knowing of this shift in the Mission's attitude until, or even some time after, their arrival in Europe.

Marshall was successful in securing Blackwood's agreement to publish the article on Japan which, Marshall assured his editor, would be "very interesting," because he was able to use special "information that no one else possess[ed]," that is, his information from Sameshima.[5] The paper was written at Dieppe, the seashore resort in Normandy. The collaboration between Marshall and Sameshima was exhausting. In a letter of 11 August, Marshall complained about the "horrible Japan article."

> I am at it literally for ten hours a day, but the difficulty of worming accurate information out of people who are afraid of making the most trifling error and whose thoughts are always tending in a direction which is not mine, is really very great. . . . And then when I think I have got it quite right, have written a couple of pages as hard as I can scribble . . . and read it to dear, good Sameshima, he gently says, three times out of four, 'no, that is not it at all,' and I have to begin all over again.[6]

But Marshall seems in some respects to have enjoyed his discussions with Sameshima:

> There is an amusing side to it, however; he is so intensely desirous to be correct, that he discusses the correct meaning of a word for half an hour, with a severity and an earnestness which we Europeans never reach.[7]

After about three weeks' turmoil, the manuscript was finally completed, and covered a number of topics unknown to Europe at the time. Among these were the Japanese government's budget table for 1872 reproduced from "a document unknown either in Europe or in Japan,"[8] details about governmental organizations and recent developments in public works and education. In conclusion, it urged readers to regard the Japanese government as an "organized and civilized Government" and supported the claim for treaty revision and Japan's sole jurisdiction within her realm.[9]

The major difficulty for Marshall and Sameshima was that they often found no correspondence between things Japanese and western, and, in such cases, were unable to translate the former into accurate European words. One such example was the *haihan chiken*, the spontaneous abolition of the feudal lord's territorial rights. Marshall explained that "history offers no parallel to it."[10] In much of Marshall's article, the impact of Sameshima's "intense desire to be correct" can be seen. For example, *dajokan* was translated into "the Great Council," whereas *sain* was not directly translated into any single English name, and its functions were explained as "analogous to those of the French Conseil d'Etat, so far as the preparation and discussion of laws is concerned." Also the short-lived institution named *shugiin* was called "a parliament," carefully avoiding capitalizing the English word.[11]

On September 1, 1871, this paper was published anonymously as was the style of many magazines of the day. Its readers could, therefore, hardly know that a Japanese diplomat was the source of its content. Blackwood, the editor, was confident that the article would attract much public attention. However, this was not the case. Perhaps at the urging of Sameshima, who thought that a reprint of it should be sold in "a six penny pamphlet for the railway stalls," Marshall suggested that Blackwood draw the attention of John Delane, editor of the *Times*, to what he had written.[12] Delane seems to have taken some interest in the article, and on September 5 did publish a short synopsis, but omitted all the expressions Marshall had used to praise Japanese progress.[13]

Within a month, a most telling criticism of Marshall's paper was published in *Macmillan's Magazine*, one of the then highly influential one-shilling London monthlies. In a short article, the anonymous author criticized Marshall:

> . . . it seems hardly to have occurred to the writer of the article that this "unknown document" may have been given to him for a purpose which he is to be the innocent means of carrying out.[14]

According to a file in the Macmillan Archive kept in the British Library, the contributor of this article was W.G. Aston, the able linguist at the British Legation in Tokyo and then interpreter for the Iwakura Mission.[15] Whether Aston criticized Marshall's article with full knowledge of its authorship is not known. Did Aston prepare the paper on his own initiative, or, was he urged by others, such as Sir Harry Parkes who was then on leave in Britain, or even the Ambassador, Iwakura Tomomi himself? A definitive answer to these questions is not possible unless, of course, new evidence turns up.

Marshall's Discovery of the Strange Europe

Sameshima and Marshall's work was not confined to shaping public opinion about Japanese questions. A more urgent task for Sameshima was to learn every detail of European diplomatic procedures, including even the choice of paper of "proper" size for writing a letter to a sovereign, or the number of lines "allowed" in one page of such a letter. How much knowledge in these matters did Sameshima have when he left Yokohama for Paris as Japan's official representative?[16] To date, no documents have been found to suggest that Sameshima had been trained in these matters before his departure. Fleury-Herard, the former Honorary Consul General of the Tokugawa government, had been in Paris, and after 1869 the Comte de Montblanc. It is possible that the latter may have given some useful knowledge to Sameshima. In the early 1870s, however, the Japanese government's notion of *gaikoku kosai* (intercourse with foreign countries) was not well defined. The very fact that Marshall was so much occupied with instructing Sameshima in various practical matters, including not only the form of treaties, but also manners of the Court, seems to speak eloquently of Sameshima's lack of formal diplomatic expertise at the beginning of his career.

In the autumn of 1873 Marshall wrote to Blackwood that "During the last two years I have had to study diplomatic details in most of these ramifications. I have written I don't know how many reports upon them—forty or fifty perhaps. . . ."[17] Books Marshall had to read for such work were numerous. Even after the absorbing months spent attending the Iwakura Mission had ended in July 1873, Sameshima and Marshall had little time to rest. They went to Trouville-sur-mer, in Normandy, where Marshall wrote for Sameshima three "very big" reports on the following topics: history of commercial treaties, extra-territoriality, and the treatment of aliens, which filled sixty-four octavo volumes.[18]

Such laborious work for Sameshima, however, brought to Marshall an unexpected by-product: a series for *Blackwood's* titled "International Vanities." Under Sameshima's "severe" questions, diplomatic customs familiar to Europe were bound to be seen in a new light and therefore to seem fresh in Marshall's eyes. For example, the habit of concluding an ambassadorial letter addressed to another ambassador from a different country:

> I beg your Excellency to be pleased to accept, with regard, the assurances of the feelings of most high and respectful consideration with which I have the honour to be . . . of your Excellency, the very humble and very obedient servant.[19]

Why "servant?" A rational explanation may be impossible. Teaching Sameshima, Marshall was led to discover a strange Europe which, in Blackwood's view, was not at all suitable for his conservative magazine. Marshall, therefore, had to promise the editor that he would not offend the diplomatic establishment in Europe:

I am not such a furious, uncompromising Tory as you are, and, possibly, I have not the same deference for ancient usages; but I promise you to be respectful enough towards these old fancies.[20]

Foreseeing that the series would sometimes read as droll satire, Marshall added that:

I should observe that I should detect illustrations from the Continent rather than from England, so as to bear the Lion and the Unicorn in un-humiliated glory. If anybody is to be found a snob it shall be the miserable foreigner, not the free born Briton—who, between ourselves, is the greatest snob on Earth.[21]

At Marshall's repeated urgings, Blackwood finally accepted the plan, and the series began from December 1873. It was to consist of the following articles and to last, with some intervals, until December 1874: I. Ceremonial, II. Forms, III. Titles, IV. Decorations, V. Emblems, VI. Diplomatic privileges, VII. Alien laws, and VIII. Glory.[22]

At the beginning of part one, Marshall wrote what could serve as a preface to the entire series:

There are some curious subjects which have . . . drifted, by degrees, so far outside the necessities of ordinary educations and occupations, that most of us grow up and live and die with but a faint perception that they exist at all, and certainly with no notion of their details.[23]

Examples of these subjects are, according to Marshall, heraldry, astrology, the art of poisoning, falconry and international law. He explained that the last form of knowledge seemed the least rare compared with the others, but that ponderous treatises on international law tended to be full of discussions using Latin words about all the theoretical questions which would look too gloomy and grave for the general reading public. Although such writings also contained various elements which might enlighten non-specialists about the nature of the human society, such topics remained, Marshall wrote, "invisible to casual eyes." He went on to suggest that: ". . . if some strange necessity should forcibly direct attention to them, they shine out like a lantern in a fog; they tell us curious stories. . . ."[24] To us, it is clear what "some strange necessity" meant, that is Marshall's employment by Sameshima. But Marshall continued, never revealing it to his readers:

. . . they show us human nature in a form which is often singularly new; and especially, they teach us . . . that nations reach a height of self-asserting vanity immeasurable beyond what any individual can possible attain.[25]

One of the early topics Marshall discussed was the problem of precedence among European monarchs and their ambassadors. It was in 1508 that the Pope Julius II "composed and promulgated a complete list of seniority for the use of ambassadors in his own chapel, recommending Europe," in vain, "to adopt it everywhere." The question had always been a vital issue among European nations, and even at the negotiation of the peace of Westphalia in the seventeenth century, it was found to be all too difficult to settle. When two nations could not settle the matter, they used to stipulate for "absolute and exact equality" between them. Marshall talks of one such example:

> This was the plan selected when Mazarin and Don Luis de Haro met to settle the conditions of the marriage between Louis XIV and Maria Theresa. In order to preserve the full dignity of their nations by yielding nothing to each other, the two Ministers stepped together, with the right foot, side by side, into a council chamber . . . and sat down at the same instant precisely opposite each other at a critically square table, on two mathematically equivalent armchairs.[26]

Marshall noted that guidebooks for diplomatic services almost identically discussed the question of forms and manners for negotiation and communication. It was in nineteenth-century Germany that treatises in this field flourished, and Marshall was obliged to read many volumes "edited beyond the Rhine." He admitted that "they [did] not constitute light reading, and, after the first three minutes, they cease even to be instructive."[27] Marshall was, however, patient and extracted some enlightenment from his reading. For example, concerning the choice of the language to be used for official communications between nations, Marshall was able to smile at the serious "Teutonic" scholars who argued that "the right of equality of nations extends to the choice of the language which their Governments employ for diplomatic communications," and he applied this theory to a case between western and non-western nations:

> Who would have suspected that when our Foreign Office...sends a telegram in English to the King of Dahomey, it is exercising "one of the rights of the equality of nations?"[28]

In fact, Marshall's language reveals how much he was enjoying detachment towards Europe.

> How proud it makes one feel to learn, in this sudden way, that the simplest acts of life may be manifestations of glorious principles, and that possibly we can do nothing without implying something that we didn't know anything about.[29]

This "sudden learning" was a product of his encounter with his inquisitive master, Sameshima.

Marshall's discussion about various modes of composing diplomatic documents, such as Bull, Brief, Capitulations, Conclusums, Concordats, etc., suggests the difficulties he must have experienced when explaining each of them to Sameshima. For example, the "French diplomatic manual alone" contained "416 separate types and models," but "how many are there of us," Marshall asked, "who [can] define, for instance, the exact difference between a Rescript and a Pragmatic Sanction . . . ? These half archaeological nomenclatures," he suggests, "mainly serve to show the vanity of nations."[30]At this point Marshall remembered his promise not to offend the "furious Tory," Blackwood:

> We will choose a few examples amongst the least solemn of the series, and will do our best to be respectful, and not to laugh at all during our explanation of them.[31]

His style of explaining Protocol and Memoire was easy for amateurs to comprehend, and far from that which ordinary diplomatic guidebooks would employ:

> A Protocol is . . . a document by which a fact is described with all its attendant circumstances, or by which an authentic and exact account of a conference or a deliberation is given. The reporters of the *Daily Telegraph* do not probably suspect that when they write soul-enthralling histories of a cricket-match at Lords...they are, in fact, composing protocols. . . . A Memoire . . . is a summary of the state of a question, or a justification of a decision adopted. Life is full of examples of it, particularly in conversations between wives and husbands.[32]

Even the vainest of wives would not ask her husband, "Could I possibly issue a Memoire?" or "Would you mind composing a Protocol?" But nations do, and this is what Marshall satirized. As "a most curious fact of all" he mentioned that:

> Letters of abolition, remission, or legitimation are sealed with green wax, because—so, at least, [a French Scholar] tells us—that colour expresses youth, honour, beauty, and especially liberty.[33]

The words "most curious" might have been uttered first by Sameshima.

Sovereign's titles were, in Marshall's eyes, particularly "aggressive form[s] of the vanity of nations." He described an Assyrian king of about 1200 B.C. as a "beginner in the art of self-laudation." Also Xerxes of the fifth century B.C. was noted as having been content with only half a dozen titles. By contrast, explained Marshall, the monarchs of modern times require "at least fifty each."[34] He classified titles into five major groups: of monarchical dignity, of territorial possession, of pseudo-family relationship with the Pope or other sovereigns, of religion, and of courtesy such as Majesty, Highness,

Monseigneur, etc. Among the titles of dignity, Emperor seems to have been one of Marshall's (and probable Sameshima's) major concerns. Marshall described the history of the denominations of "the Muscovite sovereign," and explained how the self-assumed title "Imperator" of the seventeenth century met with indignation in other European Courts for more than a century. The most offended was the Emperor of the Holy Roman Empire, Leopold I, who thought that the title was his personal monopoly.[35] Marshall counted the Honourables, the Generals, the Judges, etc., who adorned the United States, and observed that "the love of titles" never ceases even in republics.[36] In Marshall's view, there was only one exception, the sovereign of Japan:

> ... there exists a master who has held one unvarying rank since the time of Nebuchadnezzar; who would regard as a degradation any addition to the single quality by which more than a hundred and twenty of his fathers have been known before him. ... Ten-o ... "Heaven-Highest" ... is the one title of the sovereign of Japan.[37]

Marshall observed that this "solitary appellation" was "far away the grandest" and surpassed "all our vain attempts at glory." He concluded this topic, remarking that ". . . in this particular element of royal titles . . . we are not a model for other people. . . . Japan is far more worth copying that we are."[38]

The history of the orders and decorations of Europe was also a new field Sameshima had to learn in a hurry, and Marshall's detailed account on the matter illustrates the depth of his research for Sameshima. First, Marshall elaborated the history of the Crusades which brought forth the Orders of monastic military brotherhoods. Then he introduced to his readers "the great aristocratic Orders" which had been accorded only to sovereigns or great nobles since the fourteenth century—such as the Garter, the Seraphim of Sweden, the Annonciade of Savoy, etc. These matters, however, constituted the background against which Marshall maintained that a close study of the orders of the nineteenth century would deepen one's insight into human nature. He counted that there were 138 Orders in the world in 1874 and among them 86 had been created during the nineteenth century:

> Most of the old religious and strictly noble confraternities have vanished out of sight; but they have been replaced by modern institutions more in harmony with the spirit of the age.[39]

It was in the Legion d'honneur created by Napoleon I that the "knighthood for the masses" came into being, and Marshall considered this phenomenon to correspond "to one of the weak necessities of human nature."[40] He foresaw the social effects of this popularization of orders and decorations:

> Politically, this is advantageous, for free competition makes more useful citizens than monopolies can produce; but morally, the effect is probably the other way . . . we shall never be able to deny that mean and

unworthy consequences are resulting, all over Europe, from the popularization of a sort of vanity which originally influenced only a restricted section of each nation.[41]

Marshall was, however, fully aware that modern decorations and orders would go on increasing until something better was invented. They were indeed "costing little, but seeming very dear," and both givers and receivers were likely to be quite contented with them.[42] He also remarked the recent internationalization of orders in Europe and wrote that "about 55,000 crosses, of all grades," were then "bestowed outside their native soil." Thanks to Sameshima's probing, Marshall had become virtually a sober sociologist in such matters:

... it would be both amusing and instructive to look through the list of motives for which all these distinctions have been conferred. Such a study would explain to us, with a most gratifying indiscretion, what are the particular services which are most freely offered to or accepted by Continental Governments, and would, in this way afford a curious insight into a hitherto uninvestigated side of human nature.[43]

With regard to the question of monarchical and national emblems, he introduced briefly to his readers the history of these symbols in Europe:

[During the seventh century] wild animals temporarily went out of fashion in Christianity, and were replaced by flowers, figures, crosses, flames, and saints, which began to disappear again when shields of arms were invented. It is pretended that, at this time, the Germans used a serpent and a lion for their symbols; the Goths a lion, cock, and bear; the Danes three lions and a crow; the Burgundians a cat; and the Saxons a white horse.[44]

Marshall's satirical view became more clear when he proceeded to explain how all the European nations were closely attached to their national flags, mottoes and uniforms in the late nineteenth century. Obviously he had been deeply impressed by the recent invasion into Paris of the powerful Prussian Army, and became pessimistic about the future of Europe. Marshall thought that contemporary developments in weapons were bound to change national symbols and uniforms:

... the soldiers of the future will doubtless be enclosed in laboratory bottles, and be surrounded by opaque vapours; generals will wear diving-dresses ... while reconnaissances will be made by spectrum analysis. ... Under such conditions of belligerence all actual emblems would lose their value. ... France, for instance, might give up the tricolour and adopt "portable democratized earthquakes" as her badge; England might abandon the ugly Union-Jack, and send her troops to fight beneath an oriflamme of "chemistry and dynamics;" United Germany, on the other hand, would continue to employ the practical but touching motto which she has recently adopted, "Blood and Iron:" in this respect . . . she is far away ahead of her contemporaries. . . .[45]

Marshall foresaw that future fathers would take their children to a museum "to gaze with curious sympathy on the skulls and thigh-bones of the simple races which [had] used breech-loaders for weapons and coloured stuffs for emblems," and that future professors of archaeology would "teach their pupils that the Prussian Eagle [had been] an accepted sign of gentleness and maiden diffidence; that the Stars and Stripes [had] stood universally for bashful modesty; and that the British Lion [had been] a type of self-sacrificing unselfishness."[46]

Marshall's sense of detachment towards the contemporary West was also demonstrated in his discussions about diplomatic privileges and alien laws. The inviolable institution of ambassadors, he wrote, was "an essentially modern product." He observed that it had certainly occupied a high situation in European countries during the seventeenth and eighteenth centuries, when sovereigns had been "vastly bigger personages" than they were in the late nineteenth century. "Revolutions, popular education, public opinion, and the telegraph," wrote Marshall, "have dragged both [sovereigns and ambassadors] down, side by side."[47] Although the western governments were at that time loudly complaining about Japan's uncivilized treatment of foreigners, the notion of "civility to foreigners" was, in Marshall's eyes, "a new invention" even in Europe.[48] It was only in the middle of the fourteenth century that foreigners in England were relieved of all responsibility for other foreigners' debts and acts.[49] Examples of the maltreatment of foreigners had been abundant even in the nineteenth century. "It is hardly credible, but it is true, that it was not until four years ago that aliens could inherit property in England."[50] Another example was wrecking. This had been pursued as an organized occupation on the coasts of France until the end of the seventeenth century, but on some English and German coasts, the business was supported even by local churches until quite recently.[51] Marshall commented on this fact, "Europe took the curious view that a shipwrecked sailor was a foe to all humanity."[52] The depth of information which Marshall received from his encounter with Sameshima seems rather clearly shown in such a remark.

The Cold European Reading Public

The response to this series from the reading public was, however, less than enthusiastic. Marshall had been fully aware that his view would be unorthodox in Europe, and was therefore all the more anxious to know his readers' reactions. But barely any enthusiastic comment reached his ears even after the fifth part of the series had been published. He wrote to Blackwood:

I have grown somewhat discouraged about international Vanities: nobody seem to take the slightest interest in the subjects I have treated; and as the labour of getting them up has been rather serious, I hesitate a little about going on.[53]

Did his readers' silence towards "International Vanities" simply mean that they had no interest in such topics? In Marshall's discussions a radical idea was often conspicuous; that is that European manners and customs are after all of a local nature and all local traditions of the world are of equal value. But how many people in Europe at that time could really perceive both Queen Victoria and the King of Dahomey as equals? The very need for such a perception was almost nonexistent. Already, after the publication of the third part of the series, Marshall had confessed that he had heard at least one opinion from a friend of his—an opinion which might explain the nature of his readers' general silence:

A lady whose opinion I consult on many things has been abusing International Vanities—'dull and uninteresting' and I have been influenced by her hostility.[54]

The radicalness of Marshall's thought could have been quite offensive in certain quarters. This had become clearer when he had tried to publish as an article in the *Blackwood's* a more practical paper criticizing European consular jurisdiction practiced in the East. It was in the middle of January 1874, that is, after the publication of the second part of "Vanities," that Marshall sent to Blackwood a manuscript titled, "Justice Abroad." Blackwood, who had been approving, however reluctantly, the humorous aspects of "Vanities," reacted negatively when he received Marshall's manuscript urging that the British government abolish its consular jurisdiction in Japan. At Marshall's repeated request, however, Blackwood reluctantly prepared proofs for the March 1, 1874, issue of the magazine, but soon changed his mind about publishing the paper. He wrote to Marshall explaining his view of the matter:

Reading over the paper after the corrected proof came back I felt that your proposal to bring in Public Opinion to act upon minute questions in remote parts as to which only those on the spot in authority or otherwise could judge was practically impossible. Do you not feel this your self?[55]

Blackwood may have also been concerned about antagonizing his readers. At any rate, Japan was to him, as the editor of the magazine, too "remote" a country and its problem was too "minute" to be discussed in the pages of his periodical. He expressed the belief that "on the whole," the British behaved "wonderfully well to the nations" such as the Japanese and that should any misconduct occur on the part of British agents abroad, they would "speedily meet with punishment from home." Thus, Blackwood declined to publish

Marshall's paper. "I feel that in publishing it I might be making a hit in the dark on a point which I did not understand."[56] Marshall was deeply disappointed over Blackwood's decision, and he replied that:

> I am sorry you don[']t like "Justice Abroad," very sorry. But, as I have written it for a purpose, to serve a cause which, in my conscience, I believe to be an honest one, I do not see my way to altering it. May I then ask your permission . . . to publish it elsewhere?[57]

John Morley's radical periodical, the *Fortnightly Review* published Marshall's "Justice Abroad." Even Morley, however, was not altogether eager to do so, and the publication was delayed until July 1874.

But this article had far less impact on the reading public than Marshall had hoped. Marshall explained the history of European consular jurisdiction in the East from the sixteenth century, and demonstrated how European scholars in international law were inconsistent when they dealt with they question of consular jurisdiction, being, as they were, propagators of absolute national sovereignty. In Marshall's eyes, England's current usage of the word "justice" in Asian countries implied nothing but "a protection from oneselves but not as a guarantee for others."[58] Carefully avoiding the appearance of speaking only on behalf of Japan, he argued the unfairness of the system. Finally he introduced his readers to a lengthy imaginary "protest" from the sovereign of an eastern country to the British government supposedly printed in *The Times*:

> . . . as [the Government of our country] had no idea what a treaty was, or what ought to be put into it, the Government accepted, with its eyes shut, the form of treaty which the [English] captain was pleased to indicate. . . . The more Englishmen began to come to [our country], bringing with them [goods which] did damage to our people. . . . [At my Government's protest] the Consul laughed, and said, "It is in the treaty." . . . At last the Government got very angry, and told the Consul it would break so abominable and unjust a treaty, but the consul laughed once more . . . pointed to the ship, and said, "Bombardment." . . . [Our country became] a sort of property of this Consul.

Here, Marshall introduced a passage which could well remind the readers of the Iwakura Mission:

> We instituted a Commission to examine into the nature of the relations between European states. That Commission went to Paris and to London, and to many other places, under pretence of buying brandy (for Consul was so hard on us that we did not dare to let him know what we were about). . . . It has become evident to this government, that . . . we

have been constrained to adopt international obligations, which every Christian people would reject with anger and disdain, to assume a position of absolute inferiority, to abandon our sovereign right of equality and independence. . . .

Then, this king's conclusion was to take up the following policy:

We have discovered that there is in Europe a force more powerful than gunboats. . . . That force of Public Opinion, and we place ourselves in its succoring hand. We claim to fix our tariffs without dictation from abroad; we claim to judge the crimes committed by foreigners in our territory; we claim the power of punishing Englishmen who insult us . . . for these motives we declare—not to a Consul whom we fear and hate, but to the entire British nation—that we will not renew our present treaty, and then if England sends a fleet to frighten us into submission we will accept destruction rather than justice.[59]

For the sender of this protest, Marshall chose a figure, who, he thought, could be an analogy to the sovereign of Japan, and it was the King of the Gobi Desert. Marshall tried his best to attract the attention and sympathy of his readers, but his very efforts at achieving readability created a paradox; the introduction of the metaphor of the sovereign of a desert kingdom was at that time most likely to make his readers feel even more detached from the issue. In Marshall's mind, a desert kingdom may have been equal to a European empire, but it could not but be a bad joke among western societies. Most of his readers probably perceived Japan as one of those small kingdoms beyond the Near East, and considered, like Blackwood, Japan's agony to be a "minute question in remote parts." Any attempt for a readable metaphor is in a way a reconciliation between the writer's idea and the reader's supposedly familiar world. The very fact that Marshall could only choose "the Gobi Kingdom" for Japan eloquently reveals the general sense of remoteness the ordinary European reading public entertained towards Japan at that time. One can, say therefore, that Marshall was at least successful, in his series, "International Vanities," in showing Europe in a remote detachment, but was not so successful in his "Justice Abroad" in showing Japan as one of the close neighbors of European countries.

Even Blackwood was vague about the degree of coldness which the readers of Marshall's "Vanities" had exhibited. In April 1875, he published the reprint edition of the series in one small volume at 10 shillings a copy. The number of copies printed was 1,000. But this publication was a complete failure. About sixty percent of the copies printed were still on the publishers' hands four years later.[60] Already in June 1875, only two months after the publication, Marshall had to console Blackwood: "I am very sorry that the book is not selling, but much more so for you than for myself."[61]

Another Product of the Encounter

During the difficult time of publishing "Justice Abroad," Marshall's zeal for making efforts for Japan in journalistic circles seems to have cooled down. In June 1874, Marshall started, in accordance with a plan of Sameshima's, writing a guidebook for the Japanese diplomatic services. The book was planned for use at the Paris Legation, and this time Blackwood showed no reluctance in taking up the business of its printing and binding.[62] Soon its manuscripts and proofs began commuting between Paris and Edinburgh. It was decided to print 200 copies.[63] Large chunks of "International Vanities" proved useful for the book, and Sameshima demonstrated his usual "severity and earnestness" in making each word precise. Delays in returning the proofs were of course unavoidable, and Marshall sent an apology to Blackwood on October 11, 1874:

> First proofs of Chapters 14 to 18 are all in my hands now, and would
> have been already sent back if the Minister were not so slow in finally
> approving them.[64]

Until quite late in the proceedings, the author of the book had been identified as the "Foreign Office of Japan," but Sameshima seems to have concluded that this was too pretentious and decided to suppress it "both on the title page and cover."[65]

Sameshima was to leave Paris for Japan on November 20, 1875, and was very eager to acquire some copies before his departure. It would be a valuable souvenir to carry back to Japan as an example of his work in Paris during the preceding three years. It was, however, at Hyeres on the Riviera that Sameshima seems to have finally received at least one sample copy from Edinburgh. While waiting for the departure of his ship from Marseille, Sameshima was staying with Marshall at Hyeres. From here Marshall wrote to Blackwood:

> My dear Blackwood,
>   First of all Sameshima begs me to thank you very much indeed for
> all the trouble which has been taken about the Diplomatic Guide. He is
> very much pleased with it.
>   Secondly, he wants you to be so kind—unless the whole of the
> copies are already sent to Paris—as to order four copies to be at once
> proceeded here by post. He wants them to give in Japan directly he
> arrives there.[66]

The National Diet Library, Tokyo, keeps one copy of this "Guide." It was donated in 1892 to Tokyo Toshokan, one of the forerunners of the Library, from the library of the late Minister to Peking Shioda Saburo (1843-1889). It is a duodecimal book containing a four-page preface, a one-page list of contents, nineteen chapters totalling 148 pages, and a four-page index. The names of Sameshima and Marshall do not appear anywhere, and the title page reads: DIPLOMATIC GUIDE, DRAWN UP BY THE LEGATION OF JAPAN IN PARIS, PRINTED BY WILLIAM BLACKWOOD AND SONS, EDINBURGH AND LONDON, 1874. The eleven works listed in the preface as references, and the themes of those chapters are familiar to readers of "International Vanities." But there is no trace in its pages that the author is making an effort 'not to laugh.' The language is clear and very readable. To analyze each chapter and study its influence on Japanese diplomatic services would be an interesting subject, but that must remain for another time, but its contents are:

I. The right of legation; II. The composition of embassies and legations; III. Formalities of nomination; IV. Formalities of arrival; V. Precedence; VI. Ceremonial; VII. Diplomatic Privileges; VIII. The functions of a diplomatic agent; IX. Termination of diplomatic missions; X. Correspondence and forms; XI. Correspondence between sovereigns; XII. Examples of documents; XIII. Congresses and conferences; XIV. Treaties and conventions; XV. Consuls and their functions; XVI. Organization of foreign offices and diplomatic services; XVII. Rules as to decorations; XVIII. Books for a diplomatic library; XIX. International law.

Each chapter can be regarded as a product of this serious encounter between the first Japanese resident diplomat in Europe and his *Oyatoi*, or, in more general terms, as a product of joint work between East and West. Under the latter rubric, various later works by many *'Oyatoi'* can be grouped: for example, dictionaries of western languages, ethical writings by eager Christian teachers, textbooks on science and technology, etc. If they were compiled especially for a kind of reader who would be most inquisitive and obstinate, those books were bound to contain highly cross-cultural, that is more globally understandable messages because of the counter-information to which the authors had been exposed while writing. One of the conspicuous examples may be the world long-seller, *Oxford Advanced Learner's Dictionary of Current English* by A. S. Hornby, who taught English in Japan during 1924 to 1942.

Works which have been influential in the formation of the modern world may have been such products. In this perspective, the history of the nineteenth and twentieth centuries, which has so often been perceived as the process of westernization, suggests that it was a more complex process of increasingly dense interdependence and a joint-creation. Finally, on the otherwise blank page between the front cover and the title-page of the *Diplomatic Guide*, there remains a message of dedication:

Offert a Mr. [*sic*] Shioda par son ami Nakano.
Paris 23 Septembre 1875

The Secretary Nakano had been a most able aid to Sameshima in Paris and was appointed *Charge d'affaires* in April 1874 when Sameshima's health became delicate. Nakano remained in the post until January 1878 when Sameshima was appointed Minister to France again. The above handwriting, a mixture between French and English, is, however, unmistakably that of Frederic Marshall. When Nakano presented a copy to Shioda, why didn't Nakano write the dedication himself? Marshall might have been keeping at the Legation of Japan in Paris all the remaining copies of the *Guide* as if they had been his own treasure.

Notes

[1]For details, see Yokoyama Toshio, *Japan in the Victorian Mind, a Study of Stereotyped Images of a Nation, 1850-80* (London, 1987), pp. 170-175.

[2]Walter E. Houghton, (ed.), *The Wellesley Index to Victorian Periodicals 1824-1900*, vol. I (Toronto, 1966), p. 8.

[3]Mrs. Gerald Porter, *Annals of a Publishing House, John Blackwood* (Edinburgh & London, 1898), p. 306.

[4]The major part of the series was published during November 1871 (No. I) to August 1872 (No. VII), whereas No. VIII was printed in the July issue of 1873.

[5]The Blackwood Papers at the National Library of Scotland (abbreviated henceforward to NLS, BP), MS. 4294, ff. 138: Marshall to Blackwood, July 18, 1872.

[6]*Ibid.*, f. 146: Marshall to Blackwood (August 11, 1872).

[7]*Ibid.*

[8][Frederic Marshall] "Japan," *Blackwood's Edinburgh Magazine* (abbreviated henceforward to Blackw.), cxii, 380.

[9]*Ibid.*, p. 386.

[10]*Ibid.*, p. 378.

[11]*Ibid.*, p. 379.

[12]NLS, BP, MS. 4294, ff. 159: Marshall to Blackwood (August 22, 1872); *Ibid.*, Acc. 5633, D8, pp. 184-5: Blackwood to Delane (August 26, 1872).

[13]"Japan," *The Times* (September 5, 1872), p. 8.

[14][William George Aston] "Japan," *Macmillan's Magazine*, xxvi, 497.

[15]The British Library, Addit. MSS. 55392 (Macmillan Archive), f. 936; Alexander Macmillan to George Grove (September 14, 1872). See also Yokoyama, *op. cit.*, pp. 127-8, 145-6.

[16]Sameshima's title in Paris was then to be *Sho-Benmushi* (Junior Commissioner). Later he was made *Chu-Benmushi* in May 1872; *Benri Koshi* (Minister Resident) in May 1873; *Tokumei Zenken Koshi* (Envoy Extraordinary Minister Plenipotentiary) in June 1873. This last title he kept until July 1874 and resumed during November 1878 to December 1880.

[17]NLS, BP, MS. 4308, ff. 131-3: Marshall to Blackwood (September 21, 1873).

[18]*Ibid.*

[19][Marshall] "International Vanities. No. II.—Forms," *Blackw.*, cxv, 65-6.

[20]NLS, BP, VS. 4308, ff. 132-3: Marshall to Blackwood (September 21, 1873).

[21]*Ibid.*

[22][Marshall] "International Vanities," *Blackw.*, cxiv, 667-85 (No. I); cxv, 55-74 (No. II/January 1874); 172-93 (No. III/February); 486-503 (No. IV/April); 607-75 (No. V/May); cxvi, 346-64 (No. VI/September); 450-66 (No. VII/October); 723-40 (No. VIII).

[23][Marshall] "International Vanities. No. I," *op. cit.*, p. 667.

[24]*Ibid.*, p. 668.

[25]*Ibid.*

[26]*Ibid.*, p. 677.

[27][Marshall] "International Vanities." No. II, *op. cit.*, p. 56.

[28]*Ibid.*, p. 57.

[29]*Ibid.*

[30]*Ibid.*, p. 59.

[31]*Ibid.*, p. 60.

[32]*Ibid.*

[33]*Ibid.*, p. 62.

[34][Marshall] "International Vanities." No. III, *op. cit.*, pp. 173-4.

[35]*Ibid.*, pp. 180-2.

[36]*Ibid.*, p. 191.

[37]*Ibid.*, p. 192.

[38]*Ibid.*, p. 193.

[39][Marshall] "International Vanities." No. IV, *op. cit.*, p. 498.

[40]*Ibid.*, p. 499.

[41]*Ibid.*, p. 503.

[42]*Ibid.*, p. 499.

[43]*Ibid.*, p. 501.

[44][Marshall] "International Vanities." No. V, *op. cit.*, p. 609.

[45]*Ibid.*, p. 624.

[46]*Ibid.*, p. 625.

[47][Marshall] "International Vanities." No. VI, *op. cit.*, p. 346.

[48][Marshall] "International Vanities." No. VII, *op. cit.*, p. 450.

[49]*Ibid.*, pp. 458-9.

[50]*Ibid.*, p. 457.

[51]*Ibid.*, pp. 452-3.

[52]*Ibid.*, p. 452.

[53]NLS, BP, MS. 4322, f. 171: Marshall to Blackwood (June 4, 1874).

[54]*Ibid.*, f. 146: Marshall to Blackwood (February 17, 1874).

[55]NLS, BP, Acc. 5643, D8, p. 422: Blackwood to Marshall (February 17, 1874).

[56]*Ibid.*

Frederic Marshall as an Employee of the Japanese Legation

[57]NLS, BP, MS. 4322, f. 147: Marshall to Blackwood (February 19, 1874).

[58]Frederick [sic] Marshall, "Justice Abroad," *The Fortnightly Review*, xvi new series, 133.

[59]*Ibid.*, pp. 142-5.

[60]NLS, BP, Acc. 5644, F6 (Blackwood Publication Ledger, 1873-81), p. 299.

[61]NLS, BP, MS. 4336, f. 57: Marshall to Blackwood (June 16, 1875).

[62]NLS, BP, MS. 4322, f. 173: Marshall to Blackwood (June 24, 1874); Acc. 5643, D9, p. 19: W. Blackwood to Marshall (June 26, 1874).

[63]NLS, BP, MS. 4322, f. 189: Marshall to Blackwood (August 9, 1874).

[64]*Ibid.*, f. 207: Marshall to Blackwood (October 11, 1874).

[65]*Ibid.*, f. 213: Marshall to W. Blackwood & Sons (October 26, 1874).

[66]*Ibid.*, f. 230: Marshall to Blackwood (December 9, 1874).

PART FOUR

ARCHIVAL RESOURCES

16

Primary Manuscript and Printed Sources for Studying the *Yatoi*: The William Elliot Griffis Papers and Related Special Collections at Rutgers University

Clark L. Beck, Jr.

For sixty years Rutgers University has attracted scholars who have conducted research on the *yatoi* phenomenon. During the first half century, they came primarily to use the William Elliot Griffis Papers bequeathed to the University in 1928 and augmented substantially in the mid-1960's.[1] In 1980-1981, due largely to the generosity of Japanese philanthropy and the support of University Librarian Hendrik Edelman, the volume of resources around the core Griffis material increased sharply. It is now accurate to say that one can no longer seriously study the process of modernization in Japan, specifically the technical expertise lent to the Japanese by foreigners in the nineteenth century, without consulting the Griffis Papers and related primary documents. Many individuals—Japanese and Westerners—continue to aid in the creation at Rutgers of a research center for historical materials relating to the very first period of cultural and educational exchange between Japan and the West. This essay outlines the resources currently available and briefly describes their contents.

Although he spent less than four years in that country, William Elliot Griffis (1843-1928) is acknowledged widely to be America's first "old Japan hand." During the year following his 1869 graduation from Rutgers College, he tutored a number of young Japanese who had come to study in New Brunswick and late in 1870 accepted an invitation to teach science in Echizen domain (modern Fukui). He remained in Fukui until January, 1872 and then relocated to Tokyo, where he taught for two years before returning to the United States in the summer of 1874. Griffis was not to see Japan again for more than half a century, when he toured the country as an honored guest (winter of

1926-1927). In the long interim he lectured incessantly, wrote numerous books and articles, and collected voluminous amounts of material about Japan. Undoubtedly, he became the most influential writer in projecting impressions of Japan on the minds of his informed contemporaries, and for many Americans his literary activity resulted in their introduction to and primary contact with the movement analyzed in the accompanying essays.[2]

A cursory survey of the Griffis Papers reveals the exhaustive range of interests nurtured by this man. Griffis is known largely for his work on Japan, but his interests went far beyond what contemporaries considered the distant and exotic land on the other side of the world. He wrote also on European and American history, theology, Korea and China. From a biography of one of America's most obscure Presidents, Millard Fillmore; to reminiscences of his college *alma mater;* to theological treatises; to well received narratives about countries he never visited, Griffis was insatiable in his quest to appeal to the broadest spectrum of readers possible.

Perhaps more important than the activities which generated the Griffis Papers is the fact that he accumulated and saved essentially everything he wrote and everything that was written to him. It is all there, from the correspondence of a 15-year-old schoolboy to the last correspondence and diary entries of an 84-year-old man. Whether the product of an overinflated ego or of family habit, the Griffis Papers have provided generations of scholars with a wealth of resource material more significant than even its immodest creator might have imagined.

Expectedly, the volume of the Griffis Papers is enormous. They consist of some 150 manuscript boxes (fifty cubic feet), about 25 scrapbooks and approximately 450 volumes from his personal library. Most of the material is in English, and roughly half relates to Japan. The papers span nearly his entire life, from 1858 to 1929. About half the collection is available for the perusal of researchers in the reading room of Special Collections/Archives, Alexander Library, while the remainder is stored on another level of that building. Essentially all of the Japan material is housed in the Special Collections/Archives reading room, and this discussion focuses on that material.

As often is true with manuscript collections, Griffis' personal correspondence (letters received and, occasionally, drafts of letters sent) is perhaps the most revealing and fascinating part of his papers. From a slighted classmate's touching plea for young William's friendship, circa 1858, to the numerous letters of condolence to Mrs. Griffis in 1928 and 1929, the papers contain some twelve cubic feet of correspondence, about one-quarter of which relates to Japan.[3] The Japan letters are divided into four major series.

Series one consists of Griffis' correspondence from his boyhood in the 1850's to his first arrival in Japan (December 29, 1870). Although much of this does not involve Japan directly, it is important for studying the emerging character of the young man whose entire adult life was to be dominated by a country half a world away. The most frequent correspondents during these early years were family members, especially his mother, brother Montgomery, and sister Margaret (Maggie). It is in this period also that Griffis first corresponded with fellow Rutgers classmate and future *yatoi* Edward Warren Clark. Because these letters constitute only one box and the number of correspondents is not great, they are arranged by year and then alphabetically by writer within each year.

Series two comprises letters from the first Japan stay, 1871-1874. Especially illuminating are the frequent letters sent to his family (notably Maggie in the first two years), with their informative descriptions of life in Fukui and Tokyo.[4] The Fukui letters have been transcribed and published by Mr. Yamashita Eiichi, an effort for which current and future scholars are and shall continue to be grateful.[5] Correspondence from this first Japan period occupies two manuscript boxes and is arranged by year and alphabetically by writer within a given year.[6]

Series three includes all Japan related correspondence between Griffis' two experiences in that country, 1874-1926. As one might surmise, this series is the most voluminous and the number of correspondents staggering. For the present, these letters are arranged in one alphabet, by writer.[7] As the Griffis Papers are processed further this arrangement doubtlessly will be refined, probably by way of more precise chronological divisions.

The correspondence in this series, more than any other, reveals the influence of Griffis as an interpreter of Japan to the West. It is evident that people from throughout the United States and Western Europe, from varying walks of life, considered him a paramount authority not only on Japan but on Korea and China as well. Voluminous letters from friends in Japan (both Japanese and Westerners) demonstrate the extent to which he kept in close contact with his adopted land for half a century. Former students corresponded with him for decades, and his correspondents ranged from the prominent to the unknown. Among the letters in this series are many recognizable names: William G. Aston, James H. Ballagh, Samuel Robbins Brown, R. Henry Brunton, Horace Capron, Edward Warren Clark, E.W. Clement, J.H. DeForest, James Main Dixon, Harada Tasuku, Joseph Henry, James C. Hepburn, Imadate Tosui, Kaneko Kentaro, Viscount Kuroda Nagaatsu, Alfred Lucy, Benjamin Smith Lyman, J. Milne, Edward S. Morse, E.H. Mudgett (Griffis' Fukui successor), Henry L. Munro, David Murray, Nitobe Inazo, Ambassador Takahira Kogoro, Tejima Seiichi, Henry Taylor Terry, James Troup, Tsuda Ume, Guido F. Verbeck, Henry Von Rankin, John A.L. Waddell and Martin N. Wyckoff.

Important to this series is a block of responses by some 75 *yatoi* to a 1906 request from Griffis for biographical information.[8] As the self-appointed historian of these foreign employees Griffis planned to write a collective biography of as many as possible, a task he never really got underway, perhaps due to a lack of enthusiasm on the part of those from whom he solicited information. Would that everyone had shared the reaction of Edward Divers: "The author of the 'Mikado's Empire' has the strongest claim to every courtesy from any foreigner who has followed him in Japan."[9] Among the *yatoi* (or their

relatives) who did respond were S.R. Brown, C. Carrothers, Edward Warren
Clark, Henry W. Denison, F. Victor Dickins, Edward Divers, James Main
Dixon, Henry Dyer, Reverend David Grigsby, William Jaques, Alfred Lucy,
Benjamin Smith Lyman, J. Morris, Edward S. Morse, Cornelius H. Patton,
Cecil Hobart Peabody, M M. Scott, Robert A. Smith, Robert Stuart, J.B.
Unthank, Henry Van Reed, Henry Von Rankin and John A.L. Waddell.

Series four chronicles Griffis' triumphant return to Japan in 1926-1927.
After fifty years as America's "old Japan hand" (an epithet which, at 83, was apt
in more ways than one), he was in incredible demand as a speaker and/or guest,
and much of the correspondence relates to requests for such appearances.
Approximately two boxes of letters constitute this series, which is arranged
chronologically by month and then alphabetically by writer. While this trip
found Griffis at the height of his popularity, he was deeply saddened by the
growing rift he observed between Japan and the United States. In June he had an
audience with the Emperor, an occasion he no doubt considered one of the
highlights of his life. But the joy of that moment must have been tempered by
a letter he had received four months earlier from a young Fukui boy who heard
Griffis speak at the Asahi Hall on the night of January 24, 1927: "When you
return home, Please let all the Americans know that our Japanese are very
serious to restore friendship of your country and that we hope two countries
will surely develope [sic] in permanent peace."[10] Fortunately, Griffis did not
live to see the young boy's hopes shattered.

An important research source for Japan scholars continues to be the Griffis
diaries. Consisting of 23 volumes, they begin with a carefree teenage outing at
the Philadelphia Zoo and run in an almost unbroken sequence for the next 68 1/2
years to an entry by an 84 year-old man two days before his death. In
characteristic fashion, Griffis was engaged in writing yet another book when he
was stricken suddenly and died within two days. It is ironic, if not prophetic,
that the last brief entry in his diary mentions both *The Mikado's Empire* and
Corwin's *Manual of the Reformed Church in America,* thereby linking two
great devotions of his life in a final entry of less than 25 words.[11] It is as if
Griffis uncannily wrote his own epitaph.

For Japan enthusiasts, two volumes in this long sequence are essential.
First is the journal of his initial stay in Japan, 1871-1874.[12] Mr. Eiichi
Yamashita has transcribed the entries for the Fukui year, translated them into
Japanese and produced a fine volume.[13] However, the bulk of the entires cover
Griffis' 2 1/2 year stint in Tokyo and constitute a resource vital to scholarship
on the *yatoi* which should not be overlooked. The second volume recounts the
triumphant return to Japan fifty years later (1926-1927) and the many contacts
Griffis made at that time.[14] This journal has received less attention than its
earlier counterpart but it, along with the ample correspondence from the trip,
remains an underutilized source for the *yatoi* historian.

These diaries and journals are arranged chronologically. Fortunately for the
user, they are generally regular, reasonably detailed, well written and
informative.

Like her illustrious brother, Margaret Clark "Maggie" Griffis kept a diary for most of her adult life. Numbering eight volumes in all, one volume of about 250 pages details her Japan experiences, 1872-1874.[15] Although entries were made at irregular intervals, they are often quite full and informative. As a source for *yatoi* and women's history, they have not been tapped sufficiently.

One of the largest and most significant groups of resources in the Griffis Papers consists of notes, jottings, and drafts of innumerable writings (both published and unpublished) on Japan. These are perhaps the most difficult for the archivist to arrange and describe, because Griffis wrote about almost *anything* on whatever scrap of paper he could find. Such notes and drafts are scattered throughout the papers, although in several instances they are grouped with other materials on the same or similar subjects. The topics abound— Japanese art, religion, customs, economics, politics, history, language, mythology, women, urban affairs, foreign policy, folklore and *yatoi*. The longer manuscripts, for which sometimes there is more than one draft, are accessible through a topical index, circa 1960, and those from the parts of the collection acquired and/or processed since then can be located by title (key word) or by subject if no title can be ascertained.[16] The miscellaneous notes and jottings present a greater archival dilemma, however, and some sort of topical arrangement will have to be devised eventually.

Less scattered and less voluminous are photographs of Japan, the Japanese and *yatoi*. Most are actual portraits and local views dating from the Meiji era, and a number of the portraits are inscribed. Included are likenesses of Amenomori Nobushige, Awa Katsu, James Main Dixon, Harada Tasuku, Hattori Ichizo, William H. Jaques, Marquis Matsudaira, Baron Mayeshima, M. M. Scott, Saito Shinichiro, Kusakabe Taro, Tejima Seiich and Dr. David Thompson. Local subjects include depictions of various Meiji buildings and local scenes containing people, for example, the opening of Tokyo Imperial University, group portraits of Japanese students in Japan and at Rutgers, views of students at work in various Tokyo technical schools, the Russo-Japanese War, contemporary postcards and stereographs, and group photographs which include *yatoi*. Griffis has identified the subjects of many of these images on the reverse sides. The photographs largely are concentrated in two boxes and arranged by type (e.g., portraits, local views, buildings) and alphabetically by subject within each group.

Like the notes and jottings described earlier, the miscellaneous printed matter in the Griffis Papers is voluminous and scattered, and from the point of view of a workable archival arrangement, troublesome. Griffis saved offprints of many of his Japan articles, and these are arranged neatly by title (about two boxes). Various periodicals are scattered, though sometimes recorded. Pamphlets, broadsides and published reports abound, but their recording is spotty. There are a number of early Japan Society annual reports, for example, as well as copies of 1,874 examinations prepared for students at the *Kaisei Gakko*. Probably the best arrangement would be by format and date, because a strictly topical sequence could be somewhat confusing and bibliographically unsound. A further breakdown by title might be appropriate for some materials.

Griffis gathered countless newspaper clippings about Japan during his long career. It is difficult to estimate how many clippings of news stories, articles, obituaries, book reviews, etc., are among his papers, but it is doubtful that so complete a record ever was or will be compiled with this kind of material. Presently, many clippings are arranged topically, along with other formats of material on the same subject, and these subjects are accessible through an index co-compiled by Ardath Burks.[17] Many other clippings are loose. In time, a clipping file arranged alphabetically by subject probably would be the most effective means of making this valuable information available to scholars. Some comprehensive preservation efforts are in order, because these clippings generally are fragile and deteriorating, a condition aggravated further by continual use.

About 450 volumes on the Far East came to Rutgers following Griffis' death in 1928. Most are English language titles, although some rare imprints in Japanese published in late Tokugawa and early Meiji Japan are present. The library includes bound contemporary pamphlets, a number of which are official reports of both the Japanese and United States governments, and some of Griffis' own works, such as a first edition of *The Mikado's Empire*.[18] Roughly two-thirds of these books are fully cataloged using the Library of Congress classification system, although the contemporary material in Japanese remains essentially unrecorded.

A large category of miscellaneous materials rounds out the Japan portion of the Griffis Papers. About 300 essays in English by students at the Kaisei-gakko make fascinating reading, both as examples of the facility with which the young Japanese mastered English and as primary accounts of life in contemporary Japan. These essays treat such topics as "my home province or city," Japanese customs, Japanese money, the Ainu, household superstitions, the effect of theaters upon the people of a country, and "my first impressions of foreigners." An additional forty autobiographical essays by students of Griffis and sister Margaret are similiarly instructive and occasionally touching. Some 150 letters (mostly 1928) to Mrs. Frances King Griffis offer messages of condolence on the death of her husband. These letters are arranged alphabetically by writer. Fifteen volumes of *Ri-ji Kotei [A Comparison of Different Systems of Education]*, published in Japanese, were presented to the Rutgers College Library by Vice Minister of Education Fujimoro Tanaka in 1876.[19] Of some 25 scrapbooks on various subjects in the collection, two relate to Japan generally, one to Fukui, one to an 1863 military incident involving the U.S.S. Wyoming in the Straits of Shimonoseki, and three contain research materials used in the publication of Griffis' 1887 biography of Commodore Matthew C. Perry. Finally, there are Griffis' original contracts with Fukui and with the Ministry of Education in Tokyo, both in Japanese and English.

One can see easily that the Griffis Papers are a must for any serious research on the *yatoi*. Their use already has been extensive, and recent processing has rendered them still more accessible to scholars. With the anticipated publication of a catalog of the Japan material, the process of uncovering the treasure of information buried in the papers ought to be facilitated many fold.

During the past decade the research significance of the Griffis Papers has been enhanced greatly. In 1980 Rutgers received a grant from The Commemorative Association for the Japan World Exposition (1970) to identify and gather copies of appropriate primary materials to complement the Griffis resources.[20] Through the aid of this grant and additional funds provided by University Librarian Hendrik Edelman, a number of important acquisitions were made. Among these are microfilm copies of contemporary documents relating to Fukui Prefecture in the Fukui Prefectural Library, the Fukui University Library and the Local History Museum; and more general materials in the foreign Ministry Archives (Tokyo), the Tokyo Metropolitan Government Historical Institute and the Yokohama City Historical Compilation. From American institutions came copies of the papers of Thomas J. O'Brien and Milo J. Walrath (University of Michigan), Edward Sylvester Morse (Phillips Library of the Peabody Museum of Salem, Massachusetts), and Benjamin Smith Lyman (Forbes Library, Northampton, Massachusetts). The latter are particularly significant because they constitute an unusually full record of the activities of an American *yatoi* and were largely unknown before being reproduced for the Rutgers project.[21]

The newly acquired documents range from general and extensive materials on, for example, almost all the foreign employees in Meiji Japan, over to quite specific papers of an individual. A majority of the sources acquired from repositories in Japan were identified and selected by Dr. Ardath W. Burks, Professor *emeritus* of Asian Studies at Rutgers, with the able assistance of Mr. Fujimoto Hiroshi. Very few items purchased are originals, three rare maps being exceptions.[22] The bulk are microfilm and paper photocopies.

To understand the milieu of Japan in transition from the twilight of the Tokugawa era (1600-1867) to the dawn of modern, Meiji Japan (1868-1912), one could, of course, focus on the center of power. There is a voluminous literature, both in Japanese and English, about the regime of the *shogun* in Edo (modern Tokyo). Or one could, with rich rewards, dip into extant sources on regional societies, local regimes, and the cultures of the celebrated castle towns. The Rutgers acquisitions reflecting the latter approach concentrate on Fukui, to which Griffis repaired on the very eve of the collapse of the old orders and the rise of the new.[23]

Materials from the Fukui Prefectural Library include documents relating to the ruling Matsudaira family, such as "An Inquiry into the Flowering of Old Fukui Education"; reports on the *Meidokan* and the *Meishinkan*, domain academies which Griffis found surprisingly advanced; and parts of the Yagi family archives, including the only biography of a young samurai who became a Rutgers man and, after his death, a cultural hero, Kusakabe Taro.[24]

A much larger quantity of documents was copied from the Fukui University Library, which had access also to materials in the Fukui City Local History Museum. Some 48 sources were selected, including a 567 page history of Fukui Prefecture; a local history time chart prepared by the Museum; materials on the Asakura family (who first settled the Fukui region in the early fourteenth century); documents relating to Echizen domain under the Matsudaira, a family collateral to the Tokugawa *shogun;* and geographic monographs, gazeteers and maps.[25] With the aid of such resources, scholars can now (as Griffis could not in the nineteenth century) trace most of the employed foreigners who worked for the new Meiji government.

Additionally, Rutgers now contains copies of basic materials housed in the Foreign Ministry Archives, in the Azabu section of Tokyo. These comprise indices, tables and lists of foreigners employed at all levels of Japan's government; in many cases specifications, salary schedules, and contracts between the Foreign Ministry and the *yatoi*; some correspondence (in Japanese, Dutch, French, German and English) between parties; and even lists of aliens in private employment.[26]

Through the Foreign Ministry archives march the familiar figures in the drama of Japanese-Western relations in the nineteenth century. There are the diplomats: among others Sir Harry Parkes (Great Britain); chiefs of the French Legation, Yokohama, and of the Naval Mission, Yokosuka; and Charles DeLong (American Minister). On the Japanese side appear such names as Mori Arinori, Kuroda Kiyotaka, Inoue Kaoru, Iwakura Tomomi and Okuma Shigenobu. And there are, of course, the foreign employees, ranging from Francois Coignet (in Japan 1868-1877), who was the first *yatoi* hired by the regime, through the Americans (Griffis, Murray, Morse, Capron, Clark and many others), the Dutch, the French, the British and the Germans, over to the last of the hired foreigners toward the end of the century.[27]

In the process of acquisition, copies of documents chosen from the Tokyo Metropolitan Government Historical Institute were made as well. These include lists of foreigners resident in Edo (modern Tokyo); of those employed in higher education; and of those in private status, for example, hired by the Mitsubishi Company, missionaries and teachers.[28]

In November, 1982 Dr. Burks visited the newly opened library of the Yokohama Archives of History to acquire copies of additional materials. It is expected that these will reveal such details, for instance, as residence plots, special police provisions to protect aliens, and correspondence and contracts relating to the original foreign settlement on the Yamate Bluff in Yokohama.

The remainder of the acquisitions made under the Japan World Exposition Fund grant relates to individuals and their careers. They represent an interesting variety of professions (engineering, science, teaching and diplomacy), archival formats (correspondence, journals and memorabilia), and span the entire Meiji period.

In June of 1981, the author and Dr. Burks visited the Forbes Library (Northampton) and in the Phillips Library (Peabody Museum of Salem) in

Massachusetts to identify relevant sources in their archives.. Housed at Forbes are the personal papers of Benjamin Smith Lyman (1835-1920), a geologist and mining engineer who worked in Japan, particularly in Hokkaido, in the period 1873-1880. They consist of correspondence, field notebooks, journals, photographs, and even his original contract with the Japanese government. The bulk of the papers are in the form of letterpress copies, sheets of soft, translucent paper on which brownish impressions were left when moistened and blotted on to the originals before their ink dried. The secondary copies were at the point of extinction, when they would be lost to the scholarly world. At the direction of Rutgers archivists and using advanced techniques, the Northeast Documentation and Conservation Center enhanced the dim sheets, filmed them, and salvaged the papers. *Yatoi* historians doubtlessly will greet the recovery with enthusiasm, for the Lyman material is unique.[29]

Perhaps most valuable among the papers are Lyman's detailed accounts of surveys conducted in remote Hokkaido. His notes reflect experiences of the very first outsiders to visit the region inhabited by Ainu aborigines. Lyman's assistants were, in fact, the first *Japanese* to go into, for example, the Ishikari River basin, north of Sapporo. The documents show that Lyman spent winters at the compound of the Hokkaido Colonization Commission (*Kaitakushi*) at Shiba, in Tokyo. His letters and notes faithfully record the contemporary Tokyo scene. The field notebooks document the activities of the summer months, topographic surveying and assaying of mineral deposits in the remote northern island.

Lyman's letters reveal clearly the difficulties of a foreigner trying to understand a strange culture and resulting mutual tensions. One experienced foreign employee of the era concluded, "everywhere was tension, fatigue, and the cry for relief."[30] Documents demonstrate that Lyman, like Griffis, became enthusiastic about many aspects of Japanese life. They also show, however, that he was, like Griffis, often frustrated, suffered from communications failures and several times threatened to resign.

An equally fascinating figure of quite a different sort was Edward S. Morse (1838-1925), whose papers are located in the Peabody Museum of Salem. Trained as a biologist under Louis Agassiz of Harvard, Morse came to specialize in sea creatures, specifically, the brachiopods. It was the search for examples of that species that eventually took him to Japan in three periods of residence (1877, 1878-1879, 1882-1883). It has been said that he went to Japan because, as an ardent Darwinist, he could not find employment in an American college at the time. It is certainly true that Morse gave the first public lecture on Darwin in Japan (October 6, 1877). A brilliant lecturer, he fascinated the Japanese with his ability to illustrate his remarks at the blackboard by drawing with both hands simultaneously. Technically defined, Morse's position was not that of "foreign employee" of the government; rather, he was a "hired professor."[31]

In addition to his regular assignment, collecting specimens for the Peabody Museum of Salem, Morse lectured at the new Tokyo Imperial University;

began what was to be that institution's first scholarly memoirs devoted to science; and laid down the foundations of Japanese archeology. He discovered the celebrated Omori Shell Mounds, a find that shifted the whole perspective of Japan's ancient history. While travelling, digging and lecturing, Morse set down notes for what eventually would be his monumental published travelogue, *Japan Day by Day*. Meanwhile, using his superb skill as a draftsman, he also recorded in sketches details of Japanese houses, their interiors, joints, walls, doors and furnishings as well as exteriors, gardens, fences, walls, gates, warehouses and tools.[32]

Much of the raw material for these publications—as well as notes for scientific papers—was identified and copied. Acquisitions include copies of Morse's "Japan Journal" (doubtless the foundation for *Japan Day by Day*) drafts, textual materials and original sketches (for his books); letters commenting on his publications; lecture notes; and correspondence relating to Japanese potteries. Morse brought back one of the first collections of Japanese pottery to be seen in America, now housed at the Museum of Fine Arts, Boston.[33] Finally, he built in Salem one of the first and greatest collections of artifacts illustrating ethnography. Fortunately, the harvest of his labors has been arranged there for all to see.[34]

Papers of two remaining individuals, Milo Jay Walrath (1888-1913) and Thomas J. O'Brien (1842-1933), offer scholars the opportunity to sample experiences in the period toward the end of the transition, at the close of the Meiji era. Already, by the turn of the century, Japan had jumped from feudal isolation into the promises and perils of modernity. The opening of Japan had led not only to steam trains between Yokohama and Tokyo, red brick buildings on the Ginza, and street lamps in the capital, but also to smoky industries in Osaka, substandard housing in Tokyo, and a formidable Imperial Navy at Yokosuka. The sometimes sharp, sometimes subtle shifts in Japan's society and in Japanese attitudes and behavior are reflected in the papers from the late Meiji era, materials copied from the originals in the Bentley Historical Library, University of Michigan.

Milo Jay Walrath was an Iowa native who taught for two years (1911-1913) at Doshisha, a university in Kyoto long linked with both Japan's fledgling Christian community and, in the United States, with Amherst College. His papers include a rather detailed diary (1911-1913), some correspondence home, and notes. There is also a marvellous scrapbook of old postcards, a collection of old Japanese bookmarks and other memorabilia.[35]

In one way Walrath was the American counterpart of the Japanese overseas student Kusakabe Taro, who came to Rutgers and died in New Brunswick. Walrath had returned to the University of Chicago in 1913 to pursue work on his Ph.D. (Acquisitions include his student notes and papers, which clearly reflect his recent experiences in Japan.) On September 1, 1913 he drowned in a boating accident during an outing on a Michigan lake.[36]

Quite opposite was His Excellency, Thomas J. O'Brien. A lawyer and a Republican politician, he served as United States Minister to Denmark (1905-

1907) and, after his Japan tour of duty, as Ambassador to Italy (1911-1913). From 1907 to 1911 he was Ambassador to Japan.

The O'Brien material clearly reflects a different status, a different experience, as compared with that of the young, humble, Doshisha tutor, Walrath. Scrapbooks faithfully kept by family and staff reflect the pomp and circumstance by then surrounding United States-Japan relations. There is a folder of news clippings relating to O'Brien's appointment (1907). Quite intriguing are photographs, notes and memorabilia of the voyage out to Japan, where O'Brien accompanied Vice President William Howard Taft. Then there is a myriad of formal notes, invitations, acceptances, photographs and news clippings relating to the ambassadorship in Tokyo. More substantive is a folder of papers on American-Japanese diplomatic relations.[37]

One body of papers lends an ominous note, reminding the scholar that the Tokyo-Washington axis has always alternated between well-oiled, smooth operation and squeaky, rough movement filled with the torque of tension. O'Brien arrived in Tokyo just after the infamous racially discriminatory treatment aimed at Japanese in San Francisco in 1906. Although the Gentlemen's Agreement (1907) defused the trouble, Japan and the United States immediately plunged into their first "war crisis." This in turn was defused when, in October, 1908 the potentially threatening arrival in Tokyo Bay of the U.S. Fleet turned out to be a friendly exchange visit. Certainly O'Brien's calm handling of the affair contributed to an easing of tensions.

A final group of O'Brien papers deals with the visits of American, Russian and British naval components late in 1908.[38] The documents reveal clearly that, despite the idealism of the early *yatoi*, later representatives of the West are successively seized with thorny diplomatic, security and trade issues involving Japan, problems that continue to the present day.

Although Rutgers possesses a wealth of primary materials on the *yatoi*, its collections are by no means exhaustive. For example, the Horace Capron Papers at Yale University, the David Murray Papers at the Library of Congress, the materials on William S. Clark at the University of Massachusetts (Amherst), and the Griffis Collection of Japanese Books at Cornell University are extremely important sources not currently available at Rutgers.[39] Resources permitting, it is likely that additional acquisitions will enhance further the value of this unique research center which continues to be the most logical place to begin a study of the overseas employees in Meiji Japan.

Notes

[1] The additional materials resulted from the activities of Mr. Kaneko Tadashi, a Japanese graduate assistant studying at Rutgers in 1963-1964 and 1964-1965. While vacationing in California he met a granddaughter of Griffis, Mrs. Katherine G.M. Johnson, who agreed to donate to Rutgers papers which increased the volume of Griffis materials by about thirty percent.

[2]John Whitney Hall, A. Whitney Griswold Professor *Emeritus* of History at Yale University, has nominated Griffis' volume *The Mikado's Empire* as the single most influential book on Japan published prior to World War I. John W. Hall, *Japanese History: New Dimensions of Approach and Understanding* (Washington, D. C., 1966)

[3]Griffis' life-long obsession with saving his papers had taken hold already as a teenager, when he ignored his young friend's instructions to "Tear this up when you read it. Do not let anybody see this." J.G. Darlington to Griffis, [1858?]. Griffis Papers, Special Collections/Archives, Rutgers University Libraries. (Hereafter cited as SC/A, RUL.)

[4]William Elliot Griffis to Margaret Clark Griffis and other family members (June 30, 1870-December 22, 1874), Griffis Papers, SC/A, RUL. Because they were retained by the family, this is the one instance where a significant quantity of letters sent by Griffis remains among his papers. Likewise, the family saved many letters sent by Margaret from Japan. Margaret Clark Griffis to various family members (July 20-November 22, 1872; January 8-May 8, 1874); Griffis Papers, SC/A, RUL.

[5]Eiichi Yamashita, *Letters of William Elliot Griffis: The Fukui Letters 1871-1872* ([Fukui, 1982]).

[6]Any retained drafts of letters Griffis wrote to others are arranged by the name of the intended recipient. The same is true for letters he wrote to and which were received by various family members. This rule holds true for all series.

[7]Some exceptions to the writer arrangement rule have been made based on professional judgement. E.g., Griffis frequently sought information about a Japan "helper" by writing to the latter's relatives or friends. In most cases, their replies are filed under the name of the subject described. Utmost caution was exercised to insure that this exception was used only when potential research interest is overwhelmingly likely to be in the subject, rather than in the writer, of the particular letter involved.

[8]Griffis sent out countless postcards with the printed request. The request is headed "To the *Yatoi* (Foreigners in the Service of the Japanese Government), 1858-1900, or their Children, Relatives or Friends." Sample cards are available in the Griffis Papers, SC/A, RUL.

[9]Edward Divers to Griffis (September 24, 1906), Griffis Papers, SC/A, RUL.

[10]S. Nishio to Griffis (January 25, 1927), Griffis Papers, SC/A, RUL.

[11]Griffis, Diary (January 13-February 3, 1928), Griffis Papers, SC/A, RUL.

[12]Griffis, Journal (January 1, 1871-July 19, 1874), Griffis Papers, SC/A, RUL.

[13]Eiichi Yamashita, *Gurifuisu to Fukui* [Griffis and Fukui] (Fukui, 1979).

[14]Griffis, Journal (September 17, 1926-July 2, 1927), Griffis Papers, SC/A, RUL. With understandable excitement, Griffis labelled the journal "The Japan Year!"

[15]Margaret Clark Griffis, Journal (March 7, 1871-July 19, 1874), Griffis Papers, SC/A, RUL.

[16]See Ardath W. Burks and Jerome Cooperman, "The William Elliot Griffis Collection," *The Journal of Asian Studies*, XXI (November 1960) pp. 61-68.

[17]*Ibid.*

[18]Griffis, *The Mikado's Empire* (New York, 1876).

[19]Japan. Ministry of Education, *Ri-ji Kotei* [A Comparison of Different Systems of Education] (Tokyo, 1873), Griffis Papers, SC/A, RUL. Inserted in the first volume is Tanaka's presentation letter to [Rutgers] President [William Henry Campbell] (August 8, 1876).

[20]Formally established on September 1, 1971, the JEC Fund has provided grants and subsidies for endeavors in cultural exchange. The Fund has become well known in the United States for its support of library collections which specialize on Japan.

[21]The ensuing discussion is based largely on a 1983 article co-written by the author. See Clark L. Beck, Jr. and Ardath W. Burks, "Additional Archives of the *Yatoi*," *The Journal of the Rutgers University Libraries*, XLVI (June 1983), pp. 25-37.

[22]Several maps of Japan were acquired including an 1871 map of Japan, an 1859 map of Tokyo and an 1855-1860 road map of Japan. Each map measures several square feet, and two are richly hand colored.

[23]Griffis arrived in the period which the Japanese call *bakumatsu* ("the end of the *bakufu*"). The *bakufu,* or military headquarters of the Tokugawa *shogun* (military dictator), was in Edo (modern Tokyo). Echizen-*han* (the domain) was under the quidance of a wise *daimyo* (lord), Matsudaira Shungaku (1829-1890). His enlightened administration saw steady gains in the field of education, and he was instrumental in the decision to invite a foreign teacher to the domain to aid in the introduction of Western science.

[24]Kusakabe Taro (his original samurai family name was Yagi; 1845-1870) first studied Dutch in Nagasaki. He arrived in New Brunswick in 1867, and there Griffis tutored him in Latin. In 1870, just before his graduation, Kusakabe died of tuberculosis. He was the first Japanese elected to Phi Beta Kappa in an American college. The biography was written by Nagai Tamaki, *Kusakabe Taro den* [Biography of Taro Kusakabe] (Fukui, 1930). One microfilm reel.

[25]See *Fukui Daigaku* (Fukui University), *Kyodo shiryo mokuroku* [Index of Local History Materials] (Fukui, 1976), 166 pp., from which the 48 selections were identified. Among the copies obtained were: Fukui Shiritsu Kyodo Rekishikan [Fukui City Local History Museum], *Shiryo mokuroku* [An Index of Materials] and *Fukui-ken shi* [A History of Fukui Prefecture], 4 volumes. The 48 items occupy 10 microfilm reels.

[26]Gaiko Shiryokan [Foreign Ministry Archives], *Gaimusho kiroku* [Foreign Military Records], *Kaku shocho fuken gaikokujin kanyatoi ikken* [Index of Foreign Employees in Various Ministries, Agencies, and Prefectures] (Meiji 2 [1869]), 1 microfilm reel.

[27]Gaiko Shiryokan [Foreign Ministry Archives]. *Gaikokujin yatoi nyumei* [Table of Foreign Employees] (Meiji 3 [1870]), 1 microfilm reel.

[28]Tokyo-to Kobunshokan (Tokyo Metropolitan Government Historical Institute), *Kanyatoi gaikokujin kanriroku* [Control Lists of Government Foreign Employees] (Meiji 16 [1883]), 3 microfilm reels.

[29]Forbes Library, Northampton, Massachusetts, Benjamin Smith Lyman Papers: letterpress copybooks (October 4, 1872-April 4, 1882); series "L" field notebooks, Japan (1873-1882); unbound letterpress copybook (July 8-November 1, 1877); Peter and Susan Lesley letters (January 21, 1867-1885); correspondence (1883-1910); photographs of Japan, 1880's-1900's, 32 microfilm reels.

[30]See Hazel J. Jones, *Live Machines: Hired Foreigners and Meiji Japan* (Vancouver, 1980) p. 123. Jones quotes from Edmund G. Holtham (*Eight Years in Japan, 1873-1881*) (London, 1883).

[31]The Japanese term was *oyatoi kyoshi*.

[32]Edward S. Morse, *Japan Day by Day* (Boston, 1917); also *Japanese Homes and their Surroundings*, with illustrations by the author (Boston, 1886). The latter volume has been reprinted, with a new introduction by Clay Lancaster (New York, 1961).

[33]Museum of Fine Arts, Boston, *Catalogue of the Morse Collection of Japanese Pottery* (Boston, 1901).

[34]Phillips Library, Peabody Museum of Salem, Edward S. Morse Papers: correspondence (Box 8.1); "Japan Journal," 1873+ (boxes 14-15); drafts, *Japan Day by Day* (Box 59); lecture notes (Box 87); folder, "A Day Among the Kyoto Potteries" (Box 107); scattered correspondence (Boxes 121-143), 3 microfilm reels. In 1977 the Peabody Museum mounted a special exhibition honoring Morse and commemorating the centennial of his arrival in Japan. The catalog borrowed the title of Morse's book, *Japan Day by Day*, ed. by Money Hickman and Peter Fetchko (Salem, 1977).

[35]Michigan Historical Collections, Bentley Historical Library, University of Michigan, Milo Jay Walrath Papers, 1 microfilm reel.

[36]A sister, Ester Lash, added an introduction to Walrath's diaries (1911-1913) and, in effect, also his obituary. Walrath Papers, *loc. cit.*, part 4.

[37]Michigan Historical Collections, Bentley Historical Library, University of Michigan, Thomas J. O'Brien Papers, 1 microfilm reel. See folder, part 2, "Papers re. Japan-U.S. Relations."

[38]O'Brien Papers, *loc. cit.*, part 7, "Scrapbook June-December 1908 (Russia, England and U.S. fleet to Yokohama)."

[39]Some 483 titles from Griffis' Japanese language library have been identified in Diane E. Perushek, ed., *The Griffis Collection of Japanese Books: An Annotated Bibliography* (Ithaca, 1982). The volume is No. 28 in the Cornell University East Asia Papers series.

Selected Bibliography

Alcock, Sir Rutherford. *The Capital of the Tycoon: A Narrative of Three Years' Residence in Japan.* 2 volumes (London, 1863).

Allen, George C. *Appointment in Japan: Memories of Sixty Years* (London, 1983).

Ames, Mary Lesley (editor). *Life and Letters of Peter and Susan Lesley.* 2 volumes (New York, 1909).

Amioka, Shiro. "Changes in Educational Ideals and Objectives (From selected Documents, Tokugawa Era to the Meiji Period)." In Ardath Burks (editor), *The Modernizers: Overseas Students, Foreign Employees and Meiji Japan* (Boulder, 1985), pp. 323-357.

Annual Report of Sapporo Agricultural College. Numbers 1-6 (1877, 1878, 1879, 1879-80, 1881, 1881-1886). Reprint Edition (Sapporo, 1976).

Anthony, David F. "The Western Influence on Japanese Military Science, Shipbuilding and Navigational." *Monumenta Nipponica* 14 (1964), pp. 352-379.

Ashmead Jr., John. "The Idea of Japan 1853-1895: Japan as Described by Americans and Other Travelers from the West." 2 volumes. Unpublished Ph.D. Dissertation, Harvard University, 1951.

Bacon, Alice Mabel. *Japanese Girls and Women* (Boston, 1894).

_____. *A Japanese Interior.* (Boston, 1894).

Baelz, Erwin O. E. *Awakening Japan: The Diary of a German Doctor; Erwin Baelz.* Edited by his son, Toku Baelz. (Bloomington, 1974). Reprint of 1932 edition.

Ballagh, Margaret T. *Glimpse of Old Japan, 1861-1866* (Tokyo, 1908).

Barr, Pat. *The Coming of the Barbarians: The Opening of Japan to the West, 1853-1870* (New York, 1967).

_____. *The Deer Cry Pavilion: A Story of Westerners in Japan, 1868-1905* (New York, 1968).

Beauchamp, Edward R. *An American Teacher in Early Meiji Japan* (Honolulu, 1976).

Beck, Clark L. and Burks, Ardath W. (editors). *Aspects of Meiji Modernization: The Japan Helpers and the Helped* (New Brunswick, 1983).

Berry, Katherine Fisk. *A Pioneer Doctor in Old Japan: The Story of John C. Berry, M. D.* (New York, 1940).

Bickersteth, Mary. *Japan as We Saw It* (London, 1893).

Bird, Isabella L. *Unbeaten Tracks in Japan.* 2 volumes (New York, 1880).

Bisland, Elizabeth (editor). *The Life and Letters of Lafcadio Hearn*, 2 volumes (Boston, 1906).
_____. *The Japanese Letters of Lafcadio Hearn* (Boston, 1910).
Black, John R. *Young Japan: Yokohama and Yedo: A Narrative of the Settlement and the City from the Signing of the Treaties in 1858, to the Closing of the Year 1879.* 2 volumes (Yokohama, 1883).
Blakiston, Thomas W. *Japan in Yezo: A Series of Papers Descriptive of Journeys Undertaken in the Island of Yezo at Intervals Between 1862 and 1882* (Yokohama, 1883).
Blum, Paul C. *Yokohama in 1872, A Rambling Account of the Community in Which the Asiatic Society of Japan was Founded* (Tokyo, 1963).
Boxer, C. R. *Christian Century in Japan, 1549-1660* (Berkeley, 1951).
_____. *Jan Campagnie in Japan, 1600-1850.* 2nd Revised Edition. (The Hague, 1959).
Brooks, Van Wyck. *Fenollosa and his Circle* (New York, 1962).
Brunton, Richard H. "The Japan Lights." *Minutes of the Proceedings of the Institution of Civil Engineers*, Session 1876-7, Part I (London, 1877).
Burks, Ardath W. "William Elliot Griffis: Class of 1869." *The Journal of the Rutgers University Library* (1966).
_____. (editor). *The Modernizers: Overseas Students, Foreign Employees and Meiji Japan* (Boulder, 1985).
Burns, Edward M. *The American Idea of Mission* (New Brunswick, 1957).
Capron, Horace. *"Agriculture in Japan." In Report of the Commissioner of Agriculture for the Year 1873* (Washington, D. C. , 1874), pp. 364-374.
_____. *Japan: Some Remarks in Connection with the Visit of Horace Capron to Japan in 1871-1875* (Philadelphia, 1876).
_____. *Reports and Official Letters to the Kaitakushi* (Tokyo, 1875).
Carey, Otis. *A History of Christianity in Japan*, 2 volumes (New York, 1909).
Chisolm, Lawrence W. *Fenollosa: The Far East and American Culture* (New Haven, 1963).
Church, Deborah C. "The Role of American Diplomatic Advisors to the Japanese Foreign Ministry, 1872-1887." Unpublished Ph.D. Dissertation, University of Hawaii, 1978.
Clark, Edward W. *Life and Adventures in Japan* (New York, 1878).
Cole, Allan B. (editor). "The Private Journal of Henry A. Wise, U. S. N.." *Pacific Historical Review* 11 (September 1942).
Cortazzi, Sir Hugh. *Dr. Willis in Japan: British Medical Pioneer, 1862-1877* (London, 1985.
_____. *Victorians in Japan: In and Around the Treaty Ports* (London, 1987).
_____. "Yokohama, Frontier Town, 1859-1866." *Royal Society of Asian Affairs Bulletin*, 17, Part 1 (February 1986).
_____. *Mitford's Japan: The Memoirs and Recollections, 1866-1906, of Algernon Bertram Mitford, The First Lord Redesdale* (London, 1985).
Crew, Henry. "Thomas Corwin Mendenhall, 1841-1924." In National Academy of Sciences, *Biographical Memoirs* 16 (1936), pp. 331-351.

Curti, Merle and Birr, Kendall. *Prelude to Point Four: American Technical Missions Overseas, 1838-1938* (Madison, 1954).

Dennett, Tyler. *Americans in Eastern Asia* (New York, 1922).

Department of State. *Papers Relating to the Foreign Relations of the United States, 1879* (Washington, 1879).

Dulles, Foster Rhea. *Yankees and Samurai: America's Role in the Emergence of Modern Japan, 1791-1900* (New York, 1965).

Fox, Grace. *Britain and Japan, 1858-1883* (New York, 1968).

Fraser, Mary Crawford (Edited by Hugh Cortazzi). *A Diplomat's Wife in Japan: Sketches at the Turn of the Century* (Tokyo, 1982).

Fujita, Fumiko. " 'Boys, Be Ambitious': American Pioneers on their Japanese Frontier, 1871-1882." Unpublished Ph.D. Dissertation, City University of New York, 1988.

Girling, Katherine Peabody. *Selim Hobart Peabody: A Biography by his Daughter* (Champagne, 1923).

Goodman, Grant K. *Japan: The Dutch Experience* (London, 1986).

Gordon, M. L. *An American Missionary in Japan* (Boston, 1892).

_____. *Thirty Eventful Years: The Story of the American Board's Mission in Japan, 1869-1899* (Boston, 1901).

Gowen, Herbert H. "An American Pioneer in Japan." *Washington Historical Quarterly* 20 (January 1929), pp. 12-23.

_____. Five Foreigners in Japan (New York, 1936).

Greene, Evarts Boutell. *A New Englander in Japan: Daniel Crosby Greene* (Boston, 1927).

Griffis, William Elliot. *America in the East: A Glance at our History, Prospects, Problems and Duties in the Pacific Ocean* (New York, 1899).

_____. "American Relations with Japan." *Magazine of American History* 27 (1892), p. 449.

_____. "Chemical Libraries in Japan." *Nature* 6 (1872), p. 422.

_____. "The Department of Education in Japan." *American Education Monthly* 10 (May 1873), pp. 217-218.

_____. *Dux Christus, An Outline Study of Japan* (New York, 1904).

_____. "Education in Japan." *The College Courant* 14 (May 16, 1874), n.p.

_____. "Griffis' Laboratory of Physical Science in Fukuwi [sic]." *Nature* 6 (1872), p. 352.

_____. *Hepburn of Japan and his Wife and Helpmate: A Life Story of Toil for Christ* (Philadelphia, 1913).

_____. "Introduction of Chemistry into Japan: An Appreciation of the Service of Charles William Elliot as a Chemist." *Chemical Age* 3 (April 17, 1924), n.p.

_____. *A Maker of the New Orient, Samuel Robbins Brown, Pioneer Educator in China, America and Japan, The Story of his Life and Work* (New York, 1902).

_____. *The Mikado's Empire.* 2 volumes (New York, 1877. Reprinted, Tokyo, 1977).

_____. "Pioneering Chemistry in Japan." *Industrial and Engineering Chemistry* 16, 11 (1924), p. 1165.

_____. *Rutgers Graduates in Japan* (New Brunswick, 1916).

_____. *Verbeck of Japan: A Citizen of No Country* (New York, 1900).

Hara, Yoshio. "From Westernization to Japanization: The Replacement of Foreign Teachers by Japanese Who Studied Abroad." *The Developing Economies* (Tokyo) 15, 4 (December 1977), pp. 440-461.

Harris, Neil. "All the World a Melting Pot? Japan at American Fairs, 1876-1904." In *Mutual Images: Essays in American-Japanese Relations* (Cambridge, 1975), pp. 24-54.

Harrison, John A. "The Capron Mission and the Colonization of Hokkaido, 1868-1875." *Agricultural History* 25 (July 1951), pp. 135-142.

_____. *Japan's Northern Frontier: A Preliminary Study in Colonization and Expansion with Special Reference to the Relations of Japan and Russia* (Gainesville, 1953).

Hawkes, Francis L. (Compiler). *Narrative of the Expedition of an American Squadron to the China Seas and Japan Performed in the Years 1852, 1853 and 1854 Under the Command of Commodore M. C. Perry.* 3 volumes (Washington D. C., 1856. Reprinted New York, 1967).

Helbig, Frances Y. "William Elliot Griffis: Entrepreneur of Ideas." Unpublished M. A. Thesis, University of Rochester, 1966.

Henry, Joseph (edited by Nathan Reingold) *The Papers of Joseph Henry.* Volume I (Washington, D. C. , 1972).

Heusken, Henry (translated and edited by J. Van der Corput and R. A. Wilson) *Japan Journal* (New Brunswick, 1965).

Hodgson, Christopher P. *A Residence at Nagasaki and Hakodate in 1859-1860* (London, 1861).

Hokkaido Imperial University. *The Development of Hokkaido Imperial University , Japan, 1876-1926* (Sapporo, 1923).

_____. *The Semi-Centennial of the Hokkaido Imperial University, Japan, 1876-1926* (Sapporo, 1927).

Hokkaido Prefectural Government (Archives Section, General Affairs Department). *Foreign Pioneers: A Short History of the Contributions of Foreigners to the Development of Hokkaido* (Sapporo, 1968).

Holden, Frereick A. *The Capron Family Book: Genealogy of the Descendants of Banfield Capron from A. D. 1660 to A. D. 1859* (Boston, 1859).

Holtham, Edmund G. *Eight Years in Japan, 1873-1881* (London, 1883).

Hopper, Helen M. "The Conflict between Japanese Tradition and Western Learning in the Meiji Intellectual Mori Ogai (1862-1922)." Unpublished Ph.D. D. Dissertation, Washington University, 1976.

Huffman, James L. "Edward Howard House: In the Service of Meiji Japan." *Pacific Historical Review* 56 (May 1987), pp. 231-258.

Hyman, Albert. *The Dutch in the Far East* (Ann Arbor, George Wahr, 1942).

Iglehart, Charles W. *A Century of Protestant Christianity in Japan* (Tokyo, 1960).

Ike, Nobutaka. "Western Influences on the Meiji Restoration." *Pacific Historical Review* 17, 1 (February 1948), pp. 1-9.

Iriye, Akira. *Across the Pacific: An Inner History of American-East Asian Relations* (New York, 1967).

Ishizuki, Minoru. "Overseas Study by Japanese in the Early Meiji Period." In Ardath Burks (editor), *The Modernizers: Overseas Students, Foreign Employees, and Meiji Japan* (Boulder, 1985), pp. 161-186.

Iwao, Seiichi. "A Dutch Doctor in Old Japan." *Japan Quarterly* 8, 2 (April-June 1961), pp. 170-178.

Jephson, R. and Elmhirst, E. *Our Life in Japan* (London, 1869).

Jones, Francis C. *Extraterritoriality in Japan* (New Haven, 1931).

Jones, Hazel J. "Bakumatsu Foreign Employees." *Monumenta Nipponica* 29, 3 (1974), pp. 305-327.

_____. "The Formulation of Meiji Policy Toward the Employment of Foreigners." *Monumenta Nipponica* 23 (1968), pp. 9-30.

_____. "The Griffis Thesis and Meiji Policy Toward Hired Foreigners." In Ardath Burks (editor), *The Modernizers: Overseas Students, Foreign Employees, and Meiji Japan* (Boulder, 1985), pp. 301-321.

_____. *Live Machines: Hired Foreigners and Meiji Japan* (Vancouver, 1980).

_____. "The Meiji Government and Foreign Employees, 1868-1900." Unpublished Ph.d. Dissertation, University of Michigan, 1967.

Kaneko, Tadashi. "Contributions of David Murray to the Modernization of School Administration in Japan." In Ardath Burks (editor), *The Modernizers: Students, Foreign Employees, and Meiji Japan* (Boulder, 1985), pp. 301-321.

Krieger, C. C. *The Infiltration of European Civilization into Japan During the 18th Century* (Leiden, 1940).

Kuwada, Gompei. *Biography of Benjamin Smith Lyman* (Tokyo, 1937).

Lane-Poole, Stanley and Dickens, Frederic V. *The Life of Sir Harry Parkes*, 2 volumes (London, 1894).

Lehmann, Jean-Pierre. *The Image of Japan: From Feudal Isolation to World Power, 1850-1905* (London, 1978).

Lincicome, Mark E. "Educational Discourse and the Dimensions of Reform in Meiji Japan." Unpublished Ph.D. Dissertation, University of Chicago, 1985.

MacCauley, Clay. *Memories and Memorials: Gatherings from an Eventful Life* (Tokyo, 1914).

Maclay, Arthur Collins. *A Budget of Letters from Japan: Reminiscences of Work and Travel in Japan* (New York, 1886).

Mayo, Marlene J. "The Iwakura Mission to the United States and Europe, 1871-1873." In *Columbia University East Asian Institute Studies* 5 (New York, 1959).

Medzini, Meron. *French Policy in Japan During the Closing Years of the Tokugawa Regime* (Cambridge, 1971).

_____. "Leon Roches in Japan (1864-1868)," In *Papers on Japan* Volume II (Cambridge, 1963).

Merrill, George P. *The First One Hundred Years of American Geology* (New Haven, 1924. Reprinted New York, 1964).

Metraux, Daniel A. "Lay Proselytization of Christianity in Japan in the Meiji Period: The Career of Edward Warren Clark." *New England Social Studies Bulletin* 44, 3 (June 1986) 40-50.

Morse, Edward S. "Biographical Memoir of Charles Otis Whitmen, 1842-1910." In National Academy of Sciences, *Biographical Memoirs*, 7 (August 1912), pp. 269-288.

_____. *Japan Day by Day 1877, 1878-79, 1882-83*. 2 volumes (Boston, 1917).

Mossman Samuel. *New Japan: The Land of the Rising Sun* (London, 1873).

Motoyama, Yukihiko. "The Educational Policy of Fukui and William Elliot Griffis." In Ardath Burks, *The Modernizers: Overseas Students, Foreign Employees and Meiji Japan* (Boulder, 1985), pp. 265-300.

Nakamura, Hiroshi. "The Contribution of Foreigners." *Journal of World History* (Geneva) 9, 2 (1965), pp. 294-319.

Nakayama, Shigeru. "The Role Played by Universities in Scientific and Technological Development in Japan." *Journal of World History* (Geneva) 9, 2 (1965).

Netherlands Association of Japanese Studies. *Phillip Franz von Siebold: A Contribution to the Study of Historical Relations Between Japan and the Netherlands* (Leiden, 1978).

Neu, Charles. *The Troubled Encounter: The United States and Japan* (New York, 1975).

Newman, William L. *America Encounters Japan* (Baltimore, 1963).

Nishihira, Isao. "Western Influences on the Modernization of Japanese Education, 1868-1912." Unpublished Ph.D. Dissertation, The Ohio State University, 1972.

Nitobe, Inazo. *The Imperial Agricultural College of Sapporo, Japan* (Sapporo, 1893).

_____. *The Intercourse Between Japan and the United States: An Historical Sketch* (Baltimore, 1891).

_____. et al. *Western Influences in Modern Japan* (Chicago, 1931).

Notehelfer, Fred G. *American Samurai: Captain L. L. Janes and Japan* (Princeton, 1985).

Okuma, Shigenobu (Editor). *Fifty Years of the New Japan*. 2 volumes (New York, 1909).

Oshima, Masatake. "Reminiscences of Dr. W. S. Clark." *The Japan Christian Intelligencer* 1 (April 5, 1926), pp. 54-62.

Penhallow, David P. "Japan." *McGill University Magazine* 3 (April 1904), pp. 80-103.

_____. "William Smith Clark: His Place as a Scientist and His Relation to the Development of Scientific Agriculture." *Science* 28 (January 31, 1908), pp. 172-180.

Piggott, Francis S. J. *Broken Thread: An Autobiography* (Aldershot, 1950).

Pressesian, Ernest L. *Before Aggression: Europeans Prepare the Japanese Army* (Tucson, 1965).

Pumpelly, Ralphael. *Across America and Asia*. 2nd Revised Edition (New York, 1870).

Redesdale, Algernon Bertram Freeman-Mitford, Baron. *Memories*. 5th Revised Edition, 2 volumes (London, 1915).

Reed, James E. *The Missionary Mind and American East Asian Policy, 1911-1915* (Cambridge, 1983).

Roden, Donald. In Search of the Real Horace Capron: A Historiographical Perspective on Japanese-American Relations. *Pacific Historical Review* 55 (November 1986), pp. 549-575.

Rogers, Eustace B. "Life in the Foreign Settlements of Japan." *Harpers Weekly* 38 (December 29, 1894).

Rohan, Kieran M. "Lighthouses and the Yatoi Experiences of R. H. Brunton." *Monumenta Nipponica* 20, 1 (1965), pp. 65-80.

Rosenberg, Emily S. *Spreading the American Dream: American Economic and Cultural Expansion, 1890-1945* (New York, 1982).

Rosenstone, Robert A. "Learning from Those 'Imitative' Japanese: Another Side of the American Experience in the Mikado's Empire." *The American Historical Review* 85 (June 1980), pp. 572-595.

_____. *Mirror in the Shrine: American Encounters with Meiji Japan* (Cambridge, 1988).

Rubinger, Richard (ed). *An American Scientist in Early Meiji Japan: The Autobiographical Notes of Thomas C. Mendenhall* (Honolulu, 1989).

Saito Masaru. "Introduction of Foreign Technology in the Industrialization Process—Japanese Experience Since the Meiji Restoration (1868)." *The Developing Economies* 13, 2 (June 1975), pp. 168-186.

Sakamaki, Shunzo. Japan and the United States, 1790-1853. *Transactions of the Asiatic Society of Japan*, 2nd Series, 18 (December 1939), pp. 1-204.

Sansom, Sir George B. *The Western World and Japan: A Study in the Interaction of European and Asiatic Cultures* (New York, 1950).

Satow, Earnest. *A Diplomat in Japan* (London, 1921).

Scherer, James A. B. "With the Passing of Four Decades." *Japan* 21 (December 1932), pp. 17-19, 38-40.

_____. "Foreign Employees in the Development of Japan." In Ardath Burks (editor), *The Modernizers: Overseas Students, Foreign Employees, and Meiji Japan* (Boulder, 1985), pp. 207-217.

_____. *Japanese and Americans: A Century of Cultural Relations* (New York, 1955).

Shimmura, Izuru. *Western Influences on Japanese History and Culture in Earlier Periods (1540-1860)* (Tokyo, 1936).

Starr, Merritt. "General Horace Capron, 1804-1855." *Journal of the Illinois State Historical Society* 18 (July 1925), pp. 276-295.

Storry, Dorothie. *Second Country: The Story of Richard Storry and Japan, 1913-1982* (Woodchurch, 1986).

Taylor, Sandra C. *Advocate of Understanding: Sidney Gulick and the Search for Peace with Japan* (Kent, 1984).

Thiers, Louisa Kerwin. "An American Advisor to the Japanese Government." *Journal of American History* 7 (October-December, 1913), pp. 1415-1425.

_____. "Dr. Seth Capron." *Journal of American History* 17 (January-March, 1923), pp. 32-41.

Thomas, Winburn T. *Protestant Beginnings in Japan* (Tokyo, 1959).

Thompson, James C. Jr., Stanley, Peter W. and Perry, John C. *Sentimental Imperialists: The American Experience in East Asia* (New York, 1981).

Tohoku Imperial University. College of Agriculture. *American Influence Upon the Agriculture of Hokkaido, Japan* (Sapporo, 1915).

Umetani, Noboru. "Foreign Nationals Employed in Japan During the Years of Modernization." *East Asian Cultural Studies* (1971).

_____. *The Role of Foreign Employees in the Meiji Era in Japan* (Tokyo, 1971).

_____. "William Elliot Griffis' Studies in Japanese History: Their Significance." In Ardath Burks (editor), *The Modernizers: Overseas Students, Foreign Employees, and Meiji Japan* (Boulder, 1985), pp. 393-407.

Vories, William M. *A Mustard-Seed in Japan*, 5th Edition (Tokyo, 1925).

Watanabe, Masao. "American Science Teachers in the Early Meiji Period." *Japanese Studies in the History of Science* (Tokyo) 15 (1976), pp. 127-144.

_____. "Science Across the Pacific: American-Japanese Scientific and Cultural Contacts in the late Nineteenth Century." In Ardath Burks (editor), *The Modernizers: Students, Foreign Employees, and Meiji Japan* (Boulder, 1985), pp. 369-392.

Watanabe, Minoru. "Japanese Students Abroad and the Acquisition of Scientific and Technical Knowledge." *Journal of World History* 9, 1 (1965), pp. 254-293.

Wayman, Dorothy G. *Edward Sylvester Morse: A Biography* (Cambridge, 1942).

Welch, Herbert. *Men of the Outposts: The Romance of the Modern Christian Movement* (Cincinnati, 1937).

Wheeler, William. "Japan's Colonial College." *The Cycle* 2 (June 23, 1880), pp. 6-11.

Whitman, C. O. *Zoology in the University of Tokio* (Yokohama, 1881).

Whitney, Clara A. N. Edited by M. William Steele and Tamiko Ichimata. *Clara's Diary: An American Girl in Meiji Japan* (Tokyo, 1979).

Williams, Harold S. *Foreigners in Mikadoland* (Tokyo, 1963).

_____. *Shades of the Past, Or Indiscreet Tales of Japan* (Tokyo, 1960).

_____. *Tales of the Foreign Settlements in Japan* (Tokyo, 1958).

Yamamoto, Masaya. "Image-Makers of Japan: A Case Study in the Impact of the American Protestant Foreign Missionary Movement, 1859-1905." Unpublished Ph.D. Dissertation, Ohio State University, 1967.

Yokoyama, Toshio. *Japan in the Victorian Mind: A Study of Stereotyped Images of a Nation, 1850-1880* (London, 1987).

About the Contributors

Akizuki Toshiyuki, Curator, Hokkaido University Library.

Edward R. Beauchamp, Professor of History of Education and Comparative Education, University of Hawaii.

Clark Beck, Curator, William Elliot Griffis Collection, Alexander Library, Rutgers University.

Ardath W. Burks, Professor *emeritus*, Asian Studies, Rutgers University.

Ellen Conant, Art Historian, New York City.

Fujita Fumiko, Associate Professor of History, Tsuda College.

John W. Hall, Professor of History, Yale University.

Imatsu Kenji, Professor of History, Kobe University.

A. Hamish Ion, Professor of History, Royal Military College of Canada.

Iriye Akira, Professor of History, Harvard University.

Isa Kimio, Professor of Chemistry, Fukui University.

Isono Naohide, Professor of Biology, Keio University.

Hazel J. Jones, Professor of History, University of Alberta.

John Maki, Professor *emeritus*, Political Science, University of Massachusetts.

Nakata Ryuji, Professor of Chemistry, Fukui University.

Oki Hisaya, Professor of Chemistry, Fukui University.

Dorothy Robins-Mowry, Retired United States Information Agency officer.

Richard Rubinger, Professor of Japanese and Adjunct Professor of History, Indiana University.

Sakan Fujio, Professor of Chemistry, Fukui University.

Uchida Takane, Professor of Chemistry, Fukui University.

Usui Chizuko, Assistant Professor of History, Tokai Gakuen Women's University.

Yokoyama Toshio, Associate Professor of the History of Modern Japanese Culture, Kyoto University.

Index

Ministry of Education (*Mombusho*),
    38, 40, 42, 55, 57, 139, 156
Mishima Sumie, 133
Mitsukuri Rinsho, 43
Mombusho, see Ministry of
    Education
Mori Arinori, 11, 40, 43, 72, 73,
    122, 123, 124, 130, 288
Morse, Edward S., 11, 13, 25, 52,
    59, 61, 155, 193-212, 283,
    289
    contract, 194-196
    Darwinism, 202-204
    Enoshima Laboratory, 196
    publications, 197-199
    University of Tokyo, 199-201
Motoyama Yukihiko, 1
Mudgett, E.H., 283
Munro, Henry L., 283
Murray, David L., 11, 42, 122, 217,
    218, 219, 283

Nagai Michio, 36
Nagai Shigeko, 124, 125
Nagasaki, description, 54
Nakamura Masanao, 172, 173, 175,
    182, 183, 184, 186
Nakayama Shigeru, 49
National Museum of Ethnography,
    25
Natsume Soseki, 26, 27
Naumann, Edward, 104
Niijima Jo, 230
Niikapu Farm, 108
Niishima, Joseph Hardy, 72, 83
Nishi, Amane, 43
Nishimura Shigeki, 43
Nitobe Inazo, 283
Northrop, B.C., 231
Numazu Military Academy, 180

O'Brien, Thomas J., 290
Okakura Kazuko, 156
Okubo Ichio, 176, 184
Okubo Toshimichi, 153
Okuma Shigenobu, 21, 121
Oyama Iwao, 153

Oyatoi Gaikokujin (foreign
    employees), vii, 5, 6, 7, 8, 9,
    10, 11, 12, 13, 17, 19, 20, 21,
    22, 23, 25, 27, 34, 49, 55, 56,
    57, 62, 63, 64, 69, 70, 139,
    140, 151, 154, 155, 156, 157,
    158, 171, 193, 241, 245, 260,
    275, 283, 284, 287
Oyatoi Kyoshi, 229
Ozaki Takafumi, 147

Parkes, Sir Harry, 263, 268
Penhallow, David, 74, 76, 80, 231,
    234
Public Works Department (*Kubusho*),
    20, 104, 140, 154, 241, 242,
    244

Ragusa, Vicenzo, 146, 147, 150,
    157
Rangaku, see Dutch Studies
Regulations of Girls' High Schools
    (1886), 123; (1895), 123
Religious teaching, 81, 82
Research needs, 21-27
Rockefeller Foundation, 8
Rokumeikan, 142
Rose, Clara, 128
Russo-Japanese War, 143
Ryugakusei, 5, 9

Sadamotu Yuichi, 233
Saigo Takamori, 153
Saigo Tsugumichi, 153
Saigo Tsugumichi, Mrs., 185
Saigusa Hirota, 17
Sakata Yoshio, 18
Salary of *yatoi*, 20
Sameshima Naonobu, 260, 262, 263,
    264, 266, 268, 274, 275
Sanai Hashimoto, 11
Santo Yone, see Aoki Koto
Sapporo Agricultural College (SAC),
    71, 73, 76, 80, 81, 82, 110,
    229-239
Sapporo Agricultural College (SAC)
    Barn, 77, 78